Business

Tutor Resource File and CD-ROM

Carol Carysforth

Mike Neild

Endorsed by Edexcel

www.heinemann.co.uk
✓ Free online support
✓ Useful weblinks
✓ 24 hour online ordering

01865 888058

Heinemann

Inspiring generations

Heinemann Educational Publishers
Halley Court, Jordan Hill, Oxford OX2 8EJ
Part of Harcourt Education

Heinemann is the registered trademark of
Harcourt Education Limited

Text © Carol Carysforth, Mike Neild 2004

First published 2004

09 08 07 06 05 04
10 9 8 7 6 5 4 3 2 1

British Library Cataloguing in Publication Data is available
from the British Library on request.

ISBN 0 435 401351

Typeset and illustrated by TechType, Abingdon, Oxon
Original illustrations © Harcourt Education Limited 2004
Cover photo: © Corbis
Printed in the UK by Athenæum Press

Acknowledgements
Every effort has been made to contact copyright holders of material reproduced in this
book. Any omissions will be rectified in subsequent printings if notice is given to the
publishers.

Websites
There are links to relevant websites in this book. In order to ensure that the links are up to
date, that the links work, and that the sites aren't inadvertently linked to sites that could be
considered offensive, we have made the links available in the Heinemann website at
www.heinemann.co.uk/hotlinks. When you access the site the express code is **1351T**.

Contents

CD-ROM

The accompanying CD ROM contains PDFs of the contents of this file plus the following additional material:

Unit 1 Introduction to business activity
PowerPoint presentations

Unit 2 Introduction to exploring business pressures
PowerPoint presentations

Unit 3 Investigating financial control
PowerPoint presentations

Unit 4 Business communication
Student Book chapter

Unit 6 Introduction to business administration
Student Book chapter

Unit 9 Starting up a new business
Student Book chapter

Acknowledgements

The authors would like to express their personal appreciation to all those who helped in the production of this pack and in the creation of the extended Richer Sounds StudentZone.

Firstly, our grateful thanks go to the many hawk-eyed editors who worked on the tutor resource file at different stages for their continual care and meticulous attention to detail: Linda Mellor, Gavin Fidler, Camilla Thomas, Nigel Copeland, David Kershaw, Victoria Dutchman-Smith and Stig Vatland. The word 'thanks' seems totally inadequate to express our tremendous admiration for the work carried out by Julia Bruce, senior editor, who not only calmly, carefully and cheerfully kept the project on track and coordinated all the different contributions (a mammoth task in itself) but also found time to keep us sane and focused as well!

For the StudentZone, huge thanks are due to Paul Carysforth for his skill in redesigning the website and doing all the technical wizardry that is beyond our understanding, and to Brian Penton, at Heinemann, for his help and assistance in launching the new site. Many thanks, too, to Antony Carysforth for his help and expertise in manipulating the graphics we wanted to include.

At Richer Sounds, our thanks as ever are due to Julian Richer, the owner and founder; and to David Robinson, MD, for continuing to support our work. We are also grateful to the numerous Directors and colleagues who continue to help us by providing updates and additional information. They include: Jez Avens, Deputy MD; John Currier, Financial Director; John Clayton, Operation and Training Director; Claudia Vernon, Marketing Director; Solomon Essah Essel, Distribution Director; Julie Abraham, IT and Stock Control Director; Gary Woodward, Purchasing Director; Dan Burnham, Merchandising Director, Matt Oxer, Group Property Director and Darren Woodward, IT Manager. We are also grateful to Lee Nelson, James Donnan, Lol Lecanu, Paul Stephens and Dani Delany for letting us include their colleague profiles on the StudentZone and to Julia Eastwood, PA to Gary Woodward, Kim Morgan of Persula and Ricky Faust, head of Corporate Sales for their help also. A special thanks is also due to Julie McCabe, David Robinson's PA, not just for her colleague profile but also for her invaluable assistance in coordinating all our requests.

The authors and publishers would also like to thank the following individuals and organisations their assistance and for permission to reproduce copyright material: Adidas; Business in the Community; The Carphone Warehouse; Duchy Originals; Friends of the Earth (England, Wales and Northern Ireland); HM Treasury; IKEA; Indesit (Hotpoint); the LEGO Company; Marks & Spencer; Mothercare; Office of Fair Trading; RNLI; Royal Bank of Scotland; RSPCA; Ryanair; UNISON.

Introduction

This resource pack has been devised to provide all the additional materials you might need to help your students to achieve the best grades possible in the BTEC First Diploma (or Certificate) in Business. It also supports all the information provided in the Student Book and has been endorsed by Edexcel.

It consists of a Tutor Resource File and a CD-ROM which can be used together to support your teaching.

In the Tutor Resource File you will find organised by unit:

* A guide to teaching Core Units 1, 2 and 3.
* Photocopiable **additional activities**, to reinforce student understanding of the core units. Many of these have been cross-referenced to relevant specialist units with which they may also be used.
* **Background information** and suggested **answers** to the additional activities.
* Photocopiable **sample assessments** for all units, based on the Edexcel assessment grading criteria. For Unit 1, the sample assessment provides students with appropriate practice for their IVA.
* **Answers** to the sample assessments where applicable.
* **Answers** to all the exercises in the Student Book and the additional specialist units on the CD-ROM, i.e. the Over to you! sections and the Section reviews.
* **Supporting tutor materials** for Unit 4, Business communication. These provide ideas for practical activities and assessments related to the student notes.

In addition, you will find **IVA guidance notes** which give detailed information for students on the Integrated Vocational Assignment they will undertake for Unit 1 and specific information on the

Richer Sounds StudentZone. A dedicated section of the StudentZone has been created for BTEC First students to give them a unique opportunity to find out appropriate information about a business relevant to their studies for the BTEC First award. The information on the StudentZone can be linked, in many cases, with the sample assessments. This means that your students can research a business easily online and compare their findings. This also enables you to check their work easily and quickly.

On the CD-ROM you will find all of the above plus:

* **Additional student chapters** to cover Specialist Units 4, 6 and 9 which do not appear in the Student Book.
* **PowerPoint presentations** for Core Units 1, 2 and 3 to help you to introduce each section of the core units by summarising the key points. Full teaching notes are included. If you prefer, you can photocopy the slides to use as OHTs.

The resources on the CD-ROM can be printed off and used with your students. They can also be customised to suit your own teaching needs.

We hope that you will find this resource pack useful in helping to devise topical, interesting and enjoyable lessons for your students within a busy teaching schedule.

Carol Carysforth and Mike Neild
December 2004

The Richer Sounds StudentZone

The Richer Sounds StudentZone is available via the Richer Sounds main website at **www.richersounds.com** and clicking on the StudentZone option on the menu. Alternatively, students can go direct to the site at **www.richerstudentzone.co.uk**. Students are welcomed to the site by Julian Richer, the owner and founder of the business. Students must then enter the password RICHERLEARNING to obtain access to the StudentZone itself. This password is included in the introduction to the site on page viii of the Heinemann BTEC First Diploma Student Book.

On entering the site, students are asked to identify the course they are following. This then enables them to enter the area of the site which links to the units of their scheme. The information is, of course, specific to Richer Sounds. Links have been created between pages to help students find relevant material quickly and easily.

The StudentZone was originally prepared for GCSE Applied Business students but has been specially extended and customised specifically for BTEC First Diploma students. It is updated each summer so that it remains current and relevant.

Why Richer Sounds?

Richer Sounds is an ideal organisation to follow, particularly in view of the content of the BTEC First scheme, which introduces students to issues such as business ethics and corporate social responsibility alongside the importance of profit in the private sector.

- Richer Sounds is a national organisation with stores all around the country. Many students may have visited a store already or will certainly be capable of doing so quite easily.
- It sells audio separates and related equipment such as DVDs and MP3 players. Its products are of interest to young people.
- It has a very distinctive culture. It is renowned for selling excellent value products and providing superb customer service. It is also highly committed to its staff and provides a range of benefits which is second to none, including many reward systems and holiday homes. For the last three years it has consistently been highly placed in the Sunday Times *100 Best Companies to Work for in the UK*. In 2002 and 2003 it was the top UK company listed.

- It is owned by Julian Richer who, at 19, set up his first store and is now worth more than £40 million. Julian Richer is honest about the fact that he was more interested in business opportunities than academic studies – and this affected his school grades. He therefore provides an excellent role model for students who may feel that high-level academic achievement is not their forte and who prefer a practical, vocational route.
- The organisation has strict ethical principles. It gives 22 per cent of its profits back to its staff in its profit-sharing and hardship schemes as well as to charity. Its Persula Foundation distributes the 5 per cent of its annual profits that are spent on charitable projects and, in the last 10 years, the company's total charitable gifts have amounted to well over £1 million. The company is registered in Britain and pays all its taxes in Britain. It pays its staff at the top rates for the jobs they do and has an excellent retention record. Julian Richer sees no conflict in aims and objectives that include making a profit and providing excellent service, good staff benefits and having strong business ethics. This is a useful balance for BTEC First students who may, during Unit 2, come to the conclusion that all businesses which focus on profits are, by definition, unethical or have 'fat cats' as managers!

Guidance for tutors

The section of the StudentZone devised for BTEC First students covers all nine units. Before viewing the site, the following points should be noted.

- It is often very difficult to divide the activities of a modern, organic enterprise so that it conforms to specific headings. Richer Sounds is truly organic in the sense that, whilst it is structured and organised, it is non-bureaucratic and extremely flexible in relation to its methods of working. It does not, for example, have job descriptions, annual or bi-annual appraisals or 'administrators' per se. It refers to all staff as 'colleagues'. For this reason, you will find that some information repeats between sections. In other cases, the reason for a lack of information is given. This should be seen positively as it is unrealistic for students to think that any 'real' organisation automatically conforms to theoretical business models and practices. The key question to ask is whether the business is successful. If it is, then the method used obviously works, whether or not it is to be found in current textbooks or business schemes.

- Within the site is included an organisation chart and the colleague profiles of several employees. Although organisation charts are not a specific feature of the BTEC First scheme, they do relate to 'management processes' and 'hierarchies' in Unit 1. The profiles are included to give students a better insight of the job roles of staff and how each person views the business.

Core units

- **Unit 1 Introduction to business activity** has been structured to provide information which students could use for their sample IVA. It is, of course, possible for students to use Richer Sounds as one of their sources for the actual IVA. However, in this case tutors will have to take steps to ensure that the students supplement information on the StudentZone with additional independent research and use the StudentZone to produce original work. There would be an obvious issue if all the students in one group wanted to use the same organisation in the same way. For that reason, it may be advisable to use the StudentZone for the 'practice' IVA and/or reserve it for one or two students who have problems obtaining information elsewhere.
- **Unit 2 Introduction to exploring business pressures** includes a sample assessment which also requires investigation into a 'real' business and the StudentZone could be used as a focus. Again, if Richer Sounds was chosen for the 'real' investigation then steps would have to be taken to ensure all work submitted was original.
- **Unit 3 Investigating financial control** relates to key areas of financial information and issues of fraud. The information on the StudentZone will hopefully enable students to understand how these areas apply in a real organisation and will supplement their theoretical knowledge even though only a few specific figures are given. In general, Richer Sounds has a positive approach to preventing fraud by having an excellent staff welfare system and paying good wages, but reinforces this with a strict but fair disciplinary policy. The combined 'stick' and 'carrot' approach should enable students to gain a balanced appreciation of potential employer initiatives in this area.

Specialist units

- **Unit 4 Business communication** is possibly the least appropriate to include on the website, particularly given the practical nature of this unit. However, issues such as the dress code, confidentiality, business meetings and the wide range of communication methods used at Richer Sounds can help to provide an additional perspective to this unit.
- **Unit 5 Employee contribution to working conditions** relates to terms of employment, recruitment procedures and appraisals. Richer Sounds does not produce job descriptions and colleagues can request a review at any time. Richer Sounds prefers this method to an official, routine appraisal process. However, the conditions of employment for colleagues are both excellent and comprehensive and the recruitment procedures and benefits are imaginative and effective. There is also a wide range of policies to prevent discrimination and protect colleagues and customers. Richer Sounds has consistently been ranked highly by its staff in the annual Sunday Times *100 Best Companies to Work For* list – achieving second place in 2003. How this is achieved will give students studying Specialist Unit 5 an additional insight into this area.
- **Unit 6 Introduction to business administration** may seem a misnomer for Richer Sounds which does not have a separate administration function or department. However, because of the way the unit is structured, there are several useful and important aspects of Richer Sounds which relate. Core systems at Richer Sounds link to sales figures and profit statements, the business is highly dependent upon its EPOS and IT systems and has taken steps to minimise possible disruption in both areas and health and safety is obviously an important area and relates to both customers and colleagues.
- **Unit 7 Sales and customer service** is tailor-made for Richer Sounds! Tutors should note that although both the unit and the assessment criteria refer to FMCGs, Edexcel expect this definition to be taken in its widest sense to include consumer durables and the practices of Richer Sounds are noted on page 88 of the Edexcel scheme. The StudentZone contains relevant information on customer service, the policy on returns and the training of sales colleagues. This will provide an additional insight as to how Richer Sounds specifically addresses these areas and should be used to

supplement the basic information given in the Student Book.

- **Unit 8 Business online** is also appropriate because Richer Sounds achieves several of its objectives via its website, although its main site includes a warning that it actually prefers to do business 'face-to-face'. Richer Sounds not only sells goods and provides information online but achieves its social objectives through the StudentZone and through the site for the Persula Foundation at **www.persula.org**. This information is also relevant to stakeholders and links to its corporate social objectives (Unit 2).

- **Unit 9 Starting up a new business** focuses on the activities of business entrepreneurs. Julian Richer opened his first shop at the age of 19. How he started in business and his early mistakes are described on the site. As he now regularly makes the *Sunday Times Rich List* with more than £40 million of assets he would appear to be a very good role model for students interested in working for themselves.

Using the StudentZone

We would recommend that you start by studying the StudentZone yourself and printing out any materials you require. Whether you are using the StudentZone to supplement your teaching, or to allow your students to investigate the organisation, there are obvious benefits to introducing your students to the StudentZone relatively early in the course. You can then reinforce the points made in the Student Book by relating key issues to Richer Sounds. This is virtually essential if you are teaching Specialist Unit 7.

As your students progress through their course, they can gain greater in-depth knowledge of the business, stage by stage. This will also be invaluable when or if they are investigating other businesses as it gives them a readily identifiable point of comparison.

Additional materials

Relevant sources of supplementary materials related to Richer Sounds are listed below. These are particularly important if your students are investigating the company for their 'real' IVA as their use will help to prove independent research has been undertaken.

- **The main Richer Sounds website** has a wide variety of information for private and business customers and should be fully explored by students.
- **Copies of the latest in-store catalogues and newsletters**. These are available from any store or by telephone on 0845 1 300 200 (calls are charged at local rate). These provide product information, a list of stores, a FAQs page and other information relevant to marketing and promotion.

- **Company advertisements** in newspapers, *What HiFi? Sound and Vision* and other related magazines. Newspaper advertisements normally focus on special offers and include a 'free tape' voucher. Magazine advertisements are normally more technical and aimed at hi-fi 'buffs' (see also marketing page on the StudentZone).

- **Email updates** of new products and special offers which are sent to anyone registering via the website.

- **Comparative shopping reports** from one or more of the many websites that offer these, such as Kelkoo and Pricerunner, also see Unit 8, page 378. They are compiled by people who give their own account of shopping experiences – both positive and negative – and give students good practice in evaluating a variety of reports and deciding upon their validity.

- **News reports**, on both Richer Sounds and their main competitors, either from a good search engine such as Google, or a general news site, such as the BBC or Ananova. The British Companies website can be used to find current information on the 100 best companies to work for in the UK.

The Richer Way

Two books have been written by the founder, Julian Richer. One of these, *The Richer Way*, is suggested reading in the Edexcel scheme notes for Unit 7, Sales and Customer Service. BTEC First tutors can obtain both this book, and *Richer on Leadership*, the second book, at a discounted price by completing the form on page 308.

In conclusion

The Richer Sounds StudentZone has proved an invaluable source of information for GCSE Applied Business students and is now accessed by well over 10,000 students every day.

The area of the site developed for BTEC First is completely new and has been customised for the award. We hope that both you and your students will find it invaluable in obtaining detailed, relevant and topical information on a very successful business which manages to combine well-motivated, committed staff, legendary customer service, excellent profits and a social conscience.

Student guide to preparing for and producing your IVA

For the first unit of your BTEC First award you must complete an Integrated Vocational Assignment (IVA). This is set by Edexcel and covers all the topics and the assessment criteria for Unit 1.

Completing the IVA and obtaining a good mark is not difficult, but many people panic if they have to carry out a special type of assignment. This is why these notes have been written. Read them now, so that you know you have nothing to worry about! Then read them again when you are about to start your IVA.

Understanding the basics

- The IVA is a set of tasks you have to do. You do not have to do these tasks all at once, but can tackle them one at a time. Apart from Task 1, these will all relate to a selected business of your choice
- The tasks only relate to Unit 1. To give you an idea of what to expect, your tutor may give you a sample IVA for practice. If you do these tasks and exchange ideas and answers with other members of your group then this will help you to prepare for the IVA itself.
- Your answers and responses to the IVA questions must be based on a real organisation. This means that you have to choose a business to investigate and write about. This must be a business for which you can obtain a certain amount of information so discuss any choices with your tutor before making your mind up. You might like to start thinking about this now.
  - Normally the best business to choose is one you know yourself. This could be a local business, a business where your work part-time or where one of your family works. Or you could choose a well-known business that you can research on the Internet.
  - It is normally easier to choose just one organisation for answering all the questions but you can, if necessary, choose a different organisation for some tasks. Only do this if it will definitely help you and won't cause any confusion.
- The actual IVA *must* be all your own work. You cannot normally submit any group work. If you find that you have chosen the same business to investigate as another member of your class then you *must not* work together, or share your ideas and research information.

- The IVA is *not* an exam or test. It is a way of checking that you understand Unit 1 and can apply it to a real organisation. You can therefore refer to books – like this one – or to information that you have downloaded from the Internet. However, any sources you use or quote *must* be listed and identified. Never try to pass them off as your own work. You can check how to list them on page two of these notes.
- **Do *NOT* use your chosen business for any of the sample assessments**. These have been written to give you practice and to help you understand the topics. This helps you to carry out the IVA tasks more easily because you know how to apply what you have learned to a chosen business. However, they also involve discussions with other people whereas you must not, of course, share your ideas for your actual IVA with other students.
- The IVA can be done over a period of time. Your tutor will tell you how long you have to complete it when you are given it. Make sure you know your deadlines for each stage and for any reviews that you have with your tutor – and stick to them!
- If you have problems or worries about your IVA then talk to your tutor.

Preparation and planning

You are unlikely to be expected to start your IVA until you have completed most, if not all, of Unit 1. However, you may be given it sooner so that you know what to expect and you can see the actual tasks that you will have to answer.

The IVA changes each year, so make sure you have your own copy of the *Edexcel IVA Learner Instructions* clearly issued for your year. Then read it very, very carefully.

- Check that you understand the general instructions for completing it.
- Read the tasks that you will have to do, but don't worry if you don't understand all of these, particularly if you are still studying Unit 1.
- Check the summary of the tasks and what you will need to hand in.
- Check how your work must be presented for question 5 and make sure you understand this.

Your tutor will tell you the resources you can use and the schedule that you must follow. This is likely to include:

- Regular review meetings to check your progress.
- Submission dates for each individual task.
- A final submission date.

Put all these dates in your diary. It's a good idea, too, to put a 'warning' in it for the week before, to remind you that an important date is coming up.

You are allowed to ask your tutor for guidance and can discuss your ideas for answering a question – just like you would for an internal assessment. If you have a problem, therefore, or are stuck on a task then talk to your tutor. *Don't* put off doing work so that you miss your deadline.

Practical hints and tips

These cover researching the information you need, listing your sources and writing your answers.

Researching information

When you are researching, the main dangers are that you can have too much or too little, you lose important information or don't know what to do with what you've got! The following points may help.

- It is sensible to start collecting information as soon as you have agreed with your tutor on the business you are investigating. This will help to give you a 'picture' of the business from the outset – so that you can see how the topics you are studying apply to it.
- Buy a box file and label it. If you cannot afford one then find an empty cardboard box. In this you will be putting every scrap of information you obtain about your business. You now need four folders. Label these as follows:
  - Unit 1.1 – Business activities, sectors and key goals
  - Unit 1.2 – Industrial sectors
  - Unit 1.3 – Resources and aims and objectives
  - Unit 1.4 – Management processes, e.g. departments, managers, targets etc.
- Decide your best sources of information. If it is a local business, a place where you work part-time, or where one of your family works, then you may need to talk to a manager about the topics you are covering. In this case too, it is courtesy to offer to give them a copy of your final work! It is also polite to prepare for the meeting beforehand by writing down the questions you need to cover. Then make a clear note of the answers so you can read your own writing afterwards!
- If you are investigating a national or international organisation and using printed sources, then you will need to visit your college library. If you take photocopies of newspaper, magazine or journal articles then write the name and date of publication on the top.
- If you are printing out information, such as company data, from the Internet, do the same thing, unless this is an article where the date is clearly shown. Remember to restrict your searches to what is relevant. This will save you money (if you have to pay for print-outs), time and storage space.
- Put the information you obtain in your folders promptly, then you always know where it is.
- Don't throw away information you have used, in case it comes in useful for a later question.

Listing your sources

Put this at the end of your report on a separate sheet headed 'Sources of information'.

- If your source is a newspaper or magazine, state the title of the article, the title of the publication and the date.
- If your source is a book, give the title, the author and the publisher.
- If your source is from the Internet give the name of the site, the heading on the page and the URL (this is the address line that shows on screen and is normally printed at the bottom of the page).

Starting work and writing your answers

When you have obtained the information you need then it's time to start work!

- Choose a quiet time and a place where you can concentrate.
- Re-read your Edexcel Learner Instructions to refresh your memory.
- Read and re-read the question.
- Read through your information on that topic.
- Think carefully about what to write and then draft your answer.
- Make sure you stick to what is relevant – talking about how friendly the staff are or how jazzy the website is won't get you any marks!
- If you have to compare two businesses you may find it easier to write about one first and then the second. Then you can expand your answer to cover any comparisons you need to make.
- Your information will be clearer if it is written in separate sections. The easy way is to copy the task title as your main heading, then use section headings and bullet points so that your answers are easy to read.

- Include graphics where you can, such as tables, charts and diagrams. For example, you may want to include a graphic about the way the business is organised or which resources are used.
- Don't confuse quantity with quality! Writing one page which states the key points clearly is far better than writing six pages which miss the point.
- Don't copy out lengthy extracts from your source material. Instead, refer to it as evidence to support what you are saying – then include the source on your sources of information sheet.
- Expect to think more – and write more – if you are tackling a merit or distinction task. You may have to draft these out two or three times before you are satisfied. This isn't unusual! This is because the skills required and the way in which you must use your information are different:
  - **At pass grade** you will normally be asked to describe something – so you need to give a clear, factual description.
  - **At merit grade** you will be expected to explain something. This means going into more detail to give reasons for things, backed by examples.
  - **At distinction grade** you will be expected to evaluate the business in certain ways. This

means looking at what is done, how it is done, how effective it is and the factors that contribute towards this. It means making links between all the different items of information you have obtained. You may also be asked to suggest improvements or make recommendations. If so, you should support these with appropriate evidence or sensible reasoning to justify your views and opinions.
- Never think that something is impossible because you don't understand it first time. Sometimes it's just the words that may be confusing or the fact that you are panicking! Re-read the appropriate section in this book and, if that doesn't help, talk to your tutor.
- Don't miss out a part of any question in your IVA, otherwise this will affect your marks. It is always better to attempt something than to miss it out altogether.
- If you think you are going around in circles, especially with a difficult or high grade question, then write down what you can and ask your tutor to read it and comment. This might help to steer you forwards again in the right direction!

Good luck!

Cross-referenced additional activities grid

Several of the additional activities in this TRF can be cross-referenced with other units, particularly the specialist units. This grid shows you all these cross-references, but there are also reminders at the beginning of each unit.

Activity no.	Core Unit 1	Core Unit 2	Core Unit 3	Spec. Unit 4	Spec. Unit 5	Spec. Unit 6	Spec. Unit 7	Spec. Unit 8	Spec. Unit 9
1.1.4		2.4.7							
1.1.5							7.1		
1.1.7		2.3.8							
1.2.3									9.1
1.2.4		2.4.8							
1.4.1						6.1			
1.4.3							7.2		
1.4.6					5.1				
1.4.8								8.1	
1.4.9		2.2.7							
1.4.10				4.1		6.2			
2.1.1									9.2
2.1.3							7.3		
2.1.4								8.2	
2.1.5									9.3
2.2.5									9.4
2.3.3			3.1.7						
2.3.4					5.2	6.3			
2.3.5							7.4		
2.4.1				4.2					
2.4.4								8.3	

Unit overview and tutor guidelines

Unit 1 provides students with a basic introduction to how businesses operate i.e. their main activities; how they are classified; their resources, aims and objectives and their management processes. Tutors may like to bear the following in mind when teaching this unit.

- All students are familiar with the business world as customers. Some may also work on a part-time basis, others may have family involved in business. It is unlikely that anyone whose family owns a business will not know the importance of profit! Most students will also be aware of the services locally that they can access free of charge (their current course of study is one!). Many students may therefore be surprised at the business knowledge they have already, and this can be used to develop many of the early themes in Unit 1.

- Examples of well-known business organisations, products and services have been used because virtually all students will be familiar with them. Tutors can consolidate understanding further by applying many of the principles covered to local firms, the school or college, and organisations where the students may work. This is very appropriate when teaching resources, aims and objectives, as students can identify those that apply in firms they know well. It is helpful, at this point, to look at how and why managers control the use of resources. If students have to pay for computer printouts or for a parking permit, or if rooming issues are sometimes a problem, then this is a good starting point for a discussion about scarce resources and helps to prepare students for the final part of the unit.

- Students should be encouraged to think broadly about business concepts and to see that, in business, there are no neat subdivisions between different areas. This is evident on the Richer Sounds StudentZone. Students reading any pages will see a number of links to other pages, in different units, because of content overlaps. If

students appreciate this from the outset, they are more likely to grasp new concepts and apply new knowledge more readily. This is particularly relevant for Unit 3, as financial aspects permeate all areas of business planning and operation. The sooner students realise that any division of topics into 'units' is purely for educational convenience and does not reflect business practices, the better!

- The most difficult part of this unit is the concept of management processes – the longest and final section. Again school or college can provide an excellent starting point with the separation into different specialist departments overseen by a hierarchy of managers, from the head teacher or principal downwards. Targets for enrolment, retention and achievement will be readily understandable – as will monitoring of attendance! The actions tutors take to improve student performance can be developed to include the actions managers take to improve school or college performance. It is then a short step to apply this to a more standard business model – the Richer Sounds StudentZone provides excellent examples of the types of targets that are set and monitored.

- The final step is for students to judge whether identified management processes are likely to be effective in the use and control of resources and achieving aims and objectives. Dividing students into teams, giving them problems related to managing a business such as Richer Sounds and asking them to report ideas back is both useful and illuminating. It is often salutary for students to realise that all managers aim to run a successful business, so even when they read about business disasters in the press, it is likely to be for other reasons than the fact the managers couldn't manage! Try playing devil's advocate by introducing factors such as unexpected outside events or the actions of competitors into the mix and then ask students what they would do. This helps students to think more broadly and introduces them to some of the concepts in Unit 2.

This section contains 28 additional activities and case studies designed to reinforce learning and understanding. Each covers a key area of the mandatory units in the scheme where you may wish to provide additional practical activities for your students.

The content of some activities overlaps sufficiently with either another mandatory unit or a specialist unit to be marked as a cross-referenced activity. A full list of these is summarised here for ease of reference. Tutors are recommended to check the content before these are issued as, in some cases, there may be one or more terms which need a little extra explanation if students have yet to study the overlapping unit. This can be advantageous as students can be introduced to a new concept or topic almost incidentally and this also illustrates the strong links that are to be found between virtually all business studies topics.

Activity	Cross-reference
1.1.4	2.4.7
1.1.5	7.1
1.1.7	2.3.8
1.2.3	9.1
1.2.4	2.4.8
1.4.1	6.1
1.4.3	7.2
1.4.6	5.1
1.4.8	8.1
1.4.9	2.2.7
1.4.10	4.1, 6.2

The following is a summary of the activities for this unit with answers, where relevant.

1.1 – Business activities

Activity 1.1.1 – Key aspects of well-known businesses

This activity builds on the first three main areas of Unit 1.1 and asks students to identify the activity, sector and main aim for each of 16 businesses and then add four suggestions of their own. It should be noted that the final column links to the type of financial goals identified in 1.1 (i.e. sale at a profit, free, at or below cost etc.) rather than business aims as identified in 1.3 – although there is obviously some overlap in the real world.

The fact that the term 'business' is used for charities, universities and even the local register office should help students to realise that the term can be used for a far wider range of activities than they might have first thought.

Answer

Business	Activity	Sector	Financial goal
B & Q	Retailer of DIY/household goods	Private	Make profit
Connexions	Careers advice	Public	Supply free
NSPCC	Helps children in need	Voluntary	Supply free
Local register office	Records local births, marriages and deaths	Public	Contribution
BT	Telecommunications services	Private	Make profit
Manchester University	Educates students	Public	Contribution
PC World	Retailer of computers and related supplies	Private	Make profit
Council-run leisure centre	Provide leisure facilities and classes	Public	Contribution
Hotpoint	Manufacturer of domestic appliances	Private	Make profit
Local library	Lends books and CDs	Public	Supply free
Local water company	Purifies/provides water to homes/industry	Private	Make profit
Shelter	Assists the homeless	Voluntary	Supply free
Sony	Manufactures digital and electronic equipment	Private	Make profit
Automobile Association	Provides assistance and service to motorists	Private	Make profit
RSPCA	Animal welfare	Voluntary	Supply free
TUC	Represents trade unions and lobbies government on employment issues	Voluntary	Contribution

Students may do the task individually or work in small groups and compare their answers and/or do all those they can and leave the rest for discussion later. This will enable new terms or concepts (e.g. TUC) to be introduced easily.

Tutors could make the activity a little more difficult by specifying that the student's own suggestions should cover all the different sectors.

Activity 1.1.2 – Deciding on key financial goals in the public sector

Most students find the public sector harder to understand than the private sector (with its basic profit motive). The first part of this activity puts students into the role of making decisions about goals which will affect overall finances for four public sector organisations. The aim is to give them greater insight about this sector. An obvious strategy would be to divide the students into four groups with each group considering one type of business. However, as groups vary in size the rubric has been written to enable you to change this approach if you wish.

The inclusion of universities may be particularly relevant to students who may not be aware that overseas students are charged the full cost of a course (in 2004, this ranged from £8,000 to £20,000 a year, depending upon subject), while UK/ European students pay a contribution (currently £1,125 but set to increase to £3,000 in 2006). Even allowing for government funding, overseas (i.e. non-European) students are more profitable for universities.

In 2004, NHS dentists were paid £7.05 for a basic examination with patients paying £5.64 of this. Private dentists could set their own rate. Equally, NHS dentists proposing radical treatment (such as crowns) have to obtain permission beforehand with an agreement of the NHS/patient contribution. Private dentists do not have to do this. Students thinking about the dental issue could be asked also to consider the issue from a national perspective (i.e. too few NHS dentists to go round) and identify a possible solution from that point of view.

Free museum admission was introduced by the Labour government in 2002. Museums receive government grants and were also compensated through a change in VAT rules. Many, however, claim that government funding covers less than half the actual costs of running the business.

Most students will be aware of NHS hospital car parking and charges. This is a social issue as the reasons for parking will be many and various. In some cases there are few problems about charging a fee. In other cases the policy is more contentious. Ironically, car parking is free at most private hospitals. (If the college charges students and/or staff for parking, this activity could obviously be extended to include a fifth student group.)

Answer

1   **University** Advantages: more income so can improve facilities, upgrade equipment, employ more staff. Disadvantages: fewer places would be available for UK/European students. In addition, the expansion of the EU is likely to result in a higher demand for places by other European nationals which could 'squeeze out' some British students, especially those with borderline grades.

Possible solution would be to operate fixed quota system for foreign students to achieve minimum level of income from that area and use this money to expand facilities so that more students overall could be taken.

Dentist Advantages: overall income will increase, longer time can be spent with patients, greater range of treatments can be offered, patients can pay for treatment through private insurance schemes. Disadvantages: few disadvantages for the dentist concerned (unless a social conscience!). In general terms, disadvantages are that not all patients can afford private insurance and there are not enough NHS dentists so some people struggle to find one in their area.

The dentist cannot solve the national problem by individual actions but will choose one action or the other. The government could solve the problem by raising NHS funding levels (but this may mean higher taxes) or by recruiting more dentists and perhaps by trying to introduce a contract to make them work for the NHS for a specific length of time after qualifying. It could also try to recruit more dentists from abroad.

Museum Advantages: if income increased staff levels could be restored and closed areas could be reopened. Disadvantages: the main problem is that income could fall if fewer visitors came *and* the government withdrew the increased funding because of the reintroduction of fees.

Possible solution: it would be difficult for the museum to earn enough in income to compensate for loss of government funding, especially as fewer visitors are likely to attend if fees are charged. It may be better to organise special activities or exhibitions and charge an extra fee for 'free' visitors to access these areas, issue audio guides for a fee and try to increase takings through a museum restaurant or shop. It could also try to attract business sponsorship and donations.

Hospital Advantages: income should definitely increase because hospital car parking is always in demand by visitors and outpatients attending appointments. Disadvantages: parking in neighbouring streets could increase and become a nuisance to residents, it would be very expensive for people to pay to park for long periods and this could be at a time when they were under severe emotional stress.

Possible solution: the charging system should be considered carefully. Parking could perhaps be free after 8 pm and a special disc could be issued to visitors who were visiting for long periods on compassionate grounds.

Any other appropriate solutions should be accepted.

2   Some suggestions are given below but any appropriate suggestions should be accepted. Tutors may like to introduce the idea of targets at this stage and ask students to think about targets each organisation would set. It is then a small step to identify areas where performance could be improved. This will also start to prepare students for Unit 1.4.

University Fewer student withdrawals, improved student results, improved destination results.

Dentist Fewer 'no-shows' for appointments, improved follow-up system for routine check-ups, extension of expertise, e.g. into cosmetic dentistry.

Museum Improved new acquisitions or restorations, introduction of new or original exhibitions or displays, improved feedback from visitors, greater number of sponsors.

Hospital Improved recovery rates, reduction of waiting times (for example in A & E, both for clinic appointments and, on arrival, to see a doctor, and for operations), reduction in number of 're-admittance' cases.

Activity 1.1.3 – What should we do about council tax?

This case study focuses on the topical issue of council tax. The aim is to provide students with a greater appreciation of the overall problem of financing the public sector which is that people dislike paying tax but like good public services! Students could be asked to prepare for the activity by finding out how much their family pays in council tax, although this issue will have to be handled sensitively if some families are likely to be on housing benefits and therefore exempt. All local authorities issue booklets about the way the money is spent when council tax bills are sent at the beginning of the year – or students can look on the local council website.

Tutors may want to discuss the history of the poll tax in 1990 when protests and demonstrations resulted in the tax being dropped and contributed towards Margaret Thatcher's demise. (Many students may have covered this in history at school.)

There is widespread acceptance that the current system cannot continue for two reasons. The first is that, because business rates are linked to inflation and if central government provides no extra money, the only way councils can raise more revenue if costs are rising is to increase council tax. So the whole burden falls on council tax. Therefore a 1 per cent rise in budgets means an increase of 4 per cent on council tax because the latter is only meant to fund a quarter of the budget. The second is that the value of people's homes is not always a good measure of their overall wealth or income, certainly at a time when house prices are rising. So an elderly person living in their traditional 'family home' may have a low income but a high value property; hence the pensioner protests. For that reason it is widely accepted that some new initiatives will have to be considered. Tutors can therefore make the activity more topical by including any further ideas that are discussed – or by linking the activity to the changes that are eventually introduced.

Answer

1   Because they have to pay the council more money for local services.

2   Because many rely on the state pension which has risen very little over the past few years. They therefore cannot afford large council tax increases.

3   (6 of) Social services, schools, road maintenance, refuse collection, police, fire services etc. (see Figure 1.2, page 14 of Student Book).

4   To increase their revenue, particularly for services which are an 'optional extra' for people, rather than essential.

5   Because the government would have to increase taxes and this could be unpopular with the electorate.

6 **a** Pest control = free because essential service. Could cause environmental health problems if pests not controlled so council really has no choice.

b Entry to pool = contribution. This is because charging full fee to cover all costs of running the pool would make it too expensive for many people in the community.

c Replacement rubbish bin = free for normal bin, perhaps contribution for large size bin. Their provision is essential but some councils may charge for special bins.

d Car parking = full charge to make a profit because this is an optional extra for visitors and not a social necessity. However, if shoppers were dissuaded from coming to the area then the council could be criticised by traders in the town.

7 No specific answer possible, it will depend upon the opinions of the group. There is no 'right' answer, although experts argued in 2004 that the best answer would be for councils to be able to set a local business rate which took account of inflation.

8 There is some overlap between this question and question 3 on page 90 of the Student Book although that question involves researching the council site and does not just focus on monetary savings/efficiencies. Any appropriate suggestions should be accepted e.g. reducing overall wastage, buying supplies more cheaply, reducing maintenance costs, making staff efficiencies.

Activity 1.1.4 – Finding the money when you're all at sea

(Cross-references to Unit 2.4 External influences)
The aim of this activity is not just to illustrate how charities need and raise money but how they try to do this in imaginative ways. The use of new technology by the RNLI is an example of how technological advances affect the way we live and work and links to issues the students will study in Unit 2.4. Equally, the impact of stock market variations is also studied in Unit 2.4. For that reason this activity is cross-referenced with Unit 2.4 External influences. If the activity is set to consolidate Unit 1.1 tutors should provide a basic explanation of the concept of the stock market before the students start work.

Students who live in inland areas may never have heard of the charity, which will justify the RNLI's

view that it needs to improve awareness of its activities amongst young people.

The case study also enables the students to see some real costs of running a charity and to make a few simple calculations themselves. It also includes the concept of surpluses, which are first introduced in the Student Book on page 15. Again, tutors may find it useful to check that students understand the meaning of the term and, broadly, equate it to saving for the future.

A link to **www.rnli.org.uk** is available to students through **hotlinks**.

Answer

1 Royal National Lifeboat Institution.

2 (3 of) Running the lifeboat service, launching rescues, maintaining its fleet, giving information on safety at sea, fundraising (which also includes selling goods in its shops, online and by mail order), free health check of small boats. Any other appropriate suggestions should be accepted and there are several other activities identified on the website.

3 The not-for-profit/voluntary sector.

4 Any appropriate suggestions should be encouraged – and some student ideas may be enlightening. Ideas could include: the fact some students don't live near the coast, the fact that the RNLI isn't often featured in the media, the fact it isn't as famous as charities such as Oxfam and NSPCC, the fact it doesn't have charity shops in every town.

5 Money from profits or surpluses which are retained and invested to use in the future.

6 Because the stock market fell so the value of its investments was worth less.

7 **a** £274,000 × 365 is just over £100 million (i.e. £100,010,0000).

b 3 per cent of £15,000 = £450.

8 It is concerned that boat owners in danger wouldn't ask for help because they would be worried about the cost.

9 (3 of) Cameras in helmets to record rescues, installing satellite transponders in small boats, running courses for owners of small boats.

10 Any appropriate ideas should be encouraged. Students may want to refer to Figure 1.3 on page 15 of the Student Book but should also gain ideas from the website which gives information on RNLI events in different regions.

Activity 1.1.5 – What's the catch?

Students will be surrounded by special offers and freebies all the time. They may never challenge how these are compatible with the private sector motive of profit maximisation. This activity prompts students to think about the motives behind many offers.

The activity (particularly the answers) can be used to introduce many important related business concepts that students will meet in Units 1 and 2, such as business responses to competition and the importance of getting rid of unsold stock, as well as terms such as 'mark-up', 'market dominance', 'break-even' and issues such as the power of supermarkets over their suppliers.

You may prefer students to work on this in small groups and then compare ideas rather than do the activity alone.

Answer

1   Buyers are tied to buy specific printer cartridges which are sold with huge mark-ups.

2   The newspaper makes its money through selling advertising space. This is more attractive if its circulation rates are high.

3   This was Sky's response to the success of the BBC-backed Freeview service which, in June 2004, had half as many subscribers as Sky. Sky wants to reassert its market dominance. The Freeview service offers 26 channels. Sky's free service will cover 115 TV channels, 81 radio stations and 13 interactive channels including BBCi. Sky is hoping that subscribers will want to buy an upgrade and will be willing to pay up to £40 to access up to 455 channels and major sports and film packages. Sky will obviously want to keep its market leadership to guarantee future advertising revenue.

4   The recruitment agency needs both jobs and applicants to function. It tempts applicants to register because this is a free service and earns its money by charging employers when it fills a vacancy. For temporary work, the agency charges the firm more than it pays the temp and the difference is its income.

5   The airline wants to recoup the cost of operating the flight. It prefers to break even than make a loss so, as every empty seat is money lost, it would prefer to cover some of the costs than none of them.

6   Carphone Warehouse introduced the service (in conjunction with an advertising campaign) to challenge BT's dominance of the residential telecoms market. BT still has more than 70 per cent of the market even though it is not the most cost effective. Carphone Warehouse aims to make money by charging for calls to national, international and mobile numbers.

7   Supermarkets frequently engage in price wars against each other. These include 'loss leaders' to tempt customers into the store or persuade them to stay loyal. Supermarkets can often dictate terms to suppliers so the amount they are actually 'losing' by giving away some items is very small.

8   More consumers may be tempted to sign up to loyalty schemes or similar to receive a copy. Once the magazine arrives it is not only giving advice, information and new ideas to readers (as well as subtly promoting products) but if it is left around the house, many people read it or it may even find its way into a variety of waiting rooms – so the promotional message continues, free of charge. In addition, adverts can be included and the advertisers pay for these.

9   The aim of giving free samples is to impress the customer and persuade him/her to return to buy these on a return visit. Make-overs have a similar role but also engage the interest of passers-by. Both methods are far cheaper than national advertising!

10 The aim here is to free up space for new stock and to cut any losses. Unsold stock is dead money. Selling unsold stock cheaply means that financial losses are less than if the stock was not sold at all. The store should learn from its mistakes but use the money it receives to invest in new, fashionable items for next season.

Activity 1.1.6 – A question of size and scale

The aim of this activity is to reinforce the difference between size and scale and the fact that, whereas there are some general indications that can be applied, there are always exceptions. Students who are using the Student Book should have little difficulty with questions 1 and 2 but will need to think about some of the issues raised in question 3, such as the disadvantages and/or costs of operating over a wider area. They may find this easier if they think of specific examples rather than generalities, such as transporting fresh sandwiches rather than making them up each day in a local shop.

Answer

1 a Micro = sandwich shop; small = primary school; medium = department store; large = hospital.

   b No answer possible.

   c i Many employees may be part-time in some types of organisations, which will increase the overall number.

   ii Looking at other indicators, e.g. its sales turnover or scale of operations.

2 a Local = Derby County football club; Regional = Thames Water; National = Royal Mail; European = easyJet; Global = Shell.

   b Only local people will be interested (normally) in their own football team as each locality has its own team. Water suppliers are responsible for sourcing/treating/supplying water over a wide area. This is sensible given the way the supplies are sourced and the cost of treatment and supplies. The Royal Mail delivers mail all over the country because it would not be economic to have different providers covering different areas of the country. Users would not want to deal with different regional providers. EasyJet provides low cost flights mainly to holiday makers. An airline will obviously operate internationally. Easyjet does not offer transatlantic travel because this would not be cost effective, but it could not survive if it only offered domestic flights. Shell extracts oil, refines it and sells petroleum products. The cost of exploration, extraction and refinery facilities, plus the cost of transporting crude oil, is only cost effective on a global basis.

   c No specific answers possible but if students are struggling for ideas, tutors could ask them to consider which businesses are purely local, regional and so on. Ideas could include local newspapers, radio stations and cinemas. At regional level multiplexes, garden centres and shopping malls. At national level, television companies, daily and Sunday newspapers, magazines. At European level many large clothing outlets and stores. At global level Microsoft and other large computer companies (Apple, IBM etc.), drug companies and film makers/distributors (Warner Bros, Universal, Dreamworks etc.).

3 a No answer possible but ideas include sandwich shops (many local but compare Pret a Manger); pizza outlets (many local but compare Pizza Express); car rental firms (many local but compare Hertz and Avis); travel agents (some small and local but compare Thomas Cook); clothes outlets (local independent shops versus Next, Top Shop or River Island); local small inns and hotels against national chains, such as Holiday Inn or Travelodge.

   b (Benefits: 2 of) Economies of scale mean that it is cheaper to produce or buy goods in bulk, national advertising is cheaper per item sold, the overall cost of stocking and selling each item is likely to be less through reduced storage and distribution costs, having a well-known name/brand will attract customers. Any other appropriate suggestions should be accepted.

   (Disadvantages: 2 of) Regional differences/preferences are more difficult to take into account, there will be national competitors to consider, additional costs are incurred when operating over a wider area, many people may prefer to use a known, trusted local firm. Again any other appropriate suggestions should be accepted.

Activity 1.1.7 – If superstores ruled the world . . .

(Cross-references to Unit 2.3 Stakeholders)

The aim of this activity is to encourage students to evaluate the role and benefit of modern superstores and the consequences for other types of businesses, such as small retailers and suppliers. The activity has strong links with Unit 2 in relation to stakeholders (2.3) and corporate social responsibility (2.3 and 2.4). As such, the unit is cross-referenced to 2.3.

The obvious arguments are that superstores bring us cheap goods under one roof which equates to mass convenience to the financially constrained or time-poor customer. However, if they are allowed to sell a greater range of goods, this is likely to impact on more and more individual, local retailers as well as national businesses selling items from cosmetics and clothing to DVDs, books and greetings cards. Could we eventually end up with a world consisting only of superstores? It could be argued that the diversity of our towns and cities is being destroyed through the continual growth of national and multinational retail businesses.

Painting this type of picture may seem alarmist but may shock students into evaluating a gradual evolutionary type of change which they have probably taken for granted and never challenged. Rather than ask specific questions, students are asked to consider the effects on a variety of other types of organisations (or stakeholders).

Answer

1 See table below.

Action by superstore	Effect on
Sell pharmaceutical products and toiletries	Boots and local chemists shops
Sell flowers from stores and website	Local florists and Interflora shops
Sell books, DVDs and greetings cards	W H Smith, Blockbuster and high street card shops
Buy up corner shops	Independent grocers, cash and carry wholesalers
Sell cut price milk	Local farmers and milk delivery people
Sell cut price fruit and vegetables	Local markets
Sell cut price petrol	Local/independent petrol stations
Expand clothing ranges	High street stores, small clothes shops
Sell garden products	Local garden centres
Expand throughout the nation	High streets in every town, diversity of different areas
Expand throughout the world	Local cultures and diversity of different countries

2 Good = prices lower. Bad = smaller outlets cannot compete and must close.

3 Possibly only a few very large stores who dictate terms to suppliers but are competitive for customers; little variety or individuality; very convenient and cheap. **Or**: shoppers bored with lack of variety and prepared to pay more for individuality so local shops and small traders start to appear again. Students should be encouraged to let their imaginations run amok a little with this question.

4 FoE and other pressure groups do not think superstores should be allowed to expand unchecked. They do not consider it right that the acquisition of corner shops and/or convenience stores is considered as a separate issue and does not count towards their overall market share. They also believe that investigations into buyer power have not been rigorous enough. Whilst there is obviously a middle view, they do provide a useful balancing force. Students should be encouraged to access the FoE website before they prepare an answer to this question.

Activity 1.1.8 – Don't bank on it!

The aim of this activity is to allow students to discover for themselves how different types of data can be used to assess size and scale, and the strengths and weaknesses of each. Students may enjoy this task more if they work on it in small groups and then compare their answers, ideas and suggestions as a class. In addition, in the first question, scope is allowed for students to be asked to update some of the information provided. Whilst this was current in 2004, if you are undertaking this activity in 2006 or 2007, for example, this may be worthwhile.

Quality national newspapers routinely report bank profits – in August (for half-year results) and February. Alternatively, you may prefer students to research themselves through the bank websites (see hotlinks) or good news-sites.

The activity includes the concept of market capitalisation which is above the level of BTEC First but is explained within the task as the value assigned by the financial markets.

If students struggle with question 8 they could be advised to give a score to the rank in each table and then add them up. A more sophisticated method would be to weight each table and then assign a ranking score.

Answer

1

Banking tables				
Number of bank branches				
HBOS	Barclays	HSBC	Lloyds TSB	RBS group
1,000	1,700	1,700	1,800	2,277
Total number of employees				
HBOS	Barclays	HSBC	Lloyds TSB	RBS group
60,000	74,800	232,000	79,000	125,000
Number of UK customers				
HBOS	Barclays	HSBC	Lloyds TSB	RBS group
25 million	14 million	8.5 million	16 million	22 million
Foreign operations (by number of countries)				
HBOS	Barclays	HSBC	Lloyds TSB	RBS group
6	60 plus	79	27	26
Net profit 2003				
HBOS	Barclays	HSBC	Lloyds TSB	RBS group
£3.8 billion	£3.8 billion	£7.8 billion	£1.89 billion	£6.16 billion
Value of business 2003 (market capitalisation)				
HBOS	Barclays	HSBC	Lloyds TSB	RBS group
£29 billion	£24 billion	£95 billion	£25 billion	£51 billion

2 a In 2004 the order was RBS, Lloyds TSB, (joint) Barclays and HSBC then HBOS.

  b Branches are costly and banks closed branches to reduce costs and increase profitability. They considered (hoped?) that fewer customers wanted to use branches because of increased access to cash machines, telephone and Internet banking and because they could phone through enquiries to call centres. *Note*: many banks are now reconsidering these strategies and increasing staff who deal with customers in local branches.

3 a HBOS, RBS, Lloyds TSB, Barclays, HSBC.

  b A better measure than branches but depends how accurate bank claims are. For example, how do you define a 'customer'? In some cases, banks may just calculate the number of sales of investment products (e.g. the number of customers buying one cash ISA) rather than numbers of personal and business account holders so data is not always comparable.

4 a This is the foreign operations part of the table.

  b Ranking is HSBC, Barclays, Lloyds TSB, RBS and HBOS.

5 a HSBC, RBS, Lloyds TSB, Barclays, HBOS.

  b HSBC has both the greatest scale and the most employees, but this correlation fails in relation to Barclays, Lloyds TSB and RBS!

  c Not very, given that there is only a link for the highest and the lowest ranked bank.

6 a HSBC, RBS, HBOS and Barclays, Lloyds TSB.

  b Good because a small bank is unlikely to make the highest profits, so likely to be some link (correlation) between size and profits. Bad because profits may be increased mainly because of lower costs (e.g. closing branches) rather than doing more business so for one year may give a false picture.

7 a HSBC, RBS, HBOS, Lloyds TSB, Barclays.

  b The official calculation is done by multiplying the number of shares by the current share price but it is the factors that influence both of these that result in the value. These include the overall assets, financial security, past performance and current prospects both of the individual business and the sector as a whole.

8 a The answers will depend upon how the students use the data. The easiest is to assign a score (1 to 5) to the banks in each table and add them up. A more sophisticated method would be to weight the tables. It should be expected that the highest ranked bank is either HSBC (market capitalisation/employees/scale and profits) or RBS (number of UK branches) and the lowest is HBOS (branches/foreign operations) or Lloyds TSB (profits).

  b Students should be able to justify the method used and answers obtained.

  c Comparing answers as a group will enable students to see which other methods have been used and why and to obtain a final list.

9 a No specific answer possible, it depends upon student views and perceptions.

  b Students may suggest factors such as: total assets or worth, profits over a longer time period, number of UK employees.

10 Banks are ranked on market capitalisation. On this basis, for the banks listed in 2004, HSBC is the largest, then RBS, HBOS, Lloyds TSB and Barclays.

The reason is that this valuation takes account of a variety of key variables (see answer to 7c).

Note: The world's largest bank by market capitalisation in 2004 was Citigroup (£124.4bn) with Bank of America in second place (£93.9bn) and HSBC in third place (£88.1 bn).

1.2 – Classification of business activities

Activity 1.2.1 – Sectors, activities and organisations

The aim of this activity is to check whether students have understood the basic divisions of private, secondary and tertiary sectors and can place business activities and then business organisations in the correct sector.

Students then have to think of additional business activities *and* organisations for each column. Students who struggle to name organisations could find it helpful to refer to their local Yellow Pages.

Answer

Sector	Activities	Organisations
Primary	Pig farm Christmas tree grower Fish farm	UK Coal Castle Cement
Secondary	Sawmill Chemical works Shoemaker Drug company Boat builder Road builder	LEGO Kelloggs Levi Toyota Powergen
Tertiary	Doctors Architects Hotels Call centres Universities Garden centre	Esure British Museum Hertz Amazon Samaritans B & Q Thomas Cook Securicor

Activity 1.2.2 – When the consumer is king!

This activity aims to show students that there is a knock-on effect on business of all decisions made by any type of consumers. For the first set of business activities the students simply need to identify the sector and the effect of each change (i.e. positive or negative). For the second set, students are asked to suggest business activities (an indicated number is given) as well as completing the last two columns.

For the last five activities students may, of course, suggest additional business activities to those shown. For example, under rising house prices it would be fair to identify landlords (tertiary/negative) and under drink driving laws to identify breweries (secondary – though effect is probably broadly neutral). Under Apple i-Pods and download services the effect on music bands is again probably broadly neutral. However, any creative thoughts and ideas should be encouraged provided the business activity identified is being classified correctly.

Answer

Change	Business activity	Sector	Impact
EU fish quotas restrict catches of many types of deep sea fish	Fishing Fishmonger	Primary Tertiary	Negative Negative
Health scares and high cost mean fewer people are smoking	Tobacco production	Secondary	Negative
Clean air laws means fewer coal fires and also less electricity is produced using coal	Coal mining	Primary	Negative
Chilled ready meals are often preferred by busy people	Food production	Secondary	Positive
Arguably organic fruit and vegetables have more flavour	Fruit and vegetable growers	Primary	Positive
Skin cancer scares mean more people are using fake tanning products	Cosmetic firms Sunbed producers Tanning salons	Secondary Secondary Tertiary	Positive Negative Negative
New occupations linked to lifestyle include personal trainers and personal shoppers	Personal services Retailing	Tertiary Tertiary	Positive Positive
The Atkins low carbohydrate diet proved hugely popular even though it was criticised on medical grounds	Atkins Foundation Potato growers Bakers (bread/cake) Egg producers Butchers	Tertiary Primary Secondary Primary Secondary	Positive Negative Negative Positive Positive
Increased house prices mean more people want to buy their own home	House builders Estate agents Solicitors	Secondary Tertiary Tertiary	Positive Positive Positive
Drink driving laws mean fewer people want to drive if they go out at night or prefer to drink at home	Taxis Retailers Pubs	Tertiary Tertiary Tertiary	Positive Positive Negative
Most people have a computer and mobile phone and send both emails and text messages to friends	Computer and phone manufacturers Telecom companies (e.g. BT, T-Mobile) Internet Service Providers Royal Mail	Secondary Tertiary Tertiary Tertiary	Positive Positive Positive Negative
i-Pods and download services have changed demand for single CDs	Apple Manufacturers of blank CDs CD creators/ producers (e.g. music companies) Download services	Secondary Secondary Tertiary Tertiary	Positive Negative Negative Positive

Activity 1.2.3 – Pets R Us!

(Cross-references to Unit 9 Starting up a new business)

This activity brings together the classification of business activities and the size and scale of businesses from Unit 1.1. It also extends this to include small businesses and thereby provides a cross-reference link to Specialist Unit 9, Starting up a new business.

There is no requirement for students to be studying Unit 9 to do this activity. Indeed, in this case tutors may wish to extend the activity by asking students to identify the type of business ownership they would prefer and prepare a summarised business plan. Fundamentally, however, the activity has been designed to consolidate previous concepts and to encourage creativity in a novel and interesting way.

Answer

1   The following is indicative only. Any appropriate ideas should be approved.

Primary Breeders

Secondary Manufacture of: pet food; pet toys; collars, tags and leads; pet carriers; dog kennels; hutches; cat flaps; shampoos/combs; pet mats and dishes; pet clothing; goldfish bowls/tanks; pet baskets; horse riding equipment (saddles, bridles etc.) and clothing; bird/rodent cages; pet passports; miniature ornaments; books/magazines on training/breeding/caring for animals.

Tertiary Pet shop (could specialise in rare breeds); pet portraits and photos; dog walking, grooming salons/mobile services; pet insurance; boarding kennels/catteries; vets; animal behaviourists; animal trainers; pet cemeteries; pet clubs; bird/animal sanctuaries; animal charities; pony clubs; riding stables.

2   Breeding. Manufacture of speciality items – most are a possibility particularly if they are a little bit different e.g. organic shampoos. (Students could be introduced to the concept of USP at this point.) Most tertiary services apart from insurance.

3   No specific answer possible.

4   No specific answer possible – it depends upon the business chosen.

5   No specific answer possible – again it depends upon the business chosen. However, students should be guided away from any idea where specialist skills would be required (e.g. vet, animal behaviourist) and/or where substantial capital would be needed (e.g. mass production of pet food).

Activity 1.2.4 – Nerves of steel!

(Cross-references to Unit 2.4 External influences)

This case study is cross-referenced to Unit 2.4 because it links the changes in the British steel industry with the economic influences that caused these. It reinforces the concepts of employment trends, output and productivity and also includes information on economic recessions and downturns, demand and supply (and the effect on prices) and exchange rates.

If the activity is undertaken whilst studying Unit 1.2, the students can absorb the basic economic facts as background information. In this case, time should be taken to ensure students understand the points that are made in the case study and it may be more appropriate to ask them to work on the questions in small groups. Students doing the activity as part of Unit 2 may be expected to have a greater understanding of the influence of economic variables.

Tutors can find additional useful information at the websites shown (Corus, the UK Steel Association and the Iron and Steel Statistics Bureau) or can set additional tasks for students to research on these sites.

Answer

1   233,500 (268,500 – 35,000).

2   A worldwide recession and the fact British steel was expensive because of poor productivity. It couldn't compete against cheaper steel on the world markets.

3   About 133 tonnes (2 million/15,000).

4   1,655 tonnes (4.8 million/2,900).

5   Productivity.

6   Higher productivity means goods cost less to produce because each worker is producing more. They can therefore be sold more cheaply so prices are more competitive.

7   **a**   Tutor to check bar chart.

   b   **ii** and **iii**.

8   They fall because everyone is keen to sell the steel they are holding in stock so they lower prices.

9   It will fall because it takes fewer people to make the same amount of steel.

10 Corus is optimistic, otherwise it would not be investing money in new plant and equipment. It thinks productivity will increase and has targets for 2006 but does not see employment falling

because it thinks demand will remain high and so will prices because of the growth of the Chinese economy.

Activity 1.2.5 – Investigate the growth and decline of business activities in your area

The aim of this activity is to enable students to see the practical effects of the growth and decline of sectors in their own locality. Some students may have undertaken a similar study at school, so it would be useful to check this first. This may give the whole group a flying start, unless the main findings have all been forgotten!

The nine regional development agencies in England are identified as a useful source in the research list. In many cases they highlight key sectors in the area. However, students need to look carefully as in some cases, e.g. **www.nwda.co.uk** t, here are links to an associated site with that information, i.e. **www.englandnorthwest.com**. Links are available for students through Heinemann hotlinks, but for tutor information the full list in 2004 is given below.

www.advantage-westmidlands.co.uk
www.eeda.org.uk (Eastern England)
www.emda.org.uk (East Midlands)
www.lda.org.uk (London)
www.onenortheast.co.uk
www.nwda.co.uk (North West)
www.seeda.co.uk (South East)
www.southwestengland.co.uk
www.yorkshire-forward.com

In addition there are development agencies for Northern Ireland (**www.investni.co.uk**), Scotland (**www.scotland.gov.uk**) and Wales (**www.wda.co.uk**).

Another excellent resource could be a good speaker (such as another member of staff) who has an excellent historical knowledge of the local area and could visit the class to give a personal account of different changes. Equally, students should be encouraged to ask older relatives for their reminiscences.

It is useful, when the information has been obtained, to analyse it from the point of view of changes which are in accordance with national sector changes and those that are not.

This activity can easily be extended, for example by: including more visiting speakers; asking different student groups to present their findings to the class or to summarise their findings on a handout; asking student groups to prepare a summary poster about their findings on a flip chart and present this to the group.

Answer

No specific answer possible.

1.3 – Resources, aims and objectives

Activity 1.3.1 – Whose business is it anyway?

This activity introduces students to the fact that aims are likely to differ depending upon the type of business organisation. Students have to agree on the main activity of several organisations and then link these to their published aims. In some cases this provides an introduction to organisations the students will meet later in their studies, i.e. OFT, the Foreign Office (Unit 2.3), The Treasury (Unit 2.4) and UNISON as an example of a trade union.

The requirement to divide organisations into those which represent different sectors is useful revision.

Answer

1   a   Tate Modern – world famous museum showing international modern art such as that produced by artists like Tracy Emin and Damien Hirst. OFT – government agency responsible for ensuring open and fair trading in accordance with EC competition laws.

Mothercare – private retailer of clothes, toys and equipment for mothers-to-be and young children. RSPCA – charity concerned with the welfare of animals.

Carphone Warehouse – private retailer of mobile phones and telecommunications systems. Foreign Office – government department concerned with international relations. UNISON – largest union in Britain representing 1.3 million public service workers. The Treasury – government department concerned with managing government finances.

b   A = **b** (OFT); B = **a** (Tate Modern); C = **g** (UNISON); D = **d** (RSPCA); E = **h** (Treasury); F = **f** (Foreign Office); G = **e** (Carphone Warehouse); H = **c** (Mothercare).

c   Private = Carphone Warehouse and Mothercare; Public = Tate Modern, OFT, Foreign Office, The Treasury; Voluntary = RSPCA, UNISON.

2   Any appropriate suggestions should be accepted but students should preferably be focused on

identifying key resources, e.g. Tate Modern = large building, works of modern art; OFT = premises, expert staff; Mothercare = retail stores, appropriate stock for resale; RSPCA = expert staff, transport, kennels/sanctuaries; Carphone Warehouse = retail stores, stocks for resale; Foreign Office = overseas locations, contacts with foreign governments; UNISON = branch officials, researchers who can provide information for members; Treasury = expert staff, liaison/networking with government officials, central location.

Activity 1.3.2 – Matching activities and resources

This activity links resources to business activities and shows that resources may vary depending upon the core business activity. It provides a 'prompt' in the form of a table so that students do not have to remember the main types of resources but simply have to apply these to different types of businesses.

Answer

1 The following are suggested resources but other appropriate suggestions should be accepted.

Grotto at Xmas. A sandwich shop – an email/fax order service with deliveries for firms, hot and cold foods, mobile vans to local industrial estates. A security firm – distinctive uniforms, multi-lingual staff, high ratio of female staff.

b No specific answer possible, it will depend upon the suggestions made.

Activity 1.3.3 – Key resources

This activity focuses on the key resources required for a business to be successful, using business models familiar to the students. It also encourages students to think about resources to achieve the aim of raising money for charity in a fun day. The aim is to help students to think about resources more broadly and to encourage creative thinking amongst the group!

Answer

1 Suggested essential resources are listed below. Students should be expected to provide reasons which link to the needs of customers.

a up-to-date attractions, good locations, reputation for safety, additional amenities, such as cafes and restaurants.

Resource	Garden centre	Self-employed website designer	Toy shop	Sandwich shop	Firm supplying security guards
Land	✓*				
Premises	✓	✓	✓*	✓*	✓
Equipment	✓*	✓*	✓	✓*	
Vehicles	✓			✓*	
Money	✓*	✓*	✓*	✓*	✓
Managers	✓		✓	✓	
Skilled/expert staff	✓			✓	✓*
Business skills of owner	✓*	✓*	✓*	✓*	✓*
Personal skills of owner	✓	✓*	✓		✓
Location	✓*		✓*	✓*	
Brand name			✓		✓*
Reputation	✓	✓*	✓*	✓*	✓*
Good supply chain	✓*		✓*		
Good customer relations	✓*	✓*	✓*	✓*	✓*
Industry contacts		✓*			✓*

2 Any of the resources marked with * in the table above should be accepted.

3 a The following ideas are only indicative of the type of suggestions that should be accepted. Any other appropriate ideas should be accepted. A garden centre – café, children's play area, garden design service. A website designer – good website with online help/contact. A toy shop – website to sell goods online, gift wrap service, Super Santa's

b wide range of courses, good IT facilities, excellent tutors, excellent reputation for good results.

c excellent reputation, good DJ, good music, stylish premises.

d good equipment, skilled staff, good location, good reputation.

e good range of stock, good location, helpful staff, spacious premises.

f good location, good reputation/brand name, spacious premises, good chef.

2 No specific answer possible as it will depend upon the type of suggestions made by students.

Activity 1.3.4 – Aims and SMART objectives

This activity asks the students to identify the main aims of different companies from published statements of future aims and objectives. It also asks students to identify SMART objectives when these have been given. The activity illustrates the wide range of aims and objectives which are identified by business organisations each year. Students should understand that these are constantly changing, depending upon the current market and the position of the business within that market.

Answer

1 Dixons – to make a profit, to cut costs; Caffé Nero – to expand, to maximise profit; Eidos – to survive, to break even; Burger King – to cut costs, to maximise profit, to expand; BA – to cut costs, to break even, to increase market share; Levi's – to increase market share, to make a profit; B & Q – to increase market share, to maximise profit; John Lewis – to expand, to maximise profit; Dell – to maximise profit, to offer new services; Arla – to cut costs, to offer new services, to maximise profit.

2 B & Q, John Lewis, Burger King, BA. Note that some students may select Caffé Nero but strictly speaking this is not SMART because there is no target date.

3 In many cases figures for expansion are given without a specific time period. Students could be guided by listing the SMART criteria and then adding any factors which have not been included in the statements.

Activity 1.3.5 – More money but awful performance!

This case study focuses on the Royal Mail. Much has been written in the press about changes in, problems with and performance of the Royal Mail so that it is extremely easy for tutors to extend this case study if they wish. As written, it simply focuses on the aims and objectives of the Royal Mail service and does not enter into complexities of ownership or government interference.

The Royal Mail service has been used not just because it has had problems relating to service delivery (which link to the scheme criteria) but also because the Royal Mail and post offices will be well known to all students. There is therefore no need to explain the business activity. In addition, the type of resources required should be easily appreciable, even without direct experience. Tutors may find it useful to explain how the Royal Mail will have to face increased competition over the next few years, especially if this is imminent when the case study is being undertaken.

Answer

1 To make a profit, to reduce costs, to meet performance targets.

2 It made a profit and reduced costs.

3 It failed to achieve its service standards.

4 It didn't deliver 92.5 per cent of first class letters the following day and also failed to deliver 97.8 per cent of second class mail on time.

5 It cut jobs, it closed post offices, it only delivered post once a day.

6 Because postmen and women would deliver to more addresses every day.

7 Any six appropriate resources should be accepted, for example: sorting staff, postal delivery workers, post boxes, post vans, sorting offices, sorting equipment.

8 **a** Because mail gets lost and because mail is delivered late.

   b People won't trust it and will want to use another service.

9 To meet performance targets – because then he will get his bonus!

10 **a** Useful but they are not the key concerns of customers.

   b To meet performance targets and not to lose mail – so the public will trust it and choose it above its competitors.

1.4 – Management processes

Activity 1.4.1 – Information handling and administration

(Cross-references to Unit 6 Business administration)

This activity focuses on a key task for all administrators of searching for information. It links to Specialist Unit 6, where information sources are identified in 6.1 Core administrative systems. It involves the work of a sales office and so enables students to gain a simple overview of the type of information which would be handled by sales administrators who are supporting the sales staff, rather than actually selling goods themselves. Because several types of information could be obtained from more than one source, the activity also encourages students to think about alternative options, rather than just having one idea.

Answer

Information required	Source
The correct type of paper to order for the fax machine	H
The email address of a French customer	B, G, J
The date of the next sales meeting	A, D
The price you paid for photocopying paper last month	K
The name of a 4 star hotel in Milan	F
The name of the customer service manager's administrator	J, L
A competitive price for buying printer cartridges	E, F
Last month's sales figures	A, C
The number of two local taxi firms	F, I
The date when your boss is going on holiday	D
The date when an order was despatched to a customer	B, G
The arrival time of a flight from New York	F
The date arranged for the budget planning meeting	D
The name of your usual stationery supplier	K
How to insert envelopes into the new printer	H
The date your boss last wrote to a particular customer	G
Exchange rate of Euros to Pounds sterling	F
The value of a recent customer order	B, C, G
The postcode of a customer in Exeter	B, C, G, F
The dates of public holidays in Australia	F
Contact details for your firm's health and safety officer	J, L

Activity 1.4.2 – The specialisation of labour at Unicorn Floorings

This activity revises the concept of decentralisation and uses administration to review the different types of activities carried out within different departments in a business. The activity can be given as a revision exercise once the students have learned about different functional areas *or* it could be given beforehand – to provoke discussion and debate about the work that is carried out in different functional areas. In this case tutors may want students to work on the tasks in pairs, rather than alone. Many students will have some general ideas themselves from their own experiences, particularly about standard departments such as Sales or Finance, and could be encouraged to make an educated guess at less familiar titles (e.g. Facilities Management).

Tutors should note that the title Human Resources has been given rather than Personnel Management (which is the title in the scheme), given that the former is in more general use today.

Students could be referred to the summary key task tables in the Student Book when answering question 2, but should then convert the information they read to a task which would be carried out by an administrator in that department.

Answer

1 Kelly – Human Resources; Sam – Customer Services; Jo – IT Services; Emily – Sales; Jack – Purchasing; Jon – Facilities Management; Kim – Research and Development; Saeed – Finance; Nasreen – Production; Jenna – Marketing; David – Distribution.

2 No specific answer possible as a wide range of additional tasks may be suggested. These include: Human resources – sending out interview letters, helping to arrange staff training events, maintaining staff records: Customer Services – writing to customers, recording/analysing customer feedback, arranging for replacement goods to be supplied etc; IT services – logging repairs and maintenance work carried out, ordering new software or computer supplies; Sales – responding to customer enquiries, updating sales information and price lists, producing quotations for customers; Purchasing – keeping supplier details and the database up-to-date, liaising with suppliers; Facilities Management – helping to prepare documentation related to health and safety risk assessments, ordering new items of equipment and furniture and arranging for repairs to be undertaken; R & D – arranging for tests to be carried out, recording results, keeping records of investigations on performance and new materials/applications; Finance – producing invoices, sending out letters to remind customers about late payments, preparing spreadsheets; Production – checking supplies of raw materials, ensuring data on finished stock levels is accurate; Marketing – sending out/analysing market research questionnaires, making arrangements

for meetings of customer panels, updating company website, helping to prepare/place advertisements; Distribution – helping to prepare delivery schedules, contacting suppliers or customers. Any other appropriate suggestions should be accepted.

Activity 1.4.3 – Improving customer service

(Cross-references to Unit 7, Sales and customer service)

This activity enables students to put their own experiences as shoppers to good use by identifying their pet hates or things that annoy them the most when shopping and then suggesting ways in which retailers can improve customer service by reducing the number of irritants for their customers. A list of pet hates is given but students are asked to add two of their own. Additional ones, for example, could include: lack of car parking, no delivery service, extra charges for deliveries, many empty spaces on shelves at busy times and so on.

The activity is structured so that students have to negotiate, on two occasions, with their colleagues. This links to the negotiation skills included in the scheme in Unit 7, i.e. negotiating with customers. There is also an overlap with Unit 5, where students have to negotiate on behalf of others for improvements in working conditions.

Answer

No specific answer is possible because the result will depend upon individual students' views and the outcome of the negotiations.

Activity 1.4.4 – To outsource or not – that is the question!

This activity revises the concept of outsourcing and uses this as a means of revising the different types of functional tasks and areas in a business. It also reintroduces the concept of core business activity. The students are presented with two opposite viewpoints for outsourcing a range of different functions and need to be able to identify with both – and then evaluate them. Tutors may wish to re-iterate the main points about outsourcing before students start the activity.

It is sometimes quite enlightening for students to learn that there is often no single right answer in business! Any or all of the functions listed could be outsourced. In reality it is the cost, the specification, the wording of the contract (especially in case things go wrong) and the relationship between the two

businesses that is most important to its potential success.

Answer

1   Below are given indicative answers but any other appropriate ideas should be encouraged.

   a   R & D: there are specialist organisations with a wider range of facilities for food testing, they could analyse a wider range of possible ingredients in a shorter time. Distribution: vans and maintenance/drivers are expensive, we are only a small business so don't need large lorries. It is cheaper to use specialists who will despatch our items with others at a competitive rate.

   b   Marketing: we will have more control over our advertisements and the amount of money spent on this area if we do it ourselves. Facilities Management: we can control costs better if we arrange repairs ourselves and how do we know whom we can trust for security?

2   (2 of) Purchasing, Personnel (or Human Resources), Sales. Purchasing because the quality/type of raw materials is probably crucial to their success; Personnel because their staff are a key resource and recruitment, training, review needs to be kept within the company; Sales because good contacts with retail buyers will be vital and sales is one of the most critical areas of the business. They cannot trust this area to anyone else.

3   The core business is developing, producing and selling their sauces. Any other areas could be outsourced, i.e. IT, Marketing, Facilities Management, Distribution and Finance. However, apart from specialist tasks (e.g. debt collection/preparation of statutory accounts) most businesses prefer to keep finance operations in-house given the importance of frequent management accounts in monitoring business performance.

Activity 1.4.5 – Investigating functional departments and management jobs

This activity enables students to enhance their knowledge of the work carried out in functional departments and by managers by undertaking research activities. Tutors may wish to sub-divide all the tasks between different student groups with a brief to report back to compare their findings at a later, specified date. For task 3, tutors may prefer to bring newspapers into class for students to read advertisements or give specific types of jobs to investigate online. The aim is to give students an appreciation of the role and responsibilities of different managers to help them understand more about how managerial authority works in a hierarchy and how it relates to functional tasks and departments.

Answer

No specific answer possible.

Activity 1.4.6 – Know your legal rights!

(Cross-references to Unit 5, Employee contribution to working conditions)

All students are normally interested in their legal rights as existing or future employees. This activity is in the form of a short quiz which asks students to decide if various employees have been lawfully, or unlawfully, dismissed from their jobs.

Whilst this area is obviously part of the function of personnel management it is covered in more depth by students who are studying Specialist Unit 5. For that reason it has been cross-referenced to that unit so that, if preferred, tutors can use it just with students studying that area. However, there are also links with Unit 2.4 and students may find the information on page 192 of the Student Book useful when researching their answers.

Answer

1   Fair – she is in breach of the terms of her contract in respect of her uniform and hygiene regulations.

2   Unfair – part-time employees should be treated in the same way as full-time workers and given the same training opportunities, otherwise this is discrimination.

3   Unfair – the problem should be investigated and Tom should be given a free eye test (see the Display Screen Equipment Regulations). Even if his eyesight is failing, under the Disability Discrimination Act his employer still has a legal obligation to make appropriate adjustments to his job.

4   Fair – not reading the IT policy is no excuse!

5   Fair as she deceived the company by lying about her qualifications.

6   Fair. Theft is classed as gross misconduct.

7   Unfair. Under the terms of the Employment Rights Act the company cannot insist on Sunday working.

8   Unfair. Dismissal because of pregnancy is automatically unfair.

9   Unfair because harassment is unlawful and the employer must take immediate steps to prevent this and remedy the situation.

10 Fair as he has been accepting bribes.

11 Unfair. She has this right under the Data Protection Act.

12 Fair because the employer can reasonably expect employees to keep up-to-date and to change when the job changes, e.g. with the introduction of new technology.

13 Fair – the members of staff are redundant because there is no work for them to do and as all the staff in the Midlands have been dismissed there is no discrimination.

14 Unfair. Under the terms of the Employment Relations Act workers have the right to take time off in a family emergency.

15 Fair. Although lateness is a minor offence, if the disciplinary procedure has been followed correctly he cannot argue that the dismissal is unfair.

16 Fair. Employees have to comply with other laws that are related to their work. In this case, to be able to drive is a key requirement of the job.

Activity 1.4.7 – Thinking on your feet!

The idea of R & D is sometimes difficult for students to comprehend, particularly in relation to day-to-day products they use, with the possible exception of electronic goods. Therefore this case study, which looks at R & D in relation to sports shoes and trainers, should help students to appreciate its value in relation to more basic types of items.

The final question extends the activity to ask students to identify how the functional activities/departments at Adidas will link over the design, development and selling of the new shoe.

Tutors may wish to extend the discussion to include the possible future actions of other possible competitors besides Nike. The main four players in the market are Adidas, Nike, Reebok and Puma. It may also be enlightening to discuss the role of fashion and trends in this market and the way in which this can influence choice – and prices! The willingness of many young people to pay exorbitant amounts to wear a brand seen as 'cool' by their peer group – and the way in which manufacturers can exploit this to enhance their profits – may make an interesting talking point!

Answer

1   (3 of) Nike Air Max shoes, Reebok air pump shoes, Adidas ClimaCool shoes, Adidas 1 shoes.

2   The market is very competitive and it is a key way in which they can differentiate their product and make it more attractive than those of their competitors. It also links to the customer's wishes to own the latest or most fashionable brand/type of shoe.

3   So that their competitors would not find out what they were doing and/or beat them to market with the first 'intelligent' shoe.

4   a   USA and Germany

    b   China and Malaysia

    c   Because production costs are kept as low as possible as wages are lower and the cost of living is less in China and Malaysia.

5   (1 of) Most probably to make them more desirable by limiting the supply. It could also be testing demand, given the price, before making too many which could result in unsold stocks or having to lower the price.

6

Functional area	Activity
R & D	Design and test new intelligent running shoe
Marketing	Notify press about shoes and arrange for advertising
Production	Manufacture shoes
Distribution	Distribute finished shoes to stores
Sales	Sell shoes to customers
Finance	Receive payments and calculate total sales profit.

Activity 1.4.8 – Functions online and a new strategy for the LEGO Company

(Cross-references to Unit 8 Business online)

Students will need to be able to access the LEGO Company website to be able to do this activity. If they have Flash Player installed they will be able to view the Flash film showing the production process which is carefully explained so that it is easily understandable. This will help students to understand the type of automated processes commonly used in manufacturing, especially in relation to a well-known product. Students will need Acrobat installed to download the reports mentioned and tutors may wish to do this in advance of the activity. It would be helpful for students to refer to hard copies.

The LEGO Company website is so comprehensive that there is scope for far more detailed examination of the business than is given here. Tutors may wish to investigate it themselves first, to add any additional questions or activities which would be particularly useful for their group.

The activity is cross-referenced with Unit 8, Business online, and provides a useful way for students to identify features of an online operation (8.1) and benefits (8.2). Tutors setting the activity for this specialist unit may wish to discuss other aspects of the online operation with students.

Finally, students may need some assistance with the numeracy question to convert Danish krone into pounds sterling, especially if they do not have access to an online converter.

Answer

1   To nurture the child in each of us.

2   Safety is crucial to its brand image. Parents can trust LEGO® brand products. One accident because of a faulty brick could lose thousands of customers.

3   Most of the production process is automated for safety, efficiency and quality reasons.

4   a   (3 of) Downloading building instructions, finding nearest store, technical support, FAQs, parts replacement, catalogue request, contact us, order checker.

    b   (2 of) Easier for customers, customers obtain information more quickly, easier for LEGO Company staff, reduces costs of sending out information by post.

5   (2 of) Saves advertising and administration costs, reaches broader market (i.e. worldwide), is read by people interested in the LEGO® brand.

6   a   Any three aspects of the PLAY section, such as LEGO club, message boards, games, films, comics.

    b   (3 of) Product finder, information on products, buying online, information about LEGOLAND Windsor for visitors or other appropriate suggestions.

7 (2 of) The LEGO Company is a global operation, the website enables it to reach all customers instantly. Selling goods online increases profits. Providing customer service online improves customer relationships. The LEGO club helps customer loyalty. Customers have access 24/7 plus any other appropriate suggestions.

8 The amounts will depend upon the exchange rate at the time that students undertake this activity. Tutors should check this either online or in a national newspaper.

9 No specific answer possible. Tutors will be able to find this information by downloading the latest company report and accounts.

10 No specific answer required. It will depend upon student views. However, tutors can use this question to explore with the group the limitations of management processes, particularly if a product or service has reached the end of its natural life cycle and/or is now considered unfashionable.

Activity 1.4.9 – Organisational plans and the hierarchy at M & S

This activity can be undertaken to help students understand how plans are formed and put into action through a management hierarchy.

In July 2004 Philip Green was unsuccessful with his bid to buy M & S but has the right to submit a new bid after 6 months. Students are asked, as question 4, to find out current M & S performance against targets from the website and also from news websites. It will then be useful to review why any targets have been missed, the type of corrective action that has been taken and whether or not this has been successful.

Answer

Extract from Marks & Spencer Action Plan

Weaknesses	Action	Executive responsible	Information needed to monitor performance	Effect on store managers
Business too complicated	Sell the Money business (which sells M & S financial products).	F (loses job)	Sale contracts completed.	Aware but no direct effect.
Competitors stealing core customers	Win back 35–55-year-old core women shoppers by stocking the right goods at right price.	D and possibly C	Carry out survey to check how many women in this category are shopping at M & S again.	Stock items would change.
Stores too cluttered	Improve store layouts/displays and modernise store space.	A	Senior managers to visit stores to check and report back.	Managers should have a say in this.
Too many lines stocked	Reduce number of lines stocked in food (–500), clothing (–1000) and home goods (–4,000).	B, C, D	Check product lists.	Fewer number of stock items to look after and display.
Lack of brand confidence	Review (and possibly axe) new brands e.g. Sp menswear and Per Una Due young fashion. Focus on quality, value, service, innovation and trust and start new marketing campaign with slogan 'Your M & S'.	A, B, D	Customer attitude surveys. Could also mention results from focus groups.	Need to retrain staff to match new ideals.
Supply chain slow	Renegotiate to pay suppliers less and save £140 million by 2006/7. Save a further £35 million by reducing stock levels. Continue policy of sourcing more goods abroad.	E	Prices paid to suppliers. Stock level checks. Survey of sourcing from home versus abroad.	Probably little or no effect.
Costs too high	Stock fewer goods to save £35 million and reduce markdowns and amount of food wastage to save up to £50 million by 2006/7.	B, C, D	Check number of markdowns and amount of food discarded.	Involved in number and types of items to stock to minimise wastage.

Activity 1.4.10 – Could you control a business?

(Cross-references to Unit 4 Business communications and Unit 6 Introduction to business administration)

This activity involves the students in making plans, setting targets for a business and taking corrective action at a later date. The aim is to familiarise students with the type of plans made by managers and how these are monitored. The scenario given relates to running a magazine and links to the idea of a magazine raised in Specialist Unit 4 (page 21) and the costing of *Chatter* magazine in the PowerPoint slides relating to Unit 3.1. However, if the students are involved in a Young Enterprise activity then this would probably be the natural choice and, fairly easily, the basic instructions can be customised to allow this.

Because the activity involves meetings between the managers of the business, it is cross-referenced to Unit 4, Business communication, as Unit 4.4 involves preparing for and running a business meeting and to Unit 6, as Unit 6.3 involves organising meeting arrangements. However, for the first meeting the agenda is given to help to focus the students on the key areas for discussion. The students are required to prepare the minutes for the meeting and both the agenda and minutes for the second meeting. However, tutors may wish to drop this requirement if the meeting participants are not studying Specialist Units 4 or 6.

Tutors can, of course, add or delete management roles to suit the size of their group and it is expected that for most classes there would be a division into different teams to undertake this activity. This is useful because, at the end of the whole activity, feedback from the different teams and a comparison of ideas and performance is an extremely valuable plenary activity.

At the outset tutors should be prepared to discuss the background information with the students to give more depth if necessary. Depending upon the ability level of the group, tutors should also be prepared to prompt or encourage students in the early stages.

After the first meeting, tutors need to receive a copy of the business plan and the targets that have been agreed.

Assuming that the business is only discussed on a theoretical level and students don't actually try to produce a magazine, then the achievement of targets is up to the tutor's discretion. It is recommended that tutors review the business plan and the targets and identify those which are unrealistic (either too high or too low), over-ambitious or unachievable and substitute more realistic figures!

The students should then be given feedback on their performance which identifies those targets which have been achieved and those which have not – with variances (and their scale!) highlighted.

For the second meeting students have to produce their own agenda and are reminded that this should also include the two standard items of 'Minutes of the last meeting' and 'Matters arising'.

The students then have to decide the corrective action that can be taken to try to match actual performance more closely to planned performance. It is suggested that core targets should be the main ones for attention, e.g. sales targets, production levels and expenditure targets.

Answer

No specific answer possible.

Key aspects of well-known businesses

1 For each business listed below, identify

  a Its main activity

  b The sector it is in (i.e. private, public or not-for-profit/voluntary)

  c Whether it *normally* aims to:

    i make a profit

    ii supply goods or services free of charge

    iii charge users only a contribution towards the full cost.

2 Add **four** businesses to the list and complete each column. You can choose from the logos here, or think of your own.

Hotpoint registered trade mark reproduced by kind permission of Indesit Company UK Ltd

RSPCA name and logo are registered trademarks of the RSPCA, reproduced with their kind permission

Business	Activity	Sector	Financial goal
B&Q			
Connexions			
NSPCC			
Local register office			
BT			
Manchester University			
PC World			
Council-run leisure centre			
Hotpoint			
Local library			
Local water company			
Shelter			
Sony			
Automobile Association			
RSPCA			
TUC			

Deciding on key financial goals in the public sector

All businesses in the public sector receive money from the government, but they often argue that this isn't enough for their needs. They must therefore decide whether to:

- supply all goods and services free
- make a small charge for some items which contributes towards, or covers, the costs
- sell some items to make a profit.

The decisions they make will affect the total revenue they receive.

1 As instructed by your tutor, divide into groups to decide the advantages and disadvantages of each of the following ideas and then recommend the action that should be taken.

A university has places for 2,500 undergraduates a year. It knows it can increase its income by recruiting more overseas students, because they have to pay higher fees than British or European students.

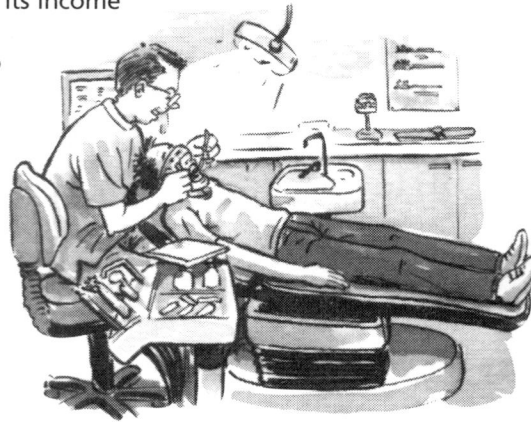

An NHS dentist is considering rejecting NHS patients and only accepting private ones from now on.

A museum is considering re-introducing entrance fees in defiance of the government's wish that entry should be free to everyone in return for higher state funding. The museum claims it doesn't receive enough funding to pay for its day to day running costs and has had to lay off staff and close down some areas. Voluntary collection boxes have not raised enough extra money.

A hospital wants to increase its income. It is thinking of installing 'pay and display' machines on its visitor car parks, with quite high charges.

2 A key goal of many organisations is continually to improve their performance.

Suggest **two** goals *each* of the businesses above could have in relation to improving performance.

What should we do about council tax?

Read the case study below. Then answer the questions that follow.

Case study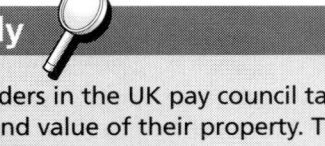

All householders in the UK pay council tax, based on the size and value of their property. This money goes towards paying for council services in their local area. In 2004, fears about more increases in council tax saw pensioners marching to Downing Street. This tax has increased by 60 per cent since Labour was elected in 1997 – which isn't much fun when you are living on a state pension which has hardly increased at all.

Who is to blame – and what should be done? Councils blame the government for making them provide more and more services without enough money. The government blames councils for over-spending and being inefficient and wasteful. It currently gives them over £54 billion a year and argues this is enough. The councils disagree.

Councils receive most of their money from three sources: government grants, business rates and council tax. The government decides how much money it will provide in grants and also sets business rates. So the only way councils can raise more money is to increase council tax, or charge for their services.

Recently, however, another idea has been put forward. This is to introduce other ways of raising money, such as the suggestions in the box below.

Other ideas for raising money	
Local income tax	A small charge on everyone who works (so pensioners exempt).
Local sales tax	An extra tax is added to goods purchased in the area.
Tourist tax	Added on to hotel bills and leisure facility charges.
Congestion charge	Charge all motorists for entering the town/city area.
Local business rates	Allow local councils to set and collect business rates themselves.

Questions

1 Why do local people dislike rises in council tax?

2 Why are pensioners especially affected by council tax increases?

3 Identify **six** services provided by your local council.

4 Why do councils charge for some services?

5 If the government gave a lot more money to councils, every service could be provided free of charge. Why won't the government do this?

6 You are on your local council. For each of the following services you can:
   i   charge the full amount to make a profit
   ii charge a lower amount, to obtain a contribution
   iii provide the service free.

Match up the following services with their most appropriate charge, in your opinion, and give a reason for your choices.

   a pest control
   b entry to local swimming pool
   c a replacement refuse bin
   d car parking in the town centre

7 As a group, discuss the advantages and disadvantages of each of the new ideas to raise money listed in the table 'Other ideas for raising money' and rank them in the order you think would be best.

8 Many people think that councils would spend less if they improved their performance. As a group, suggest **two** goals a council could set related to improving performance to reduce the money they spend.

Finding the money when you're all at sea

(Cross-references to Unit 2.4 External influences Activity 2.4.7)

Read the case study below and then answer the questions that follow.

Case study

The Royal National Lifeboat Institution (RNLI) is equipping lifeboat crews with helmet-mounted cameras so that rescue operations can be beamed to TV news programmes. The aim is to boost fundraising and to increase awareness of RNLI work, especially amongst the young.

The RNLI offers more free services than its sister organisations in other parts of the world. In French waters, for example, a small boat owner in difficulties would have to pay to be rescued – but not in Britain. The RNLI is concerned that people would then hesitate to call them out because of the possible bill.

Whilst such sentiments are admirable, some people say that the RNLI cannot afford to think like this. Stock market fluctuations in 2001/2 more than halved its reserves to £90.4 million – which is less than the amount needed to run the charity each year and keep intact its 231 stations, 451 boats (some costing £2 million each) and reserve fleet.

The RNLI needs nearly £274,000 a day to operate but is proud that for every £1 raised, 80 pence is spent on maintaining and replacing its existing fleet, 17 pence is spent on fundraising and only 3 pence is spent on administration. It is equally proud that it rescues about 3,000 people a year and saves the lives of at least 1,000 people.

In an attempt to increase funds, the RNLI now recruits donors 'face-to-face' in the street by persuading them to sign up to give monthly donations by direct debit. Since 2000, this has resulted in an extra £500,000 being raised – worth £640,000 with tax rebates through gift aid. But the RNLI isn't happy about these aggressive fund-raising techniques. Hence its interest in new technology. In addition to tiny cameras and webcams it is also looking at tracking devices using satellite transponders which signal the RNLI every 30 minutes to give the position or an alert if something has gone wrong. Installing these on small boats could be a useful additional source of income from the RNLI. In another initiative it is opening a training college for small boat owners. Not only will this earn money for the RNLI, it should also reduce the number of rescues it needs to make.

For additional information go to **www.heinemann.co.uk/hotlinks** (express code 1351T)

Questions

1 What is the RNLI?

2 Identify **three** activities of the RNLI.

3 In which sector is the RNLI?

4 Suggest two reasons why young people may be unaware of the RNLI and its work.

5 What are 'reserves'?

6 Explain why the RNLI lost money in 2001/2.

7 Calculate:

  a how much the RNLI needs each year to do its work

  b how much, from a gift of £15,000, it would spend on administration.

8 Why does the RNLI feel it would be unwise to charge for any of its rescue services?

9 Identify **three** new ways in which the RNLI is raising money.

10 Investigate the RNLI further at its website. Then, as a group, suggest two other ways in which you think it could increase its income.

What's the catch?

(Cross-references to Unit 7 Sales and customer service Activity 7.1)

In the private sector, businesses aim to make a profit. Ideally they aim for profit maximisation – which means making as much profit as possible. Normally this would mean charging the highest price possible and keeping costs as low as possible. So why do businesses often give things away for nothing? Or sell them for below cost prices?

This is usually because it is in their interests to do so. So, for each example below, can you decide what the business gains from the deal?

1. Most suppliers, e.g. Hewlett Packard and Lexmark, sell their computer printers at cost price (or just above).

2. Once a week, a completely free local newspaper may drop through your door.

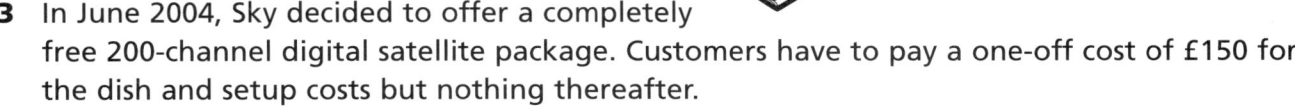

3. In June 2004, Sky decided to offer a completely free 200-channel digital satellite package. Customers have to pay a one-off cost of £150 for the dish and setup costs but nothing thereafter.

4. A recruitment agency allows customers free registration and makes no charge for finding them jobs.

5. Ryanair, the cut price airline, frequently offers bargain tickets for sale at well below cost price.

6. Carphone Warehouse introduced free local telephone calls between users of its new fixed line Talktalk service.

7. Supermarkets have BOGOFs (buy one get one free) offers on a whole range of goods.

8. Free glossy customer magazines are given by retailers, travel companies and car producers e.g. Boots, Marks & Spencer, Thomas Cook, Volvo and Mazda.

9. Free samples and make-overs are provided by cosmetic companies in department stores.

10. Summer sales are held by clothing retailers with prices slashed until the goods are sold.

Activity 1.1.6

A question of size and scale

The size and scale of a business are sometimes determined by the product or service offered – but not always. Do the activities below to find out more!

1 a Enter each of the following businesses in column (a) of table below, in its most likely position.

   Hospital   **Sandwich shop**   **Department store**   **Primary school**

b From your own knowledge of your local area, add **one** more type of business to each category.

c A small business which provides cleaning services employs over 100 people.

   i Suggest **one** reason why the number of employees is not always a good guide to business size.
   ii Suggest **one** other way of identifying the size of a business.

Table 1

Size of business	Type of business (a)	Own ideas (b)
Micro (under 10 employees)		
Small (10–50 employees)		
Medium (50–250 emp's)		
Large (250+ employees)		

2 The scale of a business often relates to the type of goods or services offered.

a Enter each of the following businesses in its correct place in column (a) in Table 2 below.

   Thames Water   **easyJet**   **Shell**   **Royal Mail**   **Derby County football club**

b For **each** business, explain the link between the goods or services provided and the scale of operations.

c In column (b) suggest **one** other type of business that could be included in **each** category.

Table 2

3

Scale of business	Name (a)	Own ideas (b)
Local		
Regional		
National		
European		
Global/ multinational		

Products and services are not always an accurate guide. For example, most chemists serve only their local area, but Boots and Superdrug operate nationwide.

a Suggest **two** other types of businesses which could operate either on a local basis or nationally.

b Identify **two** benefits and **two** disadvantages to a business that decides to operate on a large scale.

If superstores ruled the world . . .

(Cross-references to Unit 2.3 Stakeholders Activity 2.3.8)

Case study

When ASDA announced plans to open new stores and expand existing stores and create a further 4,300 jobs, it was criticised by Friends of the Earth (FoE). The pressure group argued that new and bigger ASDAs would be bad news for everyone.

Friends of the Earth

When Tesco widened its product range to non-food goods that included garden products, DVDs, televisions and books – and announced plans to operate 1,000 convenience stores around the UK – many shoppers were pleased, but others shuddered. Tesco already boasts that it receives £1 out of every £8 spent in Britain. It is now aiming for £1 out of every £7, then £1 out of every £6 and so on. FoE protested both before and outside the 2004 Tesco Annual General Meeting that Tesco was damaging local communities, small retailers, suppliers and customers.

Why all the moans about superstores? With cheap food aplenty and the convenience of buying everything under one roof, what could be the problem? Surely, the bigger the stores, the better for everyone? In addition, both Tesco and Asda argue that they are responsible companies that create jobs for local people.

You can find out more at **www.heinemann.co.uk/hotlinks** (express code 1351T).

Your tasks

Work in small groups to do the following:

1 Decide the organisations or other groups that would be affected by each of the superstore actions listed in the table on the next page. To help, the first is done for you.

2 Identify **one** good outcome and **one** bad outcome of selling more and more non-food products.

3 Suggest what shopping and employment would be like in 2100 if the increase in size and scale of superstores continues.

4 Assume you are a well-known pressure group such as Friends of the Earth and you want the government to take action. What would you want it to do? (Bear in mind your suggestions should be both realistic and legal!)

Now compare your answers and your ideas and decide which are the best.

Activity 1.1.7 If superstores ruled the world . . . (cont'd)

Action by superstore	Those affected
Sell pharmaceutical products and toiletries	Boots and local chemist shops
Sell flowers in stores and from website	
Sell books, DVDs and greetings cards	
Buy corner shops	
Sell cut-price milk	
Sell cut-price fruit and vegetables	
Sell cut-price petrol	
Expand clothing ranges	
Sell garden products	
Expand throughout the nation	
Expand throughout the world	

Don't bank on it!

Everyone knows that banks are big. In banking size is important, because banks must be financially secure. For many years the largest banks in Britain were the Big Four – Barclays, HSBC, Lloyds TSB and RBS Group (which owns NatWest and the Royal Bank of Scotland). More recently they have been joined by a fifth – HBOS – which resulted when the Halifax and the Bank of Scotland merged.

How can you tell which bank is the largest? Would you count the number of branches or customers or employees? Or would you prefer to look at profit? How could you tell which bank operates on the largest scale? Read the key facts about the banks below and answer the questions that follow to see which methods work out the best – and which don't!

Barclays
In 1987 there were over 2,700 branches but by 2004 these had fallen to fewer than 1,700. The group operates in over 60 countries and employs 74,800 staff. It claims to have 14 million UK customers and it made £3.8 billion profit in 2003. The overall value of the business is £24 billion.

HBOS
HBOS is the name of the merged Bank of Scotland/Halifax group, valued at £29 billion. It operates in the UK and in 6 overseas countries and has 60,000 employees. It has over 1,000 branches, 25 million UK customers and made profits of £3.8 billion in 2003.

Lloyds TSB
The sign of the black horse is found over 1,800 branches today – 300 less than in 1987. The group operates in 27 countries and employs 79,000 staff – 39,000 of them in the UK – to serve its 16 million UK customers. In 2003 its profits were £1.89 billion and it was valued at £25 billion.

RBS
The RBS Group includes the Royal Bank of Scotland and NatWest. In 2003 it announced group profits of £6.16 billion. In 2004 it operated 2,277 branches – 650 for the Royal Bank of Scotland and over 1,600 NatWest branches. In 1987 the two operated 3,900 branches but in the 1990s before its acquisition by RBS, NatWest closed nearly 1,500 branches. The group operates in 26 countries with a worldwide staff of 125,000 and serves 22 million UK customers. It is valued at £51 billion.

HSBC
In 1987 HSBC had 2,127 branches. Today it operates 1,700 branches in the UK for its 6.5 million UK customers. It is also active in 79 countries around the world with a total workforce of 232,000. In 2003 it was valued at £95 billion and announced record pre-tax profits of £8.5 billion.

Activity 1.1.8 Don't bank on it! (cont'd)

Questions

1. Either on your own, or working in small groups, use the key facts about the banks to complete the tables on the next page. Your tutor may want you to find out additional or updated facts by referring to the banks' websites. Links are available through **www.heinemann.co.uk/hotlinks** (express code 1351T).

2. **a** Rank the banks from 1 to 5 by number of branches they had in 2004.

   b Suggest **two** reasons why all banks decided to reduce the number of branches between 1987 and 2004.

3. **a** Rank the banks by number of UK customers.

   b Do you think this is a better guide to size than number of branches? Give a reason for your answer.

4. **a** Identify the part of the table which indicates each bank's scale of operation.

   b Now rank your banks to obtain this information.

5. **a** Rank your banks by numbers of employees.

   b To what extent does this link to each bank's scale of operation?

   c How useful do you think this is as a measure of size?

6. **a** Rank your banks by profits in 2003.

   b Suggest one reason why profit is a useful guide to size and one reason why it is not!

7. **a** Rank the banks in terms of how they are valued by the financial markets. The formal term for this is **market capitalisation**.

   b What aspects of the business do you think the financial markets – who represent investors – take into account when they value a bank? Compare your ideas with other members of your group.

8. **a** As a group, decide a method of using all your data to rank the banks from 1 to 5 in terms of overall size and scale.

   b Justify your answer, based on the way you used your data to get this result.

   c Compare your answers, as a class, to see if you all agree and if not, why not!

9. **a** As a class, decide which of your tables has been the most useful for assessing bank size and scale, with reasons.

   b Suggest any further information you think would be useful to obtain more precise answers.

10. One of the tables you have prepared is officially used to rank banks on a worldwide basis. Decide which you think is the most likely and give reasons for your choice.

Activity 1.1.8 Don't bank on it! (cont'd)

BANKING TABLES

Number of bank branches

HBOS	Barclays	HSBC	Lloyds TSB	RBS Group

Total number of employees

HBOS	Barclays	HSBC	Lloyds TSB	RBS Group

Number of UK customers

HBOS	Barclays	HSBC	Lloyds TSB	RBS Group

Foreign operations (by number of countries)

HBOS	Barclays	HSBC	Lloyds TSB	RBS Group

Net profit 2003

HBOS	Barclays	HSBC	Lloyds TSB	RBS Group

Value of business 2003 (market capitalisation)

HBOS	Barclays	HSBC	Lloyds TSB	RBS Group

Sectors, activities and organisations

Complete the table below by putting each of the business activities/occupations *and* each of the organisations listed in Table 1 into the correct sector in Table 2.

Then add **six** suggestions of your own to each column. In the first column add **six** types of business activities. In the second column add **six** names of well-known organisations.

Table 1

Business activities and occupations		Organisations	
Doctors	Shoemaker	LEGO®	Amazon
Pig farm	Universities	UK Coal	Samaritans
Architects	Drug company	Esure	B & Q
Sawmill	Fish farm	British Museum	Thomas Cook
Christmas tree grower	Garden centre	Kelloggs	Toyota
Chemical works	Boat builder	Castle Cement Ltd	Powergen
Hotels	Road builder	Hertz	Securicor
Call centres		Levi	

Table 2

Sector	Activities and occupations	Organisations
Primary		
Secondary		
Tertiary		

When the consumer is king!

The goods and services we buy are constantly changing, depending upon fashion, lifestyles and technological developments. What we buy affects what is made. If demand for something falls then eventually it will no longer be produced, or only in very small quantities. However, if demand increases then more will be produced.

1 Each of the changes in the table below has affected at least one business activity and often several. Your task is to complete the table.

   a For the first **seven** changes, the business activities are identified for you. You must enter the sector and state the impact. This is either

positive (more is demanded) or negative (less is demanded). To help, the first one is done for you.

   b For the last **five** changes you must identify the activities as well. To help, the suggested number of activities involved is shown in brackets – although you may be able to think of more!

2 Suggest **two** changes yourself that have occurred over the last few years and explain their effect on the relevant activities and sector(s). Compare your ideas with other members of your class.

Change	Business activity	Sector	Impact
EU fish quotas restrict catches of many types of deep-sea fish	Fishing Fishmonger	Primary Tertiary	Negative Negative
Health scares and the high cost mean fewer people are smoking	Tobacco production		
Clean air laws mean fewer coal fires and also less electricity is produced using coal	Coal mining		
Chilled ready meals are often preferred by busy people.	Food production		
Arguably organic fruit and vegetables have more flavour	Fruit & veg growers		
Skin cancer scares mean more people are using fake tanning products	Cosmetic firms Sunbed producers Tanning salons		
New occupations linked to lifestyle include personal trainers and personal shoppers	Personal services Retailing		
The Atkins low carbohydrate diet proved hugely popular even though it was criticised on medical grounds	(5)		
Increased house prices mean more people want to buy their own home	(3)		
Drink driving laws mean fewer people want to drive if they go out at night or prefer to drink at home	(3)		
Most people have a computer and mobile phone and send both emails and text messages to friends	(5)		
i-Pods and downloads have changed demand for single CDs	(4)		

Pets R Us!

(Cross-references to Unit 9 Starting up a new business Activity 9.1)

Read the information below and then do the tasks that follow.

Background information

Anyone who wants to start their own business first needs to identify a growing market and then to select a niche within that market which they think they could fill.

The pet market in Britain has been growing every year. According to the market research firm Mintel, pet owners were spending almost £3.5 billion a year on their animals in 2002 – and this figure had increased by almost 25 per cent over 5 years. By 2007, it is forecast that spending will have increased to over £5 billion a year.

Today cat ownership is increasing whereas dog ownership is falling a little, mainly because cats are seen as more independent and easier to care for. But both types of animals are very pampered! A survey by Argos in December 2003 found that we spend over £6 on a pet's birthday present and over £15 on its Christmas present. The Blue Cross, an animal welfare charity, also carried out a survey and found that pet owners cook their animals special Christmas dinners and even send them Christmas cards! It estimated that about £100 million was spent on animals at Christmas 2003.

Of course, Christmas gifts are only one type of spending on pets – there are dozens of other ways of making pet owners happily part with their money. So as a growing market, with lots of opportunities, the pet industry is hard to beat. Especially if you are an animal lover yourself!!

Task 1

Working in a small group, brainstorm as many different types of business activities as you can that are linked to the pet industry. Aim to identify *at least* 20!

Then divide these into different sectors, i.e. primary, secondary and tertiary.

Task 2

From your list, identify all those activities that could be undertaken on a small scale or by a small sized organisation.

Task 3

As a group, select the activity which would appeal to you most if you were starting your own business.

Then research the competition in your own area. This means identifying other businesses in your locality or region which offer the same goods or services.

Task 4

List the personality attributes and skills that you think someone working in this business would need to possess. Then identify how many of these fit you and your team!

Task 5

As a group, give a brief presentation to your class which identifies the business you have selected, explains the products or service you would offer, and gives reasons for your choice linked to your local market and your own skills and abilities.

Nerves of steel!

(Cross-references to Unit 2 External influences Activity 2.4.8)

Read the case study below and then answer the questions that follow.

Case study

Steel is all around us. It is used in trains, buses, cars, boats, bridges and buildings. At home it is used in kitchen appliances, sinks, cutlery, saucepans and radiators. Despite this, the British steel industry has a very turbulent history. In 1967 it employed 268,500 workers. By 1980 this had fallen to 130,000 and by 2000 to 35,000. Today the largest steel producer in the UK is Corus, which employs 25,000 workers at its plants in Port Talbot, Scunthorpe and Teesside.

What caused the decline of the British steel industry – and how safe are the jobs of today's steel workers?

Demand for steel depends upon other countries doing well and wanting to buy steel to use in their manufactured goods. Steel is made all over the world – so prices are very competitive. If demand falls then many countries are affected. Demand fell sharply in the 1980s because of a worldwide recession. At that time, too, British steel was expensive because productivity was poor. In Port Talbot, it took 15,000 workers to make 2 million tonnes

of steel in 1980. In 2003, 2,900 workers made over twice that amount. The company now aims to invest in £150 million in new equipment to increase output at Port Talbot to 4.8 million tonnes by 2006.

These efforts are starting to pay off. In 2004 the Chief Executive of Corus announced that the company had made a profit of £163 million in the first six months of the year – as against a £89 million loss in 2003. This is the first time the company has made a profit since 1997/8 when demand for UK steel fell because of an economic slowdown. This was made worse by a strong pound which meant UK steel was very expensive. The turnaround now is partly because Corus is more competitive. It is helped by an increase in the demand for steel, particularly from China, which has also resulted in a sharp increase in prices. The steel workers of Britain are hoping this trend continues.

You can find out more at **www.heinemann.co.uk/hotlinks** (express code 1351T).

Questions

1 How many people lost their jobs in the UK steel industry between 1967 and 2000?

2 State **two** reasons why demand for UK steel fell in the 1980s.

3 In Port Talbot how much steel was *each worker* producing in 1980?

4 If Port Talbot increases its output to 4.8 million tonnes by 2006 with the same workforce it had in 2003, how much will each worker then be producing?

5 What is the term used to describe 'output per worker'?

6 Why is increasing output per worker considered so important?

7 In 1997 UK steel production was 18.5 million tonnes a year, in 2000 it was 15.2 million tonnes a year and in 2003 it was 13.3 million tonnes.

   a Draw a bar chart to show UK output between 1997 and 2003.

   b Which **two** of the following statements explains why output fell over this period?

     i There weren't enough people to make steel because employment had fallen.

     ii Demand had fallen so less was required.

     iii British steel was too expensive because the pound was strong.

     iv The workers were on strike.

     v British steel was too expensive because output per worker was still poor.

8 If output increases and demand stays the same what do you think happens to prices – and why?

9 If output per worker continues to increase, yet demand for steel stays the same, what is likely to happen to overall employment? Discuss your ideas as a group.

10 Is Corus optimistic or not about output and employment in the future? Give a reason for your answer.

Investigate the growth and decline of business activities in your area

Your tutor will tell you whether you should do this activity on your own or as a member of a group.

1 Your aim is to find out how your own town, area or region has changed over the last fifty years and find out whether it matches the national pattern, i.e.

- a decline in the primary sector
- a decline in the secondary sector
- an increase in the tertiary sector.

Do this by finding out the pattern of business activities in your area around 1950, the pattern today and the reasons for the changes.

You can find out this information in several ways. Your tutor may allocate a specific research activity to different groups and then expect you to compare your answers.

2 Compare your information as a class and identify the major changes that have taken place, with reasons.

3 Identify the main growth business activities in your area today and their sectors.

Research activities

- Visit your local library and look at maps and street plans to see which businesses existed in your area in 1950. Identify which are still there, which have moved and which have closed – and why.
- At your local or college library find information on businesses and employment in reference books such as *Social Trends*, *Economic Trends* and *Labour Market Trends.*
- Check online information and statistics at the Office of National Statistics and (under sectors) at the Department for Trade and Industry. Links are available through **www.heinemann.co.uk/ hotlinks** (express code 1351T).
- Find out what your local newspaper keeps in its archives. Find out about major closures or the arrival of any major new employers. Have they got a summary of businesses in your area today? Compare job advertisements 50 years ago with those of today!
- Talk to people who have lived or worked in the area since the 1950s to find out the key industries and employers. Remember to prepare your questions carefully beforehand!
- Check the website of your local council or visit the offices. They will have an economic development department involved in encouraging businesses into your town which will know about key business activities in your area.
- Go online to find out about sectors in your area at your Regional Development Agency. You will either find key sectors listed on the site, or you will be given a link to another site with this information. Links are available at **www.heinemann.co.uk/hotlinks** (express code 1351T) and your tutor will tell you which site represents your area.
- Find the top 100 technology companies, the top 100 most profitable companies, the top 100 fastest growing companies and the top 100 private companies through links at **www.heinemann.co.uk/hotlinks** (express code 1351T). On the site you can select the year you want to view and select the top companies in your geographical area. This helps you to identify the sectors which are growing the fastest in your area. Each league table is also published in the *Sunday Times*.
- Use the Internet to find specific information on a particular industry in your area.
- Check the different service industries listed in the Student Book and look in local Yellow Pages to see how many of these are in your own area.
- Talk to your tutor about any other useful reference sources for your area. Or access the fasttrack site through **www.heinemann.co.uk/hotlinks** (express code 1351T).

Whose business is it anyway?

Below are the aims of eight British organisations. The name of each organisation is shown in the box below.

1 **a** As a group, agree on the main activity of each organisation.

   b Match each organisation with the most likely statement of its aims.

   c Divide your organisations into those which represent the private, public and voluntary sectors.

a **TATE MODERN**

b OFFICE OF FAIR TRADING

f **FOREIGN AND COMMONWEALTH OFFICE**

e **THE Carphone Warehouse** ...*for a better mobile life*

c mothercare

d RSPCA

g UNISON

h HM TREASURY

RSPCA name and logo are registered trademarks of the RSPCA, reproduced with their kind permission

A Our goal is to make markets work well for consumers. Markets work well when there is vigorous competition between fair-dealing businesses. When markets work well, good businesses flourish.

B To increase public awareness, understanding and appreciation of British art from the sixteenth century to the present day and of modern and contemporary art from around the world.

C To represent members and negotiate for improved pay and conditions in the workplace.

D To promote kindness and to prevent or suppress cruelty to animals.

E To raise the rate of sustainable growth and achieve rising prosperity and a better quality of life for all.

F To work for the United Kingdom's interests in a safe, just and prosperous world.

G To exceed our customers' expectations by providing an innovative approach to service.

H To be the leading specialist retailer for the mother-to-be and parents of young children, offering the widest range of clothing, hardware and toys for the pre-school child, in the UK and internationally.

2 All organisations need resources to achieve their aims and objectives. For each of the organisations listed suggest **two** key resources each business would need to achieve its aims.

Activity 1.3.2

Matching activities and resources

All businesses need resources – but these are often different depending upon the type of business activity.

Your tasks

1   For each of the businesses in the table below tick each type of resource you think would be needed.

2   Select **three** of the businesses and describe for each, in detail, **six** resources that you think would be essential.

3   The ability to have good ideas is a resource. This is doubly valuable if it helps a business to stand out from its competitors. For each of your selected businesses:

   a   suggest **one** special feature that could help to set it apart it from its competitors and be more successful.

   b   identify the main additional resources this would require.

Resource	Garden centre	Self-employed web designer	Toy shop	Sandwich shop	Security guard firm
Land					
Premises					
Equipment					
Vehicles					
Money					
Managers					
Skilled/expert staff					
Business skills of owner					
Personal skills of owner					
Location					
Brand name					
Reputation					
Good supply chain					
Good customer relations					
Industry contacts					

Key resources

Background information

In some cases, certain resources are more important than others. These could be described as the key resources – and sometimes they are not the most obvious ones! For example, the organisers of the Glastonbury festival consider that one key resource is the acts that they book to appear on the main (Pyramid) stage but this isn't the crucial one. Even more important, in their view, are the number of lavatories on site and the sanitation arrangements!

1 For each of the following types of business, suggest **four** vital resources which will contribute to its success or failure and give reasons for your choice.

    a a theme park

    b a college

    c a night club

    d a gym

    e a clothes shop

    f a hotel

2 The Glastonbury festival has to import most of its resources for three days a year! It is not alone in this. Many large sporting events are very similar – such as the British Open Golf Championship. On all these occasions the organisers need to hire everything from marquees to catering equipment and – as you have already seen – portable loos!

Assume you and your group are organising a charity fun day at your college. It will be held one Saturday in May. Your aim is to raise at least £1,000 for the charity of your choice.

    a Working in small groups, decide the types of activities you would have and list the resources you think you will need to make your day a success.

    b Identify the resources on your list that you think are the most important and critical to your success.

    c Compare your ideas with other groups to identify the types of resources which everyone thinks are the most essential.

Aims and SMART objectives

Businesses may have different aims and may have more than one aim. They are also likely to have SMART objectives to help them achieve their aims.

Below are the aims announced by **ten** business organisations in 2004. Read these carefully and then answer the questions that follow.

A Dixons is closing 106 underperforming stores in town centres to reduce costs. Instead it will buy out-of-town stores.

B After announcing increased profits in 2003, Caffé Nero said it aimed to have 400 new stores in the UK. The coffee bar operator currently has 145 stores in 47 towns and cities.

C Eidos, the computer games company behind Lara Croft, is struggling. It might not make a profit because of problems in the games market and may even have to sell the company.

D Burger King plans to spend £3–4 million opening at least 25 new outlets. Eventually it aims to have 1,000 UK outlets, although many will be small with fewer seats. The chain claims this will cut costs without reducing sales.

E BA announced that its recent economy drive had resulted in savings of £850 million. The cuts have been necessary because BA has lost market share to easyJet and Ryanair. The company has simplified its fare structure, reduced its prices and now sells short-haul tickets on the Internet. BA's short-haul network has been losing £300 million a year but it now aims to break even by the end of 2004.

F Levi's announced it was spending £10 million redesigning its 501s to make them more appealing to the youth market. Apparently too many of its jeans are being worn by middle-aged men, such

as Tony Blair and Jeremy Clarkson, and this was damaging its image and affecting sales.

G B & Q announced plans to more than double its sales of electrical goods in direct competition with firms like Curry's, Comet and MFI. It aims to increase sales of appliances from £60 million to £150 million by 2007 to obtain a 3.5 per cent share of the UK household appliances market.

H John Lewis, the largest private company in Britain, announced an increase in profits and a new expansion plan. It wants to open 10 new stores from 2008 in locations such as Cardiff, Yorkshire and Manchester's Trafford Centre.

I Dell Computers continues to go from strength to strength. Not content with an increase of 22 per cent in its profits it has expanded its range of products and now aims to introduce new services to help small and medium sized business with their IT support.

J Despite announcing profits of £21 million for 2003, Arla – the Danish group that owns Express Dairies – announced the closure of its dairy near Preston with the loss of 240 jobs because of a need to reduce milk production. At the same time it announced a two year deal with TNT Mail to deliver catalogues and magazines to 6 million households along with the milk.

Questions

1 Identify the main aims of each company from the list below. Remember that a business may have more than one aim.

a To make a profit	**b** To maximise profit	**c** To break even
d To survive	**e** To expand	**f** To offer new services
g To increase market share	**h** To cut costs	

2 Select **two** examples of businesses that have set SMART objectives to help to achieve their aims.

3 Select **two** examples of businesses where SMART objectives have not been given and write **two** objectives that would be appropriate in each case.

More money but awful performance!

Read the following case study and answer the questions that follow.

Case study: the Royal Mail

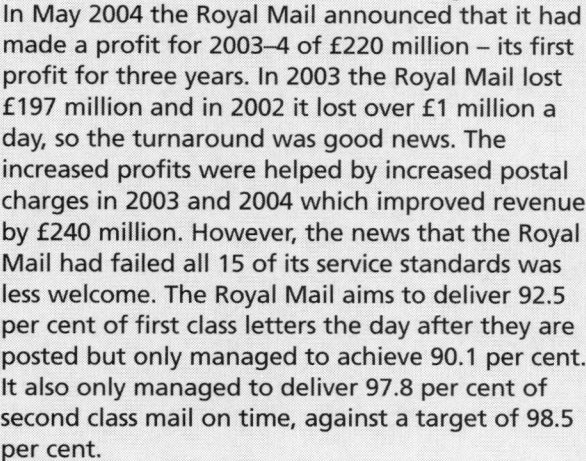

In May 2004 the Royal Mail announced that it had made a profit for 2003–4 of £220 million – its first profit for three years. In 2003 the Royal Mail lost £197 million and in 2002 it lost over £1 million a day, so the turnaround was good news. The increased profits were helped by increased postal charges in 2003 and 2004 which improved revenue by £240 million. However, the news that the Royal Mail had failed all 15 of its service standards was less welcome. The Royal Mail aims to deliver 92.5 per cent of first class letters the day after they are posted but only managed to achieve 90.1 per cent. It also only managed to deliver 97.8 per cent of second class mail on time, against a target of 98.5 per cent.

For the past two years, modernisation of the Royal Mail service has concentrated mainly on reducing costs. This has resulted in over 32,000 job losses, over 1,100 post office closures, a new sorting system and the new 'one-a-day' delivery system to utilise better existing resources. These changes led to problems with the unions and strikes in both 2003 and 2004. The Chairman of Royal Mail, Allan

Leighton, blamed the strikes for failure to achieve delivery standards but argued, too, that the scale of the changes had also caused problems. For Postwatch, the consumer group, these include the 14.4 million lost letters a year with 60 per cent apparently being put through the wrong letter box. Allan Leighton now wants to improve services and announced he would defer his bonus until key targets are met. Other senior managers made similar commitments.

The Royal Mail improvement programme ends in 2005. By then the organisation will have other challenges to face because the letter market will be open to new competition. This means customers can choose which service to use – and their decisions will depend on how much they trust the Royal Mail to deliver their post safely and on time.

You can find out more at **www.heinemann.co.uk/ hotlinks** (express code 1351T).

Questions

1   Identify **three** key aims of the Royal Mail.

2   Which **two** aims did it achieve in 2004?

3   Which aim did it fail to achieve?

4   Identify **two** SMART targets it failed in 2004.

5   Identify **three** actions the Royal Mail took to save money.

6   Explain why reducing postal deliveries from two per day to one per day utilises resources more efficiently.

7   Identify **six** other resources the Royal Mail service needs to function efficiently.

8   The Royal Mail brand name was identified by consumers as representing an organisation which is untrustworthy and inefficient.

a   Identify **two** reasons why consumers think like this.

b   Suggest a major danger for the Royal Mail of tarnishing its brand name.

9   Identify Allan Leighton's top priority now and give a reason for your choice.

10 The Royal Mail has had several new ideas – such as a digital stamp which can be used by small and medium sized businesses. You can find out more about this idea and others on the Royal Mail website.

a   How effective do you think new ideas will be in improving the reputation of the Royal Mail service?

b   In your view, what should be the key aims of the Royal Mail over the next few years – and why?

Information handling and administration

(Cross-references to Unit 6 Introduction to business administration Activity 6.1)

All administrators are 'information handlers'. They receive it, read it, store it, process it, copy it and transmit it – on a daily basis! They also often need to find information using a variety of sources.

You work in the sales department of a large business and have been asked to find the following items of information. Identify the source you would select in each case from the options below. In some cases you may have several choices – in which case try to find all of them!

Sources

A Minutes of weekly meetings	B Customer database	C Sales orders file
D Office diary	E Stationery catalogue	F Internet
G Customer files	H Equipment handbook	I Phone book
J Electronic address book	K Purchase orders file	L Internal telephone directory

Information required	Source
The correct type of paper to order for the fax machine	
The email address of a French customer	
The date of the next sales meeting	
The price you paid for photocopying paper last month	
The name of a 4 star hotel in Milan	
The name of the customer service manager's administrator	
A competitive price for buying printer cartridges	
Last month's sales figures	
The number of two local taxi firms	
The date when your boss is going on holiday	
The date when an order was despatched to a customer	
The arrival time of a flight from New York	
The date arranged for the budget planning meeting	
The name of your usual stationery supplier	
How to insert envelopes into the new printer	
The date your boss last wrote to a particular customer	
Exchange rate of Euros to Pounds sterling	
The value of a recent customer order	
The postcode of a customer in Exeter	
The dates of public holidays in Australia	
Contact details for your firm's health and safety officer	

The specialisation of labour at Unicorn Floorings

At Unicorn Floorings administration is decentralised. This means that administrators work in each of the 11 departments.

1 From the departments listed, and the statements made by the following administrators about their work, identify where each person works.

2 Then, from your knowledge of the work that is carried out in different departments, suggest one additional task each person might do.

Use the table to record your answers.

Departments at Unicorn Floorings	
Sales	Research and Development
Customer Service	Distribution
Finance	IT services
Human Resources	Production
Marketing	Facilities Management
Purchasing	

Kelly: I keep records of staff absences and holidays. I also help to prepare advertisements for new staff and greet people coming for interview.

Sam: I keep records of all returned goods and any complaints received. Each month we analyse these to see if there are any areas we need to improve.

Kim: I receive the lab reports on different fibre tests. Recently we have been using CAD packages to produce new floor designs for next season.

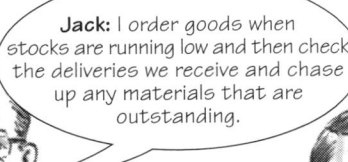

Jack: I order goods when stocks are running low and then check the deliveries we receive and chase up any materials that are outstanding.

Jon: I keep records of all the building repairs and improvements that are carried out by our approved contractors. I also receive and file the reports sent in by the overnight security guards.

David: I prepare documents for our transport dispatchers so that they can check everything is being sent out correctly. This is particularly important when goods are being shipped abroad.

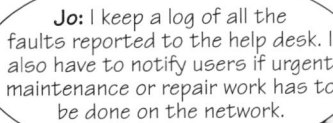

Jo: I keep a log of all the faults reported to the help desk. I also have to notify users if urgent maintenance or repair work has to be done on the network.

Jenna: I help to prepare promotional materials. Unicorn has a stand at both British and European exhibitions each year which I help to organise.

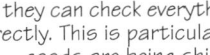

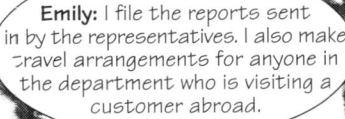

Nasreen: I keep records of the output from different machines and make sure that our schedules are kept up-to-date every day.

Emily: I file the reports sent in by the representatives. I also make travel arrangements for anyone in the department who is visiting a customer abroad.

Saeed: I check all the invoices we get and make sure that these match the goods we have received before they are paid.

Activity 1.4.2 The specialisation of labour at Unicorn Floorings (cont'd)

Administrator	Department	Additional task
Kelly		
Sam		
Jo		
Emily		
Jack		
Jon		
Kim		
Saeed		
Nasreen		
Jenna		
David		

Improving customer service

(Cross-references to Unit 7 Sales and customer service Activity 7.1)

We all have pet hates when we go shopping. We also have individual preferences which influence our choice of shopping outlets. The shop which attracts new customers and then delights them with its service has obviously a far greater chance of being successful than one which does not. However, deciding how to do this is not always easy, because all customers are different!

As a group, decide which are your pet hates and preferences by doing the following activity.

1 On your own, read the following list of customer pet hates. Add two of your own, from your own experience as a shopper. Then rank all the suggestions with the one that annoys you the most as number one.

2 With one other member of your group, combine your lists and decide your top ten items. If you disagree over the rankings or what to include then you must resolve the problem by negotiation!

3 As a pair, join with another pair to make a foursome and combine your lists. Again,

you have to reach a joint list of 10 items, in order, which you all agree on by negotiation.

4 In your foursome, decide:

a the **six** top 'hates' which could result in a serious loss of customers

b the action that should be taken by a retail organisation to prevent this.

Then compare your ideas with those of other groups in your class.

Pet hates	Ranking
Long queues of people waiting to be served	
Tills not staffed at busy times	
No staff around to answer customer queries	
Pushy staff who pester you to buy something	
Scruffy assistants	
Assistants who don't know what's in stock or where to find it	
Assistants who talk to each other (or tidy up) and ignore waiting customers	
Stock frequently being moved so you can't find what you want	
Poor range of products	
Unhelpful staff	
Poor signage so you can never find what you want	
Late opening and early closing times	
Grubby or damaged stock	
Untrained staff who constantly ask for help	
A policy that displayed items can't be sold but items are regularly out of stock when you ask	

To outsource or not – that is the question!

Farhana and Samira set up a business three years ago producing specialist sauces and flavourings. Demand has increased rapidly and they now have the opportunity of supplying a large supermarket. Farhana thinks they should grow as large as they can but keep control of all the functions themselves. Samira thinks this is impractical and is in favour of outsourcing to help.

Below are all the functions they could outsource – with both Farhana's and Samira's arguments.

1 Read the comments carefully. Then suggest:

    a the arguments Samira would use to support the outsourcing of R & D and Distribution.

    b the arguments Farhana would use to keep Marketing and Facilities Management in house.

2 Farhana and Samira haven't listed all their functional areas. Identify **two** important functions that are missing and suggest **one** reason why these haven't been included.

3 Their business adviser tells them that they need to consider which functions are the core ones for their business as these would have the biggest impact on their customers if something went wrong.

Bearing this in mind, decide the **four** most sensible functions to outsource and give your reasons in each case.

	Farhana's view	**Samira's view**
Finance	We need to keep a close watch on our money and our financial affairs are private. We are better employing our own finance staff.	We need to hire accountants anyway, because we are not professionals. Paying a firm to chase up late payments would be in our interests.
IT	Our computer systems hold confidential information. If there is a breakdown we need it repaired quickly. We need our own staff.	IT developments happen all the time. To stay up to date and to ensure our systems are secure we need specialist advice and support.
Production	We must prepare our own sauces and flavourings as only then can we ensure quality is correct. We also want to keep our recipes confidential.	We can expand production quickly and easily by outsourcing this activity. Guaranteeing quality would be part of the contract.
R & D	We must be the ones who develop new products. No-one else could do this for us.	
Distribution	If we have our own fleet of vans we can ensure goods are despatched on time and to the right people.	
Marketing		It is only good sense to employ a specialist agency to prepare our advertisements and to carry out market research for us.
Facilities Management (including security)		Maintaining buildings is a specialist job. In addition the premises need monitoring and protecting 24 hours a day. We need professional help here.

Investigating functional departments and management jobs

There are several ways in which you can find out more about the work undertaken by functional departments. Discuss the following options with your tutor.

You can visit your careers section to find further information on the work undertaken by trained accountants, IT professionals, marketing staff and many others, to see the range of tasks they do and the qualifications they need.

You can read job advertisements in the national newspapers and make a collection of those which relate to different functional areas and to different types of jobs. For example, in Sunday newspapers you will find jobs for senior executives and managers. You can find out the difference between the responsibilities of a senior director and a more junior manager – and how much they are paid. Alternatively you can investigate these type of jobs online at career sites accessible from **www.heinemann.co.uk/ hotlinks** (express code 1351T).

B.SC R.I.C.S. A.C.C.A.
M.B.A. C.I.P.F.A. C.I.M.
M.A. I.E.E.E. I.Mech.E. B.A.
L.L.B. P.G.C.E.
Q.T.S.

You can visit your college library and ask to see examples of some of the specialist magazines published, such as *Practical Facilities Management*, *Distribution* and *New Media*. There are magazines for professionals working in virtually every function in business – your librarian will be able to give you other examples. Look through these to see the type of articles they contain and the advertisements. These will also show you how businesses target each other to sell their goods and services.

Know your legal rights!

(Cross-references to Unit 5 Employee contribution to working conditions Activity 5.1)

Jennifer has just started work in the human resources department of a large business. She is really interested in the work and decides she wants to study personnel management and make this her career. One area which fascinates her is employment law and she asks her supervisor, Rob, for advice. Rob suggests that Jennifer tries the quiz below and, if she is stuck, that she looks at the TUC website to find the answers. See **www.heinemann.co.uk/hotlinks** (express code 1351T).

Employment rights quiz

Each of the employees below is dismissed. In each case, decide whether the dismissal was fair or unfair.

1 A canteen worker refuses to wear a hat because she says she looks silly, even though her uniform is fully described in her contract of employment.

2 A part-time female worker complains that she should have been included on a training course run for her department and is sacked for being argumentative.

3 Tom, who works in sales, has been having headaches recently which he blames on his computer. He thinks his eyesight is failing. He is sacked because his boss argues that using a computer is a critical part of his job.

4 A male administrator is sacked for downloading offensive material from the Internet during working hours. He says he was too busy to read the IT policy.

5 An administrator is sacked for not having the IT qualifications she claimed to have at her interview. Despite extra training she still cannot cope with the work.

6 A member of staff is sacked for stealing computer supplies from the stock cupboard.

7 A cashier in a supermarket is sacked because she refuses to work on a Sunday.

8 A female administrator is sacked when her boss finds out she is pregnant. He says the firm is too small to cope with people being away on maternity leave.

9 A female Asian employee complains that a more senior member of staff has been harassing her and making racist comments which upset her. She is sacked for causing trouble.

10 A purchasing clerk is sacked for accepting money from a supplier in return for ensuring that the supplier's company received all his orders.

11 An administrator asks if she can see a copy of her personnel record but is refused. When she insists she is sacked for being a trouble maker.

12 A sales representative refuses to use a laptop computer because he says it isn't necessary to understand IT to sell things. He refuses to go on a training course and eventually the company dismisses him.

13 Falling sales and increased losses mean that a company is reducing the number of branches and five members of staff in the Midlands are dismissed when their office closes.

14 An employee asks if she can have time off because her child has had a serious accident and has been rushed to hospital. Her boss refuses because the firm is very busy. The employee is sacked when she ignores him and takes time off anyway.

15 An employee is eventually sacked for lateness. Despite being warned and warned he has never improved his time-keeping, but he argues no-one can be sacked for such a minor offence.

16 A member of the technical service staff, who regularly travels as part of his work, is caught speeding again on a speed camera and loses his licence. He is sacked because he can no longer do his job.

Thinking on your feet!

Read the following case study and answer the questions that follow.

Case study

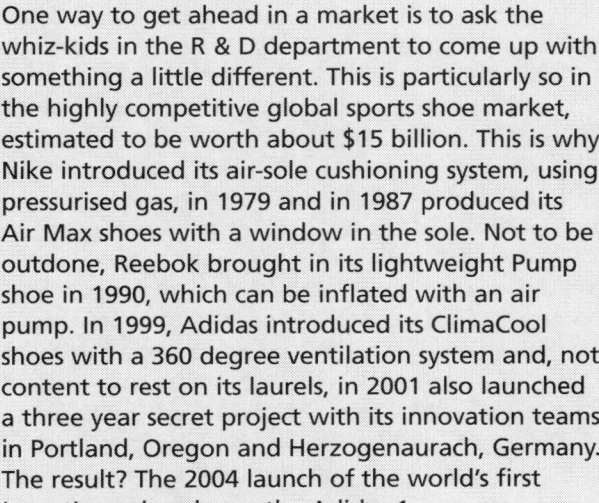

One way to get ahead in a market is to ask the whiz-kids in the R & D department to come up with something a little different. This is particularly so in the highly competitive global sports shoe market, estimated to be worth about $15 billion. This is why Nike introduced its air-sole cushioning system, using pressurised gas, in 1979 and in 1987 produced its Air Max shoes with a window in the sole. Not to be outdone, Reebok brought in its lightweight Pump shoe in 1990, which can be inflated with an air pump. In 1999, Adidas introduced its ClimaCool shoes with a 360 degree ventilation system and, not content to rest on its laurels, in 2001 also launched a three year secret project with its innovation teams in Portland, Oregon and Herzogenaurach, Germany. The result? The 2004 launch of the world's first 'smart' running shoe – the Adidas 1.

The Adidas 1 is the world's first shoe which is controlled by a microprocessor contained in the arch. This adjusts the heel cushion to the needs of its wearer based on the signals it receives. The power comes from a three volt battery which has to be changed after every 100 hours of wear. The shoe is being manufactured in China and Malaysia and the first batch will be limited to 25,000 pairs which will be distributed to selected retailers and Sport Performance stores from December 2004.

With a price tag of $250 (about £170) it isn't cheap – but the Adidas 1 may become the latest 'must have' for sports fashionistas. That is, of course, until Nike comes up with its own version!

Questions

1 Give **three** examples of the way in which R & D has affected sports or running shoes.

2 Explain why sports shoe manufacturers are prepared to spend money on R & D.

3 Why do you think the project to develop the Adidas 1 was secret?

4 **a** In which countries do its innovation teams work?

   b In which countries will the shoes be manufactured?

   c Suggest one reason why the shoes will not be manufactured in the same places as they were designed.

5 Suggest one reason why Adidas is limiting the number of shoes initially produced and only distributing them to selected outlets.

6 A project like this involves several functional areas working together. Enter each of the functional areas listed below into the table in its most logical order and then briefly describe the main activity carried out by each one. To help, the first one is done for you.

Functional areas: Distribution, Sales, Marketing, R & D, Finance, Production.

Functional area	Activity
R & D	Design and test new intelligent running shoe

Functions online and a new strategy for the LEGO Company

(Cross-references to Unit 8 Online business Activity 8.1)

Case study

Everyone is familiar with the LEGO® brand. It wasn't long after its arrival in Britain in 1959 that kids all over the country were building with bright, primary-coloured plastic bricks. Although the LEGO Company has worked hard to retain its appeal, with new ranges and LEGOLAND® Parks, it started to fight a losing battle against the increasing popularity of electronic toys and computer games. In 2000, the Danish company made a loss of Danish krone (DKK)1.07 million. How then, do you revitalise such a basic product?

In 2001 and 2002 LEGO both increased sales and reduced its costs – and made profits. It did this by expanding its product range, entering into agreements with film companies to market licensed products such as LEGO® Star Wars™ sets and also opened LEGO® Brand Stores for instance at Bluewater, Milton Keynes and Kingston. It also redesigned its website, which was visited by more than 50 million children and adults in 2003. This not only includes online games and an online store LEGO®Shop@Home but also includes in-depth information about the business – including an animated film showing the production process.

Unfortunately in 2003 sales fell by 26 per cent resulting in an overall loss of DKK 1.432 million. The problems were identified as being caused by falling sales of traditional toys and disappointing sales of the licensed products. The company is now going to concentrate on developing and marketing its basic core products, renowned for stimulating creativity and learning in children, and continue to grow its pre-school business.

Your tasks

Find the answers to the following questions by researching on the LEGO website, either in small groups or individually, as instructed by your tutor.

1 What is the LEGO Company's Mission Statement?

2 The LEGO Company is very keen on health and safety with a target of zero accidents. It is also passionate about product safety – so much so that a separate document can be downloaded giving full details about the safety of LEGO toys and packaging. Why do you think it places so much importance on this aspect of production?

3 Find out how LEGO bricks are made online! You will need Flash player installed on your computer to watch the animated film. As you watch identify the extent to which the process is automated and computerised – and why.

4 Identify **three** online customer service features at the LEGO Company and suggest **two** advantages of providing these.

5 Investigate the jobs online section – which often includes summer jobs at Legoland Windsor. Suggest **two** advantages of using the website to recruit staff.

6 The LEGO Company uses its website as a marketing tool to promote the business.

a Identify **three** key features of the site that will appeal to children.

b Identify **three** features of the site that will appeal to parents.

7 Identify **two** benefits for the LEGO Company of having a comprehensive online operation.

8 Find out the latest value of the Danish krone and work out approximately how much money the LEGO Company lost in pounds sterling in 2000 and 2003. If you want you can use an online currency converter, see **www.heinemann.co.uk/hotlinks** (express code 1351T). You will find it helpful to start by writing out the figures 1.07 million and 1.432 million in full.

9 Check the latest Annual Report or press releases on the site to see whether the company's strategy to focus on its core products has been successful and to find out its plans for the future.

10 Do you think good management processes can save the LEGO Company? Will it always be a toy children love so the management just need to concentrate on running the business profitably? Or are its days numbered no matter what managers do? Discuss your views as a class.

Organisational plans and the hierarchy at M & S

(Cross-references to Unit 2.2 Competitive pressures Activity 2.2.7)

Background information

After being given the job of new Chief Executive of Marks & Spencer, Stuart Rose reviewed the business. This was important because M & S sales and profits had been falling and Philip Green, the owner of Arcadia (i.e. Top Shop, BHS and other stores), had made a bid to buy the business. Stuart Rose could only fend him off with a plan that would improve performance and keep investors happy.

MARKS & SPENCER

Stuart Rose identified the strengths and weaknesses of the businesses. He then identified the action he was taking to remedy the problems. See his action plan overleaf.

The senior management at Marks & Spencer

Stuart Rose isn't doing all this on his own, of course. He has executives to help him. In July 2004, these included the following Directors:

A Director of marketing, store development and design

B Director of menswear

C Trading director for food

D Director of womenswear

E Director of supply chain

F Chief executive of 'Money' – M&S's financial products business.

Your tasks

To do these tasks you need a copy of the extract from the Marks & Spencer action plan with extra blank copies. Your tutor will give you this.

1 All of the executives listed above will be involved in making sure that the action plan is carried out. In the third column of your plan, identify which executive(s) would mainly be responsible for implementing each part of the plan or be affected by it and write the letter which represents that executive(s) alongside the action.

2 Action plans are all very well, but managers must ensure that they are put into action. In the second blank column list the information that would be needed, in each case, to check whether or not the individual plans would be working.

3 Imagine that you are the manager of a high street Marks & Spencer store. Some changes would affect you but others would not. Now consider how each change might

affect you and your job and enter this in the final column. In particular decide:

a Which items you would be aware of but which would be unlikely to directly affect you or your store

b Which items would affect your store but for which you would merely have to follow instructions

c Those items where you may have some say as to how the change would be implemented.

4 How successful has Stuart Rose been? By the time you do this activity Marks & Spencer may be thriving again, or not. Or Philip Green may have made another bid to buy the business! Find out what happened by checking on the corporate website through **www.heinemann.co.uk/hotlinks** (express code 1351T) and on news websites such as the BBC, Ananova and national newspaper sites and discuss your findings with your tutor.

Extract from Marks & Spencer Action Plan

Weaknesses	Action	Executive responsible	Information needed to monitor performance	Effect on store managers
Business too complicated	Sell the Money business (which sells M & S financial products).			
Competitors stealing core customers	Win back 35–55 year old core women shoppers by stocking the right goods at right price.			
Stores too cluttered	Improve store layouts/displays and modernise store space.			
Too many lines stocked	Reduce number of lines stocked in food (–500), clothing (–1000) and home goods (–4,000)			
Lack of brand confidence	Review (and possibly axe) new brands e.g. Sp menswear and Per Una Due young fashion. Focus on quality, value, service, innovation and trust and start new marketing campaign with slogan 'Your M & S'.			
Supply chain slow	Renegotiate to pay suppliers less and save £140 million by 2006/7. Save a further £35 million by reducing stock levels. Continue policy of sourcing more goods abroad.			
Costs too high	Stock fewer goods to save £35 million and reduce markdowns and amount of food wastage to save up to £50 million by 2006/7.			

Could you control a business?

(Cross-references to Unit 4 Business communication Activity 4.1, Unit 6 Introduction to business administration Activity 6.1)

For this activity you will work in a small team to run a business. You will do this by participating in at least two meetings relating to running a student business. In the first, you will help to agree on the business plan and then set short-term targets for the managers in charge of different functions – yourself included. In the second, you will evaluate the results and decide what, if any, corrective action is needed.

After the second meeting your tutor will discuss with you the likely success – or otherwise – of your business plans and targets and give you feedback on your performance.

Your tasks

Meeting one

1 Obtain information about the business from your tutor. Your tutor will also decide who will 'chair' the first meeting you have and give you the agenda for your first meeting.

2 Arrange a time and date to hold the meeting. The aim of your first meeting is to:

   a produce an overall organisational plan for your business which includes plans for future sales, profit and production.

   b decide **two** targets for each function that can be monitored to check if actual performance equals planned performance. Bear in mind that in particular you need to think about key targets, such as those relating to sales, production and expenditure.

   c allocate management job roles amongst your team.

3 Prepare for the meeting by thinking about the business and deciding how you could help. Think about jobs you would be good at. If you are creative, try to think of good ideas which would make your product appealing and popular.

4 Participate in the meeting making as many useful suggestions as you can. Help to reach agreement on all the issues discussed.

5 Help to prepare the documents to follow the meeting. As a group, you need to agree on and prepare the minutes of the meeting

with action points which state what was decided. As a group you also need to prepare a copy of your overall organisational plan and the targets which were agreed. Give your tutor a copy of both documents.

Meeting two

1 Before the meeting your tutor will give you an update on the targets which you have achieved and those which you have not. As a group, prepare and circulate an appropriate agenda for a meeting to discuss these. Remember that as this is a second meeting of the same group, your agenda must include checking that the minutes of the last meeting were correct and discussing any matters arising from these.

2 Hold the meeting and discuss the feedback you have received. Where necessary suggest appropriate corrective action that should be taken.

3 Write notes to record the decisions made at the meeting and the action points agreed. Again, give your tutor a copy.

Activity 1.4.10 Could you control a business? (cont'd)

Background information

The successor to *Chatter* magazine

Two years ago a group of students at your college issued a magazine called *Chatter*. This was very popular but when those students left, the magazine folded. No-one, last year, wanted to continue with it.

Your group has decided to resurrect the idea. Your aim is to produce an interesting magazine twice during the student year. At the end of the year profits from the magazine will go to charity.

The management team that produced *Chatter* had 9 members with the following job titles:

The Managing Editor – who was in overall charge
The Features Editor – responsible for all special features and competitions
The Assistant Features Editor – who assisted the Features Editor
The IT/Art and Design Director – responsible for the layout of the magazine and its design
The Advertising Director – responsible for the number of paid advertisements placed in the magazine (an important source of revenue)
The Sales and Marketing Director – responsible for promoting sales
The Finance Director – responsible for all the financial aspects of the magazine
The Production Director – responsible for ensuring the magazine is printed and distributed on time
The Chief Administrator – responsible for ensuring that all the meetings ran smoothly and the minutes were produced and distributed.

The new magazine may have more or less members with the same, or different, job titles. That is up to you to decide at the first meeting.

AGENDA FOR FIRST MEETING

1 Apologies for absence and introduction of group members

2 Overall aim of project

3 Formation of business plan to include:
   a   Proposed title of new magazine
   b   Proposed content and types of features
   c   Types of advertising and income from advertising
   d   Potential sales and selling price to charge
   e   Cost of production and potential profit
   f   Proposed dates of publication
   g   Other appropriate aspects raised by team

4 Identification of management job roles and allocation between members of group

5 Identification of short-term targets for each manager

6 Any other business

7 Time and date of next meeting

These sample assessments are designed as practice exercises to help your students understand the types of task they will be required to do for their IVA. Tasks can be done by individuals or by groups as indicated.

There is one sample assessment for each section of the unit:

1.1 Business activities
1.2 Classification of business activities
1.3 Resources, aims and objectives
1.4 Management processes

The structure and grading of the assessments reflect the grading criteria for the unit as provided by Edexcel. Differentiation information is given where appropriate to indicate what would be required from the student to gain pass, merit or distinction grades in the IVA. Tips to help the student

achieve a merit or distinction grade are also given. A deadline box is provided in which you can enter a submission date to familiarise your students with the idea of working to a specified date or time.

Assessments are mainly printed one to a page so that they can be easily photocopied.

Tutors are strongly recommended to familiarise themselves with the information in the current *Edexcel IVA – Centre Guidance Notes* before commencing these activities.

Answers to Unit 1 sample assessments

No specific answers are possible as it will depend upon the business investigated by the student.

Use this activity to help you to understand the type of tasks you will do for your IVA. Agree with your tutor whether you should do the work on your own or as a member of a small group.

In agreement with your tutor, select one business you will investigate for the tasks below. This could be your college, another local business or a well-known business you can research on the Internet.

Do *not* use the same business that you have chosen to investigate for your actual IVA.

Task 1 – Pass grade

1 a **Find out** and **describe THREE** main activities of your chosen business.
   b **Identify** the sector the business is in.
   c **State** why the business is in this sector.
   d **State** the size and scale of this business.
   e **Explain** what the business does and **identify** at least **ONE** key goal.

> *Deadline*

Tips to achieve a merit grade

Before you start, check that you know and understand the following:

- how the activities of your chosen business relate to the key goal
- the reason why business activities must support the achievement of the key goal
- why businesses may have different activities if they have different goals (e.g. making a profit or providing a free service)
- how to contrast or compare two different things.

Now do the following tasks.

Tasks 2, 3 and 4 – Merit grade

2 a **Explain** how the activities of your chosen business support the achievement of its key goal.
   b **Suggest** how the business activities may be different if its goal changed.

> *Deadline*

3 a **Select ONE** other business from a different sector.
   b **Identify** the activities and key goal of this business.

> *Deadline*

4 a **Contrast** both your businesses by identifying the differences between the activities and goals of each one.
   b **Briefly explain** why there are these differences.

> *Deadline*

You will find this sample assessment even more useful if you compare your findings and ideas with those of other members or groups in your class.

Use this activity to help you to understand the type of tasks you will do for your IVA. Agree with your tutor whether you should do the work on your own or as a member of a small group.

In agreement with your tutor, select one business you will investigate for the tasks below. This could be the same business you chose for the sample assessment for Unit 1.1 or a different business.

Do *not* use the same business that you have chosen to investigate for your actual IVA.

Tasks 1 and 2 – Pass grade

1 **a** Bearing in mind that businesses can be classified into primary, secondary and tertiary sectors, **identify** the sector of your chosen business.

 b **Describe** its main business activities.

 c **Explain** why your business is in that particular sector.

Deadline

2 **a** **State** the names of **TWO** other businesses which carry out the same type of business activities and are in the same sector as your chosen business.

 b **State** the names of **TWO** businesses which are in the same sector but carry out different business activities. In each case, **describe** what they do.

 c **Identify FOUR** businesses which operate in each of the other sectors to the one in which your chosen business operates. In each case, **describe** the activities the business carries out.

 d **Briefly explain** how businesses in the primary, secondary and tertiary sector may relate to each other, giving at least **ONE** example.

Deadline

You will find this sample assessment even more useful if you compare your findings and ideas with those of other members or groups in your class.

Use this activity to help you to understand the type of tasks you will do for your IVA. Agree with your tutor whether you should do the work on your own or as a member of a small group.

In agreement with your tutor, select one business you will investigate for the tasks below. If you wish you can use the same business you have used for earlier sample assessments in this unit. Then answer the following questions.

Do *not* use the same business that you have chosen to investigate for your actual IVA.

Task 1 – Pass grade

1 a **Identify** the main business activity of the organisation you have chosen.
  b **State** at least **TWO** current aims and objectives of the business.
  c **Identify FOUR** main types of business resources used by the business.
  d **Explain** how *each* of these resources is used to meet the aims and objectives of the business that you identified.

Deadline

You will find this sample assessment even more useful if you compare your findings and ideas with those of other members or groups in your class.

Use this activity to help you to understand the type of tasks you will do for your IVA. Agree with your tutor whether you should do the work on your own or as a member of a small group.

In agreement with your tutor, select one business you will investigate for the tasks below. This could be the same organisation you have used for previous sample assessments in this unit.

*Do **not** use the same business that you have chosen to investigate for your actual IVA.*

Task 1 – Pass grade

1 a Identify at least **TWO** aims or objectives of your chosen business.

   b Describe TWO management processes the business uses to enable **ONE** of these aims and objectives to be met.

Deadline

Tips to achieve a merit grade

Before you start Task 2, think about:

- the resources used by your chosen business
- how people obtain these resources
- the controls that stop people obtaining too many, spending too much, buying unsuitable resources or wasting them
- how controlling resources helps the organisation to achieve its aims and objectives.

If you used the same organisation for Unit 1.3, look back at your information for that Sample Assessment to help you.

Now carry out Task 2.

Task 2 – Merit grade

2 a Describe THREE management processes that are used in your chosen businesses to control the use of resources.

   b Explain, using examples, how controlling the use of resources helps managers to achieve the aims and objectives you identified.

Deadline

Tips to achieve a distinction grade

Before you carry out the final task, think about the following important issues.

- How useful the management processes are in achieving the goal.
- The positive (good) and negative (poor) aspects of the business.
- How the functional areas communicate and whether communications are usually good or poor.
- How often monitoring is carried out.
- The type of targets that were set, the reasons that were given if these were not met and whether these problems could be avoided.
- The corrective action that was taken when there was a problem. For example was this done quickly – and was it appropriate?
- The resources that were used. Were these used wisely or could they have been used better?

Remember that if you have to give your opinion then you **must** support this with evidence from your investigations. Finally, check the format in which you have to submit your answer and follow it!

Now answer the questions for Task 3.

Task 3 – Distinction grade

3   For this task your tutor has asked you to give your opinion of the effectiveness of the **THREE** management processes you have already identified for Task 2 and write your answers in a memo using the format given.

   a   **Explain** how successful the management processes are in making use of and controlling resources.

   b   **Assess** the success of the management process by evaluating their strengths and weaknesses.

   c   **Explain** how well you think the management processes support the main business activities. **Give reasons** for your opinion.

   d   **Describe** how successful you think your chosen business is in achieving its aims and objectives. **Give reasons** for your opinion.

   e   Imagine that you ran the business and **explain** whether you would consider the management processes are effective or not.

   - If you consider they are totally effective, **support your opinion** with evidence from your investigations.

   - If you think they are not totally effective what **suggestions** would you make to improve management processes to help them to be more effective?

Deadline

You will find this sample assessment even more useful if you compare your findings and ideas with those of other members or groups in your class.

MEMO

TO: (Put your tutor's name here)

FROM: (Put your own name here)

DATE: (Enter today's date here)

PUT YOUR MAIN HEADING HERE

Now start your memo. Use separate sections for each part of your answer and use sub-headings to make it clear where each of these starts, eg (for sub-section b):

The strengths and weaknesses of the management process

Xxxxxxxxxxxxxxxxxxxxxxxxxxxxxxxx
Xxxxxxxxxxxxxxxxxxxxxxxxxxxxxxxx

When you have finished, it is normal to initial a memo, rather than sign it in full.

1.1 – Business activities

Over to you, page 4

1 **a** Argos sells goods, easyJet provides a service, BT provides both goods and services, Pizza Express provides both goods and a service, Blockbuster provides both goods and services.

  b No specific answer possible.

2 **a** Tesco makes most of its profit from selling food, but gains additional revenue from selling other products and providing services, such as its online buying and delivery service and its financial services.

  b If Tesco reduced any one of its profitable activities its overall profits would fall.

  c Tesco sells food and non-food products (electrical and household products, clothes, mobile phones, pharmaceuticals, wine, DVDs etc.). It has the most successful online grocery operation in the business. Its services include gas and electricity, a mobile network, Internet access, home phone service, a travel service (in conjunction with Lastminute.com) and a wide range of financial products (insurance, loans, credit card, savings account etc.) and an online banking service.

  The Debut scheme was launched in October 2003 for the 30,000 students who work for the company – regardless of whether they are at school, college or university – and new, young full-time employees to give them career advice, online training and development, discounts on travel and other products, financial guidance and job opportunities. In October 2003 Tesco was piloting a Debut Pass scheme which allowed undergraduate students to job swap between home and university stores and to save as they study.

  Note: Tesco also owns the i-Village website.

  Tutors are advised to view the Tesco site and the latest media reports posted on it to check for further updates.

3 *Note*: Tutors should check the site link for the current year before supervising this task. Depending upon the level of ability and interest of the class in MU activities, it could be useful to print off the financial statement from the current Annual Report (downloaded as a pdf file). This will give a further insight into the various activities in more depth than the summary statements on the site. The Report is colourful and interesting and many students may enjoy accessing it themselves, if they have Acrobat on their computers, but should be dissuaded from printing it, given its length.

  a Playing football.

  b It sells goods in its Megastores and online, it has a mobile service, MUTV, Red Cinema and financial services. It earns money through sponsorship and from media income, e.g. TV deals, UEFA Champions League participation and when it sells players.

  c In 2003, its profit before tax was £39.3 million.

  d In 2003, its sales turnover was £173 million.

  e The key areas are 'matchday', 'media' and 'commercial'. Matchday = gate receipts, season tickets, executive boxes, the membership scheme, and matchday catering. Media = TV deals (and home and overseas), the website business (Manchester United Interactive) and UK radio. Commercial = sponsorship, MU Finance, non-matchday catering, merchandise. The split was 41 per cent, 32 per cent and 27 per cent – which means the Club made 59 per cent from non-core business revenue. (*Note*: player trading profits are listed as a separate item.)

Over to you, page 7

1 No specific answer possible.

2 **a** **i** Yes, without a profit neither the business nor Kate would survive.

    ii Selling flowers.

    iii (5 of) Ensuring her flowers are always fresh, displaying the flowers outside, advertising the business, delivering flowers, setting up displays, selling greeting cards, vases and dried displays, free gift wrap service.

    iv (1 of) To increase her profits (by maximising sales, reducing costs or improving productivity when making flower arrangements) or improving performance.

b No specific answer possible.

3 **a** They will take all the costs associated with the business away from the sales revenue. This is the costs of their raw materials and running the business.

b Making a profit means that the business can continue to prosper and they obtain a reward from their efforts and have enough money to live on.

c Maximise their sales, reduce their costs, increase their productivity.

d Their sandwiches may be too expensive and people may decide to buy elsewhere.

e £8,000.

f It would increase by £2,000.

Over to you, page 10

1 **a** A new computer from a retail store – at a profit – for the store to make a profit.

b Meals on wheels for the elderly – below cost – because although a contribution is required this is a service for a needy group.

c A passport – at cost – to meet the charges incurred in issuing it, given people gain benefits from having one.

d Tourist information leaflets – free of charge – to encourage people to visit tourist sites and spend money when they get there.

e The driving test (theory and practical) – at cost – to meet the charges incurred as people gain personal benefits from being able to drive.

f An evening foreign language course at your college – below cost – otherwise the course would be too expensive and colleges provide an educational service.

g Membership of your local community sports centre – below cost – because local authorities operate this for the benefit of the community.

h Membership of a private gym – at a profit – for the gym to make a profit.

i Planning applications for householders to change or extend their homes – at cost – to cover the cost of processing the application as householders gain a benefit from obtaining permission.

2 Below are broad guidelines of the type of information students will find. However, tutors are recommended to check the sites themselves for updates which may affect these responses and for specific local information for **2a**.

a Local councils' main goal is normally to provide services to improve the quality of life for people in their community. Activities include advice, libraries, economic regeneration, social services, roads, buildings, tourism, arts, cleanliness etc.

b Detailed information is given at **www.nhs.uk/thenhsexplained/glossary.asp**. NHS Trusts aim to offer a range of health services; some offer special expertise and others are linked to universities which provide medical training. They provide services in the community – through health centres, clinics and in people's homes and employ the majority of the NHS workforce. Primary Care Trusts are responsible for planning and providing health services and improving the health of the local population, through GPS and other local health services (hospitals, dentists, mental health care) in addition to Walk-In Centres, NHS Direct, patient transport, population screening, pharmacies and other options. They also integrate health and social care for patients.

c The goal of the ASA is to regulate marketing communications that appear in the press and online and on other non-broadcast media. This includes advertisements, sales promotions and direct marketing. Its main activities are to investigate complaints and conduct its own monitoring. It checks if advertisements are breaking the Committee of Advertising Practice (CAP) code. It provides information for consumers and advertisers (and help and guidance for students looking at advertising and marketing practices – including a guided tour). It liaises with government to influence future policy on advertising and also represents the advertising industry in Europe.

d The goal of the Samaritans is to provide 24-hour confidential emotional support for anyone experiencing feelings of distress or despair, including those which may lead to suicide. It wants to reduce the number of suicides, help people to explore their feelings and respect the feelings of others. The main activities are providing support for people who contact them by telephone or email. It also works in prisons and trains prisoners to befriend others.

e   The goal of the Environment Agency is to protect and improve the environment in England and Wales to make sure everyone looks after air, land and water so tomorrow's generations inherit a cleaner, healthier world. It regulates the release of pollutants into the air, it is involved in conservation and ecology, especially along rivers and in wetlands, it provides information to anglers and fisheries managers, it warns about flooding and builds flood defences, monitors land pollution and takes action to clean up contamination, is the major navigation authority for inland rivers, estuaries and harbours, protects, improves and promotes recreation and works with river user groups, regulates waste management and provides advice, and is responsible for water quality and water resources.

f   The goal of the Trading Standards Institute is to promote fair and honest trading by keeping consumers informed, encouraging honest businesses and targeting rogue traders. The Institute itself represents trading standards professionals and encourages the exchange of ideas between them as well as commissioning research, holding training courses, cooperating with bodies involved in consumer protection and the OFT, playing a key role with UK central government and the EU on consumer legislation and promoting TSI events. It provides services and support to its members and gives consumer education and advice – including through the Young Consumers of the Year event (for 14 to 17 year olds).

All the goals in public sector and voluntary organisations reflect the provision of services for the benefit of the public as a whole.

3   The following are examples, but students may suggest other suitable ideas.

a   A doctor's surgery – offer appointments same day or next day, reduce waiting time at surgery, reduce any delays seeing patients at home, speed up repeat prescription service, link with chemist to offer delivery service for prescription items. (Could measure appointments by assessing average wait before appointment offered/average waiting time at surgery/checking all home patients seen same day, monitoring complaints, checking all repeat prescriptions signed and ready for collection, by patient or linked pharmacy, same day.)

b   A bus company – reduce/eliminate cancelled buses, improve punctuality record, improve customer service by drivers, ensure all routes fully covered at peak times. (Check by monitoring break-downs/cancellations, employing inspectors to random check punctuality/service, monitoring complaints.)

c   A superstore – reduce/eliminate queuing at check-outs, ensuring all popular lines always stocked, improving customer service on main desk and at check-outs, offering help packing goods or taking them to car. (Check queues by monitoring visually and having spare check-out staff on hand, check complaints/type of queries made to customer service, check-out staff could ask customers if they had any problems or if there was anything they couldn't find.)

d   A restaurant – ensure telephone bookings handled professionally, improve customer service by all staff, minimise unacceptable delays in serving food, query problem if any food rejected by customers. (Most checks are visual in a restaurant and by asking customers verbally if everything is to their liking.)

e   The Royal Mail – reduce number of items lost in the post, reduce number of wrongly delivered items, increase speed of delivery and aim for 100 per cent of all first class items to be delivered following day. (Check by monitoring complaints and tracking deliveries.)

f   The fire service – reduce response times to emergency calls, ensure information service covered at all times to give guidance on fire safety issues over the phone, ensure all fires extinguished as quickly as possible bearing in mind safety of fire crew. (Monitor response times, complaints and time taken to extinguish fires.)

4   No specific answer possible – it will depend upon your college's mission statement, although the main purpose is obviously to educate, inform, guide and support students and the activities of teaching, counselling, careers guidance etc. are all undertaken to this end.

5 a The main activity is making adhesive labels. Goals include supplying high quality goods and services, meeting employee needs, maximising profit for its shareholders to receive good dividends.

b The main activity is to operate an 'no frills' online Internet café. Goals include being the cheapest by achieving the lowest cost base among competitors, providing a clean and safe environment, creating a profitable business.

c The main activity is to provide a safe online website for women plus a monitored community for women to meet up online. Goals include helping women to get the most out of life and providing up-to-date advice on key issues that concern them.

d The main activity is providing hospitality through their hotel chain. The goals are to provide outstanding service through 12 published service standards, to assist staff to achieve their personal goals and to treat all team members and job applicants equally.

e The main activity is to provide advice and consultancy services on quality management and quality control issues to SMEs, mainly in the Midlands. The main goals are to satisfy customer requirements fully and become their preferred supplier, maximise profit by using resources efficiently and effectively,

provide all employees with a satisfying career and working environment.

f The main activity is to protect and promote the health of the public by world class research. Other activities include developing better treatments, improving training and support and providing information. The main goal is to conquer and control the disease within two generations.

g The main activity is supplying business equipment (photocopiers, fax machines, AVEs, printers etc.) to organisations from the very small to the very large. The main goals are to give value for money without high pressure tactics, providing good quality, reliable equipment and a personal service.

h The main activity is to play football. The main goal is to serve the best interests of all QPR fans and to fulfil that role with diligence and integrity, through eight main actions (e.g. canvassing members regularly and acting in accordance with the majority opinion).

Over to you, page 16

1 No specific answer possible.

2 a The following gives a range of suggestions students may make. Other appropriate answers should be accepted.

*See websites for more activities, e.g. **www.dixons.co.uk** and **www.nspcc.org.uk**

Business organisation	Sector it belongs to	One main goal it may have	Two activities it undertakes to help achieve this goal
Dixons*	Private	To maximise profit To provide excellent customer service To maximise sales	Sells electronic goods at competitive prices in stores and online Operates a delivery and tracking service
A vet	Private	To make a profit To provide health care for animals To educate pet owners about animal health	Offers routine check-ups/inoculations Carries out operations on sick animals Sells pet supplies
NSPCC*	Voluntary	To eradicate child cruelty To keep people informed about child cruelty issues	Raises money Operates a Child Protection Helpline Has community based teams
The ambulance service	Public	To provide a rapid and safe transport system for hospital patients To provide emergency medical attention	Transports non-urgent patients to hospital at the request of a GP Rapid response to 999 calls Trains staff and paramedics
Your local chemist	Private	To make a profit To give accurate medical advice to customers To provide special customer services to the elderly and infirm.	Sells pharmaceutical and other products Pharmacist provides medical advice Makes up prescriptions and delivers to the elderly/infirm

b No specific answer possible.

3 a Possibly women are targeted more than men, especially when shopping or during door-to-door collections. They may also visit charity shops/buy from catalogues more often than men or be more responsive to television/press campaigns. Young people may not give because they are broke themselves, do not identify with a particular campaign or the method of collection (door-to-door/catalogues/charity shops) is not part of their lifestyle. Men may be targeted more through workplace giving schemes, raffles and television campaigns. Young people may be targeted by charity events, especially if they have chosen the charity to benefit themselves. Any other appropriate suggestions should be accepted.

b No specific answer possible as the answers will depend upon the charities for investigation selected by the students.

c (4 of) The shop will be much smaller and won't have expensive displays and fittings; stock levels/types will depend upon donations from the public, rather than regular stock deliveries; pricing goods for sale will be at the discretion of the shop manager whereas prices will be set centrally by Sainsbury's; promotional notices and signs are likely to be done by shop staff rather than received from a central office; the system for processing payments/calculating stock levels will be less sophisticated; staff will have to deal with all staff enquiries themselves, there won't be a separate customer service desk. (2 of) Discounting goods which are slow moving will be done by the shop, being friendly and helpful to customers will still be important; keeping the shop warm, safe, clean and tidy will be still be important.

4 No specific answer possible but tutors can keep up-to-date through the website of the Department of Media, Culture and Sport at **www.culture.gov.uk**.

5 The NACAB website at **www.nacab.org.uk** provides a wide range of information. Its twin aims are to give advice and to seek to influence national and local services and policies. In 2003, 79 per cent of its staff were volunteers. Specific details on its services and funding are contained in the Annual Report which can be downloaded from the site in pdf format. This covers the number of Bureaux (2,800 in 2003); the services and types/numbers and detailed information on its funding and expenditure. Tutors may wish to focus on the type of problems dealt with in the local area and amongst young people (e.g. debt counselling). It may also be possible to arrange for a CAB volunteer to visit the group to talk about their work.

Over to you, page 22

1 The following is the main information students can be expected to find on company websites. Goals and activities which link to these should be accepted. For 1b the global players are Cadbury Schweppes and Amazon, the UK companies are Carphone Warehouse and Whitbread. Innocent Drinks is the smallest but aims to become a major player in Europe.

Students should spot similarities, such as expanding, increasing market share, improving customer service, giving shareholder value (for plcs). Many also focus on employees. Differences may focus on those related to size, scale and culture (e.g. Innocent versus Cadbury's) and the need to keep shareholders happy for public limited companies.

- Carphone Warehouse has a particularly good website for students with relevant information under the 'corporate' section of the site. These include its strategy to expand retail presence (opening more stores) and gain further market share; to expand telecoms services; to develop residential fixed line etc. – all of which relate to sub-section **a**, and details of its five fundamental customer service rules and corporate responsibility stance – which relate to sub-section **b**. Information on its activities can be found under 'operations' and on other pages. These include selling mobile phones and network connections in its stores; selling accessories, selling insurance and fixed line telephone services.
- The Cadbury Schweppes site is the corporate site for Cadbury's. On the site students can find out that the core purpose of the company is 'working together to create brands people love', while their objective is to 'grow shareowner value over the long term' and they have targets relating to shareowner returns, cash flow, earnings and sales. Students can also find out details of their results and business plans – which, in 2003,

related to reducing costs (by factory closures/reducing the number of employees and spending more on marketing). Their business principles document can also be downloaded in pdf format. This concentrates on Cadbury's ethics and values and can provoke a useful discussion on cocoa farmers and fair trading (see also their FAQs page).

- Relevant information on Amazon is found under investor relations – at the foot of the page. The main goals are to 'focus relentlessly on customers, make bold investment decisions, focus on cash, work hard to spend wisely and focus on hiring and retaining versatile and talented employees. Information on current developments can be obtained from press releases and details of their activities can be seen from the variety of products they now sell online. (Their vision is to 'be the earth's most customer centric company; to build a place where people can come to find and discover anything they might want to build online'.) Goals to improve performance would logically then be related to the range of stock carried and speed of order completion.

- Whitbread sold its breweries, pubs and off-licences in 2000 and 2001 to concentrate on its new goal – to be the leading UK leisure business. The 'about Whitbread' area of its website provides useful information for students, including the business strategy to focus on the growth sectors of the UK leisure market – lodging (i.e. hotel accommodation), eating out and active leisure by growing profitability, scale and market share of leading brands, developing new brands with the potential to reach significant scale, achieving shareholder value, being brand leaders for customer service, becoming the employer of choice, meeting stakeholder responsibilities. Its activities are focused in three areas – leisure and fitness (it owns David Lloyd Leisure), hotels (it runs Marriott Hotels in the UK under a franchise agreement) plus its own Travel Inns, and Whitbread Restaurants, including Brewers Fayre, Beefeater, TGI Friday's, Pizza Hut UK and Costa Coffee outlets.

- Students may have to search rather more on the Innocent Drinks site to find the information they need, but as the site is young and jazzy, they will probably enjoy looking! The main goal of the company is to

produce 100 per cent natural drinks with no additives or flavourings. Searching through the press releases will give more information (*The Grocer* article dated 25/1/03 is particularly informative), such as current plans to grow the workforce to about 60 in the next five years, increase sales to £50 million a year and to expand into Europe to become 'Europe's favourite little juice company'. The company also supports a community project in Bangalore.

2   No specific key possible as it will depend upon the businesses selected by the students.

3   a   The magazine would need to carry gossip stories relating to American celebrities and be written in a style which would appeal to American readers (including language/spelling etc.)

     b   (2 of) Setting up an American office, employing US writers, printing the magazine in the US, setting up a distribution network.

     c   Either answer is acceptable providing it is supported by an appropriate reason, e.g. 'yes' because of size of market, many stars known on both sides of the Atlantic, similar readership etc. 'No' because costs would be too great, magazine would have to compete against established American magazines etc.

4   There are numerous possible reasons students could glean from the website including: high-quality coffee through its purchasing policy, customer service, diversity policy, focus on profits, environmental stance, steady yet rapid growth based on sound financial policy, ambitions of the owner, known brand, international 'format'.

5   a   (3 of) cost of expansion, her own ability to manage a larger scale business, competition in the new areas, size of the market, her own ambitions.

     b   (2 of) Advantages: may be able to buy some stock more cheaply, profits should increase, could include addresses of all nail bars in local adverts, customers who move or work in a different area could still use her nail bars, staff could 'cover' for each other in different shops if necessary. (2 of) Disadvantages: costs of running the business will be greater, she cannot give a personal service (herself) to every customer, she will have more administration and paperwork to do.

c (1 of) She can offer the additional services to her existing clients, new customers who attend the beauty salon will use her nail bar, it is likely to be cheaper and easier to do this than to expand the scale of her business. (1 of) Competition may be great in this area, she may not have the skills herself and will have to hire more staff, she may not have the potential for client growth that she would have in a new area.

Section review, page 24

1 a (2 of) Producing goods, selling goods, providing a service.

b One of the main targets the business wants to achieve.

c The business must make a profit to survive. It is the owner's reward and is required for further investment in stock and capital items.

d Because no business can assume it is always achieving the best results possible. Private businesses always want to improve their profits and this means increasing sales and/or reducing costs. All businesses want to improve customer service performance – which can directly affect customer satisfaction and therefore sales.

e Private individuals and shareholders (depending upon the type of business ownership).

f The state or government.

g Private sector organisations need to make a profit. Voluntary organisations are 'not for profit' and use the surplus to provide services according to their main aim or purpose.

h Profit is the difference between revenue from sales and the cost of production and supply. Turnover is the value of the goods sold in a year.

i (1 of) Number of employees, sales turnover, scale of operations.

j The size of area over which the business operates, e.g. local, regional, national, European or global.

2 a Pilkington manufactures glass and glazing products for building, automotive and related technical markets.

b Private – it became a plc in 1970.

c Its current strategy is to improve the effectiveness of its existing operations, to generate more cash from these to strengthen its financial position and to grow profitably.

d It has manufacturing operations in 24 countries in five continents and sales in 130. 54 per cent of its revenues are from Europe, 33 per cent from America and 13 per cent from the rest of the world.

1.2 – Classification of business activities

Over to you, page 27

1 Diagrams should include the following elements:

a sheep and shearing, wool processing and manufacture of product, selling of sweaters or wool carpets etc.

b petrol extraction, refinery, selling in a garage.

c potato field/farmer, processing plant, selling in retail outlet.

d trees/timber felling, furniture manufacture, selling in retail outlet.

e quarry, cement production, bags of cement for sale.

2 No specific answer possible as it will depend upon the products selected by students. Suggestions could be: increased demand for barbecues, decking, mobile phones, organic food, vegetarian meals, CDs, DVDs; decreased demand for red meat, audio tapes, video cassettes, floppy disks, fitted carpets, wallpaper.

Over to you, page 34

1 a

Primary	Secondary	Tertiary
Fisherman	Carpenter	Bank clerk
Oil driller	Engineer	Teacher
	Printer	Estate agent
		Journalist
		Website designer
		Musician
		Charity worker
		Taxi driver
		Lorry driver
		Retailer

b No specific answer possible.

2 a No specific answer possible

b (6 of) Transport and distribution, wholesale, retail, insurance, banking, advertising, accountant, solicitor, market research.

3   No specific answer possible as this will depend upon the charities selected by students. However, the main activity is normally summarised as soon as the link is clicked and each site lists the type of services undertaken.

4   The suggested order is given below, but tutors should note that some activities are interchangeable (for example numbers 3 to 6).

Activity (suggested order)	Type of business	Sector
Felling trees for converting into wood pulp	Forestry company	Primary
Converting logs into wood pulp	Processing mill	Secondary
Making card from wood pulp and other materials	Paper mill	Secondary
Manufacture of plastic box to hold CDs	Plastic manufacturer	Secondary
Manufacture of blank CDs	CD manufacturer	Secondary
Producing card for insert sleeves	Paper manufacturer	Secondary
Recording of band by technicians onto master disc	Recording studio	Secondary
Reproduction of master recording to produce multiple CDs	CD production company	Secondary
Creation of graphics and information for sleeve	Graphic designers	Tertiary
Printing of insert sleeves	Printers	Secondary
Assembling of boxes, CDs and insert sleeve	Assembly plant	Secondary
Devising advertising campaign to promote CD	Advertising agency	Tertiary
Transporting CDs to warehouses	Transport/distribution	Tertiary
Selling CDs in shops	Retailers	Tertiary

Over to you, page 39

1   a   The foot and mouth epidemic, which resulted in the slaughter of many farm animals.

b   Organic farming is ideal for small producers who can concentrate on quality produce. If demand continues to increase, British farmers could specialise and take on more workers and also concentrate on increasing output to meet demand.

c   The Defra website will help students find up-to-date information about the primary sector. Under the Farming section, Defra states that one of its major tasks is to help this industry to operate as efficiently as possible. Defra administers support policies agreed in Brussels which provide around £3 billion to UK agriculture. The headings on this area of the site include government policies on farming. Organic farmers and growers aim to provide competitive certification services to UK organic farmers and information is given on various aspects of organic farming. The Soil Association is a key site for organic food and sponsors food awards each year.

2   a

Business activity	% change in output
Weapons and ammunitions	+11 per cent
Electrical valves and tubes	+4 per cent
Wood and wood products	+2.5 per cent
Textiles, leather and clothing	+1.1 per cent
Rubber and plastic products	+0.7 per cent
Chemicals and man-made fibres	+0.3 per cent
Pulp, paper, publishing and printing	+0.2 per cent

b   It is a good sign because it indicates an increase in output.

c   Output shows a growth in items produced. Employment will vary depending upon whether an industry is labour or capital intensive. The number of firms can be misleading – there may be very many small firms in an industry. Sales may increase but may start from a very small initial level or may be caused through lower prices.

c   Output shows a growth in items produced. Employment will vary depending upon whether an industry is labour or capital intensive. The number of firms can be misleading – there may be very many small firms in an industry. Sales may increase but may start from a very small initial level or may be caused through lower prices.

d Demand increased because of the war in Iraq.

e Any appropriate suggestions should be encouraged, e.g. consumer spending on TV screens (not all are plasma or LCD as yet), people preferring the 'natural' look at home rather than plastic goods plus the demand for wooden flooring, increased demand for clothing or shoes and leather jackets becoming fashionable again etc.

f 'Flat' means that overall the increases and decreases in output virtually cancel themselves out. It can occur because an increase in output is then followed by a decrease of about the same amount.

3 a Four – retailing, hotels and restaurants, post and telecommunications, education.

b Wholesaling and reaction, sport and culture.

c Land and air transport, banking and insurance, health and social work.

d No specific answer possible but factors should be logical bearing in mind the industry chosen.

Section review, page 40

1 a (2 of) Farming, fishing, landscape gardening, horticulture, gamekeeping, forestry and logging, fishing and fish farming, mining and quarrying.

b The amount of goods (or their value) produced by an industry.

c They are concerned with the design and efficient operation of machinery and equipment, including electrical and optical equipment.

d (4 of) Any of the services listed on page 33, e.g. under the headings of retail and wholesale trade, hotels and restaurants etc.

e Secondary.

f Primary and secondary.

g Tertiary.

h The number of people employed over time shows whether an industry is increasing or decreasing in overall size.

i Employment figures do not include changes in productivity which affect output. If more automation or mechanised processes are used then output can increase when employment is falling.

j It is declining in comparison with other sectors at that time but may be doing quite well on its own.

2 No specific answer is possible but the activity should aim to increase student awareness of typical industries in their own area. Tutors can extend this discussion by looking at industries which have declined over the last 20 or 30 years – and those which have emerged.

3 No specific answer possible.

1.3 – Resources, aims and objectives
Over to you, page 44

1 Suggested answers to **a** are given below.

Type of business	Land/buildings/ location	People	Plant/equipment	Financial
Mobile hairdresser	None	None	Car or van, hairdressing equipment	Enough to obtain plant/ equipment/stock required
DJ	None	None	Car or van, decks, amplifiers and CDs etc.	Enough to obtain plant/ equipment/CDs required
Landscape gardener	Office (could be at home) for planning	Possibly labourer or general assistant	Van, basic gardening tools and equipment	Enough to obtain van and equipment required
Restaurant	Depending upon type, either in attractive rural area or preferably on main road or in distinctive area (e.g. Chinatown)	Chef Waiters	Kitchen facilities and equipment Restaurant fixtures and fittings	Enough to obtain restaurant and buy essential fixtures and fittings plus equipment

Type of business	Land/buildings/location	People	Plant/equipment	Financial
Photographer	Shop/studio – good parking desirable and accessible location	Shop or general assistant (optional)	Car plus photographic equipment – may also develop own photos	Enough to obtain car and equipment/supplies required
Taxi firm	Office and garage for cars – office preferably near station or night-club (where 'passing' trade can be gained)	Drivers Office person to take bookings	Taxis. Seating area for customers who visit office Communications equipment	Enough to obtain taxis and gain licence and provide communications equipment

Suggested answers to parts **b**, **c** and **e** are given in the table below. No specific answer is possible for **d** as this will depend upon the brand name chosen by the students which, if good enough, could be included as an intangible resource. No answer is possible for part **f**.

d Almost any suggestion can be an answer here, providing it is a famous name. *The Times*, Fairy Liquid, Simon Fuller (Pop Idol) and the BBC are all examples and should all provoke 'images' of one type or another.

Type of business	Skills/experience	Intangible resources	Market presence
Mobile hairdresser	Hairdressing skills Customer skills	Client list Trained by well-known business Unique skills, e.g. head massages	Advertise Give incentives to customers who recommend friends
DJ	Playing/mixing ability Presentational skills	Fame and reputation including previous bookings list	Advertise/Develop network through venues in the area who will make recommendation
Landscape gardener	Landscaping experience/ horticultural knowledge Design skills	Reputation plus superb design skills using different materials	Advertise/Offer free planning service/Show portfolio of completed projects to new customers
Restaurant	Catering/cooking skills Business skills	Known chef Specific theme Excellent reputation	Advertise Distinctive name Distinctive service or type of food
Photographer	Photographic skills and experience	Reputation Different approach Range of associated services, e.g. wedding DVDs/cars	Advertise Give incentives to new customers Develop corporate contacts
Taxi firm	Driving skills Previous experience with managing fleet of taxis (logistics etc.) Business skills	New fleet of cars Good reputation for safety and reliability	Advertise Have easy to remember name/phone number Give business cards to all new customers

2 No specific answer possible.

3 a The official answer relates to 'clean-cut, modern family man, healthy lifestyle, highly fashionable'.

b Because the name attracts attention and associates the product or service with the image in **a** above.

c Because her name resulted in maximum publicity for the book in the press and on TV and many fans bought the book because she had written it.

4 a Hotel – near to main town/city attractions and/or near motorway or main road, parking facilities.

b Estate agent – near to other estate agents, on main pedestrian route.

c Hospital – near to main town/city, good transport links.

d Video/DVD rental shop – easy parking, near to main road, near to local community.

e Drive-thru fast food outlet – near main road with heavy traffic, at a distance from competitors.

f Large superstore – relatively near local town/community, good transport links both for deliveries and for customers.

5 No specific answer possible.

Over to you, page 49

1 No specific answer possible.

2 a To expand abroad and to grow in the south-east and Midlands.

b To open three or four stores in Belgium within 3 months. To open another 500 stores in the next 5 years.

c Yes – because they are specific, measurable, achievable, realistic and time-related.

d If the company achieves its objectives it will be part way to achieving its main aims.

3 a (2 of) To increase profits, to increase sales (especially during weekday evenings), to reduce wastage, to minimise waiting times.

b Any appropriate objective should be accepted providing it meets SMART criteria and links to the aim identified.

c Any appropriate suggestions should be accepted.

d No specific answer possible.

Over to you, page 52

1 a Money – to enrol on the course, travel to college and to buy textbooks and other materials; time, energy and concentration – to attend regularly and do his homework. Possibly a computer, if this would help him.

b He should get the recommended textbook for the course and not waste money buying resources which are not for his level. He should attend regularly (to get his money's worth!) and plan his studying at home to get the most benefit. If he has a computer, he should find out which sites will help him the most.

c To impress his Spanish nurse.

d No specific answer possible.

2 a Important resources: staff, location, catering experience, brand name, reputation, freezer. A computer is not important, as this is not an essential requirement for the core business activity, although one would be useful for doing the accounts. Toilet facilities aren't

essential for customers, who only stay for a short time, although they must be provided for staff. Finance for expansion isn't necessary yet, as the business is not yet established.

b A large serving area, because this resource will impact on the core business activity.

3 (3 of) Order stock to reflect seasonal changes; change stock displays to reflect seasonal changes and special occasions; take on additional temporary staff at busy times; make sure additional stock items reflect seasonal demands (e.g. wrapping paper, calendars etc.); target adverts and promotions for this time – plus any other appropriate suggestions.

4 No answer required, although tutors may like to note that Blockbuster was struggling early in 2004 and there were rumours in the press that its parent company, Viacom, was looking to sell the business following three months of losses.

1.4 – Management Processes

Section review, page 53

1 a (3 of) Land, buildings, location, people, plant, equipment, financial, business skills.

b The staff employed by an organisation and the skills they possess.

c (2 of) People recognise it immediately, it creates customer loyalty, it projects a specific (hopefully positive) image.

d Any three appropriate examples can be given, for example business reliance on skilled staff, natural resources, good transport links or passing trade.

e A goal the business wants to achieve.

f (3 of) Profit maximisation, survival, to break even, to grow/expand, service provision, to expand market share.

g Specific, measurable, achievable, realistic, time-related.

h To make as much profit as possible by selling at the best price and keeping costs as low as can be achieved.

i More people buy the *Sun* than any other newspaper in the UK.

j Resources cost money so using them unwisely wastes money and increases costs which will mean profit maximisation cannot be achieved.

2 **a** Responding quickly to seasonal demand.

b Because demand will fall immediately the weather changes.

c Lorries and HGV drivers.

d Traffic congestion was holding up vehicles, but transporting goods from Humberside has meant that vehicles can travel more quickly and deliver more goods.

Over to you, page 56

1 No specific answer possible.

2 **a** To improve human rights all over the world.

b Researchers, campaigners, legal experts. Researchers are required to find out about human rights issues in different countries, campaigners look at how an issue can be promoted to the public and raised with foreign governments, legal experts will be specialists on human rights laws and the laws which apply in different countries. They will also advise on the legal implications of AI's proposed actions.

c Because this is the main way in which it raises funding and promotes awareness of human rights abuses.

d Finance and Human Resources.

e No specific answer possible.

Over to you, page 62

1 No specific answer possible.

2 **a** (2 of) It reduces the need for customers to contact the business with standard enquiries – which saves staff time and makes it easier for customers; the FAQs page can be amended and developed to take account of new enquiries and current customer concerns; it gives customers more confidence to place an order or buy goods online – which increases sales for the business.

b (2 of) Customers don't need to contact the business to query a delivery; customers can arrange to be at home to receive delivery (if necessary) if they know when it is scheduled to arrive; customers have more confidence in the service if they know what is happening.

c No specific answer possible.

3 **a** It would be too expensive to pay one person to continually replace light bulbs one by one, particular if these failed in different parts of the building so the person would keep having to backtrack.

b Have specific days for routine replacements but identify 'key areas' where replacements must be done more quickly (such as reception).

4 **a** Reduce every order by 8 (from 50 to 42).

b Send the route 1 van round in the opposite direction.

c Tell the driver to complete his delivery route and contact van 2 to arrange for him to take the flowers to the shop at the end of his run.

d Tell van 2 driver to wait. Arrange for van 1 driver to meet the driver when he has finished his route – in about half an hour – transfer the remaining flowers (including the one for the store mentioned in **c** above) to van 1 and complete the deliveries.

Over to you, page 70

1 **a** Imran should write down everything he spends for a few weeks, to see where his money is going.

b Imran could look for cheaper options, e.g. swapping computer games with friends, (legally) downloading music files, 'shopping around' for his clothes and taking advantage of sales. He should prioritise what he wants each week – so that it may be a choice between a new DVD or going out.

c **iv** is the best option as he will have longer to pay off the debt. Option **ii** would also give him an interest-free period but this only lasts 6 months and then Imran would either have to change cards again (which could affect his credit rating) or start paying interest.

2 No specific answer possible for college security, although these will include a firewall and a virus monitoring system – as well as passwords and IDs for authorised users. Firewalls and virus monitoring packages should be installed on home PCs linked to broadband. These are less sophisticated than the type that would be purchased by a large business (and cheaper) but are essential as the IP address is being communicated all the time a broadband user is online – which is likely to be much of the day. This can be an open invitation to hackers.

3 No specific answer possible as it will depend upon the student profile identified.

4 No specific answer possible – although it is interesting to develop the findings into a debate on the merits of good pay versus good conditions and a congenial environment!

Over to you, page 78

1 a A = Cutting (first stage, next to stores area)

B = Sewing (next stage, so minimum movement for cut fabric)

C = Finishing (sewn jeans moved to area for buttons, studs etc.)

D = Packing (adjacent to finishing area)

E = Despatch (next to loading bay)

b i Machine A = 6 machines; machine B = 2 machines; machine C = 3 machines; machine D = 4 machines.

ii 2,400 eggs.

c No specific answer possible.

2 a A = 1990s, B = 1960s, C = 1950s, D = 1940s, E = 1970s, F = 2000s, G = 1980s.

b Suggestions could include (4 of): To see those products/services for which demand is increasing/falling (to inform advertising/ market research); which income/age/ educational groups to target (to inform the customer profile); which regions are spending the most – and on what (for deciding on advertising/promotions); where people are most likely to buy (for placing the product and in-store promotions); trends in purchases over the Internet (for developments in this area).

Over to you, page 85

1 a No specific answer possible – it depends upon the organisation chosen.

b No specific answer possible, but decisions by top managers should link to overall planning and strategy and financial monitoring.

2 No answer possible as it depends upon the college's strategic and operational plans. *Note*: tutors unable to obtain a copy of this document can find examples on the Internet. The easiest to obtain are those from public sector organisations who publish Best Value reports each year, such as local authorities and police constabularies.

3 No specific answer possible as it depends upon the student's own aims and objectives.

Over to you, page 90

1 No specific answer possible as this is a development of the student's plan compiled earlier.

2 Any appropriate suggestions should be encouraged – unexpected events and invitations, collections at work, spending more than planned etc. Actions can include reducing general spending to compensate, staying in, saving up. Monitoring is important so that action can be taken quickly.

3 No specific answer possible as it will depend upon the details in your own local authority Best Value plan. *Note*: if this does not give clear targets then it is useful to identify another nearby authority which does. It is advisable to go through the plan to select the most appropriate and interesting pages for students, which apply to targets they can easily understand.

Section review, page 91

1 a Research and development (R & D).

b (3 of) Advertising job vacancies, receiving and recording job applications, notifying internal staff of promotion opportunities, issuing contracts of employment, arranging staff training, monitoring health and safety and keeping accident records, recording sick leave, carrying out welfare policies, providing information on company working policies, advising managers on employment law issues, keeping grievance and disciplinary records, monitoring terms and conditions of employment, monitoring working conditions, maintaining staff records, liaising with staff associations or trade unions.

c Finance who will have issued the invoice; sales who will have processed the order.

d Purchasing who have obtained the materials and must take it up with the supplier and sales who may have to contact the customers to warn them about possible delays.

e Distribution is undertaken by an external, specialist company.

f (3 of) They need information from each other, they need to support each other, they need to make mutual decisions which suit all of the different departments.

g The way in which different levels of managers are organised, with the most senior manager at the top.

h They create a departmental or operational plan, which shows what each department must do to contribute towards achieving the strategic plan.

i So that they can take prompt corrective action if a target is not being met.

j (2 of) Production targets, sales targets, expenditure targets.

2 No specific answer. Tutors may like to consider if any other areas of the college may be appropriate or invite managers from commercial organisations to give a comparison.

3 Below is a summary of the actions Thorntons took, which can be used to stimulate discussion. Students should, however, be able to identify the following priority areas:

a The main aim is to increase profits. Key objectives should relate to increasing/maintaining sales levels all year round (despite the weather) and to meeting supermarket competition. The costs of production/distribution should also be maintained or reduced.

b The main factors could include selling more branded chocolates and adding new varieties which are not currently found in supermarkets. If hot weather is a problem, Thorntons could look at developing lines which would appeal (e.g. iced or frozen products).

c Targets would relate to production (e.g. greater efficiency), sales per month, expenditure. Students should be encouraged to suggest SMART targets.

d Action on over-spending would depend upon the reason. Purchasing over-spending implies raw material costs rising, marketing implies advertising/promotional costs above budget. Raw materials may be sourced elsewhere but quality is important to Thorntons. Marketing projects can be cut but this may affect sales. A good answer would be to look elsewhere for cuts to support these increases, if possible. Sales should be analysed by store – as results may differ. Some shops may be in poor locations or too close to competitors. Launching new products could help sales, so the timing of these would be important. Production targets are important for sales to be made. Batch production will be a feature at Thorntons, so schedules could be adjusted to produce the most popular/profitable lines. Operating additional shifts would be advisable if problems occurred at a critical time of year (e.g. before Christmas).

In November 2003 Thornton's announced plans to be 'the UK's leading retailer and distributor of sweet special foods', to deliver higher sales and improve their margins. It widened the summer product range to include more ice cream and drinks, although this did not significantly benefit seasonal sales. It has increased the number of channels through which its products are made available to customers i.e. through their own stores, franchises, a gift delivery service, commercial partners (e.g. M & S) and other retailers. It is developing agreements with supermarkets and other retailers to sell its products. It is developing a new café format (five had opened by October 2003). It will provide additional services, however, in its own stores, e.g. gift wrapping, icing and advice to customers. It is increasing the money spent on developing completely new products and aims to launch new gift and impulse products. As yet it does not see a major refit of existing stores as necessary, although some adjustments may need to be made to encourage a wider cross-section of customers. It aims to improve its supply chain further to increase efficiency in the stores.

Tutors should check the website and press statements for updates to this information at the time they set the assignment for students.

In this section you will find:

Unit overview and tutor guidelines

Unit 2 focuses on the external factors that affect businesses, i.e. the expectations and behaviour of customers, the actions of competitors, stakeholder expectations and external influences. The concept of corporate social responsibility is also introduced, although it is not called by this term.

Tutors may like to bear the following points in mind when teaching this unit.

- Students normally find topics that relate to marketing and customers, such as those in Unit 2.1, interesting and relatively easy to understand. They may find the concept of 'a market' difficult at first and struggle to think beyond stalls selling fruit and vegetables! An interesting exercise is to take a standard product, such as footwear, and then subdivide it in a group brainstorming activity to see how many different markets can be identified. In this case, male, female and children's footwear are obvious categories, but another sub-division is sports and leisure footwear rather than fashion footwear. Or you can divide by materials e.g. leather and synthetic. Then there are specialist niche markets, from ski-boots to diving flippers! From here it is a relatively easy matter to look at how markets can change in different ways, for instance a decrease in demand for slippers but an increase in demand for trainers, and the effect of fashion and brand names, such as Doc Martens and Timberland. Buyer behaviour can be linked to this type of investigation as well as variations in customer attributes and how this relates to the different markets.
- All students understand the concept of competition and may enjoy carrying out a SWOT analysis on their own course, their college or any other organisation/product they know well. Tutors

should note that SWOT analyses, which take into account both internal and external factors, are introduced in Unit 2.2, whereas PESTEL analyses, which focus on different types of external influences, are introduced in Unit 2.4. In practice it would be more likely for a PESTEL analysis to be done first and for the external factors to then be divided into the opportunities and threats sections for the SWOT analysis. It is therefore recommended that SWOT analyses are revised at the end of the unit as a natural consequence from a PESTEL analysis.

- Although few students may have heard of the term 'stakeholder', very few have difficulty understanding this concept. They will certainly understand their own expectations as a customer and an employee (or student). The inclusion of sponsors is an interesting addition to the scheme, and students should be able to contribute to any discussions of sporting personalities and other stars and the fees they are paid. For example, the three year deal between Beckham and Gillette was allegedly worth $60 – $80 million. The behaviour of celebrities, and how this may affect such deals, can lead to lively discussion – as can the actions of sponsors of sporting events who ban spectators from bringing in competitive products!
- In Unit 2.3, the students are introduced to pressure groups and ethical concerns over a range of issues from child exploitation to tax evasion and the supply of harmful products such as firearms and tobacco. Current events and topical issues will always make this topic more meaningful, e.g. the plight of the cockle-pickers in Morecambe Bay, the proposals to extend smoking bans to bars and restaurants, the pressure on food producers to reduce salt and sugar in their products and on sellers of high-fat 'junk' foods to offer slimmer options. Some students may have seen the film *Super Size Me* and know how this affected

McDonald's, resulting in a change of menu. McDonald's was wise enough to turn the publicity to its advantage, arguing that it is always responsive to future trends. Students may also like to take an objective look at the film maker, Morgan Spurlock, who lived off McDonald's food for 30 days and assess the motives and financial benefits of his actions! It is useful for students to learn that not all issues are clear-cut and more informed views result from researching the facts, not jumping to conclusions, not believing everything in the newspapers and even realising that different papers have different 'slants'. A discussion on tobacco, junk food, the role of the state or even tax avoidance will normally result in some differences in opinion, and students can benefit by learning how to debate relatively contentious issues such as these in a lively yet courteous manner.

- The BTEC First scheme headings for section 2.4 are not the standard PESTEL headings, but because these are easy to remember, this is the approach used in the student book for this section. Political issues are often perceived by students as either boring or irrelevant unless there is some good reason to think otherwise. Sadly, this is the case at present, given the aftermath of the Iraq war and the taking of hostages to dissuade foreign contractors and aid agencies from working there. This has resulted in many businesses withdrawing from the region but has also provided opportunities for some western security firms to provide 24/7 protection to the workers who remain.

- The inclusion of 'macroeconomic variables' in a BTEC First scheme may seem alarming at first, particularly to tutors who are not economists. However, the topics covered under this heading are relatively straightforward. A good way of approaching the topic is from the viewpoint of young people trying to buy a house and manage their own finances – and the economic factors that will affect them (and how). If interest rates or tax rates go down they have more money in their pocket so, probably, will spend more. If interest rates and/or tax increases, they have less to spend and must make cutbacks or borrow more. It is relatively straightforward to look at how their actions affect businesses – and how these issues have an impact on businesses in much the same way. Most students will also be aware that house prices rise and fall and be interested in identifying the factors that cause this.

- Interestingly, most PESTEL analyses include social changes (for instance more women working, people living longer and so on) but in the BTEC First scheme the focus is on social issues such as GM foods and fat cat businessmen. Students should be strongly dissuaded from thinking that all managers who earn a high salary are automatically a 'fat cat'! Key business failures, such as Enron and WorldCom (and more recently, Parmalat) are now more historic, but the potential effects are still relevant. Students who study Specialist Unit 6 will also focus on the problems of business continuity in a crisis. This is a natural continuation from the type of issues introduced in this unit.

- Current news events provide an excellent resource for this unit. As useful assessment practice for Unit 2.4, students can routinely be asked to identify the type of organisations which are affected in each case and how they may adapt their activities because of these changes. Normally real-life events provide a far wider and more interesting range of scenarios than any fictitious examples.

This section contains 26 additional activities and case studies designed to reinforce learning and understanding. Each covers a key area of the mandatory units in the scheme where you may wish to provide additional practical activities for your students.

The content of some activities overlaps sufficiently with either another mandatory unit or a specialist unit to be marked as a cross-referenced activity. A full list of these is summarised here for ease of reference. Tutors are recommended to check the content before these are issued as, in some cases, there may be one or more terms which need a little extra explanation if students have yet to study the overlapping unit. This can be advantageous as students can be introduced to a new concept or topic almost incidentally and this also illustrates the strong links that are to be found between virtually all business studies topics.

Activity	Cross-reference
2.1.1	9.2
2.1.3	7.3
2.1.4	8.2
2.1.5	9.3
2.2.5	9.4
2.2.7	1.4.9
2.3.3	3.1
2.3.4	5.2, 6.3
2.3.5	7.4
2.3.8	1.1.7
2.4.1	4.2
2.4.4	8.3
2.4.7	1.1.4
2.4.8	1.2.4

2.1 – Customer expectations

Activity 2.1.1 – Taking advantage of growing markets

(Cross-references to Unit 9 Starting up a new business)

Identifying growth markets is crucial to success both for small and large businesses who will aim to match products with market demand. This first activity gives students the opportunity to be creative and exchange ideas.

Suggested answers are given in the key below but these are purely indicative and students may have several other appropriate (or better!) ideas. Those stuck for ideas of growing markets could be referred to ONS reports on Social Trends or Household Expenditure (either in the college library or online) or asked to search for examples of growth markets on the Internet by experimenting with appropriate search phrases.

Answer

Growing market	Growth and new products and services
Health and fitness	Hotels with spa facilities
	More private gyms/sports stores/fitness clothing/fitness gadgets (e.g. pedometers)/sales of home fitness equipment/activity holidays etc.
	New entrepreneur: could become personal trainer
Overseas holidays	All inclusive holidays with food/drinks paid for up front
	Cruises for young people and family/cut-price air travel/luggage/travel accessories/sun cream and safe tanning products/medicines for travellers (e.g. insect repellent)
	New entrepreneur: could offer taxi service to airport or offer house sitting service.
Childcare	24-hour nursery provision where kids can sleep overnight
	After-school clubs/holiday clubs like PGL/summer camps/restaurants with children's play areas and zones/hotels with children's clubs and babysitting service
	New entrepreneur: could train to be a child-minder or start play centre
House ownership and DIY	B&Q offering wedding list facilities
	Garden design and make-over services/interior design/decorating/wooden flooring/garden decking/supply of basic household items (e.g. IKEA)
	New entrepreneur: could start up gardening or interior design service if qualified

Growing market	Growth and new products and services
Internet access	Internet banking services
	Growth of shopping online = more online shopping sites/music download services/travel reservations online/customer service facilities online/online advertising including paying search engines for high placements/more ISPs
	New entrepreneur: setting up and installing new computer facility and doing repairs/troubleshooting. Or website development for small businesses
Healthier food	Revamped Heinz baked beans with less salt
	Low-fat products/slimming clubs/restaurants serving diet foods/organic produce/natural foods without additives/fresh fish, fruit and vegetables/bottled water/ natural supplements, health shops and herbalists
	New entrepreneur: starting sandwich shop specialising in natural, healthy food

Ideas for other growing markets could include:

- More convenience food/ready-meals/take-aways/ethnic foods.
- Cleaning and other personal services (e.g. personal shoppers and organisers) for the income-rich, time-poor.
- The 50-plus market and all associated products. Students may need to be advised that Saga's success has been based on providing holidays, insurance and financial services rather than the supply of walking frames and nursing homes! The huge growth in sales of anti-ageing skin products is part of this market.
- Alcoholic drinks (with the associated moral arguments).
- Ethical products e.g. Fairtrade coffee and bananas and ethical investments.

Activity 2.1.2 – Not the real thing!

This activity focuses on probably the biggest marketing disaster of 2004, the launch by Coca-Cola of Dasani bottled water. Background information is available on any Internet news site if tutors want more details.

The activity also relates to other issues linked to the scheme, such as product flops and disaster management. In this case Coke arguably completely misread the UK market and UK focus on natural sources of bottled water, which are less of an issue in the US. It also didn't account for the UK tabloid industry and its reaction to this type of story. Its failure to respond promptly and positively has made it difficult to relaunch the brand – but, at the time of writing, there were rumours that Coke is planning exactly that. Tutors may therefore wish to check the current situation before issuing the case study.

Answer

1 (2 of) It wanted to break into the European market; it felt there was more scope in the UK as the market still has more growth than other European countries, it wasn't fighting local firms to the same extent (Evian, Volvic and Vittel are all French companies).

2 (1 of) Coke is well known to retailers and a good seller; they were spending £7 million on their advertising campaign so customers would be aware of the brand.

3 (4 of) Safe, clean, pure, reasonably priced, fresh-tasting.

4 (2 of) Tap water is safe in Britain, it was seen as a rip-off, the idea of bottling tap water had previously been a joke on *Only Fools and Horses*, in Britain all bottled water is from natural sources, in the UK the culture and thinking is different from in the US and Coke failed to take this into account.

5 Because they were contaminated with twice the level of acceptable bromates.

6 a $95p \times 500,000 = £475,000 + £7$ million.

   b The cost of any relaunch and missed opportunities in Europe.

7 The delay in entering the European market. Coke was not concerned about losing face in the UK and in summer 2004 it was already planning how it could relaunch Dasani. (Tutors may wish to develop this question to look at some key differences between the culture of UK and US business organisations.)

8 At the time of writing the following were listed online at **www.powwow.com**: Customer expectations: a water cooler that fits their environment; properly installed with clear explanations/maintenance service; water deliveries at convenient time close to cooler; not to run out of water; to have a cooler which is always clean, hygienic and functioning well; to have an efficient and friendly relationship with the service provider within an effective administrative process. Students should be able to guess two of these by thinking of their own needs if they bought one.

9 The main benefits of a cooler are that water is always available, in large quantities if necessary, without having to buy bottles in the supermarket and carry them home. In the US this is beneficial especially when people live a long distance from the supermarket, in areas where it is very hot in summer or in remote areas with no mains supply. In the UK demand may be less because most people live near a local store, the heat is less and tap water is safe to drink.

10 No specific answer possible – but students may be encouraged to investigate this further online. Much may depend upon sales required to break-even or make a profit and the sales price. Doting pet owners may be keen, more pragmatic owners are unlikely to be very impressed.

Activity 2.1.3 – How low can they go?

(Cross-references to Unit 7 Sales and customer service)

The standard mantra of most businesses is that providing amazing customer service is an essential requirement. Yet this activity highlights two businesses which have a very different focus – and are both successful. IKEA is loved or hated by shoppers. It is loved for its cheapness (most customers leave with a large number of impulse buys because the prices are so low); it is hated for its layout, collection procedures and unintelligible instructions.

Ryanair has got probably the brashest boss in business. Michael O'Leary constantly gains publicity for all the wrong reasons (such as charging for wheelchairs) yet still fills his planes. His basic philosophy is that customers will put up with anything to travel abroad for £10!

While students are asked to think about the type of customer profiles which apply to each business – and to consider the value of these businesses to other types of customers, such as retail buyers – the main strength of this activity can be in the discussion it can provoke (see question 6) about how much inconvenience people will tolerate to save money. One way of tackling this question would be to ask students to list all the customer service factors they would sacrifice for cheapness and then decide how the increase in income would affect this list. This should enable students to see first-hand how customer wants and preferences can vary, even in their own group, and how different business models can thrive providing there is a USP that appeals to a sector of the market in each case. Tutors should note that although USPs are not introduced into the scheme formally until 2.2, they have been included in some of the activities in this section because they can quite naturally be covered as part of the area of study.

Answer

1 (2 of in each case) IKEA – flatpacks reduce transport costs from warehouses to stores, items are assembled by customers not staff, no delivery service. Ryanair – cheaper regional airports, Internet booking, low compensation and (soon) no baggage.

2 Both the national charity and the local authority will have to account publicly for their spending and will want to keep costs as low as possible. They will be particularly sensitive about the cost of travel. The new entrepreneur will want to keep all costs as low as possible and can save a considerable amount on start-up costs by furnishing the office from a business like IKEA and on running costs by travelling as cheaply as possible.

3 a IKEA – main attributes: young singles, newly-weds, families, some retired, low income. Children and the elderly might find method of shopping/self-assembly requirements difficult. Some high-income customers and empty nesters may enjoy saving money there but most would probably prefer personal service. Core customer: 18–40, students, singles, newlywed or young family, low income relative to needs.

Ryanair – Main attributes: young singles, newlyweds, retired. Families will find no baggage rule too restrictive for main holidays. Elderly will prefer more personal service and so, too, will high-income customers. Exception may be empty nesters or retired with holiday homes abroad who are frequent travellers. Core customer: 18–50, students, singles, retired, low income relative to travel needs.

b Young families will not want to use Ryanair for their holidays as they are unlikely to be able to travel without baggage.

4 a People transport their own furniture and assemble it themselves.

b (2 of) You must visit a store, have to follow a specified route, have to queue to collect the item, have to transport it and build it yourself.

c (3 of) Very cheap flights, can only book online, flies to cheaper regional airports, will not be able to take luggage.

d IKEA – cheap flatpack furniture for self-assembly.

Ryanair – most basic service possible but the cheapest prices.

5 a Customer will still expect product to fit together and function or to receive money back. This is a basic legal right. They will also expect all products to be safe to use.

   b Safety here is paramount. Ryanair could not afford a poor safety record or customers would desert it in droves.

6 No specific answer possible.

Activity 2.1.4 – Market research in action

(Cross-references to Unit 8 Online business)

This is a practical activity which will take a little time for students to do properly. However, time is needed if students are to gain the most benefit from comparing their findings and reaching conclusions. The activity is cross-referenced to Unit 8 because the group 5 activity involves comparing different online operations and suggesting new media methods of marketing. As the activity is written, there are five separate student groups but these can be further split (e.g. by sub-dividing the newspapers for investigating) or combined or some can be omitted to suit the tutor and the size of the group.

As part of the preparation required, a set of newspapers needs to be obtained. It is easier for students to compare these if they are purchased for the same day, when the way the same news items are treated can easily be seen.

Tutors should check the availability of the free Insight report from keynote before asking students to access this – and may prefer to print out a copy in pdf format for future use. Students may also need guidance reading the menus and choosing the options on some sites to get what they want unless they are relatively experienced at doing this, although no items are particularly difficult to find. Finally, group 3 will need access to free computer printing to obtain the demographic profiles for different newspapers as these often run to several pages and are difficult to compare on screen. Explain the term 'demographic profile' if necessary.

Answer

No specific answer is possible.

Activity 2.1.5 – Choosing the healthy option

(Cross-references with Unit 9 Starting up a new business)

This activity revises the basic concepts of markets and related terminology in relation to organic food and tests student understanding by identifying whether a range of statements are true or false. There is a simple numeracy question (converting sales of different market sectors into percentages and drawing a pie chart). Students are then asked to evaluate the Duchy Originals business through its website and devise a simple plan, working in a group, for their own retail organic business. This final task can be extended for students who are also studying Specialist Unit 9, to include other aspects of a standard business plan (see Unit 9, page 26). Students will gain most by comparing their ideas and answers to this question and evaluating them as a class.

Tutors should note that there is no disparity between the value of the European natural food and drinks market (£12 billion) in this activity and the value of the European bottled water market stated in Activity 2.1.2 (£10 billion) as the former does not include bottled water.

Answer

1

Statement	
By 2007, all the food and drink eaten by Europeans will be worth £12 billion.	False – this is just the value of the fresh food market
The US natural food and drink market is worth more only because America is bigger than Europe.	False – this may be a contributory factor but is not the only reason why sales are higher.
Organic food is considered a niche market because it is one part of a larger market.	True
The food market can be sub-divided into many different types: fresh food, tinned food, baby food, dairy food and frozen food are just a few examples.	True
In 2003, over £1 billion of organic food was bought in Britain.	True
The biggest selling item is organic baby food.	False – fruit and vegetables are the biggest sellers
The baby food market can be divided into organic and non-organic products.	True
More people buy organic ready meals than organic fruit and vegetables.	False – though sales of ready meals are increasing

2 Tutor to check calculations and pie-chart.

Organic food sub-markets

- Baby food 4%
- Drinks 4%
- Eggs 4%
- Cerials, bread and biscuits 13%
- Fruit/veg 39%
- Dairy 18%
- Groceries 17%

3 Strengths: (4 of) Brand name, well-established and trusted, association with the Prince of Wales (with well-known views on organic farming), excellent product reviews, good information on the site including educational information for schools, online shop, stocked in major outlets. (Any other appropriate suggestions should be accepted.) USPs: profits to Prince of Wales charity; association with Prince of Wales.

4 No specific answer possible but ideas should be appropriate in relation to the market research information provided.

Activity 2.1.6 – A definite lack of flower power!

This activity links the problem of slow (or no) adaptation despite changes in a market. In this case, the change has largely been through the emergence of greater competition, which links to the competitive pressures the students will study in Unit 2.2.

The Chief Executive of Interflora would prefer to make the business private in order to obtain finance and investment, which is not possible under the current trade association structure. This would mean individual florists receiving shares in relation to the size of their business. For the proposal to be agreed, 75 per cent of members must vote for it at the AGM in November 2004.

This detail is not given in the case study to avoid confusing students with information not specifically relevant to this unit.

However, the problems of a traditional structure of disparate members with one person one vote can be discussed with students as this obviously hampers the introduction of new ideas.

Answer

1 An association or network of independent florists who can then send flowers around the country, through the network.

2 (2 of) Because they are experiencing greater competition; because they are struggling to compete on price; because people buy flowers on impulse for themselves when they are out shopping in a supermarket or in a store.

3 Probably not if the bouquets are a lot more expensive from Interflora members. If ready-made bouquets are cheaper, look good, last a long time and are easier to buy then the competitors will win.

4 Because the members are geographically isolated and act independently. It is very difficult to get a united voice, each person will vote in his/her own interests.

5 He is suggesting champagne, chocolates and teddy bears but any other suitable product ideas should be accepted.

6 (2 of) Convert it into a private company; buy items in bulk to save money (e.g. flowers, mobile phones); use the customer database for marketing purposes.

7 Any view is acceptable here providing it is rationally argued. There is not likely to be an overnight revolution no matter what decision is reached. Some florists will no doubt still do well, and others will not and will fail if competition intensifies. Much will depend upon the individual customer base and location and whether Interflora as a network can continue.

Activity 2.1.7 – What's the point of changing?

Although this activity is the last in section 2.1 it could easily be the first in 2.2! It examines the various reasons why business adapt their product and services – and also looks at those that drag their feet or refuse to change. Two topical inclusions at the time of writing were McDonald's and Kelloggs – both under attack for the nutritional value of their food, or lack of it. In the case of Kelloggs, all its cereals, particularly those aimed at children, were criticised as containing far too high levels of salt.

Students are asked to work in small groups to suggest at least four changes or adaptations of their own. A useful start is to think about product extensions – e.g. basic soap powder was adapted to be biological, then the bleach was removed to make it colour-fast. Basic Coke was extended with Cherry Coke and Diet Coke. With services, hairdressers now often offer a range of extras from extensions to Indian head massage. The effect of technological developments is continuous – from satellite navigation and CD autochangers in cars to wall-mounted, flatscreen, interactive televisions. New ways of doing business not only include the Internet but SMS messaging (in addition to the online service BA also send text message updates to passengers). Continental and other airlines are now offering 2-way email and instant and text messaging in-flight for a small charge.

Answer

1 and **2** see table below.

3 No answer possible.

2.2 – Competitive pressures

Activity 2.2.1 – Identifying the competitive market

This activity revises the concept of the competitive market and asks students to identify the scale of the market and the degree of competition, i.e. whether competition is weak, moderate or strong. The activity starts with a brief overview of both concepts.

The second task looks at the impact of different markets on both customers and businesses. Hopefully most students will realise that the greater the scale of the market and its intensity the more likely it is that customers will have greater choice and lower prices – but that this makes it harder for businesses – especially small ones – to survive.

Change or adaptation	Reason(s)	Type
Within months of the original launch, Apple launched a 4th generation iPod (smaller, cheaper) with extended battery life and an iPod mini.	C, D, E	L
The government launched a passports online service.	A, C	F
McDonald's announced it was phasing out supersizes and introducing salads.	A, C	U
The Ford team put on heavy padded garments and goggles to restrict vision before designing the Focus car with big dials and easy access.	A, B	L
The Imperial War Museum introduced mounted flying displays to music and interactive displays.	A, B, E	L
A small town hairdresser decided to accept Switch and credit cards for payments.	A, C	F or U
A fishmonger refused to accept any cards but continued to insist on cash or cheques.		DS
The AA introduced breakdown cover for the driver not the car – so the driver is covered in a friend's car.	A, D, E	L
After seeing attendance fall for years, eventually the ECB (English and Welsh Cricket Board) introduced 20/20 cricket to liven things up.	A, C	U
Kelloggs reduced the salt in its cornflakes a little, after criticism that all its cereals had concentrations that were far too high.	A, C	U
Expedia advertised build your own holidays online.	A, D, E	L
A local fish and chip shop changed its menus to include ethnic food and pizzas and now offers a delivery service.	A, B, E	F
Dell offers a computer maintenance service for small businesses.	A, E	L
BA enhances online service so customers can check in and select their seat at home.	A, C, D, E	L
Walkers produces Lite crisps with fewer calories.	A, C	F
Fish4Homes offers to email customers with details of homes for sale in the area they want.	A, D, E	L
A hotel owner says he has no intention of having a website because he doesn't understand IT.		DS

Answer

1

Service provider/ product	Competitive market	Degree of competition
Plumber	Local	Weak
Dentist	Local	Weak
Multiplex cinema	Regional	Moderate
Night club	Local/regional	Moderate to strong
Department store	National	Moderate
Mobile phones	Global	Strong
Jeans	Global	Strong
Estate agent	Mainly local	Strong
Internet Service Provider (ISP)	National	Moderate to strong
Crisps	National	Moderate to strong
Window cleaner	Local	Weak
Cars	Global	Strong
Chain store (e.g. Boots, Next, Currys)	National	Strong
Credit cards	Global	Strong
Computer software	Global	Weak
Car maintenance	Local/regional	Weak
Bookseller	National	Strong
Washing machines	European	Strong
Jeweller	Local/regional	Moderate
Solicitor	Local	Moderate
Mail delivery	National	Weak
Supermarket	National	Strong
Cosmetics	Global	Strong
Take-aways	Local	Strong

2 a Better for business: local or otherwise small scale and weak because then customers have less choice. The business can then dictate its own terms and prices.

b Better for customers: national/global or otherwise large scale and strong competition. Businesses then have to provide competitive products/services in terms of prices, quality and other aspects of the business or they will not survive.

Activity 2.2.2 – Investigating the market for chocoholics!

This activity involves students in investigating the marketplace for chocolate in the UK. Tutors should note that chocolate is one segment of the confectionery market which includes sweets, toffees, mints and other related products. Students are warned, during their investigations, to focus only on chocolate products. This market has been chosen because it is relatively easy to understand and the products are well-known by students. The Cadbury's website, in particular, provides a wide range of useful information on the market which tutors may wish to read themselves before starting the activity. It may also help students if the most recent Confectionery Report (and any other large pdf files on other sites) are downloaded by the tutor and printed at the outset.

The market is dominated by Cadbury Trebor Bassett (CTB), Nestlé Rowntree and Masterfoods and students have to work in a group to investigate a particular supplier. Tutors with particularly large groups have two options:

- They can nominate groups to investigate smaller suppliers, e.g. Thorntons, Ferrero and Kraft Foods (who make Toblerone). Links to these sites are also provided.
- They can nominate two (or more) groups to investigate each of the large firms and consider their answers to questions 2–4 before combining to compare ideas and to prepare a joint presentation.

Tutors should also note that at the time of writing, the Cadbury site is the most informative for students although the Nestlé site is quite comprehensive. Those using the Masterfood and/or Mars sites may need additional support and guidance. It would be useful if students are guided to look for annual sales, references to direct competition with rival brands and sales trends. These are available in the Cadbury report but at Nestlé students need to look on the global site (**www.nestlé.com**) and look under Investor Relations. At present, this is not specifically available on the Mars or Masterfood sites.

A useful method of providing a visual aid of the completed SWOT analysis is on A1 flipchart paper. The final analyses for all the teams can then be left up on the wall while the teams rewrite their opportunities and threats columns in the light of the information they have received about their competitor's plans. This, hopefully, will illustrate the value of market intelligence and why companies are very keen to know about the resources and strengths of their major competitors.

The final task is simply a review to identify which company is likely to be the strongest. The answer is most likely to be one of the big three, but students should give reasons to support their views.

Answer

It is not possible to provide specific SWOT analyses for each business as these are likely to change because of business plans, market trends and the actions of their immediate competitors. However, an outline of the type of business the students could include is given below for guidance.

Strengths: Well-known brands (give examples); quality association; brands constantly revised/extended; available in wide range of outlets/vending machines; USPs of specific products (e.g. Yorkie bars/Rolo etc.); wide range of seasonal products, e.g. Easter eggs, Xmas novelties, Valentine's Day, etc.; specific snacks for eating at work/on the move; gift ranges; innovative marketing campaigns/good website.

Weaknesses: Tired brands or those which need reviving; unimaginative names or displays; lack of availability; uncompetitive prices; reduced range; high calorie product; left behind by competitors; not as well-known as competitor; 'tired' marketing campaigns/unimaginative website.

Opportunities: Extend existing ranges based on market trends such as for blocks of chocolate to share, develop new ranges based on new trends, e.g. for lower calorie/healthier options (e.g. dark chocolate); start marketing campaign on healthy option chocolate; expand into markets where there is greater demand; expand range of outlets to increase opportunities for impulse buying (if appropriate); link with associated supplier to promote specific brands (e.g sell snack chocolate in coffee shops, sell 'chocolate for sharing' with DVD rentals).

Threats: Decline in market share because of actions of competitors and their plans; decline in overall chocolate sales because of greater health concerns; arrival of new suppliers or expansion of niche suppliers (e.g. high quality European brands, particularly Swiss and Belgian chocolate makers); sale of quality chocolate on the Internet by new or niche suppliers.

Activity 2.2.3 – Know your competitors!

This activity enables students to check that they understand the concepts of direct and indirect competition by identifying specific competitors for a range of products/suppliers. Tutors may prefer to ask students to do this in pairs or small groups as the range of possible suggestions for indirect competitors is then likely to be more manageable for class discussion purposes.

Answer

The answers below are indicative only. All appropriate suggestions should be accepted.

1a See table.

Product or supplier	Direct competitor in same market	Competitor in related/wider market	Substitute products/supplies
Adidas trainers	Nike, Puma, Reebok	Doc Martens, Timberland boots	Jeans, replica football kit
Weetabix	Shreddies, Shredded Wheat	Kelloggs or own brand cereals with sugar added	Porridge, fruit juice, yoghurt, grapefruit
B & Q	Focus, Homebase, Wicks	Garden centres, hardware stores	Indoor furniture and soft furnishings
My Travel	First Choice, Thomas Cook	Cunard, Saga, PGL, Club 18–30, Disneyworld	Health farm, hotel, villa owners, camping sites
Hovis loaf	Warburton or Kingsmill brown bread	White bread, speciality bread (e.g. pitta, naan etc.)	Biscuits, cakes, crackers
Burger King	McDonald's, Wimpy	KFC, Pizza Hut, Pizza Express	Local restaurant or pub, takeaway
Walkers crisps	Smiths, Pringles, own brands (e.g. Marks & Spencer)	Wotsits, Doritos, KP Hula Hoops, Seabrook and other manufacturers of hand-made crisps	Nuts, other savoury snacks e.g. pork scratchings
HMV stores	Virgin Megastore, Woolworths and other chains, Tesco, Amazon	Independent stores specialising in specific types of music/exchanges, e.g. Fopp, Rough Trade, Vinyl Exchange	Music downloads and online services e.g. Apple iTunes site, Coke site, Napster

Product or supplier	Direct competitor in same market	Competitor in related/wider market	Substitute products/ supplies
Weight-Watchers	Slimming World, Slimmer UK, Atkins,	Online resources, diet books, diet foods e.g. SlimFast	Gyms, fitness clubs, personal trainers, fitness equipment, videos
Barclays Bank	NatWest, Halifax, Lloyds TSB	Egg, Smile, First Direct and any other phone or Internet only bank	Only a piggy bank or a safe. There are no substitutes to banking services
Marie Claire	Cosmo, Elle, Glamour, Red	Ideal Home, Autocar, Heat, Sugar, FHM	Book, newspaper, DVD, CD, TV
Monsoon	Next, Principles, Oasis, Wallis	Matalan, George at Asda, BHS, Harvey Nichols	Any shoe store or fashion accessory shop e.g. Claire's Accessories
AOL	Wanadoo, BT Yahoo, Tiscali etc.	Specialist business ISPs e.g. 100percentIT	None if you want Internet access
UCI cinemas	Odeon/Warner Village/ Cineworld	Blockbuster, Tesco, Amazon	Night club, restaurant, skating rink, bowling alley

1 **b** Banking, Internet Service Providers.

2 **a** Argos is unique in relation to its method of selling and wide range of competitively priced goods – from electrical goods and toys to household supplies. It is often described as a type of consumer warehouse driven by its catalogue. Customers can now look up product availability on the website.

b CenterParcs offers a variety of entertainments and other holiday facilities in UK and Northern Europe. Its covered areas mean that breaks are not as weather dependent as usual.

c Hamleys calls itself the biggest toyshop in the world and its size makes it unique.

d Fairtrade Products offer a fair deal to third world growers and suppliers.

Activity 2.2.4 – Market intelligence and action planning

This activity is a variation and extension of the student activity on page 139 of the Student Book. The main differences are that more details are given for different scenarios and the students are expected to research to find information out themselves. They are referred to the Hoover's Online website as a good example of a Business Intelligence source. Although this is an American site, most large British companies are included on its huge database (with the exception, it would appear, of W H Smith).

It is suggested tutors look at the website to start, as the scope for other student spin-off activities based on this is quite considerable. Although many services are chargeable, basic facts sheets and news are not. Simply looking through the information available will give students a far more realistic idea of the type of data available when businesses are researching about competitors and their activities.

Answer

1 and **2**

Business and action taken	Competitors	Main reason for action
Burberry jazzed up its lines with bright colours; hired Kate Moss as the face of the brand; and extended operations in Japan.	Aquascutum, House of Fraser, Polo, Ralph Lauren	A
Nokia announced the release by 2007 of musical handsets with a hard drive that will store thousands of songs.	Motorola, Siemens, Samsung, Ericsson	B
MFI said it was spending more on advertising, cutting prices and increasing the range of new products from 10 per cent to 25 per cent.	GUS (i.e. Argos), House of Fraser, IKEA	C

Business and action taken	Competitors	Main reason for action
Whitbread bought 150 Premier Lodge sites to add to its stock of over 400 Travel Inns. All will be renamed 'Premier Travel Inn' so customers won't confuse them with rival Travelodge.	Travelodge, Best Western, Inter-Continental Hotels, Mitchells & Butlers	A
BT reduced the price of its flagship 512K broadband service to new and existing consumers.	AOL, Wanadoo	C
Nintendo cut the price of its GameCube because of unsold stock and falling sales and launched the Nintendo DS – its entry into the hand-held game market. It will launch its successor to the GameCube in 2005.	Microsoft, Sega, Sony	C
Hoover launched 'The One', a new cleaner which can switch between carpet and hard-floor modes at a flick.	Dyson, Electrolux	B
W H Smith stopped selling singles and cut stocks of CDs and computer games to put more books, stationery and magazines on its shelves.	Tesco, Amazon, HMV	C
Mattel saw its sales of Barbie fall and profits crash following the launch of the Bratz dolls by MGA Entertainment. It hit back by launching My Scene and Fairytopia and a new adult Barbie clothing range.	Hasbro, LEGO®, MGA Entertainment	C
Tesco paid £140 million to buy a stake in Chinese hypermarket chain Hymall. This will give it a 50 per cent stake in the chain.	(In UK) Asda, Wm Morrison, Sainsbury (Worldwide), Wall-Mart and Carrefour	A

Activity 2.2.5 – Who's making music?

(Cross-references to Unit 9 Starting up a new business)

This is a comprehensive activity/case study involving three markets related to the music industry. Tutors may wish to go through the material carefully with the students at the start – and perhaps only introduce one market at a time to avoid confusion, depending upon the overall ability of the group.

The first market – audio and video production – illustrates the trends towards market concentration/consolidation that occur when businesses aim to compete by being bigger and achieving economies of scale. The downside of this can be a lack of flexibility and slow response to change. Tutors can easily add to the information given by reviewing the way in which the majors initially responded to the new threat posed by the (original) Napster site and illegal downloads by concentrating on legislative action rather than looking for ways in which they could utilise the new trend to their own advantage. Tutors should note that Impala, the European trade body for independent producers, may appeal against decision by the EU to allow the merger of Sony and BMG but this has not been mentioned in the case study. Neither is there any mention of competition law and the fact that any subsequent merger by EMI and Warner might also have to be put forward. This is

because the focus of the case study is on changing markets, rather than market dominance (or otherwise) by large businesses and possible distortion of the market. Tutors may, of course, wish to discuss this issue with students and can find further information at **www.impalasite.org**.

Information on music sales in the UK by outlet (the second market) is provided. At the time of writing this does not include download sales. It is therefore sensible for tutors (and students) to check for updates on the websites listed. The number of download sites is increasing almost continually. In July 2004, the market leader was Apple iTunes with 51 per cent of the market, but this may change in the future with the launch of the (much cheaper) easyMusic.com. In this activity students are guided to the Oxfam download site, where a contribution in each case goes to the charity.

The third market is the ringtone market. The aim of the final question is to provoke lively discussion and debate among students, who should be asked to justify opinions as to whether the current trends in the market are likely to last very long – or not.

This activity is cross-referenced to specialist Unit 9, as there is useful guidance on several of the websites for young people keen to work in the music business. Question 7 can easily be dropped for students not taking Unit 9 or extended to include the creation of a SWOT analysis for their potential business.

Answer

1 Global audio and video production; sales outlets of records in the UK; the ringtone market.

2 a It has concentrated/consolidated with the number of producers reducing but their overall size, assets and market share increasing. This has been done through mergers and takeover and is still continuing.

  b (2 of) Can afford big stars, can reduce costs, can increase profits.

  c (3 of) More flexible, respond quicker to changes, many stars prefer them because they feel they are treated better, more creative, hungry to do well so are more motivated.

3 People now can buy from supermarkets, chain stores, online or download music. Traditionally sales were mainly from specialist record stores.

4 a Internet   **b** Music stores
  c Supermarket   **d** Chain stores
  e Music stores

5 a For every track downloaded a percentage of the fee goes to Oxfam.

  b Answers may vary but should be justified. It is likely to depend on whether the cost per track is competitive and the degree to which the site is marketed. People who don't know about it can't use it!

6 a (2 of)

    i larger stock, wider range of goods, lower prices

    ii buy with shopping (convenience), impulse purchases, lower prices

    iii 24/7 availability, wide range of goods, will gift wrap and dispatch worldwide

    iv cheaper than buying a CD, can be downloaded 24/7, can be stored on iPod or other devices or on computer, can select favourite tracks from a CD or artist.

  b (2 of) Providing specialist services (e.g. finding rare tracks/specialising in certain types of music/vinyl exchange etc.); giving exceptional customer service; starting online sales/service; stocking additional goods e.g. DVDs, computer games.

7 No specific answer possible as it will depend upon the students' own ambitions.

8 No specific answer possible.

Activity 2.2.6 – Could you fight (fairly!) and survive?

This activity is meant to be as much fun as it is a learning experience. It puts the students in the role of managing a business which is threatened by a new competitor. Hopefully the students will soon realise that although some of the options are not meant to be taken too seriously, to do well they have to make proactive and practical business decisions (although there are one or two surprises with the answers!). Therefore although tutors could give it out as an individual quiz that is scored at the end, the recommended format is that teams work on it together and receive the result of each question as they go. This either increases or decreases the amount of money the business is worth and the option chosen for the final question may even be dependent on the outcome.

Answer

Tutors should note that at the start each team has £50,000 in stock and cash at the bank. They should also note that the penalties for poor decisions get worse the nearer it gets to Christmas, when there is less chance of remedying a problem.

1 a −£5,000 in potential lost sales.

  b −£5,000 in potential unsold stock as she hasn't space to display it properly.

  c −£2,000 cost of time defending action to their estate agent.

  d +£5,000 for market intelligence gained and own extra marketing potential.

2 a −£1,000 for bad publicity when thrown out by celeb's minder in front of local press.

  b +£2,000 for new sales generated as a result of contacting customers to check details.

  c −£2,000 for time off whilst sprained neck and shoulder heals

  d +£1,000 for information gained when taking a good look at the stock whilst waiting for the manager.

3 a −£5,000 for cost of lost revenue.

  b −£2,000 for cost of advertisements as only £1,000 extra sales are achieved.

  c −£3,000 for time taken trying to persuade local Trading Standards Officer it was only a joke. (Note: collusion over prices is illegal.)

  d +£5,000 in free publicity and increased sales.

4 a +£1,000 in free publicity though rain spoils impact somewhat.

b −£5,000 in lost sales as customers can't be bothered waiting to be served.

c +£5,000 in additional sales.

d +£3,000 in additional impulse gift sales.

5 a −£3,000 for being complacent.

b −£5,000 as cost of lost revenue.

c +£1,000 in additional sales (mainly of yoga mats, candles and soap).

d +£5,000 in additional sales.

6 a +£2,000 in net gain – sales are up by £3,000 but gifts cost £1,000.

b −£2,000 for cost of unsaleable stock when the same happens in her shop a few days later .

c +£5,000 in surge of new business.

d −£3,000 in cost of additional salaries.

7 a −£5,000 as cost of defending slander action by rival when claims are printed.

b −£10,000 in cost of gesture.

c −£5,000 in loss of business following scathing review about bribery.

d +£5,000 in additional business following favourable free publicity.

8 a +£5,000 as net gain after all extra salaries paid.

b +£10,000 in additional sales.

c −£3,000 as her shop has to be evacuated for 3 hours too.

d −£10,000 in lost sales on the Sunday.

9 a +£8,000 as her old stock flies out the door.

b −£5,000 in lost sales.

c +£5,000 as some of her old stock flies out the door.

d −£5,000 from lost revenue balanced by some free publicity.

10 The maximum that could have been won or lost by now is +£50K or −£50K. So the top team could have £100K and the worst team zero! This should inform the response to the final question:

a For those with £30K plus.

b For those with less than £20K (as new stock needs to be bought).

c For those with nothing!

d Only an option for those with £70K plus.

2.3 – Stakeholder expectations

Activity 2.3.1 – Whose business is it anyway?

This activity first revises the expectations of different stakeholder groups in relation to the new and rapidly growing food business EAT. It then looks at the issue of junk food and food labelling/advertising – an issue which is topical with the government and other pressure groups and relates to ethical concerns about business practices.

For Task 1, it is expected that students will find it easier to match up given expectations than think of them on their own. For this the group may need stimuli and guidance.

For Task 2, students should be encouraged to discuss the issue and put forward their own ideas, even if these are initially far-fetched or impractical. The overall aim is to stimulate interest and discussion on a topical issue.

Answer

1

Stakeholder group	Expectation of EAT
Customers	Will sell safe food Will charge a fair price/will be honest/will give a personal service/will have strict hygiene rules
Financiers	Will make its forecast profit of £2 million Will be a profitable investment/will honour its financial commitments
Online sponsors	Will attract people to its website Will promote the sponsor's business/will help to generate more business in return for sponsoring
Employees	Will pay a fair wage Will offer good working conditions/will observe health and safety/will treat staff fairly/will abide by employment legislation
Tax authorities	Will pay tax when due Will keep accurate accounts/will submit tax returns when due
Local community	Will dispose of its rubbish responsibly Will not operate noisily/will not be a health hazard/will not contribute to traffic or litter problems
Suppliers	Will pay its bills promptly Will be prepared to pay a fair price/will honour its commitments/will consider needs of suppliers
Owners	Will continue to grow and prosper Will be financially beneficial/will provide interesting and challenging work

2 **a** Gary Lineker is a stakeholder in that he has earned millions of pounds from Walker's Crisps (the 4-week salt and shake campaign alone was worth £1.5 million to Walkers). Despite his wealth, if Lineker could no longer promote the brand this would have a serious effect on his overall earnings.

b Suggestions could include: all health professionals – doctors, nurses, surgeons; other occupations related to health – dieticians, pathologists, physios etc.; all taxpayers; the government; business-related industries concerned with weight i.e. diet books/cook books, keep-fit, slimming clubs, vitamin producers/retailers, slimming pills, health clubs, exercise machines, leisure clothing, firming creams; all producers/retailers of health foods and diet foods plus calorie reduced foods; producers of health and exercise monitoring equipment e.g. pedometers, weighing scales, calorie counters.

c No specific answer possible.

Activity 2.3.2 – Identify stakeholder groups and expectations

This activity involves students in identifying the type of stakeholder groups that will have a vested interest in the issues listed. It is suggested that students do the activity in small groups to promote discussion which may have to be instigated by the tutor for some groups. Ideally any suggestions which could apply relating to stakeholder groups and their interests/expectations will be encouraged, whether or not these match to the answer shown below.

The 'head to head' issue is worthy of discussion and examples from local firms and their own college may be useful as a focus or to instigate debate.

Answer

Issue or event	Stakeholders	Expectations	Head to head
A train drivers' strike over pay	Commuters Rail company Trade union Train drivers	Major inconvenience Major disruptions to services Negotiations over pay Pay increase	Rail company and union or rail company and train drivers about whether pay award justified/size of award
A plan to site a large wind farm near a rural village	Local community Environmental groups/planners Government Energy buyers	Views/peace may be destroyed Cheap, clean energy important Clean energy targets to be met Availability of reasonably priced power	Local community and Government or local community and planners about extent of site and location
The loss of call centre jobs to India	UK employees Union UK employer Indian employees	Job losses/redundancy Negotiations but some job losses Reduced wage bill Increased number of well-paid jobs	Union and UK employer about number of job losses and compensation paid
A dispute by pilots about proposals to increase working hours	Pilots Pilot's union Passengers Airline	Working hours stay same Safety issue must be recognised Disruption to services Negotiations if costs to be lowered	Union and airline about total number of safe working hours per shift/week
Increase in speed cameras/ number of fines	Motorists Police Pressure groups e.g. AA Government	Greater danger of breaking law Reduced number of accidents/increased revenue More problems/expense for motorists Protests by pressure groups	Pressure groups and Government/police about rationale for cameras i.e. accident prevention or income source
The increase in university tuition fees	Students Parents/partners Universities Government	Higher debts More financial help needed Higher income Protests by pressure groups e.g. NUS	Students or pressure groups (e.g. NUS) and Government about total cost/repayment methods/size of grants
Financial problems at a large football club	Shareholders Spectators Players Directors/manager	Return on their investment Club success in league Competitive wages Successful business	Players and shareholders or directors about size of wages/transfers to recoup losses
Major sporting/ entertainment event, e.g. World Cup, Glastonbury Festival	Participants/teams Sponsors Local community Organisers/clubs	Good performance Increased sales through association Some disruption/noise Increased revenue	Sponsors and participants (over results/behaviour) (Organisers/local community) over disruption

Activity 2.3.3 – Financial stakeholders and the London Eye

This activity focuses on the London Eye but also asks the students to undertake some basic calculations related to revenue and profit. It highlights the fact that there can be disagreements amongst stakeholders even in relation to national icons and hopefully it sheds more light on the different expectations of stakeholders even within the same group.

Students and tutors can update the information provided by accessing the London Eye website at **www.ba-londoneye.com**.

Answer

1 3

2 That the London Eye will be profitable and provide a return on their investment.

3 In 2003 the London Eye made a profit of £12.8 million, but its total interest bill and other charges resulted in a net loss of £10.9 million. This is because £23.7 million had to be deducted in interest payments.

4 £24 million (i.e. 2 million/month).

5 The designers.

6 BA hasn't agreed because it doesn't want its interest payment revenue to fall; Tussauds hasn't agreed because it wants to own 75 per cent of the wheel first.

7 That the loan will be guaranteed by the major owner; that repayments will be made on time.

8 a £120,000 ($8 \times 15,000$)

   b £84,500

9 Some customers will pay a premium to have a capsule for themselves and a private party. Others are in a hurry. The owners of the London Eye recognise these differences and charge accordingly.

10 Customers: to have a safe ride with a fantastic view.

   Employees: to be paid a fair rate for the job and to have safe working conditions.

   Owners: to make a profit.

Activity 2.3.4 – Staff expectations on health and safety

(Cross-references to Unit 5 Employee contribution to working conditions and Unit 6 Introduction to business administration)

This activity involves a key staff expectation – health and safety in the workplace. This is also a legal requirement and is covered, in the scheme, in Unit 2.3 and also, quite comprehensively, in Unit 6 (see 6.4). In addition, the role of employee representatives also links to Unit 5, section 5.3.

The activity can therefore be given to reinforce these concepts for any of these three units. Students studying Units 2 or 5 will benefit by comparing their answers and discussing the queries in small groups. Students studying Unit 6 should have a greater insight into health and safety legislation and may therefore be expected to do more on their own first.

Answer

Problem	Action taken/advice given
Perveen argues that the new fax machine shouldn't have been put on the spare desk because the wire is trailing across the floor.	This is true but, unless the fax machine is very large and heavy, it should be a simple matter for Perveen and a colleague to move it to a safer position.
Lucy complains that she has reported the broken wheel on their only trolley three times but nothing has been done.	This needs replacing promptly as otherwise heavy items, such as large boxes of paper, cannot be moved safely. It is safer to buy a new trolley than to try to fix a damaged one.
Shazim remarks that although he has been working for the firm for 2 months, he still hasn't had any health and safety training.	The firm has a legal responsibility to provide health and safety training when people start work there. This must be arranged promptly.
Melanie complains that the electricians told her she couldn't use her portable fan heater at work unless she lets them check the wiring.	Under PUWER and the Electricity at Work regulations employers are legally responsible for checking and maintaining equipment and electrical systems. Melanie must comply with the rules.

Problem	Action taken/advice given
Farhana says she has started getting headaches when she uses her computer but when she told her manager he took no notice.	Under the Display Screen Equipment Regulations the employer must assess the risks to staff using VDUs and workstations and pay for eye tests and spectacles/lenses if these are prescribed for the work. An eye test should be arranged for Farhana and the manager reminded of the firm's legal responsibilities.
Jack says that not only are the signs and instructions relating to fire equipment torn and unreadable he doesn't think any of the extinguishers have been checked for years.	This is an offence under the Fire Precautions Act and Regulations. All fire equipment must be regularly checked and this should be arranged immediately.
Dan complains that he can't get things he needs from the hazardous substances cupboard when the manager is at lunch, because it's always kept locked.	This is good practice as the cupboard must not be left open. It may be possible to arrange for someone else to keep the key when the manager isn't in the office, otherwise Dan will have to wait until after lunch (or think ahead to get what he needs).
Emily reports that she nearly had an accident when she slipped on some paper that was lying on the floor.	Emily should have picked it up! Employees have a responsibility for their own health and safety and that of their colleagues.

Activity 2.3.5 – Problems for Sainsbury stakeholders

(Cross-references to Unit 7 Sales and customer service)

This is a topical activity as it relates to the difficulties being faced by Sainsbury's. Whilst these are not insurmountable, it is probable that any remedial actions will not benefit all stakeholder groups equally. For this activity, therefore, students are asked to identify the winners and losers in the different actions which the Sainsbury management could take.

Tutors may like to update themselves on the latest news relating to Sainsbury's before they issue this activity and customise it accordingly. Tutors should also note that they should check all students have the correct answer for question 1 before moving on to question 2.

The activity is cross-referenced to Unit 7 and tutors using it for this purpose may wish to extend question 3. This could be done by asking students to visit their nearest store to assess its layout, features, promotions etc. – or to visit Sainsbury's online and compare its site to those of Tesco or Asda, its major competitors.

Answer

1 Customers, suppliers, employees, shareholders, managers/executives, sponsors/'front men' (e.g. Jamie Oliver); local communities.

2 Below are indicative answers only. Any other appropriate suggestions should be accepted.

What Sainsbury's could do	Winners	Losers	Reason
Cut prices by 5 per cent	Customers	Suppliers Shareholders	May want to pay less for supplies Likely to reduce profits
Outsource warehousing and distribution	Customers (more goods on shelves)	Employees	Will be laid off as operation passed to another organisation
Close unprofitable shops	Shareholders	Customers Local community Employees	Less choice when buying groceries Staff laid off
Cut next dividend	Managers	Shareholders	More money retained for investment because less paid out to shareholders
Increase advertisements and promotions	Sponsors (e.g. Jamie Oliver) Advertising agents etc.	Shareholders Customers	Less money available for dividends or price cuts
Sell cheaper goods by changing suppliers	Customers	Existing suppliers	Price cutting will mean many existing (quality) suppliers lose contracts
Open more small convenience stores	Customers Local communities Employees	Shareholders Employees	Cost of buying stores, local employees may lose out if asked to work longer hours

What Sainsbury's could do	Winners	Losers	Reason
Build up online shopping operation	Customers Employees	Shareholders	Investment required plus more staff (e.g. drivers)
Revamp and modernise stores	Local community Customers	Shareholders	Cost of modernisation/more advanced stores
Sell more non-food lines	Customers	Shareholders	Investment will mean lower dividends
Freeze pay awards	Shareholders Customers	Employees	Will help to keep prices down/dividends up

3 a (3 of) Habit, nearest store to home, prefer Sainsbury to other supermarkets (on grounds of quality, layout, customer service etc.)

b (1 of) Benefit: association with well-known name, association with attributes of celebrity. In the case of Jamie Oliver this is reputation for well-sourced ingredients and quality/imaginative dishes.
(1 of) Disadvantage: will irritate those who don't like the celebrity concerned, the cost, problems if the celebrity gets bad publicity. (In the case of Jamie Oliver, the tabloids took delight in picturing his wife shopping at a different store.)

c No answer possible, it depends upon suggestions put forward by the students.

Activity 2.3.6 – Debate and decide!

(Cross-references to Unit 4 Business communications)

This activity involves students in considering a complex issue and arguing it appropriately. It is often difficult to stimulate role play at this level. To help, no false names are given and students can use their own. All they have to do is to understand their assigned role, perform the tasks requested, think about the issues raised and represent their point of view appropriately and confidently. For this reason the activity is cross-referenced to Unit 4 as it relates to the content of sections 4.1 and 4.2.

The issue relates to the use of polytunnels to grow British fruit which is considered vital by growers but is disliked by many because the view changes from green fields to one of white plastic. Many feel that the Government should provide better guidance on the issue but this is unlikely to happen (see DEFRA's statement on the British Summer Fruits site). At present the decision to restrict them or insist on planning applications seems to be dependent upon the attitude of the local council. The main point for students to realise is that there are no simplistic right and wrong answers in relation to many issues that involve different stakeholder groups. Quite simply, it is impossible to please all the people all the time.

It is suggested that tutors familiarise themselves with the issues before giving students the materials and allow enough time for those taking an active role to familiarise themselves with the situation. Added instructions should be given verbally if the students are carrying out the task for Unit 7. If the group would not be confident or happy carrying out the role play, then it is a fairly simple matter to convert the activity to a case study with the tutor putting forward the arguments for and against.

Further reference sources:
http://www.firsttunnels.co.uk/
http://www.haygrove.co.uk/
www.britishsummerfruits.co.uk
www.cpre.org.uk

Answer

No specific answer possible – it will depend upon individual/group student views.

Activity 2.3.7 – Understanding ethical business

This activity introduces students to the concept of Corporate Social Responsibility and, hopefully, through the first tasks makes it clear that this is as much an issue for small businesses as large ones.

Students are referred to the website of Business in the Community. Tutors should access the website in advance and download useful background information relating to the type of awards issued, awards given in their area, membership lists and invaluable pdf files relating to the Corporate Responsibility Index and recent reports/feedback.

Answer

1

Action	Ethical or unethical	Action to take
Selling cigarettes to a kid in school uniform	Unethical	Ask for ID whenever unsure
Buying fireworks 'from a friend of a friend' because they are cheap	Unethical	Only buy from approved sources
Selling goods which are past their sell-by date at normal prices – but reducing these by 10 per cent if challenged	Unethical	Dispose of all goods past their sell-by dates
Giving a relative a magazine to read and then putting it back on sale afterwards	Unethical	His relative must buy the magazine
Paying paperboys and girls the lowest rate in the town	Unethical	Workers should be paid a fair rate
Refusing to pay paperboys and girls when they are away on holiday	Ethical	Normally not part of the contract
Ignoring complaints that the papers are too heavy to carry on some rounds on a Sunday morning	Unethical	Could do separate deliveries of very heavy orders by car
Arguing with an elderly customer that she must pay her full bill because she cannot prove that two days' papers weren't delivered	Unethical	Should give customer the benefit of the doubt and keep accurate records to prove case if necessary
Dropping a box of pencils on the floor then putting them back on sale	Unethical	Leads will be broken. Should be disposed of
Refusing to allow part-time shop assistants to use the cash register or handle money.	Ethical	Not a problem – is a normal security measure

2 No answer possible.

2.4 – External influences
Activity 2.4.1 – Interpret the headlines!

(Cross-references to Unit 4 Business communication)

This activity aims to consolidate understanding of the different types of influences on business (and individuals) through the identification of the key issue using business terms and/or newspaper speak. This activity can, of course, easily be extended through the interpretation of actual headlines from any daily newspaper. The activity should prove useful particularly for students who aim to continue their studies at higher level when a basic understanding of contemporary issues, and how they affect business, will be crucial.

Students could be asked to write out their interpretation of the headlines or to explain them verbally. The key points tutors may wish to discuss with students are shown below, alongside the suggested categories.

The activity is cross-referenced to Unit 4 because it links to written communications and technical language (see section 4.3).

Answer

Task 1

Headline	Key points	Category or categories
Police zapper	The category is also political because the aim is to reduce accidents and crime statistics	Technology/ Political
Green tax/Heathrow breaches	Green = environmental; breach = contravening; emissions = pollution	Environmental/ Legislation
Cash spending set to fall by £17 billion by 2013	Students should understand that this refers to a switch in methods of spending, not a reduction in overall spending. Newspapers would rarely write 'spending in cash' because 'cash spending' is more punchy, though ambiguous. Student could be asked for impact on businesses – especially market traders – if debit/credit cards become even more popular	Social

Headline	Key points	Category or categories
DTI + simplifying red tape	Jargon: the term red tape = official rules and regulations; DTI = Department of Trade and Industry. This related to the fact that legislative changes which affect small business will now only be introduced on 6 April and 1 October each year	Legislation
Government + travel trade + holiday prices at peak times	Illustrates two concepts – travel trade practising price discrimination during peak times and charging high prices when demand is high and role of government re education and pupils missing school	Political/ Economic
Mi5 website (at www.mi5.gov.uk)	Example of tabloid type alliteration. For students studying Unit 6, the website gives useful hints and tips on business continuity	Political
Shareholders revolt over fat cat pay rise at AGM	Students should understand terms 'shareholders', 'AGM' and 'fat cat' but appreciate latter should be applied when pay rises out of line with performance of business	Social
Soaring house prices push up loan rates	This can stimulate a cause and effects discussion. 'Loan rates' = interest rates which have been put up to try to slow down spending. Soaring prices is evidence of demand for houses being greater than supply	Economic
Government + £1 million Bullying at Work study	Implies legislation needs updating/strengthening to give additional protection to workers	Political/Social/ Legislation
Simpay and mobile phones	This would enable payment to be made from a mobile and would provide an alternative to paying by credit card	Technology
OFT and doorstep sales	This issue can be checked on the OFT website. OFT = Office of Fair Trading; 'cowboys' refers to unscrupulous operators. The issue involves elderly people being misled into buying expensive goods/repairs on their own doorstep. Students taking Unit 7 should be more familiar with 'cooling off' periods than other students	Economic
EU rules and car makers	This could trigger discussion about why these rules will increase prices. The rules make manufacturers responsible for scrapping/recycling/ cleaner engines and therefore add to costs – though probably not to the extent currently being claimed	Environment/ Legislation
12 month maternity leave	The term 'Ministers' is often shorthand for the Government. This would be an extension of existing employment rights	Social/ Legislation
Chip and PIN reduces fraud	Refers to the credit card where holder inputs PIN number to authorise transaction and never needs to part with card	Technology

Task 2

UK in the red to the tune of a trillion

a   Combined mortgage and credit card debt in the UK passed £1 trillion in July 2004 (1 trillion = 1,000 × £1 billion).

b   Social/Economic.

c   Credit card and mortgage companies and banks would be interested – so would counselling organisations such as CAB and the Samaritans, but for different reasons.

The changing face of Europe

a   The expanded EU from 1 May 2004, now with 25 members. This number is likely to increase to 28 or more by 2007 or 2008 if Turkey and some of the Balkan members join, so at present the membership seems to be continually changing.

b   Political/Economic.

c   Businesses that export to Europe would be interested as the market has expanded, so too will businesses who could be threatened by additional imports. The market for migrant workers has also expanded for businesses that offer low-paid seasonal jobs. Universities will also have to accept EU applicants from a wider range of countries.

The science of tiny things = nanotechnology.

a Nanotechnology involves manipulating nanoparticles up to 800 times finer than a human hair. A nanometre is a billionth of a metre. Nanoparticles are already present in some products, e.g. smart fabrics that repel stains and don't wrinkle, some cosmetics and Pilkington Activ (self-cleaning glass). Future applications could include nanomachines or computers introduced into the bloodstream to fight disease.

b Technology.

c Business R & D departments, universities, doctors.

The race is on for 2012

a The London bid to host the Olympics.

b This is both political and economic as the cost of hosting the games will be considerable but the benefits to many businesses could also be great.

c Construction companies and the travel/hotel business will be particularly interested in announcements.

Search in the Blinkx of an eye

a The new search engine, Blinkx, which searches a number of sources, including files on the user's desktop, to find related information and not just websites. This is its USP in its challenge against Google. Microsoft has mounted a challenge through a new MSN toolbar to be launched in 2005.

b Technology.

c Media and broadcasting companies, publishers, advertisers – any organisation that is in the information business.

Activity 2.4.2 – Politics and economics on the road

The aim of this case study is to examine the way in which change relating to the roads affects business and is both a political and economic issue. To highlight the first point, tutors may wish to tell students about the events of August and September 2000, when protestors blockaded fuel supply depots and Britain all but ran out of petrol in protest against

fuel duty increases. The problem is always exacerbated if such increases coincide with rises in oil prices and is worse in Britain because fuel duty is higher than in other European countries. This results in all drivers of commercial vehicles crossing the Channel filling up on the continent to save money.

The difficulty for the government in raising money to build and maintain roads at a time when car ownership is continually rising could also be discussed. Particularly as increased road building to reduce congestion is not only expensive but is opposed by environmentalists. This has led to the latest ideas of building toll roads and extending congestion charging. Toll roads are a common feature on the continent, and charging a toll is a well-founded method of paying for new bridges, tunnels and motorways.

Charging for road use is unlikely to be introduced in Britain before about 2015, if ever. One vision is that all cars will be fitted with navigation systems so that all their movements can be tracked and owners will simply pay a road bill each month, rather like their electricity bill. The price per mile will, it is envisaged, depend upon the time of day, day of the week and location. All businesses, but particularly those in the haulage industry, will obviously be monitoring developments with more than a little interest.

Answer

1 a Road tax, insurance, fuel.

  b Because less business is done in the time available, wages are being paid to the driver and the vehicle is costing as much but doing fewer miles.

2 a 60p

  b 94p

3 Motorists have to pay to use a toll road.

4 a Someone who thinks there is often an ulterior motive behind something.

  b Because holiday traffic would increase the usage and families wouldn't want to be stuck in jams with young children so would prefer to pay the toll.

  c Because fewer people use it then (demand and supply).

5 (2 of) Advantages: less congestion, complete journey more quickly, economical (i.e. worth paying for economic benefits gained), fewer disappointed customers. Disadvantages: costs would increase considerably if numerous journeys done each week in large vehicles, customer's expectations will increase if toll road

can be used, if toll road is very popular then these, too, may get congested.

6   Because the Freight Transport Association is a powerful pressure group and if all hauliers had boycotted the M6 toll then MEL revenues would have gone down even further.

7   (2 of) Advantages: fewer delays on Britain's roads, roads built with private money and not out of tax (so non-road users not charged, easier to build more new roads or improve them). Disadvantages: all drivers will complain if other costs do not fall, government could lose drivers' votes in next election, businesses will transfer extra costs on to price of goods and this will trigger inflation.

8   a   Charging drivers to enter a city area.

     b   (2 of) Benefits: reduces overall traffic problems so deliveries may be more prompt, more visitors may be tempted to the area. Disadvantages: less passing trade, may create difficulties for employees, may reduce customers of some types of business (in London, for example, restaurants have said their trade has been affected).

9   Because protests became a serious political issue in 2000 and the Government would not want a repeat of this.

10   (2 of) Benefit = commuters who use public transport, the retired, those who work in rural areas or who work unsocial hours. Will not benefit = commuters by car in city areas or on major routes, those who travel on business daily, freight companies, delivery companies to businesses in major cities.

Activity 2.4.3 – The economic climate and its effect

This activity aims to help consolidate student understanding of different aspects of the economy and how they affect individuals and businesses. Tutors may prefer students to work in pairs or small groups, particularly if some are having difficulty understanding some of these concepts.

Answer

Person/business	Condition or change	Effect
Jessica Tate, who runs her own jewellery business.	Britain is in the middle of an economic boom.	Jessica will sell more goods because demand for consumer goods is high.
Usman Patel, who has just left college and is looking for a job.	Britain is in the middle of an economic slump.	Usman may struggle to find work as unemployment will be high.
Sweeneys, a large firm of housebuilders.	Spending has slowed and Britain has entered a recession.	Fewer houses are being sold, prices may be static or falling, there will be less new building work.
Alex Watson, who owes £2,500 on her credit card.	Interest rates rise by 1 per cent.	It will cost Alex more to settle her debt.
Dan and Sue Osifo, who have £5,000 in an e-savings account.	Interest rates fall by 1 per cent.	Dan and Sue will receive less interest on their account.
Javeed Patel, who runs a taxi business.	The government increases business rates and fuel duty.	It will cost Javeed more to run his business and this is likely to reduce his overall profit.
PTZ Ltd, a large furnishing store.	The government raises income tax.	People will have less to spend and may buy fewer expensive consumer goods.
Babybuzz, a European cut price airline.	The Euro has strengthened against the pound. The government has introduced a 'green tax' on airline fuel.	Holidays in the Euro-zone will be more expensive. The cost of the flights will also rise. Babybuzz is likely to find demand falls.
Astronics, which makes interactive whiteboards.	The government announces an increase in public spending, especially on health and education.	Schools will have more to spend and demand for Astronics' products could increase.
Martin and Jill, who have just bought their first house.	The government increases VAT and the local council increases council tax.	It will cost them more to buy the items they need and their running costs will also be higher than expected.

Activity 2.4.4 – The gizmo business

(Cross-references to Unit 8 Business online)

This activity links technological and social changes that might affect business. The aim of the activity is for students to investigate several issues by gender. Ideally, therefore they will be grouped into same-sex teams for this, so that key differences are accentuated during the investigative stage, rather than modified. Tutors who are teaching a unisex group or one where there is a serious imbalance may need to change the instructions – or could act as devil's advocate by taking the opposing role.

It is recommended that students are dissuaded from being too stereotypical and from taking the overall activity too seriously although there is a serious purpose. The aim is to establish the extent to which website developers should take account of different types of customer behaviour – in this case, primarily the difference between men and women online. There is a tendency for many male-dominated markets to ignore women buyers and their preferences. In the car industry, this has cost some companies dearly.

This activity has been cross-referenced to Unit 8 because of its relevance to online business.

Answer

No specific answer possible.

Activity 2.4.5 – Tracking UK stock market variations

The aim of this activity is to give students a practical insight into the variations of the stock market and why these occur. Students should understand that when share prices fall, companies are worth less and this can make them vulnerable to a take-over bid. They should also understand the type of events that can lead to falls in the stock market, including investor responses to key business failures, scandals and other events which can threaten overall peace and therefore a stable business environment.

Tutors can extend Task 3 by asking students to prepare a poster or notice which lists their holdings

and their individual value on the 'purchase' date. They can then pin this up and track their progress on (say) a weekly basis and the opportunity could be used to discuss reasons for any changes and the impact of these on the business concerned.

Answer

Task 1

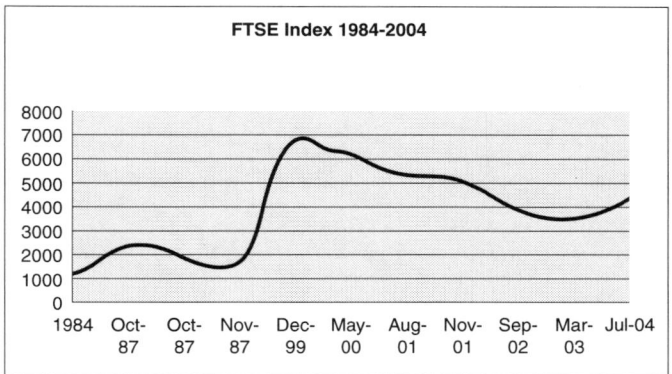

FTSE Index 1984-2004

2. No specific answer possible. Tutor to check completed chart and reasons given for changes.

3.
   a £69,506
   b £15,650
   c No specific answer possible – tutor to check.

4. No, because individual shares may behave differently if the demand for them is opposite to the main market, e.g. because they are seen as a safe investment during turbulent times.

5. Savings accounts: advantages: safe, pays interest; disadvantages: interest rate may be low, if spend interest then capital sum invested doesn't grow.

   Property: advantages: may increase rapidly in value in a boom, can rent out to receive income; disadvantages: value may stay the same over many years or fall, cost of mortgage can offset gains, needs maintenance and repairs.

   Stock market: advantages: receive dividend, shares can increase in value; disadvantages: shares can fall in value, dividend may fall or not be paid at all, difficult to predict trends accurately.

Task 2

Announcement	Effect (increase or decrease)	One business	Whole sector	Whole market
Car manufacturer announces better than expected profit figures	Increase	✓		
New gas fields are discovered in the North Sea	Increase		✓	
Assassination of American politician	Decrease			✓
UK wins Olympic bid	Increase			✓

Announcement	Effect (increase or decrease)	One business	Whole sector	Whole market
National retail chain announces increased market share	Increase	✓		
Foreign bank makes takeover bid for UK building society	Increase	✓		
Major financial scandal involving a large European business	Decrease			✓
Terrorist attack on a large city	Decrease			✓
Capture of key terrorist leaders	Increase			✓
Major medical breakthrough by leading research firm	Increase		✓	
Telecom firm announces lower profit because of increased competition	Decrease		✓	
New computer virus creates havoc with Microsoft software	Decrease			✓

Task 3

No answer possible.

Activity 2.4.6 – Changing with the times

This activity links together the various types of external influences and relates them to one business – the St John Ambulance Association – which should be known to all students on a general basis, if not specifically. Certainly football supporters will probably be used to seeing their presence at matches. Information about the Association can be found at its website at **www.sja.org.uk**.

For the first task, students are asked to place several activities undertaken by the SJA into a PESTEL analysis. To do this they need to think about the type of influence which caused the activity to be undertaken.

For the second task the students are given a series of external influences and asked to consider how these would affect the Association and what the response should be.

Answer

Task 1

PESTEL framework	St John Ambulance facts
Political	D, L, N
Economic	C, H, I
Social	A, B, G
Technological	E, J
Environmental	K, M
Legislation	F

Task 2

The following answers are purely indicative. Any other appropriate ideas should be accepted.

1   Substitute street collections with other methods of raising money, e.g. by regular subscription or by house-to-house collections.

2   This will benefit SJA in terms of any reserves it has and it would want to ensure these were in high interest accounts. It may find that its donations fall if people feel poorer as a result and may have to raise an even greater proportion of its income through training courses.

3   Training courses for carers, start 'friendly neighbour' scheme, visit elderly day centres to talk to the elderly about safety.

4   Change content of training courses to match the new legislation, advertise new courses to businesses and industry.

5   Could issue to volunteers to take photographs for newsletters and website, could give as prizes, could use to take photographs of serious injuries for immediate transmission to medical professionals for advice on treatment.

6   The SJA may have some of its reserves in shares. Rising share prices should increase their value. If not the Association should review its share holdings to make sure that its portfolio includes the market leaders.

Taking advantage of growing markets

(Cross-references to Unit 9 Starting up a new business Activity 9.2)

All businesses aim to identify markets that are growing – and to offer new products and services that link with these markets. New entrepreneurs will want to start businesses which link to growth markets. In the table below are several examples of growing markets. In each case one example of an innovation is given and in the first entry an idea for an entrepreneur starting a small business is also given.

Your tasks

1 Complete the right-hand column of the table with the following information:

   a Two new ideas of your own that link to each of these markets

   b One type of business which could be started by a new entrepreneur linked to each market.

2 At the end of the table add two additional growing markets – with your own ideas as to how these can be exploited both by established businesses and a new entrepreneur.

Growing market	Growth and new products and services
Health and fitness	Hotels with spa facilities **New entrepreneur**: could become personal trainer
Overseas holidays	All inclusive holidays with food/drinks paid for up front **New entrepreneur**:
Childcare	24-hour nursery provision where kids can sleep overnight **New entrepreneur**:
House ownership and DIY	B&Q offering wedding list facilities **New entrepreneur**:
Internet access	Internet banking services **New entrepreneur**:
Healthier food	Revamped Heinz baked beans with less salt **New entrepreneur**:
?	 **New entrepreneur**:
?	 **New entrepreneur**:

Not the real thing!

Read the case study below and then answer the questions that follow.

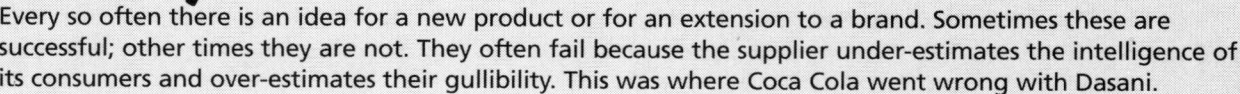

Case study

Every so often there is an idea for a new product or for an extension to a brand. Sometimes these are successful; other times they are not. They often fail because the supplier under-estimates the intelligence of its consumers and over-estimates their gullibility. This was where Coca Cola went wrong with Dasani.

Dasani is the brand name for Coke's bottled water, which is a huge success in America and the market leader there. Coke desperately wanted a share of the lucrative European bottled water market. It decided to start its European operations by introducing Dasani in the UK. Early in 2004, to the fanfare of a £7 million advertising campaign, Coke's bottled water arrived in England.

Unfortunately for Coke, the media rapidly focused on the source of Dasani. Unlike the fresh spring and mineral water sources that normally feature on bottled water products sold in the UK, Dasani was rather different. It came from the mains water supply of a factory in Sidcup, Kent. In other words, it was simply tap water. Coke defended its source by arguing that its 'highly sophisticated purification process' – perfected by Nasa – meant that Dasani was as pure as water could get.

But why pay 95p for 500 ml of tap water, asked the media? Given tap water in Sidcup costs 0.03p for 500 ml, doesn't this mean there is a mark up of about 3,000 per cent?

As if this media coverage wasn't enough, a second crisis meant that the entire UK supply of 500,000 bottles had to be removed from the shelves. Production problems contaminated the bottles with twice the acceptable level of bromates – chemicals which can cause cancer. The health scare finished off Dasani and Coke admitted defeat. Within five weeks Dasani had been launched, criticised, contaminated and withdrawn. The cost to the company ran into millions – and Coke now has to rethink its strategy of breaking into the European bottled water market.

Water facts

UK Market leaders
1	Evian
2 (joint)	Volvic, Highland Spring, Powwow
5	Vittel
6	Aqua cool

European bottled water market:
Value: £10 billion (Germany = 25%, highest consumer, then France, Italy, Spain, Poland)

UK bottled water market:
Value: £1.1 billion (20 litres per head each year compared with 150 litres per head in Italy)

Questions

1 Why did Coke decide to launch Dasani in the UK? Try to think of **two** reasons. At least one should be related to market trends.

2 Retail buyers were keen to stock Dasani. Suggest **one** reason for this.

3 Suggest **four** basic customer expectations in relation to bottled water.

4 Suggest **two** reasons why the source of Coke's bottled water was such a disaster in Britain.

5 Why did Coke finally withdraw the bottles from sale?

6 a How much did Coke lose in financial terms if you calculate the advertising campaign and the withdrawn stocks at sale price?

   b What other 'costs' could be associated with the disaster?

7 What will Coke consider is its biggest loss in the whole issue?

• Its loss of face in the UK or
• its delay in entering the European market.
Give a reason for your choice.

8 Nestlé's Powwow is bottled water provided for water coolers at work and in the home. Nestlé identify six customer expectations on their website in relation to water coolers – can you guess **two** of these?

9 Water coolers in the home are very popular in the US. Do you think they will be as popular in the UK? Give a reason for your opinion.

10 PetFresh is a new bottled water being made for animals by Springmill Products Inc (SPI), another US company. The water is being distributed in the UK by Scot Pet Foods Ltd of Glasgow. It argues the idea will be an instant success because animals hate the taste of tap water. Do you think the idea will be a success – or another flop like Dasani? Give a reason for your opinion.

How low can they go?

(Cross-references to Unit 7 Sales and customer services Activity 7.3)

Most organisations operate on the basis that if they don't keep their customers happy, they soon won't have any at all. Occasionally, however, a business seems to flout these rules – and still be successful. So will some customers put up with anything – particularly if they can save money? Read the two outlines below, see what you think, and then answer the questions on the following page.

The store the world loves to hate!

In 1955 a Swedish farmer's son struggled to get a table into the boot of his car. He solved the problem by removing the legs. With most people, that would have been the end of it, but not for the man's employer, Ingvar Kamprad. He already ran a furniture business and worked out that selling furniture in flatpacks would save a fortune. No more packing fresh air – so transport costs would be less – and no more paying staff to construct furniture. And if these savings were passed on to the customer, the effect might be even more amazing. It was. Today Ingvar Kamprad's

Swedish store operates 186 outlets in 31 countries with a sales turnover of nearly £8 billion year. Its name is IKEA.

IKEA has 76,000 co-workers (the term 'staff' isn't used), prints 130 million catalogues and serves 310 million customers each year. These are customers who don't mind having to walk on a specific route all around the store to buy one item, who don't mind crowds and queues, who don't mind that they can't buy online and who are quite happy to spend hours at home afterwards wrestling with dozens of parts and unintelligible instructions!

The true cost of cheap flights

Michael O'Leary is the boss of Ryanair, the low cost airline that is constantly making headlines for all the wrong reasons – airports miles away from city centres (because charges are less), Internet-only bookings, minimum compensation for cancelled flights, offensive and misleading adverts, extra charges to wheelchair users and non-existent customer service. But its prices are very, very low. And O'Leary plans for them to get lower still by cutting his services even more.

RYANAIR
FLY CHEAPER

Shortly, Ryanair will either introduce a £50 luggage surcharge or ban luggage altogether. Only hand baggage will be allowed. O'Leary says this won't affect demand because over 50 per cent of customers only stay away for two days and don't take luggage anyway. He argues people should buy or hire things when they get to their destination – or fly with another airline. Getting rid of baggage handling will cut Ryanair's airport costs by a third.

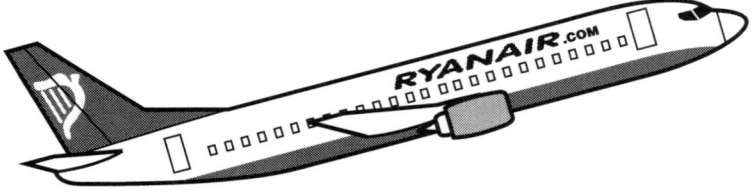

Activity 2.1.3 How low can they go? (cont'd)

Questions

1 To keep selling prices very low, costs have to be very low. Identify **two** ways in which *both* companies save money running their businesses.

2 Judith works for a national charity, Farzana started her own business last year and Martin works for a local council. Give one reason why *each* of these business buyers is more likely to be interested in low prices rather than superb customer service.

3 a Look at the following table of types of customers. Tick those that you think apply to obtain a brief profile of the core customer of each organisation.

Customer attributes	IKEA	Ryanair
Children		
Young singles (18–30)		
Newly weds		
Families		
Empty nesters (still working but family have left home)		
Retired		
Elderly		
High income		
Low income		

    b In what way do you think Ryanair's new rule may affect the profile of its core customer?

4 Both IKEA and Ryanair have adapted a product or service and offered it in a different way to exploit its market potential.

    a In what way has IKEA adapted a traditional product?

    b Identify **two** ways in which the IKEA shopping experience is unique.

    c Identify **three** ways in which Ryanair offers a different travel experience.

    d Identify **one** USP (unique selling point) of both businesses.

5 All customers have certain basic expectations which no company dares to challenge because failing to meet these would be disastrous.

    a What do you think these basic expectations are in relation to IKEA?

    b What do you think they are in relation to Ryanair?

    Discuss your ideas as a group.

6 Which is most important to you – a good deal or quality and excellent service? For example would you:

- happily get a 3 am flight if the ticket was cheap?
- queue all night to be first through the door at Next's January sale?
- buy the cheapest food possible to have more money for clothes and CDs?
- rather buy 10 bargain T-shirts than one designer T-shirt?
- love to go backpacking to see the world on a shoestring?

And to what extent do you think your opinions would change if you had more money? Take a vote to find out how customer preferences vary in your own group, especially in relation to the demand for cheap goods and services.

Market research in action

(Cross-references to Unit 8 Business online Activity 8.2)

YOUNG PEOPLE DON'T BUY NEWSPAPERS – SHOCK!

All newspapers employ strategic planners who look at the lifestyles of people who buy – or don't buy – their papers. And they have identified a problem. Unless they continue to win new, young readers each year, their circulation will fall. And young people are no longer reading newspapers.

Young people never did read newspapers very much, but today they do so less than ever. They find them boring. If they do buy, it is not for news and information. Instead men want football, women want celebrity gossip. Both like TV and 'real life' stories. If they want news they will switch on TV or go online. If they want information they will send a text message. The only way newspapers can try to win their business is to become more like celebrity magazines and carry lots of sports and gossip. At least, that is the theory. To what extent do you think these assumptions are true?

Stage one

Divide into groups as instructed by tutor. Then carry out the task you are given.

It is your job to work as a team to complete the work by the deadline you are issued.

Group one Prepare a short questionnaire for each of your class to give to 10 personal contacts of different ages and gender. Your aim is to find out which newspaper they read (if any), whether they buy one regularly or occasionally, their main reasons for buying, where they buy (e.g. newsagent, supermarket etc.), which types of features they like the most, what other sources they have of receiving news and information.

When you have drafted out the questions, check them on one or two class 'guinea pigs' to make sure they are clear and understandable. Then issue them to everyone in the group with a deadline for completion and return. When you receive the completed questionnaires, analyse them according to age and gender to see if they support the comments above and identify any differences.

Group two Form a focus group to investigate and comment on the content of the daily newspapers listed in the box below. This means looking at a sample of each one. Decide which you like the best – and why – and which you don't – and why. Then make a list of strengths and weaknesses in each case.

Group three Go online to find out the demographic profile of the national newspapers listed in the box below to see how many young people read each one, particularly in your region. You will find this information at the Newspaper Marketing Agency at **www.heinemann. co.uk/hotlinks (express code 1351T)**. Find out, too, the current net UK circulation of each of the papers under ABC data at **Heinemann hotlinks** to see which is the top seller in the UK and which is the lowest. Then, on the basis of this information, list the newspapers in relation to their current popularity with people of your age.

Activity 2.1.4 Market research in action (cont'd)

Group four Your aim is to produce a list of ways in which a newspaper could promote itself to encourage young people to buy it – apart from changing content. Check online for any existing articles or market research reports on newspapers. It is worth checking the list of free Insight reports at **www.keynote.co.uk**. In 2004, one of these reports was on newspapers. Otherwise, use a good search engine like Google to find what else is available. This will help you to learn more about the newspaper industry and the methods used to try to increase circulation and also about buyer behaviour.

Group five Check the online operations of each of the newspapers in the box below. For each website, identify its main strengths and weaknesses and decide if it could be improved in any way to appeal more to young people. Think of additional methods of new media marketing that the newspapers could use. You may also find it useful to compare the best online newspaper websites with those of major

---

Newspapers for research and comparison – groups two, three and five

Daily Mail	*Daily Express*
Daily Star	*The Guardian*
The Independent	*Daily Mirror*
The Times	*The Sun*
The Daily Telegraph	

Stage two

Each group should summarise their key findings on A1 flip chart paper and nominate a speaker who will verbally summarise these to the whole class.

Stage three

From the information you have now heard decide as a group whether, if you owned a newspaper, you would adapt your product now, wait a while to see if circulation fell and then adapt if you must or stay as you are. Give a reason for your decision.

If you would make changes, state what you would do, bearing in mind the results of the market research investigations you have all undertaken.

Activity 2.1.5

Choosing the healthy option

(Cross-references to Unit 9 Starting up a new business Activity 9.3)

Background information

Food scares and safety issues are boosting the sale of natural food and drink products. According to market research organisation Datamonitor, the European natural food and drinks market will reach £12 billion by 2007 whilst the US market will exceed £15 billion, mainly because of increased demand for organic food. Many customers today distrust mass production food processes and this has boosted the sales of organic food and drink in the

DUCHY ORIGINALS

UK from less than £4 million in 1998 to £1.1 billion in 2003. By 2007 this niche market is expected to reach £1.6 billion. Yet even this market can be sub-divided into different categories with different trends – fruit and vegetables (by far the biggest seller of all but slightly down in 2003); dairy products (rising); baby food (rising rapidly and now responsible for 50 per cent of all baby food sales); groceries; eggs; drinks; cereals, bread and biscuits. According to the Organic Consultancy, people are starting to move away from simple foods like organic vegetables and into organic ready meals.

Many businesses want a share of this market, not least the main superstores, all of which now stock organic products. Specialist suppliers include Duchy Originals, created by the Prince of Wales in 1992 because of his belief in the advantages of natural, healthy foods. All profits from sales of the products go to the Prince of Wales's Charitable Foundation and to date over £3.5 million has been raised.

There have been many research studies both in Europe and North America on the most likely type of customer to buy organic. This information is useful because it helps organic producers to target their core customers – and identify ways in which they can convert those who are more sceptical. One way is to overcome objections. Another is to provide more information to educate consumers.

Questions

1 Test your understanding of markets by identifying whether each of the following statements is true or false.

Statement	True	False
By 2007, all the food and drink eaten by Europeans will be worth £12 billion.		
The US fresh food and drink market is worth more only because America is bigger than Europe.		
Organic food is considered a niche market because it is one part of a larger market.		
The food market can be sub-divided into many different types: fresh food, tinned food, baby food, dairy food and frozen food are just a few examples.		
In 2003, over £1 billion of organic food was bought in Britain.		
The biggest selling item is organic baby food.		
The baby food market can be divided into organic and non-organic products.		
More people buy organic ready meals than organic fruit and vegetables.		

Activity 2.1.5 Choosing the healthy option (cont'd)

2 According to Organic Consultancy, this table shows the value of sales of organic food sub-markets in 2003. Work out the percentage of sales of each type of product (round this to the nearest whole number) and draw a pie chart to show these.

Fruit and vegetables	£230 million
Dairy products	£106 million
Groceries	£97 million
Cereals, bread and biscuits	£76 million
Eggs	£31 million
Drinks	£24 million
Baby food	£24 million

3 Duchy Originals has been extremely successful as an organic food business. Investigate its website at **www.heinemann.co.uk/hotlinks (express code 1351T).** and identify four strengths of the enterprise and two USPs (unique selling points).

4 You are interested in setting up an organic food retail business with a group of friends and have obtained the following market research information.

Customer profile	Reasons for buying	Reasons for not buying
Worried mothers, empty nesters (i.e. no children now at home), health conscious teenagers. Mainly female buyers. Most live in London and the south east. Well educated. Watch BBC2 or Channel 4 Read a 'serious' newspaper (e.g. *Times* or *Telegraph*).	Food safety issues. Seen as healthy and nutritious. Concerned about personal health and effect of food additives. Environmental concern. Want to support small scale producers. Desire for convenience. Fashion – 'cool' to buy. Concerned about animal welfare. Better taste. Easy to prepare. Worried about food allergies.	Cost. Bland taste. Cannot tell the difference. Doesn't stay fresh as long. Don't understand labelling. Don't understand the difference. Dislike the bruises and blemishes. Children won't eat it.

Working in a small group, devise a plan which would enable you to exploit the market potential for organic food in your own area. Do this by identifying the **three** features in each column that you think are the most important and use these as your focus to decide each of the following.

a The type of goods you would stock.

b The way you would promote and advertise your business.

c The scope of your online operation (if any).

d An appropriate name for your business.

e At least one USP for your business.

A definite lack of flower power!

Read the case study below and then answer the questions that follow.

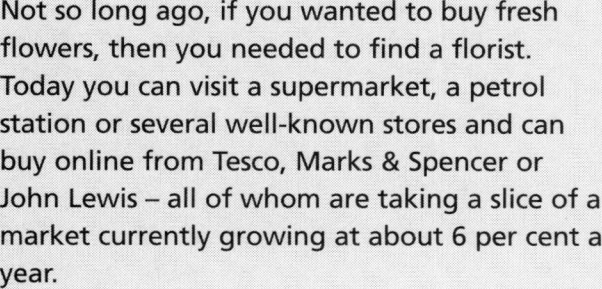

Case study

Not so long ago, if you wanted to buy fresh flowers, then you needed to find a florist. Today you can visit a supermarket, a petrol station or several well-known stores and can buy online from Tesco, Marks & Spencer or John Lewis – all of whom are taking a slice of a market currently growing at about 6 per cent a year.

You can also buy online or over the telephone from Interflora – the small florists' organisation which is owned by its members. The network unites 1,800 small florists and their staff so that they can deliver flowers around Britain at 3 hours' notice. The problem is that they struggle to compete with the larger providers on price – and cannot take advantage of the same number of impulse buys. As a result, profits at Interflora haven't increased since 1997.

In 1997 the management team at Interflora suggested several changes, all of which were blocked by the members. After a bitter disagreement the eleven members of the

management team all lost their jobs – and nothing changed. Now Steve Richards, the new Chief Executive, is proposing more changes. He wants to shake up the organisation and convert it into a private company, bring in innovations such as delivering other types of gifts, look at savings to be gained from buying flowers, or even mobile phones, in bulk and use its database more proactively – such as by reminding customers about dates they should remember. Whether Interflora members will respond positively to ideas for change this time round is as yet to be seen.

Questions

1 What is Interflora?

2 Give **two** reasons why Interflora members are struggling to increase their market share or take advantage of a growing market.

3 The Chief Executive says that a key USP of Interflora is that all bouquets are hand prepared by skilled workers, rather than mass produced in a factory. Do you think this will help the business? Give a reason for your views.

4 Each Interflora member has one vote if any change is proposed and 75 per cent of members must be in favour for a

change to be agreed. Suggest **one** reason this means it is difficult to get changes agreed.

5 The Chief Executive wants to adapt the product by delivering other types of gifts. Suggest **two** or **three** types of related gifts that could also be sent by the Interflora network.

6 Identify **two** other changes the Chief Executive wants to make.

7 If the Interflora members vote against the new ideas what do you think will be the outcome – and will it matter? Give a reason for your answer.

What's the point of changing?

Businesses adapt their products and services for several reasons.

A To respond to changing customer expectations.

B To respond to a wider range of customer needs (e.g. for the young, elderly, disabled or different ethnic groups).

C In response to feedback or criticism.

D To create new customer needs – and solutions.

E To beat (or match) their competitors.

However, there are different business reactions to change.

- The leaders (L) always want to be ahead of the rest.
- The followers (F) just copy good ideas.
- The unwilling (U) only make a certain change when they have to.
- The dinosaurs (DS) refuse to change, no matter what.

Your tasks

1 For the items in the table below where a change or adaptation was actually made, suggest the main reason(s) for this, using the A–E labels above.

2 For each item, identify whether this involved a leader (L), a follower (F), the unwilling (U) or a dinosaur (DS)!

3 Working in a small group, identify four other changes or adaptations and suggest reasons for these. If you are stuck, think of product extensions, technological developments, additional services or new ways of doing business – these may give you a few clues!

Then compare your ideas as a group.

Change or adaptation	Reason(s)	Type
Within months of the original launch, Apple launched a 4th generation iPod (smaller, cheaper) with extended battery life and an iPod mini.		
The government launched a passports online service.		
McDonald's announced it was phasing out supersize meals and introducing salads.		
The Ford team put on heavy padded garments and goggles to restrict vision before designing the Focus car with big dials and easy access.		
The Imperial War Museum introduced flying displays to music and interactive displays.		
A small town hairdresser decided to accept Switch and credit cards for payments.		
A fishmonger refused to accept any cards but continued to insist on cash or cheques.		
The AA introduced breakdown cover for the driver not the car – so the driver is covered in a friend's car.		
After seeing attendance fall for years, eventually the ECB (English and Welsh Cricket Board) introduced 20/20 cricket to liven things up.		
Kelloggs reduced the salt in its cornflakes a little, after much criticism about its cereals.		
Expedia advertised build-your-own holidays online.		
A local fish and chip shop now also serves ethnic food and pizzas and offers a delivery service.		
Dell offers a computer maintenance service for small businesses.		
BA enhances online service so customers can check in and select their seat at home.		
Walkers produces Lite crisps with fewer calories.		
Fish4Homes will email customers with details of homes for sale in the area they want.		
A hotel owner says he has no intention of having a website because he doesn't understand IT.		

Activity 2.2.1

Identifying the competitive market

Where you buy goods and services depends upon what you want and where you live. If you live in London you will have access to a greater range of suppliers than if you live in a rural area. But you may have more difficulty finding a builder or locksmith in an emergency than if you lived in a small town.

There are three reasons for these differences.

- In large cities, all major providers of goods and services are represented. These include businesses that operate in a regional, national or global market.
- In large cities there will also be local providers, but the demand for their services may be greater than in a small area.
- If competition is strong then this means there are many different firms offering the same goods or services, so it is easy to get what you want. If competition is weak, then there are far fewer suppliers, so it is harder for customers to buy what they need.

Your tasks

1 Complete the table below by identifying

a the most likely scale of the competitive market: *local*, *regional*, *national*, *European*, *global*.

b the most likely degree of competition: *strong*, *moderate* or *weak*.

Then compare your ideas with other members of your group.

2 As a group, decide which combinations are

a better for businesses

b better for customers.

Service provider/product	Competitive market	Degree of competition
Plumber		
Dentist		
Multiplex cinema		
Night club		
Department store		
Mobile phones		
Jeans		
Estate agent		
Internet Service Provider (ISP)		
Crisps		
Window cleaner		
Cars		
Chain store (e.g. Boots, Next, Currys)		
Credit cards		
Computer software		
Car maintenance		
Bookseller		
Washing machines		
Jeweller		
Solicitor		
Mail delivery		
Supermarket		
Cosmetics		
Takeaways		

Investigating the market for chocoholics!

All businesses must know their own market if they are to be successful. This means knowing their own market share, the competition and new trends and developments. They also have to be able to evaluate their own market position, by identifying their strengths, weaknesses, opportunities and threats. Then they can make plans for the future.

Your task, as a group, is to investigate the UK chocolate market and prepare SWOT analyses for competitive firms. You can then decide which, in your opinion, will prove to be the market leader in the future.

Background information

The chocolate market in the UK is a tasty chunk of the overall confectionary market which is worth £4 billion a year in sales. It is dominated by three large firms: Cadbury's Trebor Bassett (think Cadbury's Dairy Milk, Roses), Masterfoods (think Mars and Celebrations) and Nestlé Rowntree (think KitKat and Yorkie).

The problem is that chocolate sales in the UK are starting to stagnate. Some think this is because we eat as much chocolate as we can manage every year – a massive 10 kilograms each! In this case the market has probably reached saturation point and the only way suppliers can increase their market share is by outwitting each other. As

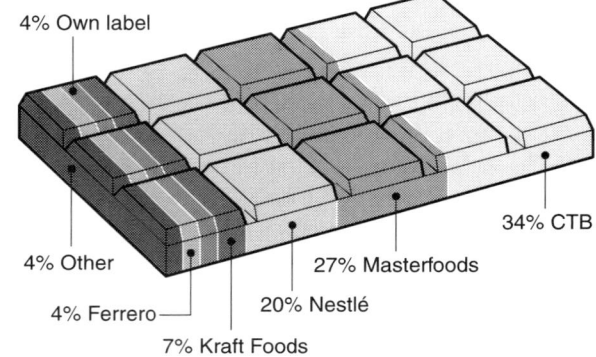

Market shares of chocolate market, 2003
(Source: *Cadbury's Confectionery Market Review* 2003)

evidence of this trend in falling sales, sales of KitKat dropped from £123 million to £116 million between 2002 and 2003 and sales of Mars bars shrank from £979 million to £943 million. As a result Nestlé brought in a new managing director to try to restore the firm to its former market leader position.

Your tasks

1   Divide into teams as instructed by your tutor to investigate the current brands offered by one of the three largest firms and obtain other information on the way they do business. Links to Cadbury, Masterfoods and Mars and Nestlé are available at **www.heinemann. co.uk/hotlinks**, (express code 1351T).

   • Cadbury has a comprehensive website and also produces a Confectionery Market Review each year which you can read for in-depth information. Remember you are only looking for information on chocolate at Cadbury's – nothing else.
   • At Mars concentrate on finding out information related only to its chocolate brands, e.g. Maltesers, Milky Way, Mars and Galaxy, particularly related to the UK.

You will also find useful additional information under the careers at Mars section of the site.
   • At Nestlé you need to download the information relating to the chocolate brands. Then check the product news, press office, about us and recruitment sections for additional information.

Your tutor may also wish other teams to investigate other suppliers, e.g. Kraft Foods for Toblerone and Chocolate Orange; Ferrero Rocher (information is available on the American site) and Thorntons (look under Investor Relations for the information you need). Links to these sites are also available at **www.heinemann.co.uk/hotlinks**, (express code 1351T).

Activity 2.2.2 Investigating the market for chocoholics! (cont'd)

2   Identify **four** strengths and weaknesses of each business and enter these on a SWOT analysis with headings as shown below

3   Identify **four** opportunities for the business. You may find it helpful here to think about specific and related aspects of the chocolate business such as

- further possible brand extensions and new products
- impulse buys – how and where they occur
- how, where and when chocolate is eaten (e.g. home, work, cinema etc.)
- consumer needs and reasons for buying (e.g. caring and sharing with a friend, giving as a present, special times of year etc.).

Try to add to these with your own ideas. Then recommend specific opportunities for the business and enter these on your analysis.

4   Think about how your competitors might take advantage of the areas you have discussed and identify **three** threats to your business from their actions. Enter these on your SWOT analysis.

5   Nominate a spokesperson (or two) and give a brief presentation about your findings to the rest of your group and answer any questions you are asked. Your presentation should include a visual aid of your completed SWOT analysis.

6   Listen to the other presentations and then review your team's opportunities and threats columns in the light of the new market intelligence you have just discovered!

7   As a class, from your investigations, decide which company is in the strongest position in the UK chocolate market today.

SWOT ANALYSIS FOR ....

Strengths	Weaknesses
Opportunities	**Threats**

Know your competitors!

It is always tougher for businesses if they have many competitors and if customers can choose alternative suppliers or substitute products. For example, if you want a packet of ordinary teabags you could buy Brooke Bond PG Tips or Tetleys or Typhoo. But you could decide instead to buy herbal tea or a specialist tea such as Earl Grey or Darjeeling, made by suppliers such as Twinings or Whittards. Or you could choose a substitute product – such as coffee, lemonade or coke.

Another way to think of this is to consider different markets. The tea market comprises the UK teabag market. The wider market includes niche markets, such as the herbal tea market, the green tea market, the organic tea market – and even the cold tea market! The soft drinks or beverage market is where you will identify the substitute products.

Ideally a business will want a unique selling point which means it has few direct competitors. Or it may want to offer a product or service which is difficult to substitute – such as petrol or diesel for cars.

Your tasks

1 **a** Complete the table below by completing the blanks.

b Highlight the **two** products or services in the chart for which there are no direct substitutes.

2 Identify a major USP of each of the following businesses which effectively limits the number of direct competitors it has.

    a Argos   **c** Hamleys Toy Store

    b CenterParcs   **d** Fairtrade products

Product or supplier	Direct competitor in same market	Competitor in related/ wider market	Substitute products/ supplies
Adidas trainers			
Weetabix			
B&Q			
My Travel			
Hovis loaf			
Burger King			
Walkers crisps			
HMV stores			
WeightWatchers			
Barclays Bank			
Marie Claire			
Monsoon			
AOL			
UCI cinemas			

Market intelligence and action planning

All businesses need market intelligence before they make plans. They need to know who their competitors are and what they might do. To find out they could use a market intelligence agency, such as Hoover's Online.

You can access Hoover's Online yourself through **www.heinemann.co.uk/hotlinks** (express code 1351T) and bring up a fact sheet on any well-known company which includes a list of major competitors. You can also bring up news reports on different companies free of charge. In-depth information is only available by subscription – but you can see the type of market intelligence that is available if you were prepared to pay for it.

Your tasks

1 Businesses might make plans to:

    A increase their overall sales and market share
    B get one step ahead of their competitors
    C simply keep up with their competitors.

For each of the plans listed in the table below:

    a identify the competitors each business will need to monitor. If you are stuck, use the Hoovers.com website to help you
    b decide whether the major reason for their actions is A, B or C as listed above.

2 In pairs, and in agreement with your tutor, select **one** of the businesses listed. This is the business you are going to advise on future action.

Find out at least **two** future plans of their competitors either by going to the news section of Hoover's Online, by looking on the competitor's own websites or by looking at other news websites.

Then identify **two** further actions your business could take linked to the aims listed in (1) above.

Business and action taken	Competitors	Major reason
Burberry jazzed up its lines with bright colours, hired Kate Moss as the face of the brand and extended operations in Japan.		
Nokia announced the release by 2007 of musical handsets with a hard drive that will store thousands of songs.		
MFI said it was spending more on advertising, cutting prices and increasing the range of new products from 10 per cent to 25 per cent.		
Whitbread bought 150 Premier Lodge sites to add to its stock of over 400 Travel Inns. All will be renamed 'Premier Travel Inn' so customers won't confuse them with rival Travelodge.		
BT reduced the price of its flagship 512K broadband service to new and existing consumers.		
Nintendo cut the price of its GameCube because of unsold stock and falling sales and launched the Nintendo DS – its entry into the hand-held game market. It will launch its successor to the GameCube in 2005.		
Hoover launched 'The One', a new cleaner which can switch between carpet and hard-floor modes at a flick.		
W H Smith stopped selling singles and cut stocks of CDs and computer games to put more books, stationery and magazines on its shelves.		
Mattel saw its sales of Barbie fall and profits crash by 73 per cent following the launch of the Bratz dolls by MGA Entertainment. It hit back by launching My Scene, Fairytopia and a new adult Barbie clothing range.		
Tesco paid £140 million to buy a stake in Chinese hypermarket chain Hymall. This will give it a 50 per cent stake in the chain.		

Who's making music?

(Cross-references to Unit 9 Starting up a new business Activity 9.4)

Rapidly changing markets present both challenges and opportunities to business. And changing faster than most today are those related to the music industry – which is worth over $40 billion a year.

Market 1 – Global audio and video production

In 1990 there were eight large production companies (the 'majors') which, between them, controlled 82 per cent of this market plus the Indies, or independent companies, which accounted for the rest. By July 2004 the market had shrunk to five majors and soon could be down to four if EMI and Warner pull off their plans to get together.

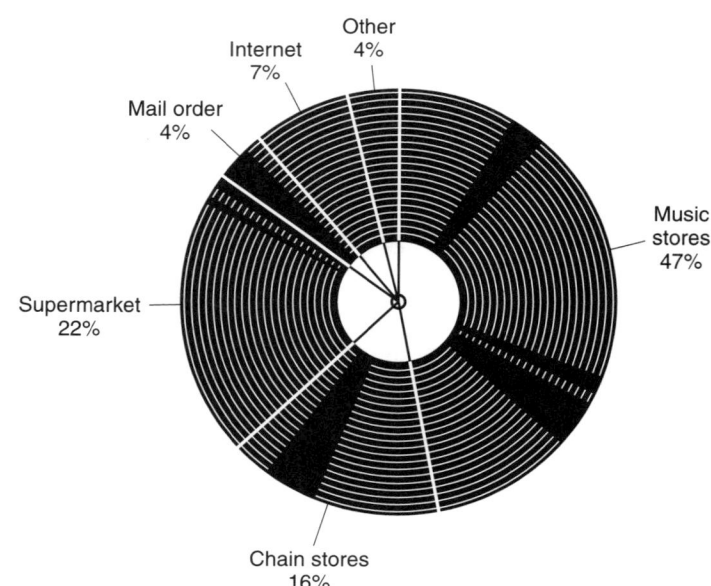

Indies 24%
Universal 24%
Warner 13%
Sony BMG 23%
EMI 13%
Sony Japan 3%

(Source: IFPI)

This type of market concentration, where businesses keep getting larger by merging with each other isn't unusual, although whether it is good for business, or customers, is another matter. The majors say they need to be big to compete, but many argue otherwise – and give the success of the Indies as evidence.

Big is beautiful	Small is better
Bigger chequebooks mean more top stars can be contracted.	Many stars prefer Indies e.g. Travis, the Prodigy, Ash, Muse, Moby.
Lower production costs per item are possible because of large scale production.	Indies are seen as creative, hungry and treat people as individuals.
Lower costs mean higher profits.	Indies can respond faster and be just as profitable.

Market 2 – UK music outlets

Today you can pick up a CD in the supermarket or buy online at stores like Amazon or download your music. Napster has predicted that there will be no high street shops left by 2014, but record shop owners disagree. They argue they can offer specialist services, such as rare vinyls, and claim many people prefer to build up a physical record collection. They also say they can diversify into selling associated products. Despite their confidence, the prediction of the British Association of Record Dealers was that downloads, which in 2004 accounted for 10 per cent of sales, would account eventually for 25 per cent – which is why the British Phonographic Industry announced the start of a download chart in September 2004.

Other 4%
Internet 7%
Mail order 4%
Music stores 47%
Supermarket 22%
Chain stores 16%

(Source: TNS Audio Visual Trak Survey)

Activity 2.2.5 Who's making music? (cont'd)

Market 3 – The ringtone market

Globally, ringtones are a £1.5 billion market and, in 2004, were worth £90 million in Britain alone. The market is booming – hence the start of the MEF Ringtones Chart, compiled by KPMG and published in *Music Week* magazine and the launch of gold and platinum disks for ringtones.

This market may go some way to making up the loss of revenue from single CD sales – down by 33.6 per cent to £64.4 million in 2004 – and will benefit writers, artists and record producers. EMI expects its revenues from ringtones to top £14 million in 2004.

Questions

1 Identify the three markets related to the music industry.

2 a Explain how the marketplace for audio and video production has changed over the last 12 years.

   b Suggest **two** benefits that major producers have gained through this.

   c Identify **three** reasons why the Indies have managed to survive despite these changes.

3 Explain how the UK marketplace for selling music to the public is changing.

4 Identify the category in which each of the following retailers will be included in the UK music outlets pie chart.

   a Amazon

   b Virgin Megastores

   c Asda

   d Woolworths

   e Your local independent record store.

5 a Oxfam has launched a charity download site – Bignoisemusic.com. What is the USP of this site?

   b How successful do you think this site is likely to be? Give a reason for your answer.

6 You want to work in the music business and are thinking of opening a small independent record store.

   a For each different type of competitive outlet listed below, identify **two** advantages they may have over you.

      i Large chain such as HMV or Virgin

      ii Supermarket chain

      iii Internet supplier, e.g. Amazon

      iv Download service, e.g. Apple iTunes or Napster.

   b Suggest **two** ways in which you could respond to the threat to your business.

7 As an alternative, you could be a DJ, form a band or even start your own label. Check out the following websites for information and guidance: the British Phonographic Industry, Music Tank and the British Association of Record Dealers, where you can also obtain an update to the market share information published above, through **www.heinemann.co.uk/hotlinks** (express code 1351T).

   Then identify the area where you think there are the most opportunities, with reasons.

8 Look at the two opinions below and, as a group, decide which you agree with.

> **View 1**: The ringtone market is overpriced and will have flopped by this time next year. Most ringtones are annoying and it's a waste of money to keep changing them.

> **View 2**: Ringtones are good fun and the market is going from strength to strength. New tunes will be written to include catchy riffs and choruses so that they feature high in the ringtone charts.

Could you fight (fairly!) and survive?

Do the quiz with a difference and find out!

 Sophie runs a small retail fashion business in her home town. She enjoys her work and earns enough for her needs. To her horror she has just found out that an empty shop four doors away has been bought by another fashion chain. They will open in a month's time – late October – to make the most of the Christmas trade in November and December.

The rules!

Divide into small groups to act as a management team for Sophie, who runs Sophie's Fashions. Each group starts with £50,000 – the combined value of Sophie's stock and cash at the bank.

After each question your tutor will tell you whether your answer has earned or lost you money – and by how much. Nominate one person to keep your score.

MAY THE BEST TEAM WIN!

1 On hearing the news about her new competitor Sophie should:

  a Reduce her Christmas stock orders, as obviously she will sell less.

  b Increase her Christmas stock orders, so she can offer more choice.

  c Ring their head office and tell them there is suspected subsidence under the new shop.

  d Check out their website for information and set up her own with more up-to-date fashion info.

2 The new store opens with a launch party, a minor celeb and huge publicity. Sophie should:

  a Crash the party to check out their stock.

  b Set up a database with full contact details for all current customers.

  c Abseil down the front of her shop in fancy dress, to get the same level of publicity.

  d Call in with a welcome gift to suss out their manager.

3 Over the next two weeks Sophie's takings are down by 25 per cent. She should:

  a Reduce all her prices by 10 per cent.

  b Advertise in the local paper for the next week, at a cost of £3,000.

  c Take the new manager out for lunch and suggest they reach a quiet deal about prices.

  d Contact local paper about planned pre-Christmas fashion show in conjunction with local beauty salon with make-over prize to one of their lucky readers.

4 Over the next two weeks takings return to normal but without the usual boost Sophie would expect just before Christmas. She should: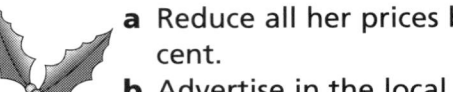

  a Bribe friends to arrive at shop on a sleigh as Father Christmas plus elves, trim up the shop artistically and get the local paper over.

  b Cancel her job ad for part-time Christmas helpers.

  c Mailshot all customers with discount tokens to be used in store between now and Christmas.

Activity 2.2.6 Could you fight (fairly!) and survive? (cont'd)

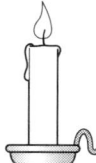

d Diversify and buy a job lot of yoga mats, yoga trousers, candles and soap to bring more people through the door.

5 Sophie learns that her competitor is having a pre-Christmas promotional event next Monday. She should:

a Laugh and realise it's just a sign of their desperation.

b Beat them at their own game by putting 'prices slashed – everything must go' stickers on her windows.

c Start a gift-wrap service.

d Announce a 10 per cent loyalty discount for any customer who brings a friend who also makes a purchase.

6 There's three weeks to go to Christmas. Sophie's takings are still lower than normal and she could do with a really big last minute boost. She should:

a Give all customers a small gift from her Christmas tree.

b Visit her rival manager for a chat and accidentally spill coffee over the party clothes rail.

c Offer all customers sales vouchers, valid after Christmas, in proportion to amount spent before Christmas.

d Poach the two best staff at the rival store by offering them a huge increase in salary to start work for her immediately.

7 The local paper has arranged interviews with Sophie and her rival for a Christmas feature and sent a journalist over. She should:

a Take him out for lunch and tip him off the other store has been carrying out a dirty tricks campaign to put her out of business.

b Announce she will give all her Christmas profits to a local children's charity this year, providing the paper will publicise this.

c Offer the journalist three designer outfits and £100 cash in return for a good review.

d Offer him a sandwich and coffee on arrival and, as he is leaving, Christmas discount vouchers for himself and a friend.

8 This year, Christmas Day is on a Monday and everyone is expecting a huge rush on the Saturday and Sunday before Christmas. She should:

a Announce she will be open from 8 am to midnight both days.

b Hire greeters and extra staff to make sure no-one goes away because they can't get served quickly.

c Ring the police on Saturday morning to say she can smell gas coming from her rival's shop and it should be evacuated.

d Open Saturday but close on Sunday to get her own Christmas shopping done.

9 Christmas is over. Sophie is concerned that there's still quite a bit of old stock left. She should:

a Start a sale on Boxing Day.

b Rest, relax and recover with two weeks in the sun and worry about the stock after- wards.

c Start a sale on 1 January.

d Get her picture in the paper giving all her remaining stock to Oxfam.

10 Immediately January starts, and based on her current finances, she should:

a Scout around for new, super spring stock at bargain prices.

b Arrange to see her bank manager for an overdraft.

c Ask her rival for a job.

d Open up a second shop in a nearby town.

Whose business is it anyway?

All stakeholders have expectations about a business – but these vary depending upon their business responsibilities.

1 Below are seven groups of stakeholders, each with an interest in EAT, a coffee and sandwich chain that is rapidly spreading across Britain.

    a Match the groups to the expectations in the chart below.

    b Then suggest **one** further expectation of each group.

Groups: EAT's owners, Niall and Faith McArthur; their financiers, 3i, who have invested £5 million in the business; EAT's customers; EAT's suppliers; EAT's employees; people in local communities who live near EAT outlets; EAT's online sponsors (Virgin Wine and Domino's Pizza); Government tax authorities.

Stakeholder group	Expectation of EAT
_____	Will sell safe food
_____	Will make its forecast profit of £2 million
_____	Will attract people to its website
_____	Will pay a fair wage
_____	Will pay tax when due
_____	Will dispose of its rubbish responsibly
_____	Will pay its bills promptly
_____	Will continue to grow and prosper

2 Many pressure groups are concerned about the business practices of the food industry following a Health and Safety Commission report that found that over two-thirds of the British public are either obese or overweight. They argue that foods should contain less saturated fat and salt, be clearly labelled and that adverts promoting junk or fast food to children should be banned. *The Lancet* (a medical journal) also wants celebrities to be banned from promoting or sponsoring junk food. Other pressure groups, such as the British Retail Consortium, which represents food shops, and the Food and Drink Federation, which represents food manufacturers, argue that it is not the role of food shops or manufacturers to tell people what to eat. They say that more laws are not necessary.

    a Gary Lineker is famous for promoting Walker's Crisps. Would you consider he is a stakeholder in the firm? Give a reason for your answer.

    b One newspaper argued that 'we are all stakeholders in the nation's health as the cost of obesity is £4.9 billion a year'. Work in small groups to identify as many 'stakeholders in the nation's health' as you can – and then compare your ideas.

    c Do you think the government should do everything in its power to improve people's diets or should people eat what they want without interference? For example, should it ban vending machines selling junk foods in schools and outlaw junk food adverts altogether? As a class decide your opinion of this issue.

    Before you discuss your views, divide into groups to find out more about the views of pressure groups both for and against tighter controls. Links are available at **www.heinemann.co.uk/ hotlinks** (express code 1351T). Then decide what you would do if you were the government.

Identify stakeholder groups and expectations

Groups of stakeholders and their expectations differ depending upon the issue involved. In some cases this means certain stakeholders going 'head to head' over particular issues.

In the chart below are 10 issues or events that affect stakeholders. For each one four groups of stakeholders are identified.

1 Decide the most likely expectations of each group.

2 In each case two or more groups may go 'head to head' by disagreeing about the issue. Identify which groups would be involved and why there might be a problem.

To help, the first is done for you.

Issue or event	Stakeholders	Expectations	Head to head
A train drivers' strike over pay	Commuters Rail company Trade union Train drivers	Major inconvenience Major disruptions to services Negotiations over pay Pay increase	Rail company and union or rail company and train strike drivers about whether pay awards justified/size of award
A plan to site a large wind farm near a rural village	Local community Environmental groups/planners Government Energy buyers		
The loss of call centre jobs to India	UK employees Union UK employer Indian employees		
A dispute by pilots about proposals to increase working hours	Pilots Pilots' union Passengers Airline		
Increase in speed cameras/number of fines	Motorists Police Pressure groups e.g. AA Government		
The increase in university tuition fees	Students Parents/partners Universities Government		
Financial problems at a large football club	Shareholders Spectators Players Directors		
Major sporting or entertainment event, e.g. World Cup/Glastonbury festival	Participants/teams Sponsors Local community Organisers/clubs		

Financial stakeholders and the London Eye

(Cross-references to Unit 3.1 Profit and break even Activity 3.1.7)

Background information

The skyline of London used to be dominated by Big Ben and St Paul's Cathedral. Now the most noticeable object is the huge big wheel next to the Thames – the London Eye. But things haven't run that smoothly at this popular tourist attraction – mainly due to rows among its three owners. These are

- Marks Barfield Architects – owned by David Marks and Julia Barfield. These are the designers who own one third of the stock.

- British Airways, which lent £130 million to fund the construction of the Eye in the late 1990s, and which is charging 25 per cent interest on the debt.

- The Tussaud's Group (which also owns Alton Towers and Madam Tussauds), which owns the third share. This group charges a 4 per cent annual management fee.

KEY FACTS ON THE LONDON EYE

There are 32 capsules

Each capsule holds up to 25 people

The flight lasts 30 minutes

There are an average 15,000 visitors a day

Adult tickets are £11.50, seniors and students are £9, children over five are £5.75

In 2003 the London Eye made a profit of £12.8 million, but its total interest bill and other charges resulted in a net loss of £10.9 million. The designers want a new deal done with the debt, so the interest payments will fall from their current level of £2 million a month. But the shareholders cannot agree on how this will be done. Any bank they approach would want the loan guaranteed by Tussauds who are only interested if they could own at least 75 per cent of the wheel – but neither BA nor the designers want to sell.

Questions

1 How many groups have a **financial** stake in the London Eye?

2 What is the main expectation of all the financial stakeholders?

3 Did the London Eye make an overall profit or loss in 2003? Give a reason for your answer.

4 How much interest is BA now receiving each year?

5 Which shareholder group wants the debt renegotiated at a lower rate of interest?

6 Why haven't the two other shareholders agreed to this?

7 State two expectations of any bank if the loan is eventually renegotiated.

8 a Can you calculate the London Eye's revenue per day in summer from the information in the Facts Box if you assume that the average ticket price is £8?

  b If the profits every day worked out at £35,500 in 2003, what must be the cost of operating the Eye each day?

9 Private capsules can be hired for £350. Fast track tickets can be bought for £25 which allow people to by-pass queues. Explain how these variations mean that the London Eye is aware of different customer expectations.

10 Identify the three major stakeholder groups involved with the London Eye and identify their key expectations.

Staff expectations on health and safety

(Cross-references to Unit 5 Employee contribution to working conditions Activity 5.2, Unit 6 Introduction to business administration Activity 6.3)

You have just been nominated as safety representative for your office. As a result, you have decided to talk to the staff to check that they are happy about health and safety. Your problem is that everyone you speak to seems to have a complaint!

How would you advise each person? And what action would you take in cases where action needs to be taken? Write down your own ideas and then compare your suggestions as a group.

Problem	Action taken/advice given
Perveen argues that the new fax machine shouldn't have been put on the spare desk because the wire is trailing across the floor.	
Lucy complains that she has reported the broken wheel on their only trolley three times but nothing has been done.	
Shazim remarks that although he has been working for the firm for 2 months, he still hasn't had any health and safety training.	
Melanie complains that the electricians told her she couldn't use her portable fan heater at work unless she lets them check the wiring.	
Farhana says she has started getting headaches when she uses her computer but when she told her manager he took no notice.	
Jack says that not only are the signs and instructions relating to fire equipment torn and unreadable he doesn't think any of the extinguishers have been checked for years.	
Dan complains that he can't get things he needs from the hazardous substances cupboard when the manager is at lunch, because it's always kept locked.	
Emily reports that she nearly had an accident when she slipped on some paper that was lying on the floor.	

Problems for Sainsbury's stakeholders

(Cross-references to Unit 7 Sales and customer service Activity 7.4)

Background information

There are four major supermarkets in Britain – Tesco, Asda, Sainsbury's and Wm Morrison. But whilst most are getting bigger and stronger, one is not – Sainsbury's. In 2004, Tesco's market share increased to 27 per cent, Asda moved to the number two slot and Morrison expanded by taking over Safeway, while Sainsbury's market share fell to 15 per cent. More importantly, Sainsbury's only made profits of £400 million – against Tesco's £1.9 billion!

What has gone wrong? Some people would say almost everything! Sainsbury's has failed to follow virtually every supermarket grocery trend to date and has hasn't responded to competitive threats. In 2004, its chief executive, Peter Davis, left and was replaced by Justin King, who cut his teeth at PepsiCo and Asda.

Can Justin King turn Sainsbury's around? Experts are advising him to cut prices by 5 per cent, to compete with Tesco and Asda, but if he does that then his small profit will rapidly turn into a loss. Another option is to cut dividends – or he could first tackle the problems with the new automated depots which don't work properly so leave shelves in the shops empty. Whatever he does, some moves will please some stakeholders and some will not!

1 Identify at least **seven** stakeholder groups that are involved with Sainsbury's. Check your answer with your tutor before you do question 2.

2 For each of the actions Sainsbury's could take that are listed in the table below, decide which stakeholder groups would be the winners and which would be the losers – and why.

What Sainsbury's could do	Winners	Losers	Reason
Cut prices by 5 per cent			
Outsource warehousing and distribution			
Close unprofitable shops			
Cut next dividend			
Increase advertisements and promotions			
Sell cheaper goods by changing suppliers			
Start own loyalty card			
Open more small convenience stores			
Build up online shopping operation			
Revamp and modernise stores			
Sell more non-food lines			
Freeze pay awards			

3 Despite Sainsbury's problems, 15 million customers still shop regularly at the store.

a Identify **three** likely reasons for this.

b Jamie Oliver is the 'face' of Sainsbury's in their sales promotions. Suggest **one** benefit and **one** disadvantage of getting a celebrity like Jamie Oliver to promote the business.

c If you were organising a sales promotion for Sainsbury's, what would you suggest is included, to set the business apart from its competitors and attract more customers? Discuss your ideas as a group.

Debate and decide!

(Cross-references to Unit 4 Business communications Activity 4.2)

FAIRFIELD FARM POLYTUNNELS

The owners of Fairfield Farm diversified last year into growing fruit – raspberries, strawberries, blackcurrants and redcurrants. In order to produce these from April to November they erected polytunnels – long white open-ended plastic covers which protects the fruit from birds, rain and wind.

However, several people in the local community have objected to the polytunnels which, they claim, not only look awful and spoil the landscape but are a hazard to wildlife. They have appealed to the council to order the removal of the polytunnels.

Your task, as a councillor, is to listen to the evidence and decide what to do.

Study the issue described above.

For this activity different members of your group will be given different roles by your tutor. These are as follows:

* The councillors of an English village who will hear the views of several different stakeholders. If you are in this group you will then debate the issue within your team and make a decision. This is likely to involve some negotiation.

* One of the stakeholders who has to put his or her case to the council. In this case your tutor will give you background notes on your role. There may also be a website listed so that you can research further.

Activity 2.3.6 Debate and decide! (cont'd)

THE ARGUMENT FOR

The two owners will argue that

- Before they erected the polytunnels they made a loss on the farm. Now they can earn a living on the farm.
- If they don't grow the fruit, then the supermarkets will simply import it from abroad. This isn't good for the British economy.
- They provide work and accommodation for 200 fruit-pickers.
- They have planted trees to screen the polytunnels from view.
- They care about the environment and wouldn't do anything to harm the wildlife.

The manager of the fruit pickers and one of his staff will argue that

- Jobs in the area are scarce and previously many people were unemployed.
- The farmer pays fair wages and doesn't exploit its fruit-pickers.
- The local community benefits because the pickers spend their wages in local shops.
- The polytunnels have improved working conditions because they give protection to the pickers out of the rain and wind.

The owner of the local store will argue that

- Sales have increased since the fruit pickers moved into the area.
- English fruit is far more popular with shoppers than foreign fruit because it tastes better.
- Many of the people who object to the polytunnels are second home owners who have no interest in the local economy.

A spokesperson for British Summer Fruits, who represents 98 per cent of growers will argue that

- Polytunnels have dramatically improved the quality and yield of a variety of British crops, including fruit, and extended the growing season.
- There is no comparable alternative.
- The demand for fruit is ever-increasing. Without polytunnels fruit would be flown in from abroad. This would result in pollution, loss of jobs and failing rural economies.
- Polytunnels do not effect soil health and reduce the need for pesticides.

THE ARGUMENT AGAINST

Three members of the local community will argue that

- The view from their homes has been ruined because all anyone can see is white plastic.
- The value of their houses has fallen because of it.
- When they applied to have extensions to their houses they were refused planning permission, yet those would have been far less of an eyesore than the polytunnels.

A local hotel owner will argue that

- His trade has fallen because tourists dislike the look of the polytunnels in the fields.
- The view from the hotel is awful and especially from his outdoor terrace which overlooks the strawberry fields.
- There is no need for English strawberries in the early spring or November.
- The strawberry trade is threatening his livelihood.
- Developers have been told they cannot build on the area because they will spoil it, yet that would also help the economy more than the fruit growing. So it doesn't make sense.

An ex-fruit picker will argue that

- Most of his co-workers were Eastern European because wages are so poor English people won't do the work.
- The other group who benefited most were students, not people with families.
- The farm therefore doesn't provide much work for local people, who are no better off.

A local member of the Campaign for the Protection of Rural England (CPRE) will argue that

- Not only are the polytunnels a visual eyesore but they create problems for wildlife and birds.
- To water the fruit can require extraction of water from boreholes which creates problems, especially during hot summers.
- It is up to the government (local and national) to set standards or the whole of England will soon be covered in plastic.

Activity 2.3.7

Understanding ethical business

In Britain, Business in the Community promotes ethical issues and social responsibility amongst UK companies. Its members commit themselves to carrying out their business in a socially responsible way and upholding the following key principles:

- to treat employees fairly and equitably
- to operate ethically and with integrity
- to respect basic human rights
- to sustain the environment for future generations
- to be a caring neighbour for their communities.

Business in the

Community

Businesses can measure their success, year by year, by completing a Corporate Responsibility Index. 'Big Tick' and Awards for Excellence are given each year to companies both large and small all over the country who have had a positive impact on society and the environment, both through their products or services and in relation to the way they relate to stakeholder groups such as employees, investors, customers, communities and suppliers.

Your tasks

1 a Check you understand what ethical business means by identifying which of the following actions taken by your local newsagent would be ethical, and which would not be.

b Then, for each action you think is unethical, say what action you think the newsagent should have taken.

2 Find out more about Business in the Community through its website. See **www.heinemann.co.uk/hotlinks** (express code 1351T). Identify three companies *in your own area* that have recently won awards and explain what they did to deserve these.

Action	Ethical or unethical	Action newsagent should have taken
Selling cigarettes to a kid in school uniform		
Buying fireworks 'from a friend of a friend' because they are cheap		
Selling goods past their sell-by date at normal prices – but reducing these by 10 per cent if challenged		
Giving a relative a magazine to read and then putting it back on sale afterwards		
Paying paperboys and girls the lowest rate in the town		
Refusing to pay paperboys and girls when they are away on holiday		
Ignoring complaints that the papers are too heavy to carry on some rounds on a Sunday morning		
Arguing with an elderly customer that she must pay her full bill because she cannot prove that two days' papers weren't delivered		
Dropping a box of pencils on the floor then putting them back on sale		
Refusing to allow part-time shop assistants to use the cash register or handle money		

Activity 2.4.1

Interpret the headlines!

(Cross-references to Unit 4 Business communications Activity 4.2)

Newspaper headlines often alert businesses to external influences that may affect them. These influences can be divided into six main categories:

Political   **Economic**   **Social**   **Technological**   **Environmental**   **Legislation**

Task 1

You have just picked up a daily newspaper and read each of the following headlines.

1   For each one identify the category or categories involved.

2   Be prepared to answer any questions your tutor might ask to check you understand the terms involved!

Headline	Category or categories
Police test zapper that stalls a speeding car at the flick of a switch	
Green tax likely as Heathrow breaches laws on aircraft emissions	
Cash spending set to fall by £17 billion by 2013	
DTI simplifies red tape for small businesses	
Rip-off travel trade slammed by Government for high-priced school breaks	
MI5's top ten tips online to tackle terrorists	
Shareholders revolt over fat cat pay rise at AGM	
Soaring house prices push up loan rates	
Government announces £1 million Bullying at Work study	
Simpay developing universal system of payments via mobile phone	
OFT demands cooling off period against doorstep cowboys	
EU green rules could add £3,000 to the cost of a car say makers	
12 month maternity leave likely say Ministers	
Chip and PIN reduces fraud	

Task 2

Newspaper headlines may sometimes be even more difficult to understand, especially if you have no background information about the topic. For each of these headlines, decide your answers to the questions that follow. Then compare your ideas as a group.

SEARCH IN THE BLINKX OF AN EYE

THE SCIENCE OF TINY THINGS

The changing face of Europe

THE RACE IS ON FOR 2012

UK IN THE RED TO THE TUNE OF A TRILLION

a   What is the topic matter being discussed?

b   In which external category or categories would it be placed?

c   Identify two types of business that would be interested in the announcement and say why in each case.

Politics and economics on the road

Read the case study below and then answer the questions that follow.

Case study

The cost of motoring is a problem for car owners, the Government and transport managers. The latter argue that the price of petrol in Britain is horrendous, largely because of fuel duty and VAT. In addition there is road tax and insurance – and the often forgotten cost of being stuck in a traffic jam. And one of the worst places in Britain for this is the M6 near Birmingham.

To help solve this problem, on 9 December 2003 the first toll road in Britain opened in Staffordshire. It charged £2 per motorist and promised 27 miles of relief. In July 2004 prices were scheduled to rise – to £3 for cars, from £10 to £11 for lorries and from £1 to £2 for motorcycles. Cynics argued the rises were timed to coincide with the holiday period. Under the terms of its contract Midland Expressway Limited (MEL) can charge anything it likes to road users and can raise its prices as often as it wants.

However, lobbying by the Freight Transport Association resulted in a decrease from the proposed £11 per lorry to a discounted £6 per lorry

until the end of 2004. According to the Association, this made the M6 toll a viable option for hauliers. In July 2004, the Chancellor suspended the intended September fuel increase. After the fuel protests of 2000, when Britain virtually came to a standstill, the Government treads far more carefully over price increases. It is well aware that every penny increase in pump prices adds £500 a year to the operating costs of a lorry.

In July the Government also announced the likelihood of a second toll road to link the M6 toll with Manchester and the possibility of extended congestion charging. London launched this system in 2003 and vehicles must now pay a fee to access central areas. One vision is to charge future motorists according to their use of the roads as recorded on GPS satellites and in-car navigation systems, and scrap road tax altogether.

Questions

1 a Identify **three** basic costs of running a commercial vehicle.

b Explain why being delayed in a traffic jam can also be considered as a cost.

2 In Britain the price of a litre of petrol can be roughly divided into 75 per cent fuel duty, 25 per cent cost of extraction, refining, distribution and selling (plus profit for the oil company and filling station). Then VAT is added.

If a litre of petrol is 80p before VAT

a how much is fuel duty?

b what is the selling price?

3 What is the difference between a toll road and an ordinary road?

4 a What is a 'cynic'?

b Why did cynics think the rises in price of the toll road were deliberately timed to coincide with the holiday period?

c Current prices can be found on the web through **www.heinemann.co.uk/hotlinks** (express code 1351T). However, you are still likely to find night prices cheaper than day prices. How would you explain this difference?

5 Suggest **two** advantages and **two** disadvantages of toll roads to business organisations.

6 MEL reduced its proposed charges for hauliers following pressure from the Freight Transport Association. Explain why MEL complied with their request – even though this meant a sharp loss in future revenues.

7 Suggest **two** arguments to support the Government's case for more toll roads and **two** arguments against.

8 a What is 'congestion charging'?

b Suggest **two** benefits and **two** disadvantages to businesses of congestion charging.

9 Why is the government very sensitive about increasing the price of fuel duty?

10 Abolishing the road tax and replacing it with congestion charges and tolls will affect both businesses and individuals. Suggest **two** groups of road users who will benefit and **two** groups who will not if these proposals go ahead.

The economic climate and its effect

Economic conditions and changes can have a number of effects on businesses and individuals. Sometimes these are good, other times they are not. In each of the cases below, explain how the change would affect the person or business described.

Person/business	Condition or change	Effect
Jessica Tate, who runs her own jewellery business.	Britain is in the middle of an economic boom.	
Usman Patel, who has just left college and is looking for a job.	Britain is in the middle of an economic slump.	
Sweeneys, a large firm of housebuilders.	Spending has slowed and Britain has entered a recession.	
Alex Watson, who owes £2,500 on her credit card.	Interest rates rise by 1 per cent.	
Dan and Sue Osifo, who have £5,000 in an e-savings account.	Interest rates fall by 1 per cent.	
Javeed Patel, who runs a taxi business.	The government increases business rates and fuel duty.	
PTZ Ltd, a large furnishing store.	The government raises income tax.	
Babybuzz, a European cut price airline.	The Euro has strengthened against the pound. The government has introduced a 'green tax' on airline fuel.	
Astronics, which makes interactive whiteboards.	The government announces a rise in public spending on health and education.	
Martin and Jill, who have just bought their first house.	The government increases VAT and the local council increases council tax.	

The gizmo business

(Cross-references to Unit 8 Online business Activity 8.3)

Case study

Changing technology not only affects how business is carried out but also, in some cases, whether a business exists at all. Without the Internet, for example, Google, Yahoo, Friends Reunited, Ebay and Lastminute.com would still be a gleam in someone's eye.

In 1998, friends Michael Smith and Tom Boardman decided to join the dotcom boom and turn their own fascination with gizmos and gadgets into an online business, initially called hotbox.co.uk. Now known as Firebox, this 'boys' toys site' has gone from strength to strength and in 2003 made a profit of £340,000 on sales of £5.3 million. Today the

business also has a mail order catalogue but still sells 85 per cent of its goods online. It prides itself on stocking the latest and most unusual gizmos it can find.

Firebox is a very male-oriented site. Extra business would be gained if Firebox could encourage more women to spend on its site. Research now shows that women spend an average £475 a year on gadgets – but what the founders of Firebox might not have realised is that this may not be for personal use. Quite simply, buying gadgets for the men in their life leaves them free to do their own thing!

Your tasks

Carry out the following investigations in small groups which *only* comprise members of your own sex. Then compare your results to find out the differences between the overall views of males and females in your group.

Finally, discuss with your tutor whether you think social divisions on gender have lessened over the years – so businesses can virtually disregard them – or whether they remain roughly the same.

Your investigation

1   Investigate the Firebox site through **www.heinemann.co.uk/hotlinks** (express code 1351T). Assess it both for its features *and* the type of goods it sells. In particular note its top 20 items and decide which you would like to buy.

2   a   You have won £1,000. How much would you want to spend on gadgets? Add your collective amounts together.
    b   Identify two other items you would spend your money on.

3   The best thing about the Apple mini I-Pod in your opinion is *either*
    a   the size and colours, *or*
    b   its functions and price.

4   You can buy any of the following. Put them in order of preference for yourself and then take a vote on each one to get your group's view.

A new mobile phone   A handheld computer
ABS brakes   Teeth whitening
A digital camera   A mini robot
Ceramic hair straighteners A new outfit

5   Score each person in your team out of 2 for each of the following statements where:

2 = Absolutely; 1 = In your opinion; 0 = You must be joking!

   a   It's easy and fun to keep up-to-date with modern technology.
   b   Shopping for clothes is a drag if it takes longer than half an hour.
   c   Solving basic software problems isn't hard – just download the latest patch.
   d   It's a lot easier to burn a CD or download an MP3 file than it is to make an omelette.
   e   Sub-woofers and tweeters make all the difference to your sound system.
   f   The key feature of a car is its engine performance.
   g   Playing with stuff like mini-racers is a good laugh.

6   You accidentally access a website for in-car gadgets. How long would you be likely to stay in the site? Give a reason for your answer. Access the site through **www.heinemann.co.uk/hotlinks** (express code 1351T).

7   Prepare to argue your team's view of the following.

A good website is a good website. There is no difference between the way men and women view a website or the products on it.

Tracking UK stock market variations

Background information

Share prices basically change because of supply and demand. If more people demand shares then the price rises. If fewer people want them, the price falls.

However, the reasons for price changes can affect individual companies, whole sectors of industry or every business in the market. This happens when the value of a whole market falls – such as the Footsie. This is the slang term for one UK index of share prices. Its full title is the Financial Times/Stock Exchange (FTSE). The FTSE 100 is the index of the prices of the leading 100 British companies whose shares are traded on the London Stock Exchange. It is calculated by adding together the value of all the shares for these companies to give a picture of what is happening to their fortunes. This index is recalculated every 15 seconds during trading hours. Other variations in the UK are the FT250 index and AIM, which is a listing of smaller companies. Foreign markets have many other names but if you hear the terms Dow Jones or Nasdaq, these refer to American markets. Often a major event in the US affects the price of UK shares.

Task 1

1   Draw a line graph to chart the rise and fall of the Footsie from the information in the box below.

2   a   Find out the value of the index today to complete your chart.

   b   Go online to find out the reasons for any major changes since this book was written. You can either ask the right questions in a good search engine or search in a good news site, such as the BBC.

3   Imagine you had invested £10,000 in a representative group of Footsie 100 shares on 1 January 1984.

   a   What is the most your investment could have been worth?

   b   After June 1987, what is the least your investment could have been worth?

   c   What would your investment be worth today?

4   Do you think all shares will follow the Footsie index? Give a reason for your answer.

5   If you inherited a large sum of money you could put it in a savings account, buy property or invest it on the Stock Exchange. As a group, decide **two** advantages and **two** disadvantages of each option.

FOOTSIE HISTORY

- The Footsie was launched on 1 January 1984 at 1,000. The easiest way to think of this is to imagine investing £1,000 and each share is worth £1.
- By 15 October 1987 the index had risen to 2,322.
- On Black Monday, 19 October 1987, the index fell to 1,801 in response to the Dow Jones crashing 22.6 per cent in a day, mainly due to panic selling.
- By 9 November 1987, the index had reached a low of 1,565.
- The dot.com bubble raised the index – to an all-time high of 6,950.6 by 30 December 1999.
- When the bubble burst, in May 2000, the Footsie fell to 6,045.5.
- By August 2001, the Footsie was standing at 5,420.
- By November it had fallen to 5,071 – mainly due to the events of 9.11.
- US accounting scandals at Enron and WorldCom shook investor confidence and by September 2002 the index was down to 3,907.
- On the 10th March 2003, with fears of the Iraq war and bad economic news, the index fell to a 7 year low of 3,436.
- By July 2004 the market had started to recover a little and was worth 4,413.

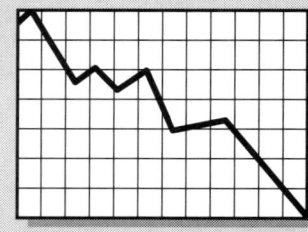

Activity 2.4.5 Tracking UK stock market variations (cont'd)

Task 2

Decide whether each of the following announcements will increase or decrease share prices and enter this in the first blank column. Then decide whether each one will affect just one business, the whole sector or the whole market and tick the correct column to indicate your choice.

Announcement	Effect (increase or decrease)	One business	Whole sector	Whole market
Car manufacturer announces better than expected profit figures				
New gas fields are discovered in the North Sea				
Assassination of American politician				
UK wins next Olympic bid				
National retail chain announces increased market share				
Foreign bank makes takeover bid for UK building society				
Major financial scandal involving a large European business				
Terrorist attack on a large city				
Capture of key terrorist leaders				
Major medical breakthrough by leading research firm				
Telecom firm announces lower profit because of increased competition				
New computer virus creates havoc with Microsoft software				

Task 3

You have £10,000 to invest in businesses of your choice. Divide into small groups and decide which **five** shares you are going to buy.

Track these from today's date (your date of purchase) and chart their highs and lows.

At **two** points during the term you can decide to sell some of your shares and switch your holdings.

On the last day of your course find out the value of your shares and see which team is worth the most!

Changing with the times

The Order of St John was founded over 900 years ago. Today you know it as the St John Ambulance. To survive all this time, it has had to adapt or change – and it has done this by observing external trends and taking advantage of them.

Task 1

Read the current facts about the St John Ambulance. Then put these into the correct categories in the PESTEL framework below by thinking about the external events which have prompted each of these initiatives.

Facts about the St John Ambulance

A Helps AIDS victims in South Africa

B Offers child-related safety training to new parents

C Makes most of its income from providing first aid training to companies

D Has remained independent from the government

E Has purchased 300 high tech Crusader ambulances

F Wants the law changed to be like France, so that anyone assisting at an accident can't be sued

G Provides First Aid training to disadvantaged Chinese communities

H Sells goods by mail order and on its website

I Runs Health and Safety courses for businesses

J Recruits volunteers from its website

K Supports the aim of a smoke-free environment

L Lends spare ambulances to help out the NHS when it can

M Offers advice for keeping cool on very hot days – even more important now with global warming

N Has welcomed the Government's guide for coping in an emergency

PESTEL framework	St John Ambulance facts
Political	
Economic	
Social	
Technological	
Environmental	
Legislation	

Task 2

As a group, suggest what impact each of the following external influences might have on the St John Ambulance and what, if anything, it should do in response. To help you may like to investigate the website through **www.heinemann.co.uk/hotlinks** (express code 1351T).

1 Changes in tax rules on street collections which reduce the overall value of each collection.

2 Increase in interest rates.

3 Increase in accident rates in elderly people living alone.

4 Changes in health and safety legislation.

5 Gift of 100 digital cameras to the Association.

6 Rising share prices.

These sample assessments are designed as practice exercises to help your students understand the types of task they will be required to do for their formal assessments. For practice, tasks can be done by individuals or by groups as indicated.

There is one sample assessment for each section of the unit:

2.1	Customer expectations
2.2	Competitive pressures
2.3	Stakeholder expectations
2.4	External influences

The structure and grading of the assessments reflect the grading criteria for the unit as provided by Edexcel. Differentiation information is given where appropriate to indicate what would be required from the student to gain pass, merit or distinction grades. Tips to help the student achieve a merit or distinction grade are also given. A deadline box is provided in which you can enter a submission date to familiarise your students with the idea of working to a specified date or time.

Assessments are mainly printed one to a page so that they can be easily photocopied.

Answers to Unit 2 sample assessments

No specific answer is possible for the assessments in this unit because it will depend upon the business selected by the student.

Choose a business you know well – either because you work there part-time or because one of your family works there.

Alternatively, select a business you would like to know more about. This should be one which you can investigate on the Internet or where you could obtain permission to visit and interview a senior manager.

Task 1 – Pass grade

1 **a** **Describe** the market in which your chosen business operates.

   b **Describe** its key customer in terms of their main attributes.

   c **Identify FOUR** key expectations of its customers.

   d **State THREE** ways in which the products or services provided meet each of these key expectations.

Deadline

Tips to achieve a merit grade

Before you start Task 2, think about the following points.

- You need to find out how the business obtains information *both* in relation to market trends *and* from customers.
- Then you need to check how the business has responded to customer feedback.
- Look especially for examples of action the business has taken to change its products or services as a result.
- Look for additional things they could do to improve their competitiveness. It may help you to do this if you look at actions taken by competitors but not by the business you are investigating.
- If you genuinely cannot suggest anything then give your reasons by explaining what it has done already, why it is ahead of its competitors and why it cannot do anything more. This could be the case, for example, if it would cost too much to make an improvement worthwhile.

Now answer the following questions.

Task 2 – Merit grade

2 **a** **Identify** at least **ONE** way in which the business finds out about market trends.

   b **Identify** at least **ONE** way in which the business obtains feedback from customers.

   c **Explain TWO** ways in which the business has responded to feedback from its key customers. At least one of these should include how the business has responded by improving or adapting its products or services.

   d **Recommend THREE** ways in which the business could become more competitive by responding to customer expectations of its products or services. If you think this is impossible, give a reason for your opinion.

Keep your information safely, as you will need to refer to it again when you reach the end of section 2.2.

Deadline

For this assessment you should use the same business to investigate that you chose for Section 2.1. Start by looking through the notes you made then, to refresh your memory about the business.

Task 1 – Pass grade

1 **a** **State** the main product or service the business provides. If it produces a range, then identify the one you have decided to focus on for this question.

    b **Identify THREE** direct competitors of the business for this product or service.

    c **Identify**, with reasons, whether the competitive market is local, regional, national, European or global.

    d **Describe** the marketplace for this product or service in terms of:

       i the approximate market share of your chosen business or the product or service you have chosen

       ii the intensity of competition (i.e. whether it is weak or strong)

       iii past market history

       iv likely future developments.

e **Suggest THREE** ways in which your selected business could respond to the key competitive forces it faces.

Deadline

Tips to achieve a merit grade

Before you start Task 2, read this information carefully.

- For this task you will prepare a SWOT analysis. You should start by identifying the internal **strengths** and **weaknesses**. You will need to include those listed in **2a** below and also add any other strengths and weaknesses you have found.
- Think about a major competitor and the competitive pressures faced by the business. This will help you to prepare the **opportunities** and **threats** section.
- Finally, you will use your SWOT analysis to improve the recommendations you made for task **2d** for Unit 2.1. You should be able to do this because the analysis should give you greater insight into the business and trigger new ideas.

Now answer the following questions.

Task 2 – Merit grade

2 **a** **Identify** the strengths and weaknesses of your chosen product or business by undertaking a SWOT analysis. In your analysis, include each of the following elements:

- product or service quality
- consistency
- customer service
- image/branding
- reputation
- USPs.

    b **List** the main resources and strengths of at least **ONE** competitor.

    c **List** the main competitive pressures which face your business.

    d **Complete** your SWOT analysis, using the information from **b** and **c** above to identify the opportunities and threats.

    e Look back at the recommendations you made for task **2d** at the end of section 2.1. Use your SWOT analysis to **suggest any other ways** in which you think the business could become more competitive in relation to customer expectations and product or service features.

Deadline

Tips to achieve a distinction grade

Before you start the final task, think about the following points.

- You need to consider the market position of the business, product or service you have selected. It will help if you can find out the market share. Alternatively assess the range of competition and the popularity of this business, product or service in the market in which it operates. Remember this might be local, regional, national or international. You can base this on sales and customer feedback, and also on the findings in your SWOT analysis.
- Now think about how the business could improve its market position and be more competitive. For example, could it change the price (by lowering costs), sell to other markets or adapt its USPs? You may find it helpful to look back at your SWOT analysis to see how many weaknesses could become strengths – and what action would be needed to change them.
- Finally, think about future developments that could affect the business. How could it take advantage of these – and perhaps turn a possible threat into an opportunity?

Remember that if you cannot make any suggestions, this conclusion must be based on evidence. However, most businesses can normally take some action to improve their market position!

Now do the following task.

Task 3 – Distinction grade

For this task you will use the information you have obtained for the tasks above, and those you carried out earlier to evaluate the market position of the business or a selected product.

Do this by answering the following question.

3   **a** **Identify** its position now in relation to its competitors.

    b Now **explain** whether you think this can be improved, and how this could be done. If you think it could not be improved at all, give a reason for your opinion.

Deadline

Unit 2.3 Stakeholder expectations

Choose a business you know well, either because you work there part-time or because one of your family works there. Alternatively, select a business you would like to know more about and which you can find out about on the Internet. You can use the same business that you investigated for sections 2.1 and 2.2, or you can choose a different business if you wish.

Task 1 – Pass grade

1 a **Identify** the key groups of stakeholders involved in the business.

b **Identify** at least **ONE** particular concern of each stakeholder group.

c **Explain** *why* each stakeholder group is likely to be interested in the activities of the business.

Deadline

Tips to achieve a merit grade

Before you start Task 2, think about the following points.

- How your business might change or adapt its activities because of stakeholder issues or concerns.
- Why it should take action. This is often easier if you think about the consequences of *not* doing anything.

Now answer the following questions.

Task 2 – Merit grade

2 a **Select THREE** stakeholder groups and **identify** one issue that may concern each group.

b For each issue you identified above, **explain**:

- how the business might adapt (or has adapted) its activities, and
- why it might need to take action (or has taken action in the past).

Deadline

Tips to achieve a distinction grade

Before you start the final task, think about the following points.

- A **key stakeholder group** is important to the business. The business cannot afford to ignore it!
- **Evaluate** means looking at the different responses the business could make and identifying the advantages and disadvantages of each one. Think about these in relation to the business *and* to the key stakeholder group *and* any other stakeholders who may be affected.
- Use this process to help you to identify which responses would be the most appropriate and the ones that would not. You are now in a position to identify these and give your reasons.

Now do the following task.

Task 3 – Distinction grade

3 a **Identify** a key stakeholder group that has an interest in your selected business and **suggest** the type of issues that would concern this group.

b For each issue you have identified, **evaluate** the different ways in which the business may respond (or has already responded) to these concerns.

Deadline

For this assessment you can choose a business you have investigated previously in this unit or a different business, if you wish.

Task 1 – Pass grade

1 a Carry out a PESTEL analysis to identify at least **SIX** key external influences which would concern your chosen business.

b In each case **identify** the effect these influences can have on the business.

Deadline

Tips to achieve a merit grade

You will find it helpful to read this before you start Task 2.

- Remember that a **key** external influence is one which has, or could have, a big impact on the business.
- Now explain what the business could do to respond to this influence. Remember that you must suggest responses which would have **successful** outcomes.
- Analyse your responses by identifying how useful each would be, so that you can decide which are the best suggestions.

Now answer the following questions.

Task 2 – Merit grade

2 a Identify at least **ONE** key external influence or event that could significantly affect your chosen business in the future.

b Suggest ways in which the business could successfully respond to the key influence(s) you identified above.

c Analyse your suggestions by explaining how each would help the business.

Deadline

Tips to achieve a distinction grade

Before you start the final task, think about the issues below.

- Refresh your memory by looking back at the key influences you have already identified.
- Then look at ways in which other businesses have adapted their activities because of these influences.
- You may be able to find specialist information and guidance about businesses on the Internet, for instance at the dti and CBI websites. See **www.heinemann.co.uk/hotlinks** (express code 1351T). Alternatively, if the influence relates to current or topical issues, you may find that many newspapers have reported on it. Another good source of information is the BBC website. Remember, then, to follow any useful links that are given.

Remember that if you genuinely think that for a particular influence, nothing could be done, then you must give a good reason why. One reason could be that the business has already taken the required or recommended action, in which case you must say what it has done.

Now do the following task.

Task 3 – Distinction grade

Recommend ways in which your selected business could successfully adapt its activities based on the key external influence(s) you have identified previously.

- If you can, **support your ideas** with recommendations and evidence obtained from at least one specialist source.
- Where you do not think adaptation would be possible or beneficial, **give evidence** to support your opinion.

Deadline

2.1 – Customer expectations

Over to you, page 97

1 **a** and **b** No specific answer possible.

c Suggested age range divisions could be: 0–10, 11–18, 19–39, 40–54, 55–65, 65+ to identify key differences in needs and wants at points where lifestyles are most likely to change.

2 This is more a question for debate than one with 'correct' answers and is meant to highlight the differences in personal expectations and also (hopefully) common elements between different age groups or even different gender groups at times. The following answers are therefore purely indicative but may be useful for tutors who want to add suggestions into the debate.

a buying this book – (key): good quality, informative, accurate/easy to understand; (important, not as critical): competitive price, interesting, rapid order processing.

b going into hospital as a patient – (key): high quality, clean, skilled/highly trained staff; (important, not as critical): comfortable, accurate information, friendly service, prompt/efficient service.

c buying a computer game – (key): exciting, competitive price, compatible with other items; (important, not as critical): good quality, challenging/meets personal needs, good availability.

d buying a television – (key): good quality, competitive price, guarantee or warranty; (important, not as critical): range of payment options, prompt delivery, expert installation/repair service.

e using an Internet banking service – (key): free of charge, meets personal needs, security of personal information; (important, not as critical): accurate, easy to understand information; not asked inappropriate personal questions, speedy/effective problem solving.

f buying an expensive photocopier for a firm – (key): competitive price, functional, regular/efficient servicing; (important, not as critical): prompt delivery, reliable performance, speedy/effective problem solving.

3 Ideas could include (from list): free of charge, interesting, challenging, meets personal needs, accurate/easy to understand information, security of personal information, not asked inappropriate personal questions, skilled/highly trained staff, friendly service, speedy/effective problem solving. Additional items could include: friendly staff, sympathetic tutor, new friends with similar interests, careers advice, range of facilities etc.

4 **a** **i** Touch of Yogurt not an appropriate name.

ii Harley Davidson image not conducive to perfume.

iii People want to see/touch pets before they buy.

iv 'Manufactured' bands often less successful over the long-term.

v Digital cameras made them obsolete.

b No specific answer possible.

Over to you, page 101

1 £1,700,000,000,000; £80,400,000,000; £5,400,000,000; £1,000,000,000.

2 The local market for used cars.

3 **a** Hire car firms, auto magazines, car ferry companies, repair garages, road builders, governments (car tax, roads), local authorities/builders (car parks), police, taxi firms, train companies, motorway service stations.

b Projected figures refer to predictions, actual figures are real sales.

c US, Canada and Mexico. (2 of) Size of country so long distances to be covered, size of population, high standard of living, cheap fuel, 'driving' culture.

d Africa, Iran, Iraq, India etc. Lower standard of living generally so few people can afford cars.

e Eastern and Central Europe, because projected growth between 2003 and 2004 is far higher than the others at +18.4 per cent. (Japan +0.9 per cent, Pacific rim +5.6 per cent, South America +8.8 per cent, Others + 9.5 per cent.)

f France – because sales are declining the most.

4 No specific answer possible, as priorities vary depending upon local needs.

Over to you, page 107

1 Suggested needs are as follows:

Retail buyers	Other business buyers	Government buyers (central and local)	Voluntary sector buyers
To buy popular goods which sell quickly to meet sales targets	Technical support and assistance	To obtain best value	To buy cheaply to minimise running costs
To maximise stock turnover – goods must sell quickly	One-to-one demonstration or presentation	To receive information on new products/services for start of budget year	Competitive discounts
To achieve margins by selling goods at best competitive price	Discounts and/or special payment terms	To receive detailed bids or tenders for expensive contracts	Ethically sourced and supplied products which link to the aims of the organisation
High quality, reliable products	Delivery and installation	For the work to be carried out as agreed in the contract and at the price stated	
Products which link with their reputation, image and ethics.	Spare parts service		
Additional benefits, e.g. known brand name or marketing campaign.	Other expert advice as required		

2 Suggestions are given below, although other appropriate examples may be found on the websites.

a Bank – business accounts, loans for businesses, business advice, merchant services (for card processing) etc.

b BT – broadband, Internet and web hosting services, wireless services to share data/Internet access/resources in a small office, contact centres, call monitoring, analysed bills, phone equipment etc.

c Office World – discounts and bulk purchasing, VAT invoices, monthly statements, free credit etc.

d Dell – servers, networking equipment, back-up equipment, workstations, networking software, technical support etc.

e Microsoft – business software and software licences, training, support services etc.

f Insurance – pensions, cargo and freight insurance, employers' liability, fleet car insurance, business advice.

g Car hire – prestige cars, leasing, preference services, replacement vehicles etc.

3 a (5 of) High quality/artistic, reasonable price, friendly service, prompt processing, skilled photographer, professional attitude, flexibility to meet specific individual needs.

b Advertisers and advertising agencies, large businesses (producing corporate booklets, college prospectuses etc.), newspapers and magazines, book illustrations.

c (4 of) Competitive price (will be more apt to shop around), cutting-edge style to differentiate from competition, prompt and efficient service, guarantee or speedy problem solving, flexibility to work around needs of the business/other integrated schedules.

d (3 of) Produce a corporate brochure to show his work, offer individual quotations, include testimonials from satisfied customers, offer guarantee of prompt delivery/successful work or free re-shoot.

Over to you, page 114

1 No specific answer possible, although ways in which this information is used include: (3 of) to improve their understanding of customers, to decide where to open/close branches, to decide which products to stock in specific branches, to identify their target markets, to decide where to advertise, to decide where to send mailshots.

2 a i *Company* magazine – single, female, employed, 21–35

ii *Esquire* magazine – single, male, employed, 21–35

iii *Country* magazine – rural, family, affluent

iv *Financial Times* – city workers, single/married, mainly male, very affluent but time-poor.

b

Publication	Car manufacturer/model
Company magazine ('for your freedom years')	Fiat Seicento, VW Beetle
Esquire magazine ('the sharper read for men')	Subaru Impreza, Audi TT
Country magazine ('when your heart is in the country')	Land Rover, Suzuki
Financial Times supplement ('how to spend it')	BMW, Jaguar

3 **a** Natural fabrics, e.g. pure wool, cashmere and leather – profile: older, affluent, professional.

   b Artificial fabrics, e.g. plastics and nylon – profile: all ages, non-affluent, probably large families.

   c Leisure wear, e.g. leggings and fleece tops – profile: young (mainly under 35), sporty/outdoor lifestyle.

   d Formal clothing, e.g. suits, overcoats, tailored skirts – profile: professional workers, older (30+), quite affluent.

   e Casual clothing, e.g. jeans, T-shirts – profile: young, students, non-affluent.

(1 of) Knowing the profile will help businesses to design and target the advertisement (e.g. which newspapers or magazines to use or which television programmes their key customers would watch), the stores in which to stock the product, the prices to charge.

Over to you, page 121

1 No specific answer possible.

2 No specific answer possible. Either decision is acceptable provided that appropriate reasons are given.

3 **a** This is a debatable issue – and depends upon the difference in interest rates. Some customers would prefer higher interest rates, no matter what. Others would prefer to sacrifice these (a little) for better service.

   b Because it costs banks less to concentrate on this.

   c **i** They think it will be a lot of work, they haven't much money saved, they can open a savings account somewhere else but still continue banking with their original bank.

      ii They can continue with their current practices until enough customers leave, then they would have to take action. They can work this out mathematically – as long as customers stay it doesn't pay them to change.

Section review, page 122

1 **a** All the possible consumers for a product or service.

   b An internal market exists when buyers and sellers are located in the same industry or business. In an external market, buyers and sellers are located in a different business.

   c (2 of) To buy goods customers will like to meet sales targets; to maximise stock turnover – goods must sell quickly; to achieve margins by selling goods at best competitive price; high quality, reliable products; products which link with their reputation, image and ethics; additional benefits, e.g. known brand name or marketing campaign.

   d (2 of) To provide one-to-one specialist/technical advice, to give demonstrations/presentations, to give after-sales advice/support, to customise a package to the customer's own needs, to arrange discounts/payment terms.

   e A group of customers who think in the same way, are attracted by the same features, use and value the product in the same way and have the same buyer behaviour.

   f (4 of) Age, gender, culture, socio-economic, family size, status in family, lifestyle.

   g Primary = original research (surveys, interviews); secondary = desk research (using files, published reports).

   h (2 of) Trade press, local newspapers, national newspapers, international publications, online sources.

   i (3 of) Changing the range, type or features of a product or service; adjusting the price; changing or increasing the source(s) of supply to improve availability; improving the benefits, e.g. better back-up or after-sales services.

   j (3 of) Respond quickly and make the necessary changes to products or services; wait and see. Only respond if absolutely necessary; disregard it and do nothing.

2 **a** It operates in a market for active, relatively affluent, mainly retired people aged 50 plus.

   b Age 50 plus, male/female, relatively affluent, children flown the nest, decision makers in family, more leisure time, not tied to school/college holidays. Culture: mainly white, middle class, but not exclusively so.

   c More people are living longer. Nearly 44 per cent of Britain's adults are over 50, by 2024, one in two adults will be over 50. As well as living longer, this group also has money to spend and is healthier than ever before. 66 per cent of this group took a holiday in 2001.

   d It has been responsive to new trends such as travel insurance, the growth in credit cards and the need for older people to obtain reliable investment advice. Its success is evidence that it has 'guessed right' in terms of the needs of its key customers.

e Possibly – but likely to be successful, initially, only in towns with a large population of retired people (e.g. some seaside towns on the south coast).

f The following are some suggestions but any other relevant ideas should be encouraged. Banks and retailers could offer special online services (with larger print screens etc.) for older people; specialist clothes shops could target older people; more products could be designed/devised for older people (e.g. easy to use microwave ovens/DVD players, small washing machines, clearer alarm clocks etc.); more frozen or chilled ready-meals for one.

2.2 – Competitive pressures

Over to you, page 126

1 **a** direct competition, **b** direct competition, **c** indirect competition, **d** indirect competition, **e** direct competition, **f** not in competition, **g** direct competition, **h** not in competition, **i** direct competition (both were in a battle for the No. 1 slot in 2000 and again released simultaneous singles at the end of 2003), **j** indirect competition.

2 **a** **i** Local – because of availability and distance customers prepared to travel. **ii** International because designer brands sell their products in many countries and compete against each other. **iii** Regional: the additional facilities/outlets/competitive advantage mean that people will travel to visit them. **iv** The cost of transporting equipment, setting it up and removing the debris all mean that these firms are apt to operate on a regional basis. **v** International: mobile phone handset manufacturers operate on a worldwide basis given the global market for phones and the fact they can gain economies of scale. **vi** Depends upon availability in the students' home area – local if more than one nearby, otherwise regional – again because of facilities. **vii** International because of costs of production and similar global tastes in relation to many forms of entertainment.

b **i** No answer possible for local/regional – depends upon students' own area. Arguably Thorpe Park, Legoland at

Windsor and Alton Towers are national attractions because of distinctive features. Legoland in Denmark and Disneyland Paris are European. Disneyworld Florida and Universal Studios in Los Angeles are international attractions.

ii Difference relates to scale and uniqueness plus attraction of brand name.

3 No specific answer possible as this will depend upon where your college is located and the courses offered. As a guide, direct competitors will include other colleges and sixth-form colleges in your locality (or 'travel' region); indirect will include private training providers, IT training facilities (e.g. at local libraries), Learn Direct, the BBC for learning materials on topics such as modern languages. The higher level the course/the more specialist the topic then the more likely it is that students will be attracted over a wide area. If your college also has a strong reputation in a specific area (or COVE status) this may increase its attraction.

4 No specific answer possible as this will depend upon current investigations. Tutors may wish to pre-select one or two which would interest students for class discussions.

Over to you, page 132

1 **a** Not competitive, because only one service covers a particular area and therefore has a monopoly; **b** very competitive, many suppliers and prices are constantly falling/special offers advertised; **c** competitive for cheaper models but less so for designer brands – price is the key indicator; **d** not competitive because the Royal Mail service currently has a monopoly; **e** very competitive because of the many greetings card shops and cut-price shops, too; **f** not very competitive because people are often desperate to find one in an emergency and there are often too few to go around – hence the increase in plumbing insurance policies from associated businesses like British Gas.

2 **a** Relatively stable, although there have been some changes in recent years, e.g. away from writing paper towards computer printing; **b** More dynamic because of fashion changes, e.g. heated brushes, hair straighteners; **c** Relatively stable, only change is in range of materials used or design; **d** Dynamic, because of growth of sales of digital cameras (although new trend for disposable cameras is increasing demand for traditional processing!); **e** Dynamic – floppy disks

to CDs to DVDs, including rewritable DVDs;
f Relatively stable although some changes to accommodate health concerns, dietary needs, age of dog etc.

3 a Growth stage – more competitors entering market, sales still rising and prices falling.

b Decline – far fewer buyers as more data is saved on CDs.

c Growth stage – sales increasing as product becomes more accepted.

d Decline – virtually obsolete as replaced by whiteboards.

e Growth stage – far more competition and sales increasing.

f Maturity stage – Buyers can 'pick and choose' from many suppliers, all of whom are keen to reduce prices to sell. Existing owners only replace in response to technological innovation.

g Development stage – new on market (2003/4), no competition as yet, additional services still to be made available in UK.

h Saturation – virtually everyone owns a washing machine. Only replaced when existing product fails. Prices now relatively low.

Over to you, page 137

1 a In a sealed carton, not a bag, so can be used over longer time without product deteriorating.

b Most well-known global online auction site.

c Simple, Scandanavian designed flat-pack furniture assembled by buyer to keep costs and prices low.

d Catalogue-based store where customers select goods from catalogue and queue to obtain, to keep costs and prices low.

e Traditional, safe (and customised) building bricks which can be assembled by very young children and by much older affectionados!

2 a Suggested completion: Opportunities: growing market for 3G, increasing demand for 3G handsets, can develop links/associations with additional related businesses, can enter into sponsorship agreements for future relevant events; Threats: four well-established, well-resourced competitors, actions by competitors to develop 3G and compete with video calls/fast

Internet access, competitors may offer 3G services at lower prices because reputation/size will enable economies of scale.

b No specific answer possible as this will depend upon the actions of competitors and the success of 3G in the future. It is suggested that tutors search online news sites (e.g. **news.bbc.co.uk**/ or **www.ananova.co.uk** or any newspaper online) to obtain the up-to-date situation. Selected reports could then be given to students for analysis.

3 This question has been included because students will be fascinated by the content of many of the websites – especially Framestore and the Moving Picture Company, and because the industry is likely to be very relevant to their interests and leisure activities. Tutors may enjoy accessing some of the sites beforehand to prepare for student feedback, particularly as the content is likely to change regularly. Suggested responses are given below although any other appropriate ideas should be encouraged based on current site content. *Note*: this activity is also very relevant to students studying Specialist Unit 8 of the award on Online Business.

a USPs will depend upon the company but are likely to include realistic effects using modern digital technology; named animators with a known reputation/track record in the industry; industry awards; previous work which has been highly regarded; a particular affinity with/reputation for certain types of effects.

b Extremely important. Each opportunity is a 'one-off' opportunity to communicate with the customer/client, the market is highly competitive yet special effects are not cheap. Customers will demand cutting-edge quality and consistency and will 'play safe' by opting for businesses with a known reputation, especially for expensive contracts.

c (4 of) Highly skilled and creative staff; cutting-edge equipment and software; finance (specifically working capital because most projects will only be paid for on completion and delivery, but may take many months); a skilled sales/promotions team to 'bid' for new projects; a cutting-edge website; industry contacts/networks (most are located in London); a good reputation in the industry.

d (2 of) Creative ideas that use existing technology in the most inventive ways; rapid adaptation of new technology to develop new effects; 'poaching' well-known creative staff from other agencies to improve own resources; minimising costs so bids are highly competitive or cheaper for same work; developing reputation for always delivering on time and within budget.

Over to you, page 139

1 i   **b** – Successful unless other leading jeans manufacturers copy it or a loophole is found to enable supermarkets to mount a new legal challenge.

ii   **b** – Cut-price airlines and Eurostar/the Channel Tunnel have all affected standard routes, e.g. Dover/Calais. Should be a successful strategy to operate such services – depending upon routes offered by other ferry operators, such as Brittany Ferries.

iii   **a** – Appropriate and should be successful as based on needs of own customers.

iv   **c** – Tesco is expanding its ranges to obtain greater market share in clothing. Debatable whether customers who want to pay more for clothes will want to buy these in Tesco.

v   **b** – Sainsbury's is responding to moves made by Tesco and Asda so is copying them. Will only be successful if brand is seen as competitive and range is equally as good – if not better.

vi   **a** – Sales of *The Independent* increased rapidly as a result. This was innovative for a broadsheet newspaper. (Expansion – option **c** – could also be argued as an acceptable response.)

vii   **b** – *The Times* was taking a more cautious approach but if sales increase is likely to roll this out across the country – with other newspapers copying the idea.

viii   **c** – Argos is likely to succeed given its reputation for good value/competitive prices. Established suppliers like IKEA may reduce prices to compete and may 'win' given Argos is untested in this market.

ix   **b** – The sofa market is highly competitive (hence all the TV adverts and discount/finance offers). Each supplier is constantly trying to think of new ways to outdo its competitors. May be successful – depends upon how many customers want to emulate Linda Barker!

x   **a** – OD2 is the main European business-to-business download service and was first in this market. It should be successful given the projected growth of this market.

2 a   The following are suggestions but students may have other, equally acceptable, ideas. (4 of) Extend opening hours, improve shopping online service, improve replacement stock procedure, change the signage, increase the number of cashpoints, reduce prices where possible, target specific promotions and make sure customers understand these.

b   (2 of) Increase range so that it is better than in superstores, offer advisory service from qualified pharmacists, reduce prices on selected products, include herbal and alternative medicines, offer first aid service, provide first aid/health leaflets. (*Note* Any suggestions relating to competitive edge or USPs should be encouraged.)

3 a   (3 of) Next, River Island, TopShop, Oasis or any other comparative outlets suggested by students.

b   (2 of) Improve stocks so current fashion trends are reflected more quickly; ensure prices are competitive; advertise in associated magazines or link to relevant TV programmes, e.g. Pop Idol; through sponsorship to improve brand recognition. Any other relevant suggestions should be encouraged.

Section review, page 140

1 a   Producing the same goods or service for the same market as other businesses.

b   Indirect competition, because these are similar goods/services for comparable markets.

c   No specific answer possible.

d   It has enabled small businesses to advertise and sell on a global basis.

e   A business with the largest market share in a market.

f   (3 of) Number of suppliers, difference between products on offer, the information available to buyers, whether suppliers can offer discounts or reduce prices, the ease of entry to the market, the availability of alternative or substitute products.

g   The point at which most people who want the product have one, sales fall, profits are reduced. The only way people can be tempted to purchase a new product is because of technological innovation or increased efficiency.

h Profits fall and sales decline so only the most efficient suppliers can afford to stay in the market.

i Strengths, weaknesses, opportunities and threats.

j Unique Selling Point. It is important because it differentiates the product or service from competitors' offerings.

k (2 of) Copy good ideas, reduce price, improve/adapt product, improve range, improve supply, increase outlets (e.g. online), expand into new markets.

2 a Strengths: USP = uniqueness, cult status, 'cool' image, brand name; good performance reports (especially Mini Cooper and Cooper S), fun to drive, wide range of fittings, many optional extras, diesel model. Weaknesses: lack of space for backseat passengers, lack of luggage space, questionable instrument layout, reports of gearbox and electrical problems. Opportunities: diesel cars and superminis very popular, sales increasing every year, best new car award in North America boosts sales, most appealing compact car vote in North America, car popular in Japan, Germany and Italy, car featured in Austin Powers films (other opportunities for similar promotions may be available given cult status). Threats: Highly competitive market, not currently in top five superminis, product reliability not as good as some competitors, improved performance/new models by competitors could threaten market share.

b No specific answer possible – it will depend upon actions by competitors and innovations by BMW reported on the websites.

c i It was different and unique, it won two awards which boosted sales, the 'cult image' appealed, drivers liked the high performance.

ii To consolidate and strengthen its market position.

iii A convertible may be popular, although probably less so than in America because of the more variable summer weather; a pick-up version is likely to be less appealing in Britain as these sell far more widely in the States.

iv Inspire, because it proves that compact cars and superminis can be successful in the American market.

d It is under considerable competitive pressure because virtually all large manufacturers have a supermini model and many have several. They are constantly improving these and including a wide range of equipment as standard.

e No specific answer possible as it will depend upon current investigations and updates. At present the Mini is increasing its market share and sales are strong in both the UK and US markets, but this may change in the future. Students should be encouraged to support any opinion with up-to-date facts, to prepare them for the type of evaluation they will do for their final assessment.

f i (1 of) Address problems of reliability and publish favourable new test reports; extend the product range still further, extend the range of optional extras, improve the instrument layout.

ii Start special promotions, copy good ideas from competitors but adapt these for the mini itself, continually improve the car, reduce the price, extend the range of standard fittings.

iii Sell in new markets, adapt the mini for new markets (e.g. a two-seater with more luggage space).

2.3 – Stakeholder expectations

Over to you, page 143

1 A wide range of acceptable answers may be given, for example:

Customers – product availability, help and advice, honest/courteous service, competitive price, product quality/safety, after-sales service etc.

Suppliers – open/honest negotiations, to be treated fairly, to be consulted about major changes to future orders.

Employees – to be treated fairly, to be paid a fair wage, to be consulted about important matters that will affect them, to have their legal rights upheld (e.g. health and safety, employment rights etc.).

Owner(s) – to receive a reward for their investment, to see the business thrive.

Banker(s) – to receive a reward for their investment, to be kept informed of important financial matters.

Trade unions/employer associations – to be consulted about proposed changes that will affect their members, to be able to represent their members' interests.

Sponsors – to receive a return on their investment and a higher profile through increased publicity and association with the event or person.

Local and national communities – to be informed about changes that will affect them, to have their views heard when they are concerned about a change or issue.

Pressure groups – to represent the views of their group to political and business leaders.

Tax collection authorities – to receive tax payments promptly and in full, according to the tax liability of individuals and businesses.

2 a (3 of) Employees, suppliers, supporters/customers, beneficiaries.

b (3 of) Employees (doctors, nurses, technicians, admin staff etc.), patients, GPs in the area, suppliers, trade unions.

c (3 of) Employees – direct and indirect e.g. pilots/crew, airport staff, airport catering workers etc.; customers, aircraft manufacturers, bankers, trade unions, environmental pressure groups, local communities, regional businesses, tax collection authorities.

d (3 of) Employees, local community, borrowers, local authority, authors, book publishers.

e (3 of) Band members, fans, recording company and associated staff involved in making/issuing/promoting CDs, record shop owners, DJs and radio presenters, MTV, tax collection authorities.

3 The aim of this question is to raise the issue of relative power of different stakeholder groups and how this can be increased by collective action or unanimous opinions. Tutors can extend the discussion to encompass the type of issues on which student views can be considered relatively easily (e.g. where they do not impact on other groups, are easy to implement) and those where action may be impossible (e.g. improving car parking or reducing course fees).

Over to you, page 149

1 No specific answer possible, but the organisations where concerns would be taken seriously should be small and quite highly dependent upon the stakeholder for some reason (e.g. as a part-time employee for a small business or a valuable customer to a local shop).

2 a i customers **ii** because they are more dependent upon their customers for profits

than their suppliers and want to please their customers – who want cheap milk.

b Break even means that there is enough income to cover all the costs. Market share relates to the percentage share of the whole market which that business has.

c If supply of milk is greater than demand, then prices will fall.

d There are a lot of suppliers so supermarkets can 'shop around'. This weakens the power of suppliers.

e Many farmers could cease milk production and diversify – if milk supplies fell this could result in a price rise; farmers could set up their own milk processing plant as a collective; milk processors could promote milk to try to increase demand; farmers could refuse to supply supermarkets at all unless they received an increase (but all would have to agree for this to be effective and they may not be able to afford to do this); farmers should form a pressure group with the aim of influencing customer opinion. Any other appropriate ideas should be encouraged.

3 A summary of some of the key facts students may be expected to find is given below, but tutors are advised to access the sites themselves for more detailed information.

a Banks – business accounts (deposit, loan, current); help with business plan; advice on starting a business; banking online; credit cards and merchant services; overdrafts, loans and other types of financing; e-commerce services; international services; business reports.

b Business Link – financing a business (types of finance, borrowing money, leasing/buying, selling shares, government support, family loans etc.); selling part of a business, business banking and services/finding the best account; grants and subsidies; cashflow management; help with financial problems.

c The Prince's Trust helps young people aged 18 to 30, who are unemployed but have an idea for a business. It provides low interest loans of (currently) up to £5,000, a grant of up to £1,500 in special circumstances, a test marketing grant of up to £250, marketing support and specialist advice plus ongoing advice from a volunteer business mentor.

d Shell LiveWIRE provides help, advice and support to entrepreneurs aged 16 to 30 on a wide range of business topics, e.g. general management, sales and marketing, business planning, finance and funding and personnel. It also runs an annual competition and gives awards totalling over £220,000 to winners.

Over to you, page 155

1 **a** It is the national organisation which represents member unions, acts as a voice for working people, promotes the rights of people at work by lobbying the government, political parties and employers. It campaigns to protect or improve people's rights at work.

b Because they are stronger and more effective if they work together with other unions. Plus they benefit from the TUC's resources and expertise.

c Support if they have a problem at work; improved pay and conditions, because many other people at work are members, they believe in trade unions, they gain industrial benefits/services and financial services.

d The TUC seeks to work with the government to win support for its policies, putting its case through research and reports and in meetings with ministers and civil servants.

e Trade unions aim to work in partnership with employers to improve businesses and services, and specifically: improving communication between employees and managers, negotiating pay and working conditions, encouraging companies to invest in training and development and acting as a positive force for change.

2 (Main points only are given. Tutors are recommended to check websites for updates.)

a BECTU – represents those working in broadcasting, film, theatre, entertainment, leisure, interactive media and allied areas, including permanently employed, contract and freelance workers in these sectors.

Member services: negotiating pay, conditions, safety and contracts; advice on copyright, credit card, financial discounts on insurance, legal services, AA membership, personal loans, mobile phone package; personal advice and representations for members, publishes *Stage, Screen and Radio* magazine.

b CWU – represents communication workers at the Post Office, BT, other telephone companies, cable TV, Girobank, Alliance and Leicester.

Member services: representation for members, legal services, financial and motoring services, education and training.

c GMB – represents various sectors, including several manufacturing and service sectors and trades, including public and private sectors.

Member services: help, assistance and advice to members, negotiate on their behalf, expertise on employment law, health and safety, pensions, terms and conditions of employment, weekly accident benefits, fatal accident benefit, funeral benefit, victimisation benefit.

d UNISON – represents workers in the public sector, in voluntary organisations and in private companies that provide services to the public.

Member services: member representation, education and training, welfare schemes, legal services, insurance and finance, holiday discounts.

e TGWU – represents a wide variety of sectors/occupations, including food and agriculture (e.g. horticultural and agricultural workers and stock handlers), manufacturing (e.g. automotive workers, engineers, textile workers, power workers), services (e.g. librarians, caretakers, rent collectors), construction (e.g. bricklayers, scaffolders), transport (e.g. bus drivers, freight and container handlers, taxi drivers) and the voluntary sector.

Member services: representation for members, education and training service, journals and information booklets, facilities for reduced-rate holidays and short breaks, special associations for young members and retired members.

f AMICAS-AEEU is the largest union representing manufacturing employees. The AEEU section includes engineers, plumbers, electricians etc.

Member services: representation for members, free legal advice, stakeholder pension, financial advice, various types of insurance, travel services, health plans and training courses.

3 **a** No answer possible.

b Benefits at Richer Sounds, like benefits at many companies, increase for long service employees to reward loyalty.

Over to you, page 166

1 a (3 of) High profile amongst football fans; association with young, sporty image; association with popular and successful event; increased promotions at a cheaper price than would be possible through normal advertising methods; greater brand recognition throughout Europe.

b No specific answer possible.

2 a Tutors are recommended to check current concerns of the Association. At the time of writing these included the extension of broadband to rural communities, tourism in rural areas, taxation on farm lettings, housing problems, farming and agricultural issues.

b (2 of) They enable similar-minded people to group together to voice concerns, they give more power to disparate or less influential stakeholder groups, they can publicise social or ethical issues that people may not otherwise know about, they can develop networks to lobby politicians in Britain and Europe.

3 There are no specific answers to this question, but the following are some suggestions.

a In all probability you would want staff to be fairly flexible, especially if other staff were absent or there was an urgent deadline to meet.

b If conditions and pay are good, career prospects excellent and relationships between employees/employer are good, then staff are more likely to be flexible or willing to work additional hours without pay than if they are in a boring or low paid job. However, even then employees will feel 'put upon' if the situation goes on too long.

c The aim of this debate should be for students to appreciate that opposing views often create a balance of power – even when they may be extreme in themselves. The CBI may be seen as having an important voice for business entrepreneurs, who need to try to make a profit whilst coping with other pressures. Yet it can also be viewed as authoritarian and repressive. The TUC and unions can be seen as an important lobby for employees, who would lack power otherwise. Alternatively, they can be seen as creating difficulties with a 'one size fits all' approach, especially for small business owners who need flexibility. Tutors are recommended to add spark to the debate by acting as devil's advocate to encourage consideration of aspects that the students may not naturally identify.

4 a Boycotts are more likely to be successful when: virtually all consumers/stakeholders support it, the boycott gets wide media coverage, the issue is emotive or almost impossible to defend, the issue is highly topical, the boycott is publicly supported by politicians/celebrities (which also sustains media coverage), taking action will save the company money, taking action will not affect other key stakeholders, not taking action could be disastrous.

b and **c** No specific answer possible.

Section review, page 167

1 a Any person or organisation that has an interest in a business.

b Because key stakeholders are important groups that businesses dare not ignore.

c (3 of) Opening hours and availability of goods; good quality or value for money; the range of goods or services, additional facilities and services (such as free delivery); the attitude of staff; the efficiency and reputation of the organisation including speed of response and staff expertise; the overall success or performance of the business.

d (2 of) There are few buyers for the product or service, there are many other suppliers, the market is highly competitive, the supplier is highly dependent upon the customer.

e (2 of) That your money is safe, that you will receive a return on your investment, that the business is financially sound.

f (4 of) To be treated fairly, to be paid a fair wage, to be consulted about important matters that will affect them, to work in a safe environment, to have a considerate boss, to work with other people who are friendly and cooperative, job security, to receive essential training/opportunities to progress.

g (3 of) To gain a better return for the cost than other methods of advertising; to get greater brand recognition among their target market; to promote the business in their own region; to demonstrate social or community responsibility; to improve or adjust their image.

h Because of scandal or controversy which they feel would affect their image or because the club's performance or pop star's following is falling.

i (2 of) Air pollution, litter and waste disposal, noise, traffic, crime or environmental health.

j (3 of) Buying goods from suppliers who exploit children or female labour in developing countries, environmental damage, dangerous working conditions, payment of unacceptably low wages, tax avoidance/evasion, supply of socially harmful products (or other appropriate suggestions).

2 a (6 of) The Environment Agency, the US Navy, the owners of Able UK, local residents, Friends of the Earth, the employees of Able UK, local people looking for a job, other conservation groups/supporters of local feeding and breeding sites.

b Yes, because he backed their opinion/campaign.

c Although Able UK was involved in a contentious issue, it followed due legal process to apply for a licence and claims it has the skills/expertise necessary and could provide work for local people. It blamed the Environment Agency for the problem. Whether it should have bid to dismantle the ships in the first place is far more debatable!

d Tutors should check the current situation on the FoE website.

2.4 – External influences

Over to you, page 171

1 a Sales increase in hot weather in cases **i**, **iv**, **vii** and **x**. Sales decline in all other areas – including cat food, because cats sleep more!

b (10 of) Ice lollies, lager, salad ingredients, mayonnaise, shower gel, portable barbecues, food for barbecues, marinades, charcoal, suntan lotion, white wine, bread rolls, cooked meats, sun hats, sunglasses – or any other appropriate ideas.

2 a Sars virus, Iraq war, 9/11, cost of aircraft fuel, increased airport tax, Bali/Turkey bombings, consumers booking later, consumers designing own holidays, consumers booking on the Internet.

b i Extra capacity would please the industry.

ii Industry would be concerned about customers losing confidence in flying.

iii Industry would consider spending on holidays will increase.

iv Additional capacity again.

v Concerns over fears of travelling affecting bookings.

vi More travel firms would find it profitable to offer Internet bookings.

vii Concerns that costs will increase and affect bookings.

viii More people choosing flexible dates/booking later/wanting off-peak holidays or short breaks.

ix Greater demand for 'singles plus kid' holidays/family hotels with kids clubs and babysitting services.

x Falling demand for expensive European holidays – more people go long haul, depending upon other factors.

c i Political, **ii** Social issue, **iii** Economic, **iv** Technology, **v** Political, **vi** Technology, **vii** Environment, **viii** Legal, **ix** Social trend, **x** Economic.

Over to you, page 182

1 a Current interest rates, proposed changes to interest rates, how quickly he can repay the money, future business prospects.

b Fixed rate – advantage is knowing the cost cannot increase, disadvantage is that if interest rates fall he will be paying above market rate.

c If business is doing well, then he will be less worried about variable rate affecting the payments. He will want the option to pay off earlier if this is possible, without any penalties.

2 a During a boom in the economy, to control or restrain consumer demand which may cause prices to increase (inflation).

b Because the effect is not felt for some time – so caution is needed. If the change is too severe, this may provoke a recession.

c i Annoyed as he will have to pay more in service charges for the loan.

ii Concerned that the increase in VAT may dampen consumer spending.

iii Pleased because their savings will earn more interest.

iv Worried that their mortgage payments and the cost of essential household items will both increase.

3 The following are suggested answers but any appropriate ideas should be accepted. Two suggestions are required in each case.

a Aircraft manufacturers, shipyards, arms manufacturers.

b Airlines with routes to that country, businesses who buy from suppliers in that country, businesses who sell to that country.

c Pubs, restaurants, hotels.

d Architects, construction companies, building material suppliers.

e Manufacturers of rolling stock and other rail equipment (positively), road builders (negatively).

f Museums, theme parks, theatres, suppliers of security staff.

4 Suggested answers only. Other appropriate ideas should be accepted.

a Local government issues (e.g. car parking for shoppers, road changes etc.), government support for small business; interest rates and taxation.

b Foreign trade regulations, FO business and travel warnings; interest rates and exchange rates.

c Foreign trade regulations, changing regimes in countries where suppliers are based; tax rates, consumer spending.

d Government priorities, government support for business; interest rates and rates of taxation (specifically fuel tax).

e Planning regulations, government priorities; business cycles, interest rates.

Over to you, page 188

1 Only **b**, **h** and **i** – the specific items – are not meaningless.

2 a Suggested answers only. Other appropriate ideas should be accepted. One trend and one issue to be identified in each case.

i Population changes, changing lifestyles (specifically drink/driving laws etc.); safety of public transport, crime and safety of individuals.

ii Changing patterns of work, home working, increased standards of living,

increase in Internet use; product quality, health scares, transport/travel safety.

iii Standards of living, changing lifestyle; product quality (specifically chemical content), garden products environmentally friendly.

iv Population changes, increased ethnic mix; product quality, animal testing.

b Suggestions may include: changing patterns of work (for own employees, also for offering flexible breaks); increased standards of living (greater demand for better quality accommodation), changing lifestyles (e.g. introduce spa/keep-fit facilities, offer no-smoking rooms and Internet access). Accept bookings over the Internet. Offer vegan/vegetarian choices in the dining room. Be aware of directors' pay concerns (promote ethical practices) and worries about health scares (train staff well, have or develop reputation for excellent hygiene standards).

3 a No specific answer possible – it will depend upon current recalls.

b (2 of) In case anyone is injured, to protect reputation, to demonstrate social responsibility.

Over to you, page 196

1 a Suggested answers only. Other appropriate answers should be accepted.

i Ability to vote by mobile phone, over the Internet or by digital television. Future – video clips to mobile phones.

ii More people buying CDs or downloading over the Internet. Future: links between record companies and websites for payable downloads.

iii Fewer people wanting video format, more people buying DVDs from superstores. Future: movie downloads on demand.

iv Computerised appointment systems and patient records. Future: digital photos of patients sent to consultants for opinions, online consultations, e-prescriptions direct from surgeries to pharmacies.

v Bar coding, electronic scanning, electronic funds transfer at point of sale (EFTPOS), computer database of customers/buying habits, online shopping. Future: electronic trolley/basket which checks out goods automatically without need for check-out operator; wireless tagging of stock.

vi Banking online, electronic transfer of funds. Future: better security of cash machines plus online sites and identification of users – including iris scanning.

vii Electronic transfer of graphics and files from reporters, electronic publishing, Internet information sites. Future: more use of colour, choice of formats (broadsheet or tabloid), e-publication of whole newspaper for subscription.

b No answer possible.

2 Suggested answers only. Appropriate alternative answers should be accepted.

a Braille buttons/verbal information in lifts, ramps for wheelchair access, disabled toilets.

b Review of pay rates and pay scales, job analyses/evaluations to check differences between jobs, monitoring of pay/equal opportunities policies.

c No-smoking areas, no-smoking workplaces, regular fire drills, risk assessments, safety notices.

d Adjusting hours for young employees, checking hours and overtime for other employees.

e Introducing family-friendly policies, ensuring there are formal grievance and disciplinary procedures in place and employees are informed.

f Issuing instructions not to use work phones when driving, issuing instructions to managers not to phone staff when driving.

3 a Suggestions could include: (3 of) fraud by a senior executive or governor, serious injustice in relation to an employee or student, scandal over results or assessments, website failure at critical time, hacker gaining access to confidential student or financial information, fire or flood.

b This will depend upon the type of issues identified. Answers should include solving problem quickly, prompt and honest communications to media and all stakeholders.

c This will depend upon the students' own values and perceptions of social issues. Some

students may only be concerned about immediate events that would affect them personally, e.g. eating at an unhygienic restaurant. Others will be more concerned about broader issues – whether or not they are likely to gain or lose personally.

Section review, page 197

1 a Political, economic, social, technological, environmental, legal.

b (2 of) Easier to trade with countries with good international relations, businesses which supply goods may not be paid if there are political problems, business which buy goods not be able to obtain them if there are political problems, business employees abroad may be in danger if there are political problems.

c (2 of) General elections, local elections, government spending priorities, local council plans and regulations.

d A boom is when the economy is doing well. Consumers are spending, there is low unemployment, businesses are producing as much as possible and are optimistic. A slump is the opposite. People are buying much less, businesses have unsold stocks and cut production, unemployment rises.

e (2 of) They pay more in service charges on their loans, they earn more on their financial reserves, they may sell less because consumers may reduce their spending.

f (2 of) GM foods, cost of energy in the future, nuclear waste, directors' pay/bonuses if not linked to company performance (or any other appropriate answers: testing on animals, content of food products, recycling etc.).

g (2 of) Ability to create/capture and transfer files, data and graphics electronically, increased home working, virtual teams, data capture whilst on the move, film clips on websites (or any other appropriate answers).

h (2 of) Health and safety laws, employment law, consumer protection laws, product safety, laws on money laundering, data protection laws, computer use laws, laws relating to methods of work, company law, partnership law.

i A general rise would mean that share prices are increasing. This will increase the overall value of the business.

j (2 of) It destroys investor confidence in business, it can trigger a fall in stock prices generally, it can have a negative effect on the economy, it puts pressure on the government to take action, it affects all stakeholders in the business.

2 Suggested answers only – other appropriate ideas should be encouraged.

a Children's nursery: (4 of) Political: type of food served to children; Economic: low unemployment/growing economy means demand for places likely to increase; Technology: CCTV security systems; Environment: emphasis on recycling; Legal: vetting of all staff, plans to extend parental leave. Action could include: (3 of) giving healthy snacks/drinks, using recycled paper for play materials, using CCTV to monitor security/check main entrances/exits; vetting law must be complied with, interview process should be rigorous and easily checked.

b Local pub: (4 of) Political: late night policing costs, no-smoking zones; Economic: increase in business rates; Social: fast-paced lifestyle, greater demand for healthy food; Technology: broadband jukeboxes; Environment: recycling; Legislation: age discrimination. Action could include: (3 of): setting up/extending no-smoking zone, serving healthy/quick snacks, installing new jukebox for entertainment, recycling plastic/glass bottles, employing older people.

c Smoothie maker manufacturer: (4 of): Economic: interest rates, economic forecasts, Social: increasing health consciousness, dislike of additives; Technology: electronic ordering, selling from website; Environment: minimising packaging materials, biodegradable materials; Legislation: mobile phone use, age discrimination. Action could include (3 of): reducing loans to avoid higher interest rate payments, expanding production to link to economic forecasts and social trends, focusing adverts on health issues, ordering components electronically, selling on-line, reviewing type of packaging materials used, ensuring travelling employees not expected/asked to use mobiles when driving, reviewing interviewing/employment policies.

d Town centre car park: (4 of) Political: congestion charging; Economic; economic forecast (growth means more spending by shoppers); Social: greater car use/ownership; Technology: machine payment by cash/credit cards, CCTV security systems; Legislation: use of mobiles when driving; age discrimination. Actions could include (3 of): expansion of car park or increasing prices if spaces are limited (or converting to 'short stay' only), installing automatic payment machines, installing better security systems, putting up notices to remind drivers about mobile phone laws; recruiting older car park attendants.

e College: (4 of) Political: content of vending machines, university top-up fees; Economic: low unemployment; Social: students have part-time jobs; Technology: ordering supplies electronically, 3G phones, growth in Internet/broadband use; Environment: recycling; Legislation: staff vetting, age discrimination, parental leave. Actions could include (3 of): reviewing content of vending machines, offering healthy food in refectories, offering financial advice workshops to students applying for university; ordering stationery and other materials online, accepting student applications online for some courses, contacting absent students by mobile/email; recycling waste paper, checking employment policies, take account of all legal issues.

f Town centre foodstore: (4 of) Political: congestion charging, economic forecast, business rates increase, house prices rising (will affect consumer spending); Social: fast paced lifestyle, organic foods, healthier options; Technology: online ordering, selling online, CCTV security; Environment: recycling; Legislation: age discrimination. Actions could include (3 of): having own car park for customers (if possible); offering home delivery service; online shopping service; reviewing stock to include more organic foods/healthier options; having 'healthy' sandwich bar for lunches, buying online, improving security systems; increasing recycling of packaging materials/waste; reviewing employment policies and employing older workers.

Unit 3 Investigating financial control

In this section you will find:

Unit overview and tutor guidelines

This unit provides a basic introduction to key financial aspects of business operations. The major topics covered are profit and loss, break even, cash flow, budgeting and recording transactions.

Tutors may wish to bear the following points in mind when teaching the unit.

- Business finance inevitably requires students to manipulate numbers. It sometimes seems as if human beings fall into two categories – those who have no problem relating to numbers and those who struggle. Students who fall into the latter category will require plenty of support. They need to realise that almost everyone who works in a business has some involvement with money – for example, the department they work in will probably have a budget. Business owners need to understand figures to be able to check they have made a profit – as they will learn if they study Specialist Unit 9. Julian Richer's early problems, detailed on the StudentZone, may also be informative! It is worth mentioning that households have to use many similar principles to manage their money. For example, not only does money have to be available for food and other daily items, some also has to be set aside for major expenditure items, such as a new car or a holiday.

- It will help if students can fully understand what the figures mean. For example small groups of students could be set up as individual businesses in a supply chain (wholesaler/retailer/customer) using Monopoly-type money and buying and selling pencils, paper clips or other low value items. This type of situation could be used to illustrate concepts such as profitability, price, profit margin and perhaps even competition.

- Students can also be helped over the numeracy hurdle by introducing topics using simplified illustrations – for example calculating profit using small, whole numbers. This is the approach adopted in the Student Book. Students who are wary of numbers but who enjoy IT should find that using spreadsheets helps their motivation and understanding.

- At any particular time there are normally newspaper headlines about businesses which are doing well and making better profits every year, such as Tesco in 2004. There will also be examples of businesses which are in trouble – Marks & Spencer had declining profits over the same period. These types of examples can be used to explain the basic concept of profitability. Individual students may have direct experiences through their part-time jobs or through relatives who have perhaps been awarded bonuses during good times or threatened with redundancy when there are problems. Obviously, sensitivity will need to be used if this type of outcome is discussed in class. Whichever examples are used, questions such as 'Where does the income come from and how can the amount be increased?' 'What does the business spend its money on and can we reduce this amount?' should help students to appreciate the relevance of profit and loss. After this, the idea of not-for-profit organisations can be introduced – including the concept of break even. Examples can be used to illustrate this – for instance, if a local council's revenue falls, it has less to spend on keeping the streets clean or maintaining the parks.

- During discussions about practical examples of expenditure students could also be introduced to the idea of fixed and variable costs – for example a café has to pay business rates even if it doesn't sell a single meal. On the other hand, the more customers it feeds, the more food it has to buy. Another useful example is the type of household expenses which must be paid even though the family has gone on holiday – and those that are not – so mortgage payments or rent are a fixed cost but the weekly spending on food is a variable cost.

- Fixed and variable costs lead nicely on to the concept of break even. A useful first step is to explain break even as total revenue = total costs. At the outset, most students find it easier to understand break even by looking at (and drawing) break even charts rather than using the formula. The easiest way is to start by drawing the chart in stages – axes, fixed cost, variable cost and income – without using figures. Ultimately, students need to practise drawing a chart (or charts) for themselves as well as putting figures into a formula to calculate break even.

- Students learning about cash flow need to realise that, at the end of the day, businesses can only survive if they have enough money in the bank to pay their bills when these are due. It may be worth describing what happens if creditors (often a bank or the Inland Revenue) force a business into bankruptcy. This often happens because bills have been left unpaid, which in turn means that the unfortunate business has not enough money in its bank account. The consequence to the workforce (who may be owed outstanding wages) also helps students to understand the ramifications of poor cash flow management.

- Students also need to understand the meaning of credit trading and the links to cash flow forecasts. Credit trading can easily be illustrated by discussing how an object in the classroom would be purchased – for example talking through the chronological sequence of events (and timescale) when the college bought a chair. It is probable that the chair was paid for several weeks after it was delivered. This discussion could be extended to what steps the furniture supplier might take if the college did not pay within a reasonable time. Students need to practise completing cash flow calculations, firstly for one month and then extending this to several consecutive months. This will help students who are overwhelmed by the design or layout of a cash flow forecast. In this case, repeating the forecast over a period of months consolidates understanding. All the time the emphasis should be on the effects the various figures have on the final bank balance. For variety, and to increase understanding, students should experiment on a spreadsheet by introducing their own changes on a 'what if' basis. For example 'What if half of the customers paid a month late?'

- Students studying credit control could be asked to draft a letter to a customer who is two weeks late paying a bill. Alternatively (or as well) students could role play a telephone call for the same scenario.

- A possible starting point with budgets is to remind students that local councils have to break even. They could then be asked to imagine that they are the manager of the department that looks after the traffic lights. They do not see the bank statements and have no idea how much money is coming in or being spent overall by the council. However they do have to authorise spending on maintenance materials, overtime etc. The basic question is – how can this spending be controlled so that, overall, the council breaks even? The answer is through a budget which tells the manager how much can be spent (normally each month) under various headings of expenditure. At the end of each month each manager is told how much has actually been spent under each heading. This provides an opportunity to correct any problems. Students can reinforce their understanding of these ideas by carrying out calculations – starting with simple ones for a single month. They could then discuss what action should be taken about any major variances. Another approach to the topic would be to suggest that everyone operates some form of budget system since they have a limited amount of income and have to make decisions about how to spend it. Tutors may also like to discuss the type of budgetary system that operates in the school or college and how this affects their own spending or that of their department.

- All students will be given receipts for some of the purchases they make and could be encouraged to provide examples. They could then be asked why they might need to retain the receipt and why the shop also needs to have a record of the transaction. The latter discussion leads ultimately to payments required to be made to the Inland Revenue and Customs and Excise (VAT). Samples of receipts can be examined to discover the various items of information they contain and to suggest why each item is included. If EPOS receipts are available, it would be interesting to look at the extra types of information (such as marketing promotions etc) which are often added. Students can also be encouraged to observe the type of cash register used when they pay for items and services. This could almost be turned into an "I-spy" game – who has spotted the most? If a significant number of students have jobs in the retail trade, their first-hand experience could be used. The discussion could be broadened to include suggestions as to why each type of business has chosen the particular type of equipment – from the market trader with a cash box to a superstore's sophisticated EPOS system.

- Students are unlikely to have direct experience of petty cash and day books. The former can be introduced by pointing out that even the largest organisations, such as Rolls-Royce, which sells aircraft engines for millions of pounds, will still pay some local tradespeople in cash – such as the newsagent who delivers the *Financial Times* to the MD's office, and the local taxi firm. In addition, even small businesses may be involved in numerous purchase and sales transactions each day. Each of these needs to be recorded in one of the day books – which allows them to be categorised before they are transferred to the main accounts.

- Fraud or theft is an unpleasant subject but, unfortunately, a reality in the business world. Tutors may like to note that although the scheme uses the term 'fraud', these types of offences are more accurately described as 'theft', as explained on page 263 of the Student Book. Students will have noticed CCTV cameras in shops, staff using a key or their own pin number before they can use a till and security guards patrolling some of the larger stores. Some may also be aware of anti-theft regulations they have had to observe in part time jobs – for example theft being punished by instant dismissal, the employer having the right to stop and search and not being allowed to serve friends or relatives who visit retail premises in which they are

This section contains 22 additional activities and case studies designed to assess progress and reinforce learning and understanding. Each covers a key area of the mandatory units in the scheme where you may wish to provide additional practical activities for your students. A cross referenced activity exists at 2.3.3.

3.1 – Profit and break even

Activity 3.1.1 – Profit and loss – true or false?

This is an introductory exercise designed to help students to grasp the key concepts in profit and loss calculations: for example that profit/loss is found by deducting expenditure from income. It will help them to understand that private/commercial organisations need to make a profit whereas governments and charities aim to break even.

Answer

The following statements are true: 2, 4, 5, 8, 11.

The correct answers to the others are given below.

1 Profit is the excess of income over expenditure. The total amount of money earned by a business is income or revenue.

3 Local governments try to balance income and expenditure.

6 Businesses need to make a profit to provide income for owners/shareholders and also from re-investment.

7 Charities receive money from many sources as well as collecting boxes. These include other forms of donations, bequests and shops.

9 Charities can only spend up to their total income.

10 Businesses make a profit when they earn more than they spend.

12 Expenditure is greater than income so the £5,000 is a loss.

Activity 3.1.2 – Profit or loss?

This activity complements the previous one. This time, students gain a further appreciation of the nature of profit and loss by carrying out calculations. They are then asked to label their result as either profit, break even or loss. It is important to emphasise that expenditure is *always* deducted from income, even if the resulting figure is negative (a loss).

Answer

Income (£)	Expenditure (£)	Difference (£)	Result
400	300	100	Profit
25,000	25,000	0	Break even
4,650	5,521	–871	Loss
105,800	96,425	9,375	Profit
5,654	5,653	1	Profit
37,522	37,522	0	Break even
52,000	61,750	–9,750	Loss
270,000	150,000	120,000	Profit

Activity 3.1.3 – Where does the money come from?

This activity helps the students to become familiar with the formula:

Revenue = number sold × selling price

It also helps them to understand that most organisations have a range of products and that this formula must be applied in each case and then the resultant totals added together to give the grand income total.

Students could also be reminded that commercial organisations may occasionally have other sources of income, such as selling property. Not-for-profit organisations normally have several sources of income.

Answer

1 £10,350 + £3,450 = £13,800

2 £10,846

3 £108,075 + £56,250 + £107,960 + £35,970 = £308,255

4 See table below.

5 £9,076

Product	Selling price (£)	Number sold	Revenue (£)
A	50.00	25	1,250.00
B	27.50	47	1,292.50
C	210.00	5	1,050.00
D	16.50	125	2,062.25
E	75.50	18	1,359.00
		Total	7,013.75

Activity 3.1.4 – Fixed or variable – that is the question!

The last activity looked at income. This one looks at the other component of profit/loss calculations – expenditure. Students should already be familiar with the fact that businesses normally have many items of expenditure and that these can be broken down into fixed and variable costs. This activity reinforces this point by asking them to split a list of expenditure items into the two categories. They could be reminded that indirect and direct costs are two terms which mean the same as fixed and variable respectively.

Answer

1

Fixed costs		Variable costs	
Item	**£**	**Item**	**£**
Rent	6,000	Cars	8,000
Business rates	1,500	Boats	3,000
Telephone	560	Planes	5,000
Gas	700	Tools	1,500
Water	300	Paint	300
Electricity	560	Packaging	900
Insurance	1,100		
Total	**10,720**	**Total**	**18,700**

2 Reduced costs, fixed = £9,648, variable = £17,765

Activity 3.1.5 – Maximising profit

This activity develops the theme of the last two exercises. Commercial organisations are always looking for ways to increase profit (or reduce losses!). There are two main ways of achieving this – increasing income and/or reducing costs. In the exercise, costs are split (as before) into fixed and variable. Students should also be reminded that *all* businesses, including those which aim to break even, try to keep costs to a minimum whilst at the same time maximising income.

Answer

Any from the lists below or other appropriate suggestions.

> **Maximise income by:**
> Attracting more customers by marketing (various methods of advertising, exhibitions, leaflets through letterboxes etc.)
> Reducing prices to increase number of customers and number of sales per customer
>
> Increasing customers by buying out a competitor
> Increasing product range
> Selling complementary products, e.g. shoe shop selling shoe polish
> Increasing prices – without losing core customers
>
> **Reduce fixed costs by:**
> Finding/negotiating better contracts for telephone, utilities, consumable materials (all acceptable as individual items)
> Buying second-hand equipment/furniture
> Reducing heating costs
> Moving to cheaper premises (less rent, rates)
> Limiting phone calls – using email more
> Mechanising manual work
>
> **Reduce variable costs by:**
> Obtaining a better deal from suppliers – reduced price, maybe for bulk purchase
> Moving to a cheaper supplier
> Using less labour
> Automating processes
> Using cheaper type of material (e.g. plastic instead of wood)
> Using less material
> Reducing scrap
> Increasing productivity

Activity 3.1.6 – Would Penny break even?

This activity brings together the individual topics already covered in this unit. Break even allows businesses to look at possible decisions and ventures to decide whether or not they are likely to be profitable. The exercise asks the students to construct a break even chart, label the main features and extract various types of information. It also asks them to use the break even formula as an alternative approach.

It could be useful to encourage students to discuss the pros and cons of the two ways of analysing break even. For example, the chart is time-consuming and less accurate *but* it produces a visual display of the overall situation.

Answers

1 and **2**   Tutor to check student chart (see overleaf).

3   125

4   75

5   £600 loss, £200 profit, £600 profit

6   Break even $= \dfrac{1,000}{12-4} = \dfrac{1,000}{8} = 125$

7   £12 − £4 = £8

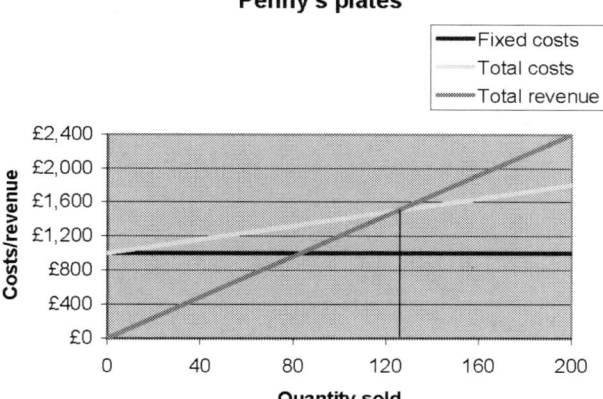

Penny's plates

Legend:
— Fixed costs
— Total costs
— Total revenue

(y-axis: Costs/revenue, £0 to £2,400; x-axis: Quantity sold, 0 to 200)

8 Firstly, by looking at the chart, Penny knows that she must sell at least 125 plates per month to break even. If she sold less than this, she would lose money. Above the break even point, she can work out how much profit she would make for any given level of sales.

A more in-depth analysis would include the fact that Penny needs to live! Even at sales of 200 plates per month she is only making £600 – about £150 a week (on which she may pay tax). She may have to decide whether she would be able to produce and sell more if she wants to improve her standard of living.

3.2 – Cash flow management

Activity 3.2.1 – Elements of a cash flow forecast

The activities in this section progressively take students from the simple structure of a cash flow chart to charts which involve several months' analysis and also the opportunity to use spreadsheets to carry out the analysis.

This first activity asks them to explain the various headings of a basic cash flow chart and then to prove that they understand the relationship by completing a forecast from a brief set of notes. The successful completion of this exercise will lay the foundations for the following activities in this section.

Answer

1 Suggested explanations are given below. Other appropriate answers should be accepted.

A **Income** The total amount of money received by the business from all sources. For commercial organisations this would be mainly from customers.

B **Expenditure** The total amount of money spent by the business – including materials, wages, heating etc. The different types of expenditure are normally itemised under this heading.

C **Net cash flow** The difference between income and expenditure (income – expenditure). This shows the net amount of money flowing into or out of the business's bank account in the period which is being assessed.

D **Monthly summary** A heading for the last three items which collectively show what has happened to the cash flow situation that month.

E **Opening bank balance** The amount of money in the bank account at the start of the month. It is identical to the closing balance figure from the month before.

F **Net cash flow** This item appears twice (see above). The second time the figure is copied from the one above.

G **Closing balance** The amount of money in the bank on the last day of the month. It is found by subtracting the net cash flow from the opening bank balance. It also becomes the opening balance for the next month. If the figure is negative, the business will probably need a loan or an overdraft.

2

Mark's cash flow forecast – March	
Income	£2,400
Expenditure	£1,100
Net cash flow	£1,300
Monthly summary	
Opening bank balance	£1,500
Net cash flow	£1,300
Closing balance	£2,800

3 It enables Mark to check that his bank balance will remain positive and allows him to take action if he is forecast to spend more than he receives in a given month. This may mean reducing spending or obtaining a bank overdraft.

Activity 3.2.2 – A1 Alarms

This is the first of a sequence of four activities based on the case study A1 Alarms, a business run by Altaf Patel. The sequence develops three themes – looking at more complex cash flow forecasts, creating and using a spreadsheet and carrying out 'what if' analysis.

This first activity extends the analysis needed for the last exercise by asking the students to complete a cash flow forecast for one month and then answer some straightforward questions to check that they understand the principles involved. A photocopiable form is provided on the page following the activities section.

Answer

1

A1 ALARMS - CASH FLOW FORECAST						
	July £	August £	Sept £	Oct £	Nov £	Dec £
INFLOWS/RECEIPTS						
Sales	200,000					
Loans received	0					
Total income	200,000					
EXPENDITURE						
Materials	70,000					
Wages/salaries	120,000					
Capital items	0					
Rent and rates	700					
Electricity	650					
Stationery	100					
Telephone	200					
Advertising	2,000					
Insurance	250					
Loan repayment	12,000					
Sub total of expenditure	205,900					
Net cash flow	-5,900					
MONTHLY SUMMARY						
Opening bank balance	10,000					
Net cash flow	-5,900					
Closing bank balance	4,100					

2 The net cash flow is negative (−£5,900) because income is less than expenditure.

3 Eventually, the closing bank balance would be negative and Altaf might have to apply for a bank loan or overdraft, at least in the short term. However, his overall aim would be to improve his cash flow to achieve a positive bank balance.

4 Manufacturing businesses need to use materials constantly to make their products. Equally, all businesses need some staff to run them.

5 **Capital** is the component of the repayment which reduces the original amount borrowed. Eventually, this will fall to zero and the loan will have been repaid. **Interest** is the money paid to the bank for agreeing to the loan. It is used to pay for administration and is a contribution to the bank's profit.

6 £4,100. Just as the opening balance for July (£10,000) would have been the closing balance for June.

Activity 3.2.3 – Cash flow spreadsheets

The main emphasis of this activity is for the students to create and use a spreadsheet to construct a six-month cash flow forecast. They are asked to start by checking the figures they enter and then enter formulae for July. This enables the student to check that these are correct by comparing the results to the answers for the previous activity. Alternatively, students could be asked to complete all the calculations manually and use a spreadsheet to confirm (or otherwise!) their results.

The final figure is given (£29,600) so that students have a quick reference point. If they disagree with Altaf's estimate, they can start looking for the reason for the difference.

This spreadsheet forms the basis for the next two activities, particularly 3.2.5, so it is important that students check that theirs is accurate and that they fully understand how it operates before moving on.

Asking more questions on specific figures could extend the exercise.

Answer

1 a The month with the lowest sales figure is August (£190,000 compared with the next lowest of £200,000).

   b Altaf would probably think that people would be on holiday and it would not be convenient to have a home alarm fitted.

Answer

A1 ALARMS - CASH FLOW FORECAST						
	July	August	Sept	Oct	Nov	Dec
	£	£	£	£	£	£
INFLOWS/RECEIPTS						
Sales	200,000	190,000	210,000	210,000	210,000	200,000
Loans received	0	0	0	0	0	0
Total income	200,000	190,000	210,000	210,000	210,000	200,000
EXPENDITURE						
Materials	70,000	70,000	70,000	70,000	70,000	70,000
Wages/salaries	120,000	105,000	105,000	115,000	115,000	115,000
Capital items	0	0	10,000	0	0	0
Rent and rates	700	700	700	700	700	700
Electricity	650	650	650	650	650	650
Stationery	100	100	100	100	100	100
Telephone	200	200	200	200	200	200
Advertising	2,000	2,000	2,000	2,000	2,000	2,000
Insurance	250	250	250	250	250	250
Loan repayment	12,000	12,000	12,000	12,000	12,000	12,000
Sub total of expenditure	205,900	190,900	200,900	200,900	200,900	200,900
Net cash flow	-5,900	-900	9,100	9,100	9,100	-900
MONTHLY SUMMARY						
Opening bank balance	10,000	4,100	3,200	12,300	21,400	30,500
Net cash flow	-5,900	-900	9,100	9,100	9,100	-900
Closing bank balance	4,100	3,200	12,300	21,400	30,500	29,600

Activity 3.2.4 – Understanding Altaf's forecast

This activity builds on the previous one by asking the students to analyse some of the features of the spreadsheet. It should help to make the point that, although they should be able to construct a cash flow chart, they must also be able to interpret it. They should be reminded that the closing bank balance is a key figure on a cash flow chart since it is a measure of the business's ability to pay its creditors.

2 The £10,000 entered under capital items in September.

3 He almost certainly looked at the previous year's figures for the same six-month period and adjusted them in the light of any changes planned or expected. For example, if he expected to increase sales by 20 per cent, all of the expenditure figures could be adjusted accordingly. On the other hand, he might also be looking for ways to economise.

4 Three loan payments would be saved, 3 × £12,000 = £36,000. The December closing balance would increase by this amount to £65,600.

5 −£900 −£3,200 = −£4,100

6 The drop in the wages bill co-incidentally occurs in the same month as the £10,000 spent on the van.

7 a £10,000 (£9,100 + £900).

b This is due to a fall in sales income of £10,000 (£210,000 − £200,000).

8 a The difference is £29,600 − £10,000 = £19,600.

b Altaf should be pleased about this since it is one indication that his business is doing well. He would also be pleased that his closing balance is always positive – he never goes into the red.

Activity 3.2.5 – Altaf thinks 'what if...?'

The last exercise asked students to interpret an existing spreadsheet. This one gives them practice in finding out what happens when figures are changed – 'what if' exercises. This technique could be used to test worst case scenarios or to discover what would happen if something new was tried.

Students again need to use the spreadsheet produced in Activity 3.2.3 – *and return to it after each individual exercise*. The answers give the closing balance for each individual exercise. This links to the format of the exercise which has been designed to save students having to take printouts after each change. As an alternative, of course, the students could be asked to do this.

The exercise could be extended by introducing other scenarios.

1

Month	July	August	Sept	Oct	Nov	Dec
	£	£	£	£	£	£
Closing bank balance	−7,900	11,200	20,300	29,400	38,500	37,600

Comments: The profit on the contract is £8,000, so on this basis it would be worthwhile. The snag is that, because the overtime has to be paid in advance, the closing balance for July is negative (−£7,900). This means that he would probably need an overdraft, unless he could reduce costs – such as ordering fewer materials.

2

Month	July	August	Sept	Oct	Nov	Dec
	£	£	£	£	£	£
Closing bank balance	7,100	9,200	21,300	33,400	45,500	47,600

Comments: On the face of it this is a straightforward gain for the business. The closing balance increases cumulatively by £3,000 each month. However Altaf would have to be sure that the quality of the material supplied is at least as good as that from his current supplier. Other factors such as reliability and credit terms would also have to be taken into account.

3

Month	July	August	Sept	Oct	Nov	Dec
	£	£	£	£	£	£
Closing bank balance	4,130	3,260	12,390	21,520	30,650	29,780

Comments: The net gain on the closing balance over 6 months is £180 – or 0.6 per cent. This is very unlikely to be worth doing at the risk of upsetting the staff.

4

Month	July	August	Sept	Oct	Nov	Dec
	£	£	£	£	£	£
Closing bank balance	4,100	3,200	12,300	3,400	24,500	35,600

Comments: The big worry would have been that the closing balance in October could be negative. However, although the figure dips, it remains positive each month and overall is £6,000 higher in December. Presumably the reason for the reduced repayment to the bank is a saving on interest repayments.

5

Month	July	August	Sept	Oct	Nov	Dec
	£	£	£	£	£	£
Closing bank balance	–900	–6,800	–2,700	6,400	15,500	14,600

Comments: This type of 'what if' analysis is useful as part of a business's risk analysis. In this case a modest reduction in sales in the first three months results in a negative closing balance figure – the worst being –£6,800 in August. Altaf would be well advised to have an overdraft facility of, say, £10,000 if this situation was likely to arise.

Activity 3.2.6 – Cash flow is king!

This exercise develops a key aspect of cash flow – the problems associated with credit trading. As an introduction, it may be worth reminding the group about the basic process of credit trading, starting with the delivery of goods then the subsequent sending of an invoice which states the terms of payment, a statement of account at the end of the month and subsequent payment.

Answer

1 A cash flow plan forecasts all of the money expected to be paid into and leaving a business's bank account over a period – often a month. This results in an estimate of the closing balance of money in the account. If the closing balance is forecast to be negative, the business would probably arrange to have an overdraft facility. It is important to stress that cash flow relates to money actually entering and leaving the account – not money owed or cheques waiting to be cleared.

The key aspect of all this is that if, for any reason, cash flows out of a bank account faster than it flows in, the business may not have enough money to pay its creditors.

2 **a** Payment is made at a later date than when the goods or services are supplied.

   b Money will be received up to one or two months later. For example, if a business

customer's car is cleaned early in a month, the invoice is sent at the end of the month and the payment will (hopefully) be made in the middle of the next month. In other words, payment could take up to six weeks, or even longer, after the service has been delivered. In the meantime Gavin has had to find the money to pay wages and other bills.

   c Problems can occur if business customers delayed payment even longer – and this can often happen. Worse still, some customers may not pay at all. Businesses can go bankrupt because of late or non-payment of debts.

3 (4 of) Looking at published accounts – particularly for public limited companies. The creditors item in the balance sheet gives some indication of how quickly the business pays its debts. Asking for bank references. Using a commercial credit reference agency. Asking for references from other suppliers.

4 (3 of) Send invoices promptly. Have a (computerised) system for flagging up overdue payments. Have a procedure for chasing late payments which begins with a polite and friendly approach but which becomes progressively more severe. Consider cancelling the contract for persistent late payers. Offer a discount for prompt payment.

Activity 3.2.7 – Carrymore's cash flow forecast

This activity gives students an opportunity to obtain practice in producing a spreadsheet from raw data. The instruction is for students to start with a manual cash flow and then construct a spreadsheet to check the result, but tutors can obviously vary this instruction.

The notes require the students to read the information carefully. For example, sales are given as three figures with a note that they are all in thousands of pounds. In the note on materials the abbreviation 'K' for thousand is given. In the expense list all the figures are per month.

Answer

	April £	May £	June £	July £	August £	Sept £
INFLOWS/RECEIPTS						
Sales	150,000	170,000	140,000	150,000	150,000	130,000
Loans received	0	0	0	0	0	0
Total income	150,000	170,000	140,000	150,000	150,000	130,000
EXPENDITURE						
Materials	75,000	75,000	75,000	75,000	75,000	75,000
Wages/salaries	65,000	65,000	65,000	65,000	65,000	65,000
Rent and rates	500	500	500	500	500	500
Electricity	1000	1000	1000	1000	1000	1000
Stationery	150	150	150	150	150	150
Telephone	200	200	200	200	200	200
Advertising	1,000	1,000	1,000	1,000	1,000	1,000
Insurance	1250	1250	1250	1250	1250	1250
Sub total of expenditure	144,100	144,100	144,100	144,100	144,100	144,100
Net cash flow	5,900	25,900	-4,100	5,900	5,900	-14,100
MONTHLY SUMMARY						
Opening bank balance	15,000	20,900	46,800	42,700	48,600	54,500
Net cash flow	5,900	25,900	-4,100	5,900	5,900	-14,100
Closing bank balance	20,900	46,800	42,700	48,600	54,500	40,400

3.3 – Budgets for planning and monitoring expenditure

Activity 3.3.1 – All about budgets

The first exercise in this activity tests the students' understanding of the terms used in a budgetary control system. The second asks them to reorder the sequence of a complete budget cycle. This is slightly different from the list in the Student Book so that students have to think about this and cannot merely copy the list! Question 3 is the most difficult and tutors may ask students to suggest ideas working in small groups.

Answer

1 **List of expenditure items** = a list of all types of items which a department uses – including salaries, if appropriate. **Budget holder** = person responsible for trying to ensure that expenditure does not exceed the amount allowed in the budget – for each item. The person is normally a middle manager such as a departmental head. **Cost centre** is a section of department in an organisation which has its own budget. **Planned expenditure amounts** are the agreed expenditure figures which are allowed for each expenditure item. **Variances** are differences between planned and actual expenditure. **Budget report** is feedback on expenditure given to the budget holder after a certain period, normally a month. **Negative variances** occur when there is an overspend.

2 C E B F A D G.

3 Similarities (2 of): Both forecast financial plans for a future period, normally a year. Both are normally broken down into monthly intervals. The actual results are regularly checked against plans.

Differences (1 of): Budgets normally relate to several individual departments whereas cash flow is monitored for the business as a whole. The finance department would be responsible for monitoring and controlling cash flow whereas individual budget holders/cost centre managers are responsible for controlling expenditure related to their own budget.

Activity 3.3.2 – Budgeting at 'Rustic Products'

This is a fairly straightforward budget exercise. Students need to know how to complete a budget chart with the information provided and are also asked to comment on the variance figures they have produced. The basic point is that only major variances attract managerial attention. The actual action taken would ultimately depend on the specifics of the situation but in broad terms, large negative variances are the major cause for concern.

Answer

1 and **2**

RUSTIC PRODUCTS

FURNITURE DEPARTMENT – MARCH BUDGET REPORT			
Item	Planned expenditure (£)	Actual expenditure (£)	Variance (£)
Poles	34,000	38,000	–4,000
Planks	28,000	27,600	400
Nails	2,500	2,400	100
Wood preserver	1,000	2,000	–1,000
Varnish	2,000	1,900	100
Saw blades	1,500	2,500	–1,000
Electricity	1,200	1,100	100
Wages	8,500	6,000	2,500
Total	78,700	81,500	–2,800

3 Poles, wood preserver and saw blades – large negative variances which require investigation and correction. One step would be to check whether there were problems with a particular supplier and whether the items could be bought more cheaply elsewhere. Another possible problem is too much material being scrapped or stolen. Serious problems may have to be referred to a senior manager if the departmental manager cannot solve it. If a problem cannot be solved at all, the next budget may have to be adjusted.

Planks, nails, varnish and electricity – small acceptable variances.

Wages – large positive variance. If this continued for two or three months, the next budget would be adjusted (reduced) accordingly.

Activity 3.3.3 – Trouble in the High Street

This activity is based on actual events which occurred at Marks & Spencer in 2004. Its fundamental theme is the new MD's attempt to reduce planned expenditure. Although the term budget is not specifically mentioned, there is an obvious link since Stuart Rose clearly thinks that expenditure is almost out of control. When undertaking the exercise, students should be encouraged to discuss fundamental principles – that businesses have to spend less than they earn and that budgetary control is a system of controlling the money spent by middle managers.

Another important theme which emerges from the activity is that some expenditure has a direct effect on sales and therefore income. On the other hand other types of expenditure do not have this effect. There is a rough comparison here between direct/indirect costs discussed in 3.1.

Answer

1 a Expenditure which has a direct effect on sales.

b (1 of) Stock items, point-of-sale materials, extra reward points for special promotions to card holders, sales staff. Note that it is surprising that he includes marketing in the restricted category since it could be argued that this would come under the same heading.

c The core business of Marks & Spencer is selling goods to the public. Anything which detracts from this would reduce income and therefore profits. This issue could be broadened into a more general discussion related to earlier sections – improving cash flow and maximising profit by reducing expenditure and increasing income.

2 Attention to health and safety matters is a legal requirement. There are also humanitarian considerations.

3 Middle and junior managers were spending money too freely – without checking that the expenditure was justified. This rule severely limits their powers to spend company money as senior managers would check that expenditure was justified before agreeing that the money could be spent. Stuart Rose actually said that all staff should 'treat every penny we spend as if it were our own money'.

4 a Stock.

   b Because reducing stock (and choice) would reduce sales and therefore income and profits.

5 a Finance, purchasing, IT and administrative staff will be examples of head office staff. None are directly involved in selling goods to customers and Stuart Rose may also feel that there are too many head office staff.

   b Because stores need sales staff to be able to sell goods and stopping these could negatively affect sales.

   c The staff remaining at head office will not be too happy, especially since some of them may have to cover the unfilled vacancies.

6 a To tighten up on, in order to reduce expenditure.

   b (2 of) Examples follow but any appropriate suggestions should be accepted. Only travel second class by train, only travel by budget airlines, only stay in (maximum) three-star hotels, no overnight accommodation without agreement of a senior manager.

7 They may not stay up-to-date with new developments directly affecting their jobs.

8 Six months.

9 The measures will have a direct effect on the budgetary control system by reducing spending as managers are no longer allowed the freedom to take as many types of financial decisions as they have taken previously.

10 a Since less money is being spent, the overall cash flow should be more positive.

   b If sales stay the same then profits will increase as there are fewer deductions from income.

3.4 – Recording transactions

Activity 3.4.1 – All about transactions

This activity tests students' fundamental understanding about what constitutes a transaction, what needs to be recorded and why. The basic messages are that:

- everyone is involved in transactions
- transactions can take many forms
- handwritten receipts are the most basic kind of record of a transaction
- almost all receipts contain standard types of information
- records of transactions are important. The Inland Revenue and HM Customs and Excise may need to examine them to verify submitted accounts.

Answer

1 (4 of) Private customers, business customers, the van hire company, garage for petrol, various material suppliers, telephone company, business stationery suppliers, Inland Revenue – or any other reasonable suggestions.

2 Because he works away from the office – he could hardly carry a cash register round with him! Also he likes to be paid as soon as he has completed a job, rather than going to the trouble of sending invoices and waiting to be paid.

3 (6 of) Rob's business name and address, his telephone number, the date, a receipt number, the amount of money (in figures and words), description of the work done, Rob's signature.

4 Rob will have to provide full and accurate information to the Inland Revenue each year so that his tax can be calculated. This will be based on his profit, which is found by deducting the total of all his expenditure transactions from his total sales transactions. If he is registered for VAT, HM Customs and Excise will also need similar information.

Activity 3.4.2 – Payment methods

This topic is not directly mentioned in the unit brief. However, an understanding of this subject will help students to appreciate the nature of the various forms of transaction and the types of records generated from them. This activity is designed to test students' understanding of the basic attributes of the various payment methods. Tutors may feel that students would benefit from a quick revision session before asking them to attempt the activity.

Answer

a direct debit, **b** cash, **c** debit card, **d** electronic credit transfer, **e** cheque, **f** cash, **g** debit card, **h** cheque, **i** credit card, **j** direct debit, **k** direct credit, **l** credit card.

Activity 3.4.3 – Cash registers and electronic recording

This activity tests students' basic understanding of how cash registers, swipe systems, EPOS systems and computer-based financial packages operate. The student is asked to evaluate a range of choices for a small gift shop. The first question looks at the essential equipment specification required for any till based transaction and the second involves adding in a swipe system for credit and debit cards. The third question relates to the security aspects of cash handling. The next two questions involve the additional facilities which can be added when computerised systems are used. The last question mainly relates to records and could produce a wide range of answers since very sophisticated packages are available. However, students will probably limit themselves to the basic functions described in the Student Book.

Answer

1 (3 of) Display of amount owed, cash drawer, buttons to input amount, device for recording each transaction amount and producing the total transaction amounts, printing receipts.

2 Kelly's mother is correct in that she will need a separate system for processing card transactions if she has a basic cash register installed. Otherwise she cannot handle card payments.

3 The benefit is that it is cheap. The disadvantage is that there is no record of transactions and little security.

4 Electronic Point of Sale.

5 (4 of) Bar code reader, updating stock records, re-ordering low stock items, identity of till user, processing credit/debit card transactions, printing detailed receipts, capturing customer information (with loyalty cards).

6 (4 of) Customer records (invoices sent, payments etc.), supplier records (invoices received, payments etc.), bank balances and statements, cash flow, produce invoices and monthly statements, produce budget forecasts, store product records and prices, produce reports such as profit and loss accounts, calculate VAT.

7 Kelly would be better, at this stage, installing a basic cash register and swipe system. An EPOS system is too elaborate and expensive, a cash drawer is too risky. She could do her accounts more easily if she used a financial software package but would only need a simple one as she is not selling goods on credit.

Activity 3.4.4 – Petty cash

The first activity asks students to demonstrate their understanding of a basic petty cash procedure by putting the various stages into the correct sequence. They could be given some initial guidance by asking them as a group where petty cash comes from in the first place and what the word 'float' means.

The second activity is a simple numeracy exercise and the third introduces basic problem solving.

After the exercise students could be asked to explain why most businesses have a petty cash system.

Answers

1 The correct sequence is: D, H, L, E, J, A, C, G, K, B, F, I

2 a £171.80   b £28.20

   c £171.80

3 a Check that the stamps have been received by the supervisor, ask the supervisor to write a note on the voucher confirming this and then reimburse the money.

   b Hopefully spot this before it happens but notify the accountant and arrange for an emergency top-up. If it happens frequently then the float amount will have to be increased permanently.

   c Refuse because the maximum amount payable in Jane's firm is £25. The member of staff should be referred to the accountant or a manager to discuss alternative methods of reimbursement (e.g. through the capital expenditure system).

Activity 3.4.5 – Retail theft in Europe steals the show!

This case study focuses on a European measure for retail crime which is updated annually. It would be useful for tutors to start by accessing the latest report, and to update the case study before it is issued to students.

Two points should be noted. This activity contains data which overlaps with that given on page 263 of the Student Book. The data is not identical because a more general picture was given for the introduction to the topic. This case study contains more detailed information therefore, for example, a precise figure for shrinkage in 2002/3 is given (16.9 per cent) against an averaged figure of 17.0 per cent in the Student Book and the different factors that account for shrinkage are described more precisely.

Students who have part-time jobs in retail may be able to answer some of the questions through personal experience of the type of events observed and precautions taken. Although the main theme is theft from retail outlets tutors may wish to extend the discussion by mentioning that other forms of business also suffer, for example, the motor mechanic who offers to service customers cars in his own time, the solicitor who uses clients' money for her own purpose etc.

These issues are raised because tutors may find a variety of approaches to this activity from students which go beyond the suggested answers. Tutors may have to use their own discretion when reviewing the students' responses. Unusual suggestions may come from first-hand experience!

Students will gain by discussing and comparing their ideas and suggestions – either by doing the case study in small groups or comparing their answers at the end. In particular tutors may need to lead a discussion focused on question 9 that will include aspects such as culture, store layout, opportunism, peer group pressure and even language. There is one argument that referring to retail theft as 'shoplifting' actually downgrades the offence and makes it more acceptable. Tutors could even be contentious and ask if there is a correlation between, say, football hooliganism in Europe and store theft!

Answer

1   Stock loss from crime or wastage.

2   **a**   Falling – from 1.45 per cent to 1.37 per cent between 2001/2 and 2002/3.

    b   Falling. It was 1.81 per cent in 2000/2001, 1.77 per cent in 2001/2 and 1.69 per cent in 2002/3.

3   (3 of) Breaking or damaging an item, mistakenly not processing it properly, not pricing it accurately, forgetting to charge for it after a distraction – or any other appropriate suggestions.

4   **a**   By not including them in the delivery (i.e. stealing at source) or by taking them out of the delivery (i.e. stealing during distribution).

    b   Always checking that all deliveries are correct and match the order and the following invoice.

5   (2 of) Deliberately not charging for some items, giving illegal discounts, giving false refunds – or any other appropriate suggestions.

6   Below are suggestions only. Other appropriate ideas should be accepted.

a   (1 of) Never leave items on a counter, make sure all displayed goods are dummies or locked away, never leave till drawers open, empty tills regularly, put cash into tills immediately on receipt.

b   (1 of) CCTV cameras, reputation for prosecuting thieves, guards over tills, tills emptied regularly.

c   (1 of) Restrict unaccompanied youngsters, do not allow 'gangs' of kids into a store, observe youngsters carefully.

7   **a**   (2 of) They can only cover a limited number of areas, they will only give a historic account, they are no substitute for good staff welfare policies and proper disciplinary procedures, they are only one of several methods of deterring customers from stealing.

    b   (1 of) They are spotted as dummies and ignored, word spreads that they are dummies, they cannot help if a theft actually occurs.

8   No specific answer possible.

Activity 3.4.6 – Catch 'em if you can!

Although the message here is serious, the activity has been lightened for students by including certain unacceptable (and illegal) actions by a store keeper with the aim of reducing or eliminating store theft.

You may wish students to do this activity in pairs or small groups and then compare their answers.

Answer

1   The unlawful actions are actually very few! Tutors may find the following observations useful:

The only unlawful actions are E, I, L, N, Q and T.

D is legal because there is no discrimination – all staff are being treated equally. However, Kala may find it difficult to run his business in this case! E is not legal because being 'new' is no criterion for deciding on guilt in a theft case.

I is illegal because a store has a legal responsibility to refund customers if goods are faulty.

L could result in Kala being sued for assault and kidnapping!

N is illegal but O is legal. This is the maximum amount that can be withheld.

Q is illegal because CCTV cameras in the toilets obviously invade employee privacy. T is illegal because all staff have a legal minimum holiday entitlement (28 days for full-time staff and pro rata for part-time staff).

J may surprise some students but is perfectly legal. The member of staff must be allowed to be accompanied by a colleague or union representative and there are obvious safeguards laid down.

K and M are representative of the fact that all store owners can decide whom to allow into the shop and whom to serve. They can refuse to sell goods to anyone at their own discretion and without giving a reason! As long as this is not discrimination it is not illegal.

2 The best ideas are A, B, F, R and S, though students may also choose C, G, H, K or P! It may be useful to discuss with students the 'carrot' ideas (F, R), 'stick' ideas (A, O) and prevention measures (G, H etc.) and to discuss that a 'mix' of these is beneficial.

3 (2 of) Empty tills regularly, reward staff who report fraud/theft, have a system where cash registers are checked when staff change, employ security staff. Any other appropriate ideas should be accepted.

Profit and loss – true or false?

Say whether you think that the following statements are true or false. For those where you think that the answer is 'false' give the correct statement.

1 Profit is the total amount of money earned by the business.

True/False _____

2 A business makes a loss if income is less than expenditure.

True/False _____

3 For local government, income has always to be much greater than expenditure.

True/False _____

4 If income is £50,000 and expenditure is £45,000, the business has made a profit of £5,000.

True/False _____

5 For a business to break even, income and expenditure must be the same.

True/False _____

6 So long as private businesses break even, they will be all right.

True/False _____

7 For a charity, the only income is the money received from collecting boxes.

True/False _____

8 Profit = Income – expenditure.

True/False _____

9 If a charity receives £100,000 in a year and spends £150,000 it will be OK.

True/False _____

10 When a business spends more than it earns, it makes a profit.

True/False _____

11 Private businesses need to make a profit so that they have enough money to invest in developing the business.

True/False _____

12 If income is £75,000 and expenditure is £80,000, the profit is £5,000.

True/False _____

Profit or loss?

The chart below shows the income and expenditure for a number of businesses. Complete the third column by calculating the difference between the figures in the first two. Finally, complete the end column by stating whether each business has made a profit, a loss, or broken even.

Income (£)	Expenditure (£)	Difference (£)	Result (profit, loss or break even)
400	300		
25,000	25,000		
4,650	5,521		
105,800	96,425		
5,654	5,653		
37,522	37,522		
52,000	61,750		
270,000	150,000		

Making a profit is critical to survival

Where does the money come from?

For each of the following situations, calculate the total revenue:

1 A farmer sells 23 cows for £450 each and 15 pigs for £230 each at a cattle market.

£ _____

2 In a year, a local charity receives £5,760 from its shop, £2,751 from door-to-door collections, £1,760 from a charity concert and £575 from collecting boxes located in town centre shops.

£ _____

3 In a month a car showroom sells 5 MPVs, 3 sports cars, 8 family saloons and 6 compacts. The prices are £21,615, £18,750, £13,495 and £5,995 respectively. £ _____

4 Complete the following table to calculate the total revenue for the business:

Product	Selling price (£)	Number sold	Revenue (£)
A	50.00	25	
B	27.50	47	
C	210.00	5	
D	16.50	125	
E	75.50	18	
		Total	

5 In task 4 above, calculate the new total revenue if the sales of product D are doubled.

£ _____

Fixed or variable – that is the question!

Julia owns a model shop which specialises in remote-controlled cars, boats and planes. Customers buy the items in kit form and build them themselves.

1 Julia's main items of expenditure are listed below. Enter these in the table below in their correct column under the headings fixed and variable costs. Then calculate the total in each case.

2 Julia wants to reduce her fixed costs by 10 per cent and her variable costs by 5 per cent. If she achieves this, what will her new total figures be?

Rent	£6,000	Model plane kits	£5,000
Business rates	£1,500	Electricity	£560
Model car kits	£8,000	Tools (to build models)	£1,500
Model boat kits	£3,000	Paint for models	£300
Telephone	£560	Insurance	£1,100
Gas	£700	Packaging (carrier bags etc.)	£900
Water	£300		

Fixed costs		Variable costs	
Item	**£**	**Item**	**£**
Total:		Total:	

Maximising profit

Use the chart below to list ways in which businesses can maximise profit by increasing income or reducing costs. Do this by listing **five** actions they could take under *each* of the three headings.

Maximise income by:

Reduce fixed costs by:

Reduce variable costs by:

SID'S SUPERSAVA STORES

Would Penny break even?

Background information

Penny has always been interested in art and at college she particularly enjoys decorating pottery. When she achieves her final qualification she wonders if she could start up her own business in this field. She has noticed that, in her own town, organisations (such as businesses, schools and charitable organisations) often celebrate anniversaries. She thinks that there is a market for commemorative anniversary plates for people to buy as a memento. She decides to look at some cost and revenue figures and to assess what could happen in a particular month.

Penny could rent premises fairly cheaply for £300 and estimates that her total monthly fixed cost figure, including the rent, would be £1,000. She also thinks that she can sell plates for £12 each and that the materials and other costs per plate would be £4. With the method of production she plans to use, the maximum number of plates she could produce a month would be 200.

Questions

1 Use this information to draw a break even chart and label all of the lines you have drawn, including the axes.

2 Label the following aspects of the chart:

Profit, loss, break even point.

3 Use the chart to read off the break even point.

4 From the chart, read off the margin of safety if sales were 200 plates.

5 From the chart, read off the profit/loss (say which) for sales of 50, 150 and 200.

6 Use the formula to confirm the break even point which you have read from the chart.

7 Calculate the profit margin per plate.

8 Explain how the break even chart can help Penny to make a decision about her business idea.

Elements of a cash flow forecast

Your friend Mark is hoping to start his own business and has to prepare a cash flow forecast. He has been given the main headings and has some figures on a list. But he isn't certain what he is doing – or how to do the forecast properly – and asks you for advice.

Your tasks

1 Look at the table for the March forecast below and explain clearly the meaning of *each* heading labelled A to G.

2 Prepare the March forecast for Mark yourself by entering his figures in the correct place and doing the calculations correctly.

3 In two or three sentences explain to Mark the benefits of doing a cash flow forecast.

Cash flow forecast – March	£
Income (A)	_____
Expenditure (B)	_____
Net cash flow (C)	_____
Monthly summary (D)	
Opening bank balance (E)	_____
Net cash flow (F)	_____
Closing balance (G)	_____

Mark's figures	
Feb closing bank balance	£1,500
Estimated income March	£2,400
Estimated costs in March	£1,100

A1 Alarms

This activity and the three that follow are based on the following case study. Read this carefully before you begin.

Case study

A1 Alarms is a small business which installs intruder alarms for businesses and private households. Most similar businesses tend to offer standardised systems to customers. However, A1 pride themselves in understanding each of their customer's individual requirements and designing a system to meet their exact needs. This means that the business has a workshop where customised alarm systems are built from basic components.

The business was started three years ago by Altaf Patel who took out a bank loan to buy the workshop/office building, vehicles and stocks of components. The business has expanded rapidly and Altaf has recently taken out a large loan to fund this growth – including buying much larger premises.

It is now June and Altaf decides to forecast his cash flow for the next six months, starting with July.

Altaf's July cash flow forecast

1   Altaf has started his cash flow forecast for July by entering his forecast sales and expenditure figures. This is shown opposite. He also tells you that his opening bank balance in July will be £10,000.

Complete the cash flow forecast for July by inserting and/or calculating the following figures:

   a   Total income
   b   Sub total of expenditure
   c   Net cash flow (twice!)
   d   Closing bank balance

2   State whether Altaf's net cash flow is positive or negative.

3   Explain what would happen if the cash flow stayed like this for the next few months.

4   The highest items of expenditure are materials and labour (wages). This is typical for most businesses like Altaf's. Suggest **one** reason for this.

5   The loan repayment consists of two components – **capital** and **interest**. Explain clearly what both of these terms mean.

6   Identify the amount of the opening bank balance for August.

A1 ALARMS - CASH FLOW FORECAST		
	July	Au
	£	£
INFLOWS/RECEIPTS		
Sales	200,000	
Loans received	0	
Total income		
EXPENDITURE		
Materials	70,000	
Wages/salaries	120,000	
Capital items	0	
Rent and rates	700	
Electricity	650	
Stationery	100	
Telephone	200	
Advertising	2,000	
Insurance	250	
Loan repayment	12,000	
Sub total of expenditure		
Net cash flow		
MONTHLY SUMMARY		
Opening bank balance		
Net cash flow		
Closing bank balance		

Cash flow spreadsheets

This activity again focuses on A1 Alarms and continues the work you started in Activity 3.2.2.

Altaf knows that the easiest way to forecast cash flow is to enter the figures into a spreadsheet. He has asked you to do this for him.

To help you, he has added all of his forecast income and expenditure items for the rest of the six-month period. This is shown in the table below.

A1 ALARMS - CASH FLOW FORECAST						
	July	August	Sept	Oct	Nov	Dec
	£	£	£	£	£	£
INFLOWS/RECEIPTS						
Sales	200,000	190,000	210,000	210,000	210,000	200,000
Loans received	0	0	0	0	0	0
Total income						
EXPENDITURE						
Materials	70,000	70,000	70,000	70,000	70,000	70,000
Wages/salaries	120,000	105,000	105,000	115,000	115,000	115,000
Capital items	0	0	10,000	0	0	0
Rent and rates	700	700	700	700	700	700
Electricity	650	650	650	650	650	650
Stationery	100	100	100	100	100	100
Telephone	200	200	200	200	200	200
Advertising	2,000	2,000	2,000	2,000	2,000	2,000
Insurance	250	250	250	250	250	250
Loan repayment	12,000	12,000	12,000	12,000	12,000	12,000
Sub total of expenditure						
Net cash flow						
MONTHLY SUMMARY						
Opening bank balance						
Net cash flow						
Closing bank balance						

Your tasks

1 Create a spreadsheet using this data. Check that you have entered all of Altaf's figures correctly.

2 Enter formulas for June to produce the correct answers to the previous activity. This will enable you to check easily that your formulas are correct.

3 Copy your formulas across for the remaining months so that the forecast is complete.

4 When Altaf drafted out his forecast he calculated that his closing bank balance for December would be £29,600. Do you agree with him?

Understanding Altaf's forecast

This activity again focuses on A1 Alarms and continues the work you started in Activities 3.2.2 and 3.2.3.

Once you have completed Altaf's spreadsheet and have confirmed that it is accurate, examine it carefully *and* answer the following questions.

Questions

1 a In which month has Altaf forecast the lowest sales figure?

   b Bearing in mind that a lot of his business is fitting alarms to domestic property, why do you think he may have done this?

2 Altaf has decided that he will need to buy an extra new van. How is this shown in the cash flow forecast?

3 How do you think Altaf decided what figures to put in for his items of expenditure?

4 If Altaf's loan repayments ended in September, rather than at the end of the year, what would be his closing bank balance in December?

5 What would the net cash flow have to be in August to make the bank balance go to zero in that month?

6 The sub total of expenditure is the same in September and October (£200,900) even though the wages bill in the first month is £10,000 less. Can you identify why is this is the case?

7 a What is the difference in net cash flow between November and December?

   b Explain why is this is the case.

8 a What is the difference between the opening bank balance in July and the closing balance in December?

   b Do you think Altaf will be pleased with this? Give a reason for your answer.

Altaf thinks 'what if...?'

This activity again focuses on A1 Alarms and continues the work you have done in Activities 3.2.2, 3.2.3 and 3.2.4.

Use the spreadsheet you produced for Activity 3.2.3 to answer these questions. Instead of printing your result each time, record your answers in the boxes below.

After you have answered a question and noted the result, remember to **go back to the original spreadsheet** before you move on to the next.

For each question say whether or not you think that Altaf's idea is a good one or not, giving your reason each time.

Questions

 **1** Altaf knows of a special contract which is coming up in August. It would increase sales income by £20,000 in that month but would require his staff to work overtime in July at a total extra cost of £12,000.

Month	July £	August £	Sept £	Oct £	Nov £	Dec £
Closing bank balance						

Your comments:

_____

_____

2 A material supplier contacts Altaf with a special deal which would mean that his material bill would be £3,000 less per month for the whole period.

Month	July £	August £	Sept £	Oct £	Nov £	Dec £
Closing bank balance						

Your comments:

_____

_____

_____

Activity 3.2.5 Altaf thinks 'what if...?' (cont'd)

3 Altaf is considering putting labels on all telephones saying, 'No private calls allowed, anyone disobeying will be disciplined'. He estimates that this will save £30 per month.

Month	July £	August £	Sept £	Oct £	Nov £	Dec £
Closing bank balance						

Your comments:

_____

_____

_____

4 Altaf contacts the bank to find out what would happen if he pays his loan off early. Payments were due to end in December. The bank says that he can pay £30,000 in October to complete the repayments early.

Month	July £	August £	Sept £	Oct £	Nov £	Dec £
Closing bank balance						

Your comments:

_____

_____

_____

5 Altaf wonders what would happen if his sales forecasts proved to be optimistic. He decides to lower the figures by £5,000 in July, August and September to see what would happen.

Month	July £	August £	Sept £	Oct £	Nov £	Dec £
Closing bank balance						

Your comments:

_____

_____

_____

Cash flow is king!

Case study

Your friend Gavin sends you a text message asking if you can meet. When you see him he is excited and full of enthusiasm about an idea to expand his business.

Gavin currently runs a car wash and valet business which caters for members of the public. Most of his customers pay cash so that he always has money in the bank to pay his bills. He has decided to expand his business by offering contracts to firms which run fleets of cars for their employees. Each business customer will pay a basic fee per month plus a special

discounted rate for every car cleaned.He plans to invoice his business customers at the end of each month and his invoices will say: 'Terms – payment within 14 working days'.

When Gavin has explained all of this to you, you ask him if he has considered his cash flow situation. He looks puzzled and asks you to explain what you mean. Answer the following questions to help Gavin to understand why it is important to monitor cash flow.

Questions

1 Explain how cash flow forecasting works and why it is important to all businesses.

2 You tell Gavin that he is moving from a situation where most of the payments he receives are in cash, to trading on a **credit basis**.

   a State what trading on credit means.

   b Explain how this can affect his cash flow, giving a specific example of a credit transaction.

   c Identify how credit trading can cause cash flow problems.

3 Having listened to your explanations, Gavin knows that he has to be careful in choosing the customers which he allows to pay on a credit basis. Suggest **four** ways in which he could check out businesses before he allows them a credit contract.

4 You also explain to him that, even when he has signed an agreement with a customer, he cannot automatically assume that bills will be paid on time. Suggest **three** actions he could take to deal with late payments.

Carrymore's cash flow forecast

Carrymore is a business that makes and sells shopping trolleys. You work for the accountant, Ben Schumaker, who is producing a cash flow forecast for six months beginning with April. The information he has been given by his staff is shown below.

Use this information to complete a cash flow forecast for Carrymore using the template below. Then construct a spreadsheet to confirm your result.

Ben

Given recent rise in interest rates, think we should avoid taking out any loans for the time being.

Jack

Ben

Projected sales figures from April to September are as follows:
150, 170, 140, 150, 150, 130.

All figs are £'000.

Jen

Ben

Materials are currently costing us £75k each month. I don't expect any major changes so suggest you can use this figure.

Hamid

Payroll data:
Wages = £65,000 a month

Carrymore Current account
31 March

Closing balance: £15,000

Ben

Expense list you asked for is given below. All figs are per month.
Rent and rates = £500
Electricity = £1,000
Stationery = £150
Telephone = £200
Advertising = £1,000
Insurance = £1,250
Katya

CARRYMORE'S CASH FLOW FORECAST						
	April	May	June	July	August	Sept
	£	£	£	£	£	£
INFLOWS/RECEIPTS						
Sales						
Loans received						
Total income						
EXPENDITURE						
Materials						
Wages/salaries						
Rent and rates						
Electricity						
Stationery						
Telephone						
Advertising						
Insurance						
Sub total of expenditure						
Net cash flow						
MONTHLY SUMMARY						
Opening bank balance						
Net cash flow						
Closing bank balance						

All about budgets

1 Gemma has just started working with you in the sales department of AB Components. On her first day, she overhears the following conversation between the sales manager, Kim, and yourself. Gemma says it was like listening to a foreign language! Can you help her by explaining the meaning of each of the terms in bold?

Kim Do you know if our **list of expenditure items** is up-to-date?

You Yes, I checked it yesterday.

Kim Good. As **budget holder** of this **cost centre** I want to make sure we keep on target this year.

You I've also checked the **planned expenditure amounts** to make sure that my list is correct, too.

Kim That's great. I want you to alert me to any potential **variances** before I see them in the **budget report**. This is especially important if we have any **negative variances** as I'll have to explain the reason for these to the MD.

2 AB Components' financial year runs from 1 April to 31 March each year and each of the following activities are key parts of the process.

Put these in the correct order for the process to work.

A Cost centre spending is checked at the end of each month

B Departmental budgets are set

C Overall business financial plan is agreed

D Cost centre spending is adjusted for the next month if there is a problem

E Budget holders attend planning meeting about their own departmental budget

F New budget year begins

G Budget plans for next year are adjusted according to experience

3 In her last job, Gemma worked with cash flow forecasts. She asks you what the similarities and the differences are.

Identify **two** similarities and **one** difference between budgets and cash flow forecasts.

Budgeting at Rustic Products

Rustic Products is a business which specialises in making wooden garden products such as fencing, sheds and furniture. You work for Tim Cryer, the manager of the furniture department. This department produces wooden tables, chairs and benches. The main types of wood used are poles to make the legs and armrests and planks to make the seats and table tops.

The department's planned expenditure each month is given below.

Furniture department – planned expenditure	
Item	**£**
Poles	34,000
Planks	28,000
Nails	2,500
Wood preserver	1,000
Varnish	2,000
Saw blades	1,500
Electricity	1,200
Wages	8,500

Tim
Statements for March are as follows:

Poles	£38,000
Planks	£27,600
Varnish	£1,900
Nails	£2,400
Saw blades	£2,500
Wood preserver	£2,000

Electricity allocation, each dept. March = £1,100.

Tim – spending on wages this month was £6,000. Sue

Your tasks

1 Use this information to produce the following budget report for the department.

RUSTIC PRODUCTS

FURNITURE DEPARTMENT – MARCH BUDGET REPORT

Item	Planned expenditure £	Actual expenditure £	Variance £
Total			

2 Create a spreadsheet using the same format and check your result.

3 Comment on each variance figure and state what (if any) action you think might be taken.

Trouble in the High Street

Read the case study below and then answer the questions that follow.

Case study

In June 2004 the newly appointed chief executive of Marks & Spencer, Stuart Rose, sent a memo to all staff about expenditure (see below). The High Street retailer had been in trouble for some time with both sales and profits falling every month. There was even talk about the business being taken over by Philip Green, who had successfully turned around other retail businesses including BHS and Topshop.

Contents of the memo

- All spending to be carefully controlled for six months.
- Expenditure must be stopped unless it is essential to drive sales or for health and safety reasons.
- All expenditure on new stores, store refurbishments, IT hardware and software, maintenance, repairs and marketing must be approved by one of three named top executives.
- All head office recruitment to be stopped.
- Staff banned from attending short courses and conferences.
- A clampdown on travelling expenses.
- The purchasing of goods for re-sale will continue as normal.

MARKS & SPENCER

Questions

1 a What do you think Stuart Rose meant by 'expenditure which drives sales'?

b Give **one** example.

c Explain why these items were exempt from the spending restrictions.

2 Suggest **one** reason why health and safety expenditure was still permitted.

3 Suggest why only very senior executives were allowed to agree expenditure items, such as store refurbishment and maintenance.

4 a What are goods called that are bought for re-sale?

b Why was the purchase of these goods allowed to continue unrestricted?

5 a What type of jobs do you think would be held by head office staff?

b Why do you think these were stopped when stores could continue to recruit new staff?

c How do you think the head office staff will feel about this rule?

6 a What is meant by the term 'clampdown'?

b If you were clamping down on travelling expenses, suggest two rules you would introduce.

7 Suggest **one** negative effect of preventing staff from attending short courses and conferences.

8 How long did Stuart Rose intend these measures to last?

9 What effect do you think that these measures would have on the normal budgetary control system?

10 What effect do you think that measures would have had on:

a the company's cash flow

b the company's profits?

Give a reason for your answers.

All about transactions

Rob runs a roofing business as a sole trader. He specialises in repairing customer's roofs – anything from replacing a few cracked tiles to complete tile replacement. He uses a hired van to travel to his jobs and to pick up materials.

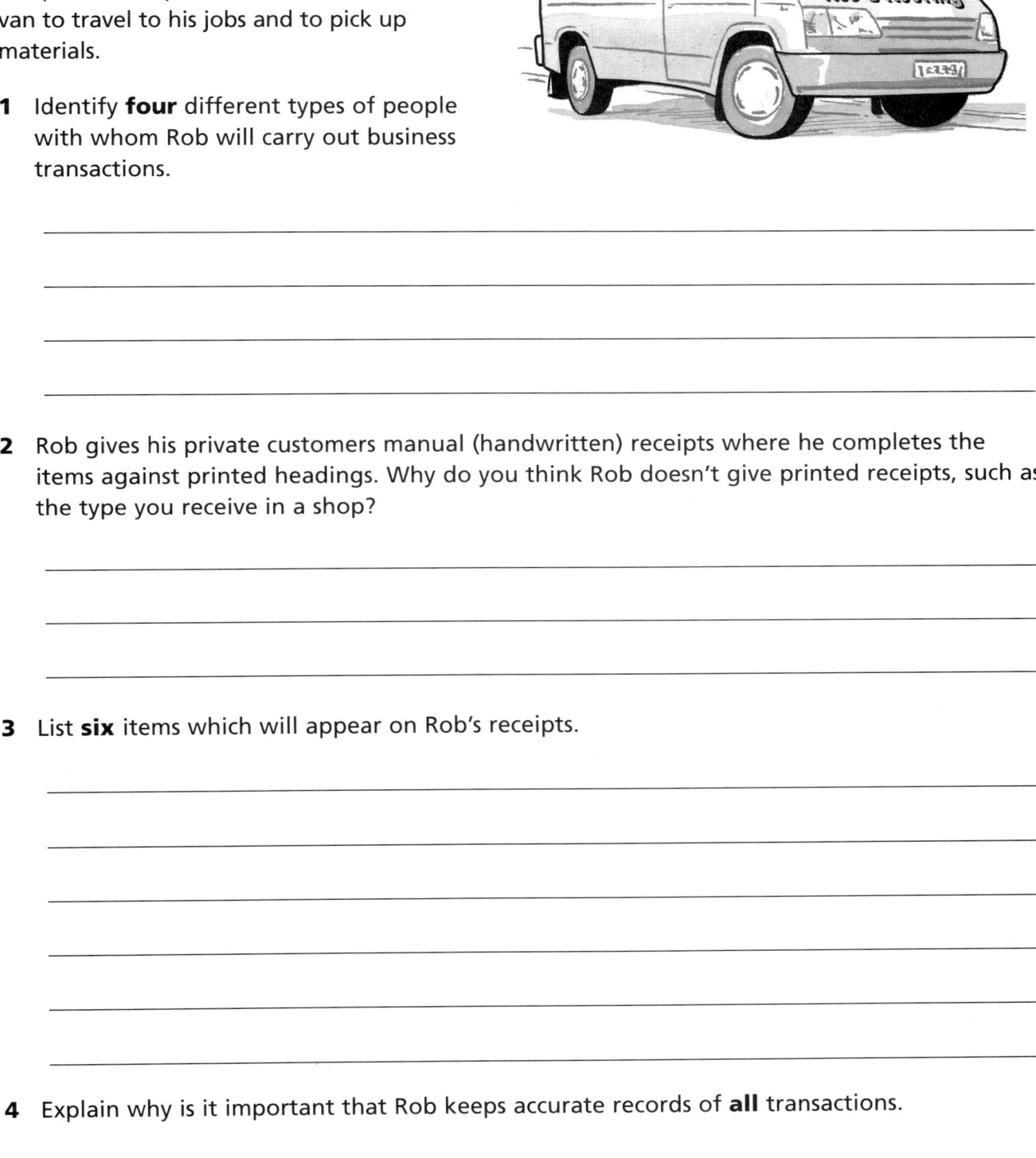

1   Identify **four** different types of people with whom Rob will carry out business transactions.

_____

_____

_____

_____

2   Rob gives his private customers manual (handwritten) receipts where he completes the items against printed headings. Why do you think Rob doesn't give printed receipts, such as the type you receive in a shop?

_____

_____

_____

3   List **six** items which will appear on Rob's receipts.

_____

_____

_____

_____

_____

_____

4   Explain why is it important that Rob keeps accurate records of **all** transactions.

_____

_____

Payment methods

Each of the statements in the chart below relates to one of the following payment methods.

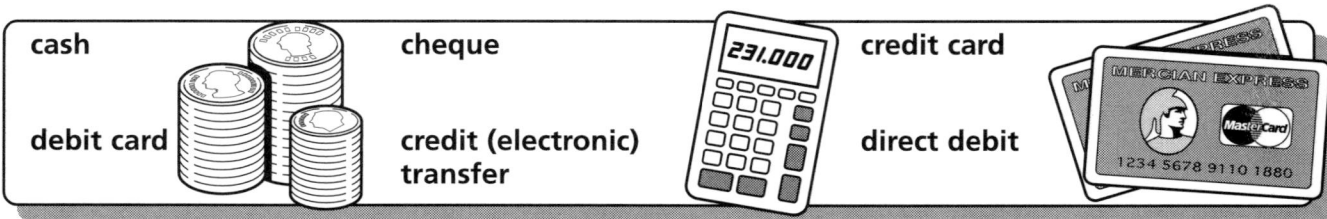

| cash | cheque | credit card |
| debit card | credit (electronic) transfer | direct debit |

In the right-hand column, write the type of payment method that is described. Note that you are expected to choose some methods more than once.

Statement	Payment method
'The money is taken from my account at the same time every month. I am notified in advance if the amount is going to change.'	a)
'I always carry a small amount in my pocket to buy a snack.'	b)
'I just hand over my card, sign the slip, and the money is taken from my account straightaway.'	c)
'The money is paid into the bank account of each of our employees on the last working day of each month.'	d)
'I always check the counterfoils in my book against the bank statement.'	e)
'We have to put a float in the till at the start of each day'.	f)
'The bank gave me this as well as a cheque book when I opened my account. It saves me having to carry a lot of cash around and I can't get into debt.'	g)
'I don't like giving my card number over the phone so I send the money by post.'	h)
'I am in so much debt that my friends say that I should cut it up and never have another one.'	i)
'I sometimes forgot to send a cheque to the electricity company each month. Now that we have set this up, the payment is made automatically each month.'	j)
'Housing benefit is a routine payment, so this is the best way of paying claimants.'	k)
'I always pay off the full amount when the statement arrives, so I never have to pay interest.'	l)

Cash registers and electronic recording

Background information

Kelly is opening a gift shop in a picturesque village well known for its tourist trade. She cannot work out which type of system to install for taking and recording transactions and has been talking to her family.

- Her father thinks a basic cash register is quite good enough for a little shop.

- Her mother tells her that she will also need a swipe system, such as PDQ, for accepting credit and debit cards.

- Her grandfather says that all this is far too elaborate and expensive. He says that when he worked in a shop, he just had a lockable drawer for cash.

- Kelly's sister works in a large superstore using an EPOS system. She thinks this would be ideal for Kelly.

- Kelly's brother is keen on IT. He argues Kelly simply needs a business financial software package installed on a computer.

Kelly is your friend and is totally confused by all these different views. She has asked for your help.

Questions

1 List **three** essential components of a basic cash register.

2 Do you agree with Kelly's mother? Give a reason for your answer.

3 Identify **one** benefit and **one** weakness of Kelly's grandfather's suggestion.

4 State the full title of the EPOS system.

5 List **four** functions which a sophisticated EPOS system can provide.

6 List **four** functions which a business financial software package can provide.

7 Recommend the most appropriate system(s) for Kelly, giving a reason for your choice.

Petty cash

1 Jane Watkins is responsible for the petty cash system at Universal Engineering. This is used for all small purchases under £25. One of Jane's colleagues is Tom, who works in the store. He sometimes comes to her for petty cash. The list below gives the various stages of the procedure which she uses – but is written in the wrong order. Starting with **D**, list the items in the correct order.

A	Tom gives Jane the receipt for the taxi fare he paid together with his completed petty cash voucher.
B	Jane totals all the amounts paid out this month.
C	Jane gives Tom the money and keeps the voucher and the receipt.
D	The petty cash float is topped up to £200 at the start of the month.
E	Tom completes and signs a petty cash voucher.
F	Jane checks that her total is the same as the amount of cash she has paid out from the float.
G	Jane transfers details of the transaction to the list in her petty cash book.
H	On the 1 May Tom obtains permission to take an injured colleague to hospital. His boss tells him to use a taxi and reclaim the money from petty cash.
I	Jane shows her balanced petty cash book to the accountant who tops up the float again.
J	Tom's boss signs the authorisation section on the petty cash voucher.
K	Jane deals with several other petty cash requests during the rest of the month.
L	Tom makes sure he gets a receipt from the taxi driver.

2 During May, the vouchers Jane received are listed in the box opposite.

   a How much money did she pay out?

   b How much money should she have left in the petty cash box?

   c How much money will she need to restore the float?

3 What do you think Jane should do in each of the following situations?

   a A colleague was told to buy some stamps but lost the receipt on the way back.

   b Because there are more purchases than normal, she runs out of money during one month.

   c A member of staff asks her to reimburse the money he has paid out to buy a small fridge for the office which cost £70.

May Vouchers	
Phone	£17.00
Newsagent	£24.00
Flowers for reception	£8.00
Jug kettle	£17.50
Taxi	£18.00
Tea and coffee	£11.30
Milkman	£15.00
Window cleaning	£17.00
Flip charts	£16.00
Velcro strips	£12.00
Stamps	£16.00

Activity 3.4.5

Retail theft in Europe steals the show!

Read the following case study and answer the questions that follow.

Case study

Each year the Centre for Retail Research in Nottingham produces the European Retail Theft Barometer. This measures retail crime across the 16 countries of Western Europe. The study is funded by Checkpoint systems.

In the 2002/3 Barometer, average shrinkage across Europe, i.e. stock loss from crime or wastage, fell from 1.45 per cent to 1.37 per cent of sales turnover. The UK, however, has the worst shrinkage rate in Europe at 1.69 per cent of sales, which works out at a cost per head of £83.20. But this was an improvement from 1.77 per cent in 2001/2 and 1.81 per cent before that. The countries with the lowest rates are Switzerland, 0.89 per cent, and Austria 0.98 per cent.

According to the research, customer thieves are responsible for 48 per cent of shrinkage, employees for 28 per cent and suppliers for 7 per cent, making 83 per cent of shrinkage crime-related. Staff mistakes cause 17 per cent.

In the UK this works out at £1,956 million lost through customer theft, £1,664 million lost through staff theft, £184 million through supplier theft and £807 million lost through errors and mistakes.

You can find out more by going to **www.heinemann.co.uk/hotlinks** (express code 1351T)

Questions

1 What is meant by the term 'shrinkage'?

2 a Is shrinkage falling or rising across Europe? Give figures to support your answer.

 b Is shrinkage falling or increasing in the UK? Again give figures to support your answer.

3 It is often said that anyone can make a mistake. Can you suggest **three** types of mistake that staff could make which could mean that an item of stock cannot be sold or isn't sold at the right price?

4 In the UK, £184 million of goods could not be sold because of supplier theft. Can you suggest:

 a one way in which suppliers can steal goods?

 b one way in which retailers could help to prevent this?

5 Staff may be in collusion with customers when goods are stolen. Can you suggest **two** ways in which staff can help customers to steal goods?

6 Studies have shown that there are different types of thieves. For each type of thief listed below, suggest **one** action a store could take to deter each of them.

 a Opportunistic thieves who do not steal regularly but will take advantage of any unexpected opportunities to do so.

 b Persistent thieves who will visit stores with the aim of stealing.

 c Juvenile thieves who steal to impress a group of friends.

7 Many stores install CCTV cameras to help them to spot thieves, but experts caution against relying too heavily on these to the exclusion of other methods. To save money, many shops also install dummy cameras.

 a Suggest **two** limitations of CCTV cameras

 b Suggest **one** danger of using dummy cameras.

8 Access the latest version of the Barometer through the link at **www.heinemann.co.uk/hotlinks** (express code 1351T) and check the latest shrinkage rates to find out if the situation is improving or worsening.

Catch 'em if you can!

Kala is opening his first store and wants to prevent theft and fraud by any means possible. He has made a list of 20 actions he can take. When you look through them you are quite surprised at some of them – and even wonder if they are legal!

Your tasks

1 Check through this list. Start by identifying all the actions that you think Kala cannot legally take. Put a cross against that item in the Lawful/Unlawful column. This then eliminates these ideas from the list.

2 Select the **five** items that you think are the most important and would be the most beneficial in helping to prevent theft in Kala's shop. Give reasons for your choice.

3 Suggest **two** more ideas of your own that you think would be useful.

	Action	Lawful/ unlawful
A	Train staff well and make sure they know that anyone who steals will be instantly dismissed.	
B	Display goods in locked glass cabinets and only use dummy product displays in the store.	
C	Put up warning signs saying all thieves will be prosecuted.	
D	Sack all the staff immediately if theft has taken place but the culprit will not own up.	
E	Sack the newest member of staff immediately if theft has taken place but the culprit will not own up.	
F	Pay fair wages and give staff discounts on goods they buy in the store.	
G	Refuse to allow junior or work experience staff to use the tills.	
H	Only allow the store supervisor to void sales or give refunds.	
I	If the supervisor is absent, refuse to give refunds to customers.	
J	Make it a condition of employment that staff will agree to be searched before they leave if theft is suspected.	
K	Refuse to have unaccompanied children under 16 in the shop.	
L	Allow unaccompanied children but if they mess about, give them a clip behind the ear and lock them in the empty storeroom for a while.	
M	Refuse to allow admittance or serve to anyone who is drunk or is a known troublemaker. Call the police if necessary.	
N	Refuse to pay a member of staff his or her wage if the till they are using has a shortfall.	
O	Pay the staff member a wage if the till has a shortfall but keep back 10 per cent.	
P	Insist all personal belongings are left in staff lockers.	
Q	Place CCTV cameras throughout the store including in break rooms and toilet areas.	
R	Operate a hardship fund for staff with financial problems.	
S	Put security tags or loop alarms on valuable goods.	
T	Refuse to allow staff to have their annual holidays if the tills they have worked on have had a shortfall on more than three occasions.	

These sample assessments are designed as practice exercises to help your students understand the types of task they will be required to do for their formal assessments. For practice, tasks can be done by individuals or by groups as indicated.

There is one sample assessment for each section of the Unit:

3.1	Profit and break even
3.2	Cash flow management
3.3	Budgets for planning and monitoring expenditure
3.4	Recording transactions

The structure and grading of the assessments reflect the grading criteria for the unit as provided by Edexcel. Differentiation information is given where appropriate to indicate what would be required from the student to gain pass, merit or distinction grades. Tips to help the student achieve a merit or distinction grade are also given. A deadline box is provided in which you can enter a submission date to familiarise your students with the idea of working to a specified date or time.

Answers to Unit 3 sample assessments

3.1 – Task 1 Pass grade

a The key points should include the fact that break even can be calculated using a chart or a formula. It enables the business to check how many sales are required, to cover costs. Below this level the business will make a loss. It also shows, at a given level of costs, how many sales are required to make a profit. It also enables the business to identify a safety margin and to identify if action is required to improve sales or reduce costs.

b The student's numeric example should correctly illustrate the points made.

3.1 – Task 2 Merit grade

a Tutor to check.

b **i** Break even = 500 hot dogs

   ii Revenue = £1,280, profit = £240

   iii Sales revenue = £480, loss = £160

   iv Margin of safety = 500

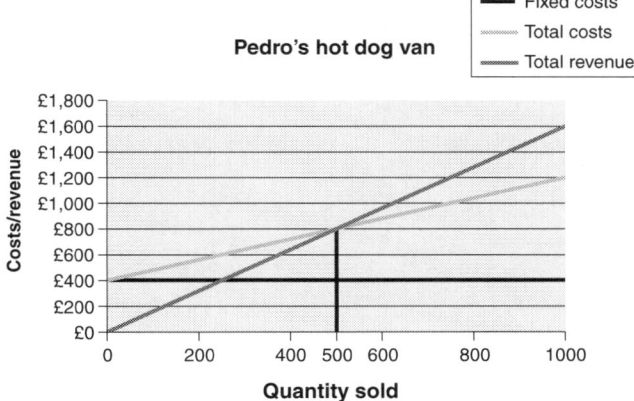

Pedro's hot dog van

Legend: Fixed costs, Total costs, Total revenue

3.1 – Task 3 Merit grade

a Break even = $\dfrac{£400}{£1.60 - £0.80} = \dfrac{£400}{£0.80} = 500$

b Profit margin = £1.60 – 80p = 80p

c **i** Break even = 571. Would need to sell at least 71 more to break even but could sell even more at the lower price.

   ii Break even = 250. Need to sell less to break even, but would he get as many customers at the new site?

   iii Break even = 444. Need to sell less to break even. Would make more profit if sales stay the same – this would depend on customers' perception of the quality of the new sausages.

   iv Break even = 333. This again is lower. Higher profit if sales stay the same, but some people may not be prepared to pay the higher price.

3.1 – Task 4 Distinction grade

Tutors may wish to instruct students to do this section in groups, providing the exercise is not being used as the formal assessment. Any appropriate recommendations should be accepted providing these are justified. Raising/lowering the price could depend upon the competition in the area and the popularity of the site. Finding a cheaper supplier for the *same quality* of sausages or rolls would reduce costs. Adding other options (e.g. hamburgers) could increase income because it would only add to variable costs and not to fixed costs. Or Pedro could reduce the price for multiple purchases with less risk of overall takings falling. Pedro may even be better paying more for a busier site (e.g. near a football ground) where he would have more regular customers.

3.2 – Task 1 Pass grade

a

BUSHRA'S BUSES - Cashflow Forecast						
	July £	August £	Sept £	Oct £	Nov £	Dec £
INCOME	20,000	20,000	18,000	16,000	15,000	15,000
EXPENDITURE						
Fuel	1,500	1,500	1,400	1,300	1,300	1,300
Insurance	1,000	1,000	1,000	1,200	1,200	1,200
Maintenance	2,000	2,000	2,000	3,000	3,000	3,000
Rent	1,800	1,800	1,800	1,800	1,800	1,800
Wages	12,000	12,000	12,000	12,000	12,000	12,000
Total expenditure	18,300	18,300	18,200	19,300	19,300	19,300
Net cash flow	1,700	1,700	-200	-3,300	-4,300	-4,300
MONTHLY SUMMARY						
Opening bank balance	10,000	11,700	13,400	13,200	9,900	5,600
Net cash flow	1,700	1,700	-200	-3,300	-4,300	-4,300
Closing bank balance	11,700	13,400	13,200	9,900	5,600	1,300

b **i** Less fuel is used because the coaches are not being used as much out of the holiday season.

ii Maintenance costs rise because refurbishment and preventative maintenance take place during the quieter months. This is sensible as Bushra would want to ensure there are minimal breakdowns during the busy summer season.

iii The money flowing into and out of Bushra's business in income and expenditure.

iv The final bank balances decrease steadily in the second half of the period. This pattern is due to falling sales income which is a seasonal issue and the increased maintenance costs identified in **ii** above. Another factor is the increase in insurance costs (presumably unavoidable) from October onwards. Despite all of this, the account is still above zero so that there is no need to use an overdraft facility – yet!.

3.2 – Task 2 Pass grade

a The revised spreadsheet has final balances from July to December respectively as £11,700 (same), £11,400, £9,200, £900, –£5,400, –£11,700.

b Both have reduced the net cash flow figures.

c This shows that in November and December Bushra needs an overdraft. Hopefully, when things started to go wrong, she realised what was going to happen and talked to the bank. The bank would want to be reassured that, soon after December, her business would become profitable again. As well as solving the temporary problems, she might be able to improve income by finding more work during the autumn/winter months or by cutting costs.

3.2 – Task 3 Merit grade

The student's explanation should include the fact that a profitable business can go bankrupt if it doesn't receive money owing. This is because it still has to make payments itself, so lack of income can create a negative cash flow. On a temporary basis a business may be able to operate an overdraft until the payment is received. However, the situation can quickly become critical if a major customer defaults on a large debt and the company already operates at the maximum overdraft level. If the bank refuses to lend any more money and the business cannot pay its own debts, it may be taken to court and forced into bankruptcy by creditors who want their money. Appropriate figures should be used to illustrate the concept.

3.2 – Task 4 Distinction grade

Answer should include the fact that Bushra needs to carry out appropriate credit checks on new customers and set an appropriate maximum credit level; forecast her cash flow and monitor that income is received as predicted and expenditure is broadly the same; introduce a system of credit control to chase up debts owing (the student should provide some details and examples here); take action to keep expenditure to target levels. If there is a problem, she should keep her bank informed. She should also look for other ways to increase income and pay suppliers on time – but not too early unless there is a financial incentive to do so.

3.3 – Task 1 Pass grade

a

EASYFOOD BUDGET - SANDWICH COST CENTRE - APRIL - SEPTEMBER							
Item	April	May	June	July	August	September	Total
Meat	2,000	2,000	2,000	2,000	2,000	2,000	12,000
Fish	2,000	2,000	2,000	2,000	2,000	2,000	12,000
Cheese	1,500	1,500	1,500	1,500	1,500	1,500	9,000
Bread and rolls	2,000	2,000	2,000	2,000	2,000	2,000	12,000
Salad/vegetables	2,000	2,000	2,000	2,000	2,000	2,000	12,000
Packaging	3,000	3,000	3,000	3,000	3,000	3,000	18,000
Wages	5,000	5,000	5,000	5,000	5,000	5,000	30,000
Margarine	1,000	1,000	1,000	1,000	1,000	1,000	6,000
Item total	18,500	18,500	18,500	18,500	18,500	18,500	111,000
Cumulative total	18,500	37,000	55,500	74,000	92,500	111,000	

b   The student should clearly explain how budgets are constructed to include agreed planned spending for each cost centre and actual expenditure is entered, usually every month. The variance is calculated and used to check spending. Action is taken when variances are unfavourable, especially if the variance is for a significant amount. Example figures should be used correctly to illustrate these principles.

3.3 – Task 2 Merit grade

a

EASYFOOD SANDWICH COST CENTRE - APRIL BUDGET REPORT			
Item	Planned	Actual	Variance
	£	£	£
Meat	2,000	2,500	-500
Fish	2,000	2,500	-500
Cheese	1,500	1,400	100
Bread and rolls	2,000	2,500	-500
Salad/vegetables	2,000	3,000	-1,000
Packaging	3,000	3,300	-300
Wages	5,000	6,000	-1,000
Margarine	1,000	500	500
Total	18,500	21,700	-3,200

b   The student should explain that budget variance information enables budget holders to check spending regularly, to report significant variances to senior managers and to take action themselves. Senior managers use budget variance information to check spending across the business against financial plans. They can claw back underspends in one department and use this for more appropriate purposes. They can take action if there are unfavourable variances and review these in relation to possible action or even a change in future business methods or activity.

3.3 – Task 3 Distinction grade

a   The total variance figure is –£9,360. In other words, the business has lost over nine thousand pounds. Many new developments lose money at the outset but Emily would be unhappy if this situation continued.

b   The trends in the total variance figures between April and August should give Emily some encouragement as these reduce from –£3,200 in April to –£250 in August. However, problems have obviously occurred again in September and these need solving.

c   i   The costs in a budget should always be readjusted if previous estimates haven't been accurate.

ii   The unfavourable variance for meat has been reduced, so staff are obviously using less per sandwich.

iii   Wages have fallen so presumably productivity has risen. It would appear staff have received some training and are now more experienced.

iv   Bread costs fell and now show a favourable variance. It is most likely that the supplier has been changed.

v Packaging is also now favourable. Perhaps the supplier has been changed or a different type of packaging is being used or a refund was received in August.

d Varying the fillings could be a good idea but should only be done on a temporary basis. Sales figures will show which are the most popular lines. Poor sellers should be scrapped. It is also always more cost effective to make larger amounts of sandwiches with the same filling, to gain discounts on larger orders, than to offer too much variety.

e Final recommendations could include the following. The area is new and the original costs may not have been accurate. These can be reviewed for the next budget in the light of experience. Meat costs are now acceptable so no action is required. Fish is still too high, could a cheaper supplier be found? There are currently no problems with cheese and bread. Salad and vegetables are showing a high unfavourable variance. This could be through wastage as these items are perishable. Either storage should be improved or fewer items ordered more frequently. The fillings may be reviewed again to select the best sellers which are the most cost effective to produce. There are no problems now with packaging and savings are being made on margarine. Wages have started to increase and the reason should be investigated. If this area continues to give problems, perhaps different ways of working could be investigated, such as greater mechanisation.

3.4 – Task 3 Distinction grade

No specific answer possible; it will depend upon the business selected by the student.

Pedro owns a hot dog van which he drives to a park on Saturdays and Sundays. He has permission from the local authority which charges rent for the site. It is now the end of June and Pedro is wondering what might happen during July, when many families are away on holiday. June has been a rainy month, and Pedro didn't do very well. You have offered to help him to see if you can suggest improvements he can make.

Task 1 – Pass grade

You tell Pedro that a business can calculate its break even to check its profitable activity levels, but he doesn't know what you mean.

1 a Briefly explain the idea of break even – what it is and how it can be calculated.

  b Include a simple numerical example of your own to demonstrate the points you are making to him.

Deadline

Tips to achieve a merit grade

For this task you will have to draw a break even chart and calculate break even by using the formula.

Drawing your chart:
* Remember to plot your axes carefully. The maximum on the horizontal axis is the greatest number that will be sold. The maximum on the vertical scale is the maximum amount of money that can be earned, i.e. the greatest number to be sold multiplied by the selling price. Don't forget to label both axes.
* Label each line as you draw it, i.e. the fixed cost line, total cost line, and the sales revenue line.
* Identify the break even point by seeing where the total cost line crosses the sales revenue line.
* Remember that sales above this point means profit; below it means loss.

Using the formula:

$$\frac{\text{Fixed costs}}{\text{Selling price per unit} - \text{variable price per unit}}$$

Simply substitute the figures you are given in the correct place in the formula.

Now do Tasks 2 and 3.

Tasks 2 and 3 – Merit grade

Pedro now writes down the following figures:

Fixed costs (rent etc.):	£400
Variable cost per hot dog (bread, sausages etc.):	80p
Selling price:	£1.60

Pedro tells you that the greatest number of hot dogs he has ever sold is 1,000.

2 a From this information, **draw** a break even chart.

  b After checking with your tutor that the chart is correct, **list** the following information for Pedro:
  i   The break even point.
  ii His sales revenue and profit/loss (say which) if 800 hot dogs are sold.
  iii His sales revenue and profit/loss if 300 hot dogs are sold.
  iv The margin of safety if 1,000 hot dogs are sold.

3 **a** Now **carry out** the same calculation, using the formula method, to show Pedro how this is done.

b **Calculate** Pedro's profit margin for each hot dog sold.

c In June, Pedro's actual sales were 700, giving a profit of £160. He would like to increase this figure and has some ideas. These include:

i Reduce the selling price to £1.50.
ii Move to a cheaper location to reduce overheads to £200.
iii Buy cheaper sausages so that the variable cost per unit would be 70p.
iv Increase the selling price to £2.00.

Re-calculate the break even point in each case and **suggest** the possible outcomes for each of the ideas, bearing in mind the new break even point and other factors.

Deadline

Tips to achieve a distinction grade

This question asks you to make recommendations based on your work. The following ideas may help you.

- Use all the calculations and the break even points you calculated in Task 3 to help you.
- Decide which types of actions help to increase the level of profit. Make a list of these.
- Apply these actions to the situation you are given. Try to be as inventive as possible!

Now do Task 4.

Task 4 – Distinction grade

During the first week of July business is very poor and Pedro makes a loss. His situation is now critical.

Recommend the action he should take immediately, based on the calculations you made for task **3c** above – and add any other ideas which you think will help.

For every suggestion you make, **explain** what will happen if Pedro takes this action.

Deadline

You work for **Bushra's Buses**. Bushra's business hires out coaches for school trips and holidays. Her busiest time is in the summer when her coaches travel all over Britain taking people on holiday tours. In the other months, most of the work comes from school contracts.

Tasks 1 and 2 – *Pass grade*

1 a Bushra has started to produce a spreadsheet to forecast her cash flow for the next six months. Her opening bank balance in July is £10,000.

She has asked you to **complete this** for her and to calculate the final bank balances for each month. Do this as requested and check your answer with your tutor.

BUSHRA'S BUSES - Cash flow forecast						
	July	August	Sept	Oct	Nov	Dec
	£	£	£	£	£	£
INCOME	20,000	20,000	18,000	16,000	15,000	15,000
EXPENDITURE						
Fuel	1,500	1,500	1,400	1,300	1,300	1,300
Insurance	1,000	1,000	1,000	1,200	1,200	1,200
Maintenance	2,000	2,000	2,000	3,000	3,000	3,000
Rent	1,800	1,800	1,800	1,800	1,800	1,800
Wages	12,000	12,000	12,000	12,000	12,000	12,000
Total expenditure						
Net cash flow						
MONTHLY SUMMARY						
Opening bank balance						
Net cash flow						
Closing bank balance						

b Study your cash flow forecast carefully. To check you understand it, answer the following:

i   **Suggest** why the amount paid for fuel decreases over the period.

ii **Suggest** a reason for the maintenance costs rising in the autumn.

iii **State** what you understand by the meaning of 'cash flow'.

iv **Give your opinion** of Bushra's cash flow over this period.

Deadline

2 Bushra's cash flow forecast does not go according to plan. At the start of August, one of her drivers is ill. He needs an operation and says that he will be off work for the rest of the year. Bushra has to employ a temporary replacement driver which costs an extra £2,000 a month.

Then, during a routine inspection, it is discovered that one of the buses requires a major overhaul. The total cost for this is £3,000. This has to be paid for in October.

a   Make these changes on your spreadsheet.
b   Comment on the effect of *each* change on Bushra's cash flow.
c   Explain what action Bushra may have to take to cope with the situation.

Deadline

Tips to achieve a merit grade

Before you do the next task, it may help if you remember the following points.

* Cash flow analysis is mainly used to provide a **forecast**.
* This helps a business to avoid serious problems because these can be seen in advance.
* Problems mean the business must plan to spend less, earn more or borrow for a short time.
* Failure to take action can lead to bankruptcy.
* Think of examples of specific things that can go wrong and the amount of money that could be involved.

Now do Task 3.

Task 3 – Merit grade

Bushra is alarmed to hear that another coach operator in the area has just gone bankrupt because of cash flow problems. She had thought that this rival firm was very profitable.

Your colleagues are worried in case this could happen to Bushra's business and you lose your jobs. They ask you to tell them how a profitable business can go bankrupt because of cash flow problems.

Explain clearly how this can occur, **using example figures** to illustrate the points you are making.

Deadline

Tips to achieve a distinction grade

Before you start the next question, think about the following points.

* Businesses must take action to reduce bad debts and late payments.
* They can do this by carrying out checks on new customers.
* They can also have a system of **credit control**.
* You need to be able to explain the detailed aspects of both these systems in your recommendations.

Now do Task 4.

Task 4 – Distinction grade

Bushra is now wondering if the failure of the rival business could provide extra opportunities for her business. There are two problems. First, some of the firms approaching her to hire coaches regularly are unknown to her. Second, the finance manager has warned that the overall level of bad debts is rising.

Bushra wants to take action. She has therefore asked you to **suggest** as many **recommendations** as you can to help her to control her cash flow as effectively as possible.

Deadline

Easyfood is a business which was started 10 years ago by Emily Brent. It makes and supplies cakes and other confectionery for canteens and shops. The business has grown and is profitable. Recently, Emily decided that she could increase sales and profits by adding pre-packed sandwiches to the product range and selling them to her existing customers. She built an extension to the factory, hired extra staff and bought equipment. She decided to treat the new venture as a separate cost centre and planned a monthly budget for it. This is shown below.

Sandwich cost centre – monthly budget	
Meat £2,000	Fish £2,000
Cheese £1,500	Bread £2,000
Salad and vegetables £2,000	Packaging £3,000
Wages £5,000	Margarine £1,000

Task 1 – Pass grade

1 a Emily asks you to set up a spreadsheet showing her proposed expenditure for the next six months, i.e. from April to September.

She has asked you to include both a monthly and a cumulative total on your spreadsheet.

Draw up the spreadsheet and take a print-out for Emily.

b A member of staff, Tim, is promoted to manage the new cost centre. He will be the budget holder. Tim is experienced in catering but new to budgets.

Emily asks you to write a note for Tim which explains how and why budgets are used in the business.

Write your own explanation and **include** some sample **figures** to illustrate to Tim the reason for budgets.

Deadline

Tips to achieve a merit grade

For the next question you have to prepare a budget and a budget report yourself. The following points may help you.

- Use the standard layout for budgets, such as that shown in your Student Book.
- Remember that you will need four columns on your spreadsheet for the items, the planned and actual expenditure and the variances.
- For the first two columns you can copy the information from your first spreadsheet.
- You can then add the expenditure and calculate the variances for the month.
- Remember that variances can be positive or negative. Whereas minor variances may be ignored, larger variances are never ignored.
- Budget holders will be expected to take action immediately, wherever possible.
- Otherwise senior managers will step in. This is particularly the case if there are large negative variances.

Now do Task 2.

Task 2 – Merit grade

2 a Tim has listed his expenditure for April.

Create a spreadsheet for his budget, include his actual spending and calculate his variances. Use the planned expenditure figures from Task one.

Save your spreadsheet and take a print-out to check with your tutor that it is correct.

Expenditure for April

Meat £2,500	Fish £2,500
Cheese £1,400	Bread £2,500
Salad and vegetables £3,000	Packaging £3,300
Wages £6,000	Margarine £500
Tim	

---

b You are about to go on holiday and a new colleague, Fatima, will be taking over some of your tasks while you are away.

Emily asks you to write a note for Fatima and **explain** the importance of budget variance information to managers like herself and Tim. Bear in mind that Emily is a senior manager and Tim is the budget holder of the cost centre.

Deadline

Tips to achieve a distinction grade

The final task tests your ability to read and understand a budget report. Before you start, you might find it useful to consider the following points.

- All managers study variances very carefully. They are particularly concerned about negative variances, especially if these are large.
- Total variance figures are very important because these show whether variances only occur occasionally – or whether there is a serious, cumulative problem.
- Finding out the reason for negative variances is important. Sometimes it may be because the budget amount was not calculated accurately.
- In other cases action must be taken. This can include buying cheaper supplies, rejecting inferior materials, using less raw material, reducing wastage, reducing wages and so on.
- In some cases no action is possible and the budget amount for that item may have to be increased.

Now do Task 3 on the next page.

Task 3 – Distinction grade

When you return from holiday you are involved with different work for several months. In September, however, Emily asks you to start working with budgets again. The financial controller has just printed out a budget report on Tim's cost centre for the last six months.

3 a You glance at the total variance figures out of interest. **State** what Emily's opinions will be, with reasons.

b Emily is studying the total variance figure for each of the six months, starting from April. **Explain** what these figures tell her.

c You ask Emily why the variances have occurred. She tells you that there have been several problems.

    i At the start, the costs weren't calculated accurately enough.

    ii Then she found that staff were putting too much meat in the sandwiches.

    iii Productivity was poor at the start so overtime was necessary.

    iv The bread supplier increased his prices.

    v There were problems with the packaging – many of the hinged lids fell off when the packets were closed.

Emily asks you to **describe** what action you think she has taken for *each* of the problems that she has listed above. She says you can gain some clues by studying the budget report up to August carefully.

d Tim now wants to vary the fillings each month to see which are the most popular. Emily is not convinced this is a good idea as some of the new fillings are more expensive, which means the selling price of those sandwiches is also quite high.
Emily asks you to **give your opinion** about this idea.

e Finally Emily has asked you to **recommend** ways in which she should deal with this new cost centre, given it is consistently recording an unfavourable budget variance.

EASYFOOD BUDGET REPORT - SANDWICH COST CENTRE - APRIL - SEPTEMBER

Item	Budget	April variances £	May variances £	June variances £	July variances £	August variances £	Sept variances £	Total £
Meat	2,000	-500	-300	-200	-200	-100	0	-1,300
Fish	2,000	-500	-300	-200	-300	-400	-500	-2,200
Cheese	1,500	100	-50	60	-100	50	50	110
Bread and rolls	2,000	-500	-300	-700	10	200	150	-1,140
Salad/vegetables	2,000	-1,000	-1,100	-500	0	-1,000	-1,200	-4,800
Packaging	3,000	-300	200	-500	-400	600	100	-300
Wages	5,000	-1,000	-500	-800	-200	-100	-300	-2,900
Margarine	1,000	500	450	650	550	500	520	3,170
Item total	18,500	-3,200	-1,900	-2,190	-640	-250	-1,180	-9,360
Cumulative total		-3,200	-5,100	-7,290	-7,930	-8,180	-9,360	

Deadline

Select one small retail business you know. This could be a local business where you are a customer, a business where you work part-time or where a member of your family works.

Task 1 – Pass grade

a **Describe** the business, the type of goods it sells and its range of customers.

b **Investigate** two or three different transactions, e.g. purchases from other businesses, purchases made by staff and sales to customers. In each case **briefly explain** how these transactions are recorded in the business.

c For each example you give, **explain** whether you think the method of recording is both effective and secure.

Deadline

Tips to obtain a merit grade

Before you start the next task, think about:

- The ways in which fraud can occur in a business.
- The types of people who may be involved.
- How fraud can take place when goods are being sold by the business.
- How fraud can take place when sales transactions are being recorded.

Now do Task 2.

Task 2 – Merit grade

Explain how fraud could take place in this business when sales transactions are being processed and recorded.

Deadline

Tips to obtain a distinction grade

Before you start the final task, think about the following points.

- The type of fraud that you have already stated could take place in the business.
- Positive methods the owner could take to reduce the risk of fraud.
- The cost of different types of prevention methods.
- Simple, sensible, precautions that would cost very little.

Now do Task 3.

Task 3 – Distinction grade

Identify and **suggest** simple fraud prevention and detection measures that could be taken by the owner.

Deadline

3.1 – Profit and break even
Over to you, page 203

1 Income and revenue. Costs and expenditure.

2

Income (£)	Expenditure (£)	Difference (£)	Result
25	20	5	Profit
37	40	–3	Loss
1,500	1,200	300	Profit
1,725	1,725	0	Break even
2,735	2,294	441	Profit
5,710	6,123	–413	Loss
100,445	97,003	3,442	Profit
47,653	47,653	0	Break even

3 **Profit** – Asda, Sky Digital, Marks & Spencer.

Break even – County council, BBC, OXFAM, Help the Aged, school/college, British government.

4 No specific answer. The aim of the exercise is to encourage students to reflect on the many facets of business and what can go wrong with them. More obvious answers are – prices too high, costs out of control, poor marketing/promotion, poor quality of services or products, products out of date.

Over to you, page 205

1 **a** £400, **b** £114, **c** £466

2 **a** £15, **b** £100, **c** £60, total = £175

3 £750,000 and £1,400,000

Over to you, page 206

1 **a** fixed, indirect

b variable, direct.

2 Fixed – wages for full-time mechanic, heating, business rates, insurance.

Variable – spare parts, oil, wages for part-time mechanic, coffee.

3 Any reasonable answers are acceptable. They could include:

Indirect – rent, loan repayment, utility bills, telephone, cleaning materials.

Direct – any number of types of bread and filling ingredients.

Over to you, page 207

1 **a** First total is 25,800

b Second total is 35,900

2 Inflation increase is 80,000 + 4,000 = 84,000

With the extra 5,000 = 89,000

Over to you, page 208

1

No. of units produced	Variable cost per unit	Total variable cost
100	50p	£50.00
250	£1.00	£250.00
375	25p	£93.75
500	£1.30	£650.00
623	£2.00	£1,246.00
57	£50.00	£2,850.00
1,374	£15.23	£20,926.02

2 £26,065.77 and £28,672.35

3 £6.85, £2.55, £3.25, £4.35

Over to you, page 212

1 A false, B true, C false, D true, E false, F true, G true, H false.

2 Revenue = unit price × number sold.

3 Negotiate a better price with material supplier, look for a cheaper supplier, reduce the amount of material used, find a cheaper material without affecting quality, or any other appropriate suggestions.

4 **a** Door-to-door collections, raffles, charity events, appeals by letter or in the press, collections at work or in pubs.

b Much depends upon whether the charity has premises. Assuming it has then (3 of) rent, heating, electricity, telephone, salaries of paid staff (not volunteers), insurance. It is important for the charity to keep its fixed costs as low as possible because every £1 saved is £1 available for the cause it supports.

Over to you, page 216

1 a   £2,400 and £7,200

   b   £3,500 and £6,500

   c   £800 loss and £400 profit

   d $(80 - 67) = 13$ mowers

2 a

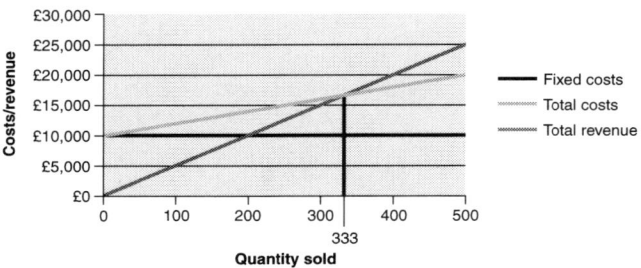

Super Smoothie Makers

   b   Tutor to check.

   c   i   The actual break even point is 333, however, given the lack of complete accuracy when using a chart, a figure close to this is acceptable. This argument also applies to other readings taken from the chart.

      ii   £16,650

      iii Income = £2,2500, expenditure = £19,000

      iv   Sales of 400 gives profit of £2,000
           Sales of 200 gives loss of £4,000

      v   Students should be able to confirm their results

Over to you, page 217

1

Business	Total fixed costs (£)	Variable cost per unit (£)	Selling price per unit (£)	Break even point
A	20	2	4	10
B	1,000	50	100	20
C	500	21	31	50
D	270	18	33	18
E	1,050	7	11	262
F	2,714	53	107	50

2

Business	Total fixed costs (£)	Variable cost /unit (£)	Selling price per unit (£)	Total sales	Total sales revenue (£)	Total variable cost (£)	Total cost (£)	Profit or loss (£)
A	20	2	4	100	400	200	220	180
B	1,000	50	100	75	7,500	3,750	4,750	2,750
C	500	21	31	700	21,700	14,700	15,200	6,500
D	270	18	33	10	330	180	450	−120
E	1,050	7	11	30	330	210	1,260	−930
F	2,714	53	107	200	21,400	10,600	13,314	8,086

Over to you, page 218

1

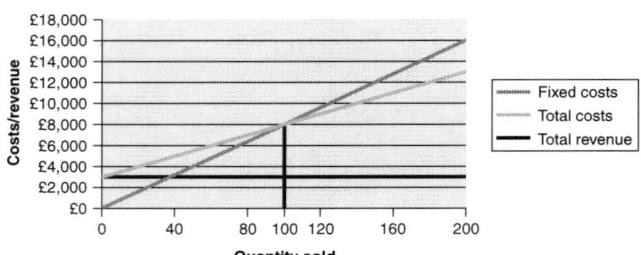

Len's lawnmowers (revisited)

   a   100

   b   No specific answer possible

   c   33

   d   Because the fixed costs have increased so he has to sell more to cover the additional cost.

   e   £12,000

   f   £1,500 profit

   g   £600 loss

   h   No specific answer possible

2   This is an open-ended question. It should stimulate a debate bringing in different issues. It should introduce the theme of the next section.

    Could Len afford to lose £1,000?

    Could he promote the product in less expensive or more effective ways?

    Could he advertise for a couple of weeks to see if sales improve?

Over to you, page 219

The answers below are indicative. Students could produce other equally valid answers.

1 This would reduce direct costs – assuming that the labour force can be expanded or contracted, depending on demand. There would be some costs involved in obtaining new premises, recruiting staff etc. Also there may be redundancy costs for UK staff. Since many companies are doing this, there is an overall cost saving. The main risk is the quality of service, given potential language problems.

2 This would reduce direct costs but would the quality of the finished product (such as windows) be affected? If the quality is lower, the business could lose customers or have higher warranty claims.

3 This would increase fixed costs – the building itself plus maintenance, cleaning etc. There would also be additional staffing costs. The key question is, would enough extra students be attracted to increase the additional income sufficiently to cover the additional costs?

4 For the sake of argument, the purchase price in either case could be called a fixed cost whereas maintenance could be called a variable cost. A lot would depend on whether the additional maintenance cost of the secondhand cars would offset the reduced capital cost. An additional consideration is that the secondhand cars would probably break down more often which in turn would affect customer satisfaction.

Section review, page 220

1 a The costs incurred from all sources, i.e. variable plus fixed costs.

b Profit of £40,000.

c Direct costs; for example (3 of) stock for resale, sales commission for staff, raw materials, spare parts, overtime (or other suitable suggestions).

d When total revenue and total costs are the same, so the business hasn't made a profit but hasn't lost any money either.

e Profit or loss = Income less total costs.

f Indirect costs; for example (3 of) electricity, rent, rates, heating, most staff wages, telephone, stationery (or other suitable suggestions).

g When calculating the break even point.

h (2 of) Sell more goods by advertising, sell more overall by reducing the price a little, find new sources of income.

i The number by which sales can fall before the break even point is reached.

j (2 of) Negotiating lower prices for bulk orders, finding a cheaper suppliers, using less material, reducing waste, using more automated systems, increasing productivity.

2 a

Fixed costs	Variable costs
Heating £500	Waterproof cloth £5,000
Business rates £1,000	Catch mechanisms £1,500
Insurance £300	Metal struts £3,000
Telephone £150	Telescopic shafts £2,000
Staff wages £20,000	
Water and electricity £1,200	
Total fixed costs = £23,150	Total variable costs = £11,500

b i £40,000

ii (4 of) 'Shop around' for cheaper electricity, cheaper heating or cheaper insurance, find a cheaper supplier of the cloth or umbrella components, buy supplies in bulk for greater discounts, reduce wastage, increase productivity.

iii If sales remain the same or increase then overall income will increase, but sales may fall. In this case overall income may be less, depending upon the number of sales lost.

iv £249,600 – profits would fall to £30,400.

v Staff could be paid a bonus if sales or profit targets were met. Commission could also be paid but this normally only benefits sales staff, rather than all staff.

3.2 – Cash flow management
Over to you, page 222

1 XYZ Trading: Net cash flow £3,000, closing balance £11,000.

2 Widgets Unlimited: Net cash flow £20,000, closing balance £70,000.

3 First Features: Net cash flow £5,940, closing balance £28,440.

4 Creative Projects: Net cash flow £2,204, closing balance £18,633.

Tutor to check layout of answers.

Over to you, page 224

The chart shows a negative cash flow figure for February, compared with January. This is due to a decrease in sales revenue and an increase in the costs of cement and wages.

GARDEN FEATURES CASH FLOW			
	January £	February £	March £
Income from sales	20,000	18,000	22,000
Expenditure			
Cement	2,000	3,000	2,500
Sand	1,000	1,000	900
Wages	14,000	15,000	14,000
Paint	500	500	500
Miscellaneous items	300	200	200
Subtotal of expenditure	17,800	19,700	18,100
Net cash flow	2,200	-1,700	3,900
Monthly summary			
Opening bank balance	3,000	5,200	3,500
Net cash flow	2,200	-1,700	3,900
Closing bank balance	5,200	3,500	7,400

Over to you, page 226

1   Tutor to check. The answer should be identical to the answer to the last 'Over to you'.

2

NIKITA'S CASH FLOW STATEMENT						
	January £	February £	March £	April £	May £	June £
Income from sales	50,000	48,000	50,000	55,000	58,000	60,000
Expenditure						
Shoes	45,000	30,000	25,000	20,000	22,000	20,000
Trainers	22,000	20,000	15,000	14,000	14,000	13,000
Wages	5,000	5,000	5,000	5,000	5,000	5,000
Rent	1,000	1,000	1,000	1,000	1,000	1,000
Miscellaneous items	500	500	500	500	500	500
Subtotal of expenditure	73,500	56,500	46,500	40,500	42,500	39,500
Net cash flow	-23,500	-8,500	3,500	14,500	15,500	20,500
Monthly Summary						
Opening bank balance	20,000	-3,500	-12,000	-8,500	6,000	21,500
Net cash flow	-23,500	-8,500	3,500	14,500	15,500	20,500
Closing bank balance	-3,500	-12,000	-8,500	6,000	21,500	42,000

3   The negative cash flow is in January and February and the closing bank balance figure is negative in January, February and March. The negative figures are due to her re-stocking in the early months of the year.

Over to you, page 228

1   Tutor to check that the student's original spreadsheet has been recalled and amended correctly and now matches the example in the book.

2   The final balances are shown for each change.

a   The overall effect is positive, although the closing bank balance is lower in March. The expenditure would appear to be worthwhile.

Closing bank balance
6,500 0 2,500 19,000 36,500 57,000

b   By June this is having a negative effect, so is probably not a good idea.

Closing bank balance
6,500 0 3,500 19,000 33,500 53,000

c   The clearance improves the final balances for every month. On this basis it would be very worthwhile – unless the stock would sell at a higher price if it were kept on display longer. . This is why the timing of sales clearances is very important.

Closing bank balance
11,500 5,000 8,500 23,000 38,500 59,000

d   i   This reduces the bank balances because of the increased expenditure. Nikita would be concerned about the negative figure in February and *may* delay the appointment until March.

Closing bank balance
6,500 –1,000 1,500 15,000 29,500 49,000

ii   This shows a net gain of £7,000 by June so is very worthwhile. Even if the sales figure is too optimistic, some additional sales should be generated. At worst, the situation would be as **i** above – which the business can still afford. However, Nikita would still think very carefully about the projected negative balance in February.

Closing bank balance
6,500 –1,000 4,500 21,000 38,500 61,000

Over to you, page 234

1   The most promising strategies are: look at published accounts, ask for bank references, use a commercial credit agency.

The others are less suitable for different reasons.

The company accountant would not release a bank statement, as it would contain many kinds of confidential information. In addition he/she could take offence since the integrity of the business is being called in question.

The appearance of the building is not a particularly good indicator of a business's willingness to pay on time. Some businesses like to project a good image whereas the substance could be entirely different.

Asking for references from other suppliers is a possibility but some may be friendly with the targeted supplier, others may be concerned about libel – and some may not take the trouble to reply.

2   The exact information will depend upon the websites investigated. Tutors may wish to subdivide the topic further if the class is large and, say, compare the relative merits/services of competing CRAs. The following are guidance notes only. Tutors are recommended to check each site themselves for updated content at the time of issuing this task.

   a   Examples of CRA services offered by one firm, Experian. These include: advice to consumers/copies of credit report/advice and assistance; business services including market trends/economic reports, advice on customer account processing/credit control; technology solutions, data application processing etc.; credit monitoring including online credit reports/email and SMS notifications.

   b   Examples of services offered by one firm, Checksure: online reports for companies; snapshot level report at discount price (currently £5.95); online updates available; discounts for multiple reports. The Company Information page is useful and includes details of the type of businesses required to file reports at Companies House and those which are not required to do so. There is also an example report on the site.

   c   The core product of CCS is Colsys, a debt collection package. Users can access the system online and CCS will act as the debt recovery agent. Larger businesses can access the system from a network and use it to produce letters, task lists and court forms. Alternatively the system can be installed on the customer's own server. The system monitors the status of every debtor, provides

a full accounting package and is designed for easier recovery of outstanding debts.

   d   This company is one of many who will provide up to 90 per cent of funds immediately for invoices. The invoices are issued by the supplier and, at a basic level, the supplier then issues statements and chases up late payments. If the supplier wishes, through its credit control service GE will also take care of everything else, i.e. issue statements, chase up payments, and keep records. Overseas transactions are included. The company also offers credit protection insurance, to insure against bad debts and non-payment.

   e   This site includes useful advice for businesses on managing cash flow which students would find both helpful and informative. Press releases provide up-to-date information on the campaign. Legal updates are included on the site and a 'site doctor' for giving advice to businesses that have a problem.

3   a   (3 of) Keeping accurate records of invoices and payment due dates, having a system of flagging up when payments are overdue, refusing to take orders from customers who persistently offend or demanding payment before delivery, having a firm but polite procedure for dealing with customers who offend.

   b   This question can be treated in a lighthearted way, but in the end the suggestions should be of a 'firm but fair' nature.

      i   This could be a genuine reason, especially during standard holiday periods. However, most businesses would not have a situation where no cheques can be provided in emergency. Pre-signed cheques could be available or someone else could have authority to sign. The customer should be questioned on this.

      ii   Computer faults are normally fixed quite quickly or the business could not operate. Manual cheques can also be written.

      iii Probably the oldest excuse. The cheque could be stopped and another issued. Also ask when the cheque was posted and confirm the address was correct.

      iv   Ask for the name and address of the debtor and expected date of payment. A bank loan could be taken out, secured against the debt so that the supplier could be paid.

v Fax a copy of the invoice straightaway. If payment is not received within a few days then the 'lost' invoice is an excuse and more questions need to be asked.

Section review, page 235

1 a Cash flow refers to the amounts of money flowing into and out of a business's bank account.

b (2 of) 'What if' calculations can be done quickly and easily; figures can quickly be amended; if the figures and formulas are correct then the calculations must be accurate; actual figures can be input (or any other appropriate answers).

c Monitoring means checking that actual income and payments occur as they were predicted. Forecasting means making predictions for future income and payments.

d The ability to 'go into the red' on the current account, i.e. spend more money than is in the account. Interest has to be paid.

e Because a business knows that it will have a negative cash flow in the near future, which could result in a negative bank balance figure.

f (2 of) Monitor the overall level of debt, arrange for action to be taken if debts are unpaid, arrange for credit checks to be carried out on new customers, set the total level of credit allowed, prevent further goods being provided if the credit limit is reached.

g Selling goods and receiving payment at a later date.

h Late payments can cause cash flow problems for the supplier, particularly if the amount owed is considerable.

i A debt which remains unpaid after a reasonable amount of time has elapsed and despite reminders.

2 a i

Income from sales	£10,000
Expenditure	£6,000
Net cash flow	£4,000

Monthly summary

Opening bank balance	£2,500
Net cash flow	£4,000
Closing bank balance	£6,500

ii She can see exactly which items of expenditure are increasing or decreasing each month and take action accordingly.

iii Jenny needs to forecast her cash flow in advance – otherwise she cannot take remedial action in good time. The first she would know of a problem would be after it had happened. Ideally she should forecast her cash flow and then monitor her actual income and spending to check it is the same – or better – than predicted.

b Before: 2, 3, 6; After 1, 4, 5.

3.3 – Budgets for planning and monitoring expenditure

Over to you, page 239

1 a False, **b** True, **c** False, **d** False, **e** True, **f** True.

2 Senior managers, budget holder, budgets, variance, budget process.

3 Tutor to check. Without going into personal detail, it may be useful for group members to compare notes in broad terms. Some will have a fairly accurate control over their spending and others may have little at all.

Over to you, page 242

1 Tutor to check against answer below.

FLEXILIGHT BUDGET REPORT - APRIL			
Item	Planned	Actual	Variance
	£	£	£
Bulbs	2,200	2,100	100
Plastic base	1,500	1,500	0
Telescopic arm	3,000	2,800	200
Switch	1,200	1,250	-50
Transformer	5,000	4,800	200
Cables and plugs	1,800	1,700	100
Screws	500	500	0
Wages	5,250	5,000	250
Total	20,450	19,650	800

2 Differences are: bulbs, telescopic arm, switches, wages. All have increased. Reasons may be: rising supplier cost/no immediate alternative source, change of supplier for improved quality/delivery, pay rise for staff, more overtime to meet production targets.

3 a – b See budget below.

c There are three major negative variances. The first is an overspend on raw plastic. The explanation for this is the incorrect setting on the moulding machine. This should be corrected and systems put in place to check the settings regularly.

PLASPRODS WASTE BIN BUDGET REPORT - JUNE			
Item	Planned	Actual	Variance
	£	£	£
Raw plastic	25,000	28,000	-3,000
Power	6,000	5,700	300
Metal brackets	3,000	2,000	1,000
Nuts and bolts	1,500	1,600	-100
Machine maintenance	2,500	4,000	-1,500
Wages	10,000	12,000	-2,000
Total	48,000	53,300	-5,300

There are two more major negative variances which are linked. The extra money spent on maintenance is due to the major breakdown. This, in turn, resulted in the increase in the wages bill due to the overtime which had to be worked to catch up. An investigation is needed into the serviceability of the moulding machine. The first problem of poor settings already mentioned could also be linked to this.

The only major positive variance is the £1,000 saving on metal brackets. This is due to the staff member's suggestion. Presumably this is a permanent saving which will continue into future months.

The overall variance figure is negative and high. Hopefully, the measures discussed above will prevent recurrence and the savings on metal brackets will help to show a positive figure in future months. This saving will also be included in the budget planning process for the next year.

Over to you, page 244

1 a The amount spent on promotional activities is the total *less* the cost of marketing administration, i.e. July £13,000; August £14,000; September £31,000; October £17,000; November £22,000; December £15,000.

   b The figure matches at £130,000.

2 a

MODELSHOP MARKETING BUDGET - JULY TO DECEMBER							
ITEM	July	August	Sept	Oct	Nov	Dec	Total
TV advertising	0	0	10,000	5,000	5,000	5,000	25,000
Sales representatives	5,000	5,000	5,000	5,000	5,000	5,000	30,000
Posters	2,000	4,000	4,000	0	0	0	10,000
Own magazine	5,000	0	5,000	0	5,000	0	15,000
Magazine advertising	0	4,000	6,000	6,000	6,000	4,000	26,000
Website	1,000	1,000	1,000	1,000	1,000	1,000	6,000
Administration	3,000	3,000	3,000	3,000	3,000	3,000	18,000
Monthly total	16,000	17,000	34,000	20,000	25,000	18,000	130,000
Cumulative total	16,000	33,000	67,000	87,000	112,000	130,000	

   b The cumulative total under December is another 'double check' because it should match the overall monthly total.

3 a £15,000

   b £7,500 each month

   c Yes, because he has simply transferred the spending to a different heading.

4 a To take advantage of additional sales opportunities.

   b £12,000 and £8,000

   c £140,000 (see budget reproduced below).

MODELSHOP MARKETING BUDGET - JULY TO DECEMBER							
ITEM	July	August	Sept	Oct	Nov	Dec	Total
TV advertising	0	0	10,000	0	0	0	10,000
Sales representatives	5,000	5,000	5,000	5,000	5,000	5,000	30,000
Posters	2,000	4,000	4,000	7,500	7,500	0	25,000
Own magazine	5,000	0	5,000	0	5,000	0	15,000
Magazine advertising	0	4,000	6,000	6,000	12,000	8,000	36,000
Website	1,000	1,000	1,000	1,000	1,000	1,000	6,000
Administration	3,000	3,000	3,000	3,000	3,000	3,000	18,000
Monthly total	16,000	17,000	34,000	22,500	33,500	17,000	140,000
Cumulative total	16,000	33,000	67,000	89,500	123,000	140,000	

Talking point, page 245

View 1 Marketing was crucial to enable us to achieve successful sales. Reducing the budget would be risky and could result in lower sales next year.

View 2 Marketing is vital to match the actions of our competitors. If we reduce the budget and divert money to customer service or the packaging design then we could lose out to the competition.

Over to you, page 248

1 **a** Senior managers should solve the problem. It is outside the scope of the Production Manager, who is the budget holder.

   b Claw back some money from the marketing budget and use it to update the file server.

   c The budget holder can solve the problem by changing the menus.

   d The variation is positive and very small. No action is required.

   e The amount allowed should be increased in the next budget.

2 He has said that he was originally allowed to use his underspend on travel to buy laptops but now the money is being taken out of his budget to be put towards new loading equipment in the warehouse.

3 **a** Suggestions include: spending is controlled and the business should make an overall profit; problems of overspending are identified reasonably quickly; budget holders have control over their own area of responsibility, so that they don't have to continuously ask senior managers for permission to do things; the process of planning a budget forces people to think about the future and any changes they may wish to make. This is particularly true when a business is trying to cut costs.

   b This is a difficult task and students may need some prompting. Some of the drawbacks of budgets are as follows. If the forecast expenditure is too high, managers may be tempted to spend the money anyway, rather than having the money clawed back or their budget reduced for the next period. It could discourage budget holders from seizing opportunities to make improvements. Operating a budgetary control system costs money – meetings to set budgets, collecting data on expenditure and producing monthly reports.

Section review, page 249

1 **a** The amount the budget holder is allowed to spend.

   b (2 of) To monitor departmental spending, to control overall spending, to identify variances, so that action can be taken on unfavourable variances. Other appropriate suggestions should be accepted.

   c The difference between allowable and actual spending.

   d A favourable variance is an underspend whereas an unfavourable variance is an overspend.

   e Unfavourable variances mean the business is spending more than is budgeted so costs increase and this will affect profits. Favourable variances are a saving.

   f A person who is responsible for managing and monitoring spending in a cost centre or department in line with the budget.

   g A flexible budget is when the budget holder is allowed some discretion on how he/she allocates money within the overall figure.

   h The money is likely to be clawed back and used for other purposes. The budget is also likely to be reduced next year.

   i He should report the problem to his own manager and give a full explanation. He should also suggest remedial action, if possible.

   j (2 of) Current spending levels, unavoidable increases, problems encountered during the current year, new ideas for saving money or doing business in a different way.

2   a and **b**

JIM'S GARAGE - 6 MONTH BUDGET							
Item	Jan	Feb	March	April	May	June	Total
	£	£	£	£	£	£	£
Wages	5,800	5,800	5,800	5,800	5,800	5,800	34,800
Heating	1,000	1,000	1,000	1,000	1,000	1,000	6,000
Telephone	200	200	200	200	200	200	1,200
Electricity	1,000	1,000	1,000	1,000	1,000	1,000	6,000
Equipment maintenance	2,500	2,500	2,500	2,500	2,500	2,500	15,000
Building maintenance	500	500	500	500	500	500	3,000
Monthly total	11,000	11,000	11,000	11,000	11,000	11,000	66,000
Cumulative total	11,000	22,000	33,000	44,000	55,000	66,000	

c

JIM'S GARAGE - 6 MONTH BUDGET REPORT									
Item	Jan	Feb	March	April	May	June	Total	Actual	Variance
	£	£	£	£	£	£	£	£	£
Wages	5,800	5,800	5,800	5,800	5,800	5,800	34,800	50,000	-15,200
Heating	1,000	1,000	1,000	1,000	1,000	1,000	6,000	5,900	100
Telephone	200	200	200	200	200	200	1,200	2,000	-800
Electricity	1,000	1,000	1,000	1,000	1,000	1,000	6,000	4,000	2,000
Equipment maintenance	2,500	2,500	2,500	2,500	2,500	2,500	15,000	16,000	-1,000
Building maintenance	500	500	500	500	500	500	3,000	6,000	-3,000
Total	11,000	11,000	11,000	11,000	11,000	11,000	66,000	83,900	-17,900
Cumulative total	11,000	22,000	33,000	44,000	55,000	66,000			

d   The comments are:

Wages –£15,200 High negative variance. Action needs to be taken. Maybe too much overtime is being worked?

Telephone –£800 Significant overspend. Why is the phone being used so much? Are people making too many personal calls? Alternatively, was the cost not realistic or has the price increased?

Electricity +£2,000 A high positive variance. Unless there is an exceptional reason, the budget could be reduced next year.

Equipment maintenance –£1,000 Not a very high overspend, but may need keeping an eye on. If the overspend was because of one problem, then it can be ignored. If it was because of continual maintenance required on one item of equipment then it may be cheaper to renew the equipment.

Building maintenance –£3,000 The amount spent was double that allowed. Unless there was an exceptional problem, the budget figure may have to be reviewed.

Finally, Jim should not have waited six months before reviewing his budget expenditure. One of the main points of the budget process is to identify problems fairly quickly (i.e. at the end of a month) and try to do something about them. Some of the problems Jim has found, such as high spending on building maintenance and wages, perhaps could have been noticed earlier and acted upon.

3.4 – Recording transactions

Over to you, page 252

a   A transaction occurs when a private individual or a business purchases goods or services from a business. Money is paid in return for the goods/services received.

b   Students should be encouraged to think of as broad a range of examples as possible. As a supplier, Oliver will cut/style hair as a service. He could also sell related items such as shampoo, conditioner and other products. As a customer he would pay for utilities, property fittings and maintenance, goods to sell on, business rates, staff wages and so on.

2 a This question has been set purely to enable students to confirm that they understand the various methods of payment which are made for different types of transaction. This is to prevent misunderstandings when they are describing transactions and how they are recorded.

b The following provides a broad indication of the content of each website relevant to a retailer but the sites should be checked at the time for updates and changes.

i This site provides details of the range of different credit cards (e.g. lifestyle cards, donation cards, affinity cards etc.), information on credit problems and merchant services and card comparisons. It also provides information on credit card jargon and tips. A retailer thinking about accepting cards would be able to obtain basic information to inform the decision. The site is also useful for anyone who wants to know more about credit cards and how they work.

ii Barclays is one of several banks which provide a merchant service facility. The site summarises the benefits for businesses, how accepting card transactions works, the equipment required and so on.

iii Switch is a UK debit card service but is now linked to Maestro – an international system. By 2005 the service will be known as Maestro only. The site includes a separate retail section that gives retailers information about accepting Switch, the benefits, the changeover to Maestro and information about the chip and PIN cards.

iv Fastpay is a NatWest merchant service which enables small businesses to receive payments on their website by credit or debit card. A button is added to the website which the customer clicks to make the payment. This saves small businesses needing technical expertise or security payment systems on their site.

v The direct debit site is part of the BACS system and gives information on the benefits to the public and to suppliers of receiving direct debit payments. The

suppliers' section also includes how to set up the system. The retailer could use this to make his or her own payments.

vi The direct credit site is also part of the BACS system and provides the same information as **v** above but on direct credit payments. This method could be used to pay suppliers electronically.

Over to you, page 259

1 a i Name and address of supplier. This identifies the supplier and the customer has proof of the business that supplied the product or service.

ii Receipt number. This makes it easier to trace the transaction if there is a query or problem.

iii Customer's name and address. This identifies the person who has paid the money. Although an address isn't essential, it is normally recommended practice to include as much information on a handwritten receipt as possible in case there are later queries (e.g. between two customers with the same name).

iv Amount of money paid. This is an essential requirement for both the customer and supplier. The customer has proof of the amount paid in case there are any later problems. The supplier needs to record this amount in the main business accounts.

v Reason for payment. This clarifies why the money was paid in case faults or problems are discovered later.

vi Signature. This identifies the member of staff who processed the transaction and received the money. It is a safeguard against fraud and any problems or queries can also be checked out with this person.

vii Date. This states when the money changed hands. It is important for the main accounts as the date of the transaction must be entered for tax purposes. It is also important for the customer, particularly if there is a warranty on the work.

b Because handwriting is sometimes poor so the words and figures are a double check, especially when large amounts of money are involved. This argument also applies to cheques and any legal contracts where sums of money are included. Both must match.

c Date and amount paid.

2 a (3 of) To prove that they have paid for the goods/service, to identify whom the payment was made to, to confirm the date of purchase, to identify the amount paid, so that bank or credit card statements can be checked.

b (3 of) For tax purposes, to produce the business accounts, to calculate actual cash flow, to calculate profit/loss and the annual accounts, to deal with any subsequent customer queries/complaints.

3 a (2 of) To keep track of withdrawals, to check against the bank statement, in case the money issued isn't correct.

b The receipt can be used for identity theft because of the information it contains (in addition to being litter!).

c Refuse help and refuse to re-enter the PIN. Report the loss to the bank immediately. This is often a scam where the card isn't really stuck (for references see press reports on 'Lebanese loop scam'). The 'helper' can retrieve it when the cardholder has gone and obtain cash using the demonstrated PIN number.

d Keeping the money is technically theft! The bank can trace the problem (even if a receipt has been refused) because of its cash machine records. It can then write to customers who visited the machine and request the money back (although, interestingly, it can't insist on payment). Sometimes, however, honesty pays. A couple who found their bank account with Egg had been overcredited by several thousand pounds reported the error immediately – and were rewarded by being able to keep the interest, which amounted to over £1,000.

4 Answers may vary depending upon where individual students have worked and the equipment they have used. Alternative suggestions should be encouraged to illustrate the differences in working practices – and common practices, often for security reasons.

a To ensure all employees handling cash have been properly trained, have been vetted, have demonstrated loyalty to the organisation.

b Numeric keys, total key, amount tendered, refund key. Any students who have operated an EPOS system should be encouraged to contribute to this debate.

c So that the takings can be balanced for that particular operator.

d To prevent the till being broken into if there is a robbery as theives can see there is no cash.

e The owner, manager or senior member of staff

in a small business, trained accounts staff/cashiers in a large business who work in a separate, secure area.

f Normally only a supervisor or manager can do this as a security precaution.

g The answer is given on page 266 of the student book. There are three conditions for this to be legal. First, there must be a procedure which ensures that any discrepancy can only have occurred when one person was operating the cash register. Staff cannot be penalised for a mistake which could have been made by someone else. Second, the penalty system must be stated clearly in the contract of employment and have been agreed with the member of staff at the outset. The manager cannot just introduce it as a new term of employment. Third, the amount of the deduction is limited to 10 per cent of total pay.

Over to you, page 262

1 a A cash register, probably linked to the computer system. This system will be used because many sales transactions are processed every day by River Island branch shops and the information will be needed at head office.

b A hand-written receipt because it isn't worthwhile for the dentist to install a cash register yet a record is needed. The dentist will keep a copy.

c Direct on to computer because payments will mainly be made by direct debit, credit card or cheque to an administration office.

d A cash register which may or may not be linked to an EPOS system (depending upon the size of the club, overall value of sales transaction). This is because most sales will be made at the club shop and be recorded separately from gate receipts or other sources of income.

e Petty cash because the cash sale needs recording and so, too, does the fact that the member of staff was reimbursed.

f Purchase Day Book, so that there is an immediate check on the number of transactions and the value of each one.

2 Students could role play this exercise or simply discuss the action Samira should take, with reasons.

a £750 is too much to pay out of petty cash and is likely to exceed the authorisation limit for any one transaction. Someone needs to contact the garage to persuade them to send an invoice and release the van. If the garage is particularly awkward, perhaps the van driver could be given a cheque for the amount to take to the garage.

b Samira should pay this.

c Petty cash cannot be used to pay for personal items. This could be a misunderstanding but the assistant needs to get the money from the Administration Manager.

d Again, petty cash can only be used for official purchases. The crisps and coke should be crossed off the receipt and only the £5 reimbursed. Jan could ask her boss if she could leave early since she had given up part of her lunch hour.

e If Tom is persistent, he may have to continue to be paid out of petty cash. The canteen manager could try to persuade him to supply invoices. If the business feels particularly strongly, it might look for a milk supplier who does not insist on being paid in cash.

f A legitimate business expense. Gail should be paid when she produces the receipt.

g On the face of it, tough luck for Patrick. However, if a senior manager is prepared to support his action – and countersign a petty cash voucher – Patrick could obtain a duplicate receipt and be paid.

3 **a** Total amount spent £112.30 leaving £87.70 in the tin.

b It doesn't matter (apart from inconvenience if stocks are low) because blank vouchers are useless. Only when they have been signed and approved – and a receipt attached – can anyone claim repayment.

4 **a** True, **b** False, **c** True, **d** False, **e** True.

Over to you, page 267

1 The goods are easy to carry and small enough to conceal (or wear). They are mostly relatively valuable for their size – e.g. bottles of whisky, not beer. Top of the range items and recognisable brands which are easy to sell are also more likely to be stolen. It could only be classed as shrinkage if the stock could not be sold.

2 **a** False. Shrinkage is the difference between the amount of stock bought and the amount actually sold.

b False. It is thought that about half of theft is carried out by customers and half by staff.

c True.

d True.

e False. The rest of the shrinkage amount after theft is because of damage to stock, obsolescence etc.

f True.

3 **a** (4 of) Stealing money from the cash register, not recording cash received, recording a smaller amount than received and keeping the difference, undercharging friends or relatives, over-ringing a refund, recording a non-existent refund, keeping a customer receipt, using own store card.

b **i** (2 of) Pay well, offer general staff discounts, have good staff benefits, counsel staff with financial problems, operate a hardship fund, look after staff welfare.

ii (2 of) Have clear policies for dealing with fraud, check all references, have induction training and explain disciplinary procedures, limit staff using tills, ensure staff 'swipe' or 'log' on to use a till, do not allow staff to serve friends/relatives, ensure staff purchases are authorised by a manager, deduct shortfalls from salaries, use bar codes to prevent under-ringing, position tills so customers can see display, have strict procedures for 'voiding' a sale.

iii (2 of) Install CCTV cameras at sales points, reward staff who report fraud, have cash registers which can be quickly checked by managers, include the right to 'stop and search' employees if theft is suspected.

Section review, page 268

1 **a** To record small cash purchases made by employees who are then reimbursed by the business.

b (2 of) Date, amount paid, item purchased, method of payment, name of supplier (or any other appropriate answer).

c Making a written entry of a sale, often in a receipt book, where duplicate entries are then copied into the business's accounts.

d (2 of) They incorporate bar code readers, stock records are updated, the identity of the assistant who processed each transaction is known, credit/debit cards can be swiped, detailed receipts are printed, customer details can be captured.

e To list all sales transactions in date order.

f (2 of) For tax purposes, to produce the business accounts, for auditing purposes, to calculate profit and loss, to calculate actual cash flow.

g (2 of) Stealing money from the cash register, not recording cash received, recording a smaller amount than received and keeping the difference, undercharging friends or relatives, over-ringing a refund, recording a non-existent refund, using own store card to 'steal' points.

h (2 of) Have clear policies about which staff can use tills, do not allow staff to serve friends or relatives, only allow manager to give refunds or void a sale, install CCTV cameras, deduct shortages from wages, pay fair wages, reward staff who report thefts (or any other appropriate answers).

i The float is the amount of money put into the petty cash system at the start of the accounting period. It is topped up after the accounts have been balanced at the end of the period to the fixed amount. The term is also used for the amount of money (for change) put into a cash register at the start of a day's trading.

j (2 of) It directly reduces profits, security costs money, it disrupts and upsets honest staff when investigations are taking place.

2 The aim of this exercise is to allow students to think about the effects of different theft prevention measures. It could be argued that sound recruitment and induction procedures are a universal requirement. Within reason, any other well reasoned answers could be accepted, however the particular circumstances of each shop need to be considered.

- College bookshop – temptation for students to steal textbooks for themselves and friends. A till which incorporated a bar code reader and CCTV would help.
- Newsagent. Deals mainly in cash, so theft of money is relatively easy. Cash register important and strict rules about use. CCTV again useful. 'Grazing' would be relatively easy, as would be discounting to friends/relatives. Main control would be reconciling cash with

till records. Above all, having trustworthy staff would be a key factor.

- Clothes shop. Bar code reader is a must. Limit the number of staff who actually process the transactions. Have strict rules about authority to discount prices. Tag clothes so that alarm sounds unless tag is removed.
- Hotel. Two recording systems are needed. Cheques and credit/debit cards will be used for large accounts and need to be processed. Normally the transactions are logged on computer against each guest's bill. A small cash fund may be available for other purchases. These could be processed in a cash register although some hotels seem content to use cash boxes! Prevention measures may include issue of receipts for all transactions, restricted access to cash, limit to amount of cash that is kept on reception, only small sums handled and cashed up regularly, especially on shift changes.
- Doctor's practice. Normally a manual recording system with a receipt book. Precautions include nominated members of staff to handle money, regular cashing up of money received against receipts.
- Jeweller's shop. This is probably the most susceptible to staff theft since items are of relatively high value and small, although cash is unlikely to be used for most transactions. There may be a stop and search policy if staff theft is suspected and staff will not be allowed to take personal belongings (e.g. bags) into the sales area. CCTV cameras are likely to be installed.

3 Tutors should check the Richer Sounds StudentZone for any changes in precautions against fraud that have happened since 2004. The following answers were right at the time of writing in 2004.

a (3 of) Excellent staff benefits, good terms and conditions of employment, good pay, hardship fund for staff with financial problems, good communications between staff and managers, staff work as a team etc.

b (2 of) Only sales colleagues who have completed induction can process payments, EPOS tills record identity of user, store managers must carry out certain operations, strict procedures for handling sales/issuing receipts, staff encouraged to tell the manager if they suspect a colleague is stealing.

c It is a sackable offence. All staff are aware that the outcome would be instant dismissal.

Unit 4 Business communication

3.4 – Recording transactions

Cross-referenced additional activities can be found at:

These sample assessments are designed as practice exercises to help your students understand the types of task they will be required to do for their formal assessments. For practice, tasks can be done by individuals or by groups as indicated.

There is one sample assessment for each section of the Unit:

4.1	Verbal instructions
4.2	Representation in personal dealings
4.3	Written business communication
4.4	Preparation for business meetings

The structure and grading of the assessments reflect the grading criteria for the Unit as provided by Edexcel. Differentiation information is given where appropriate to indicate what would be required from the student to gain pass, merit or distinction grades. Tips to help the student achieve a merit or distinction grade are also given. A deadline box is provided in which you can enter a submission date to familiarise your students with the idea of working to a specified date or time.

Assessments are mainly printed one to a page so that they can be easily photocopied.

Notes and suggestions for sample assessments

4.1 – Verbal instructions

Students can be asked to undertake tasks following verbal instructions in a variety of contexts. This could include working in a training office or being on work experience. Although some could be given to small teams working together, others must be given to individual students to enable accurate assessment of ability to take place. Tutors may also like to check with their External Verifier if confirmatory evidence from a workplace supervisor would be admissible towards the assessment for this section.

4.2 – Representation in personal dealings

The scheme grid gives the example of retail sales as an occasion for a structured business interaction. This may be suitable for students who work part-time in a retail environment and who will have received specific training for this type of activity. In this case, students will hopefully also be studying Specialist Unit 7, Sales and customer service. Section 7.3 in particular – Effective sales practice – provides useful information on this area.

Unit 4 has been written bearing in mind the many occasions when students can represent their group, department or college at a variety of events, such as open days, parents' evenings, meetings of governors and so on. These would be equally valid for this type of business interaction, providing students had 'rehearsed' and prepared for the event beforehand.

4.3 – Written business communication

The pass grade requirement for the assessment specifies 'restricted internal matters'. Therefore business letters are not appropriate. It is sufficient for the student to communicate in writing on restricted internal matters.

Suggested investigations that student groups could undertake are given below. The aim is that the students will work in small teams to decide the method of investigation and will communicate with each other in writing as they make arrangements and share information. They will then discuss their ideas and, finally, write an individual (short) report. Quite obviously, if there is a specific topic which would be particularly relevant to the group/college, this should ideally be substituted for any or all of the suggestions below.

1   Investigate the range of business textbooks in their library, compare these with publishers' catalogues and recommend additional texts.

2   Investigate places of interest that their group could visit within a specific radius of the college and the cost/possible methods of transport.

3   Investigate a specific career in business (e.g. marketing, accountancy, human resources etc.) and identify the qualifications required, salary levels and where to find out further information.

4   Investigate signage around the college for strangers (both internal and external) and recommend improvements.

5   Investigate student opinions of common room facilities and suggest how these could be improved.

6   Investigate student views of the college induction programme and recommend improvements.

4.4 – Preparation for business meetings

If each student is to be given the chance to run the meeting/take notes, then you need at least as many meetings as there are students unless you split them into smaller groups. Students need to be given the opportunity to run a meeting to achieve a distinction grade.

Below are 12 suggestions that have all been based on the college experience, so that you could form a 'mini council' which could have weekly meetings and bring forward items from one week to the next. You can obviously add to this with ideas from the students themselves (which could be an agenda item on the first meeting!) and also those which are relevant to your own organisation.

It is suggested that you, as tutor, chair the first meeting and check the notes of that meeting. This gives all the students an example to follow for subsequent meetings and records of the meeting. You may wish to point out that, on the first set of notes, there is obviously no AOB item!

Meeting suggestions:

1 To decide a student charity of their choice.

2 To agree a day out at the end of term.

3 To decide on three changes which would improve the student experience at the college.

4 To decide the content of a 'welcome pack' from the students on this year's course to next year's students.

5 To come up with three ideas for improving the course next year.

6 To suggest ways in which more students could be attracted to the college (or course) next September.

7 To suggest a new uniform for college administrative staff/receptionists.

8 To discuss/suggest displays for a parents' evening.

9 To suggest improvements to induction week.

10 To suggest/agree on a team-building event that the group could attend.

11 To improve facilities in the student common room.

12 To identify the most important information they need to move onwards next year.

Answers to Unit 4 sample assessments

4.1

No specific answer is possible because it depends upon the tasks students are asked to carry out. Tutors must decide the number/complexity of tasks to give for parity – and the degree to which instructions will be explicit/implied.

It is suggested that, say, two or three tasks are done over a short period of time, with at least one to do as a team, rather than one very complex task. This is more realistic and will also give students more practice at learning to think for themselves.

4.2

No specific answer is possible. However, tutors should note that, in line with the assessment guidance, students should be well prepared and trained to cope with the limited interactions they are asked to undertake.

4.3

No answer is possible.

4.4

No specific answer is given as, to some extent, the overall requirements of the students will be determined by the actual meetings with which they are involved and, more specifically, whether they will prepare notes and/or run only one meeting or more than one. However, it is suggested that specific criteria for each grade of the assessment are drawn up and discussed with the students. (This could even be a topic discussed at a student meeting!) Peer group evaluation would also be a useful component to determine the overall score for each grade, but against strict criteria to prevent students simply praising their friends.

Some of your assessments for this unit involve specific instructions from your tutor. These may be verbal or you may be given additional written details. Remember that you should make careful notes if you are given information verbally. If you are given information in writing, read it carefully and keep it safely for future reference.

Task 1 – Pass grade

Your tutor will give you explicit verbal instructions for specific tasks. You must carry these out correctly and to the required timescale.

1   a   **Carry out** each task correctly, and

   b   **Write down** each task you were given and **give a brief description** of the actions you took in each case.

Deadline

Tips to achieve a merit grade

This will involve you using your common sense to identify the **implicit aspects** of a task.

- This means that every single step will not be spelled out for you. Instead you will have to use your own initiative in regard to certain aspects.
- This doesn't mean that you cannot query something which is unclear or something which you did not understand. If this is the case then talk to the correct person to find out what you need to know.

Task 2 – Merit grade

Your tutor will give you verbal instructions for specific tasks. You must carry these out correctly and to the required timescale to complete each task. This will also require that you understand the implicit aspects of each task yourself. These will not be spelled out to you.

2   a   **Carry out** each task as instructed.

   b   **Write a brief description** of the actions you took, any aspects of the task you checked or clarified and the person with whom you liaised over these.

Deadline

For this assessment you must represent your group or college appropriately at a specific event.

Tasks 1 and 2 – Pass grade

1   At an event chosen by your tutor, **represent your group appropriately**. This will mean dressing appropriately, talking to people courteously, being diplomatic and tactful, and correctly representing both your college and your group.

2   a   After the event, **write a brief account** that summarises how you prepared for the event and what you did at the time.

    b   In your account, make sure that you **identify any difficulties** or problems you faced. Then **suggest** ways in which you could overcome these on a future occasion.

Deadline

For this assessment you will work in a small team to carry out an investigation.

Tasks 1 and 2 – *Pass grade*

1   Work in a small group of two or three to **carry out a particular investigation**. You will receive your instructions by email and must respond to your tutor, and communicate with other members of your group, mainly by email.

Carry out the instructions you are given and undertake the investigation. Make sure that you make a full contribution to the team effort.

2   **a**   At the end of the investigation **write a short informal report** which summarises your findings and conclusions. Your tutor will tell you whether any recommendations are required.

The report must be all your own work although some of the information it contains may be common to reports other than yours.

b   When you submit your report for assessment, you must also **submit copies of the emails** you have both sent and received from other members of your group.

Deadline

Sample assessment

This assessment relates to meetings you will attend with other students in your group. Your tutor will give you detailed information about the arrangements.

Task 1 – Pass grade

Prepare for these meetings appropriately so that you are a responsible and committed participant.

1 a After the first meeting, write a brief account of the preparations you made.

b In your account, consider whether you could improve your behaviour or contribution to future meetings you attend. Then suggest how you could do this.

Deadline

Tips to achieve a merit grade

For this task you will have to prepare meetings documents.

- Check the format that is used by referring to previous documents that have been issued. Then use this as your guide.
- Remember that minutes only give a summary of the key points that were discussed.
- If you cannot read any part of your notes, check your understanding of what happened with the chairperson.
- Don't forget to add action points to your minutes.
- Always proof-read all your documents *very* carefully before you issue them.

Now carry out the task below.

Task 2 – Merit grade

2 a As instructed by your tutor, **prepare and distribute a notice and agenda** of one or more of the meetings of your student group.

b Also as instructed by your tutor, **prepare prompt and accurate minutes** of the meeting, with clear action points.

c After your tutor has checked your minutes, **distribute these** to all participants promptly.

Deadline

Tips to achieve a distinction grade

This task involves you in running a meeting. The job of chairperson can be difficult. Before you start, note the points below.

- To do the job well, you *must* be well organised. Prepare by obtaining all the relevant documents and reading them carefully.
- Arrive in good time and start promptly.
- Remember to follow the agenda.
- Speak clearly, so that everyone can hear you.
- Give people time to speak, but keep contributions short and to the point.
- Thank people who contribute.
- Sum up the discussions at the end of each agenda item and any decisions that were reached.

Now do the next task.

Task 3 – Distinction grade

As instructed by your tutor, run at least one of your student meetings.

3 a Prepare for this task properly so that you are familiar with the purpose of the meeting and the time available.

   b Run the meeting in such a way that communications are good, contributions from others are invited and everyone understands what is being discussed and what is agreed.

   c Afterwards, **write a brief account** of the experience. Say what you think you did well, what caused you problems and the ways in which you think you could improve your meetings skills with more practice.

    Attach a copy of the agenda of the meeting and the minutes of the meeting to your account for information.

Deadline

This section includes additional materials and suggestions for the activities which may be undertaken for this particular unit.

Artwork for Over to you, page 10, q3

Diagram 1

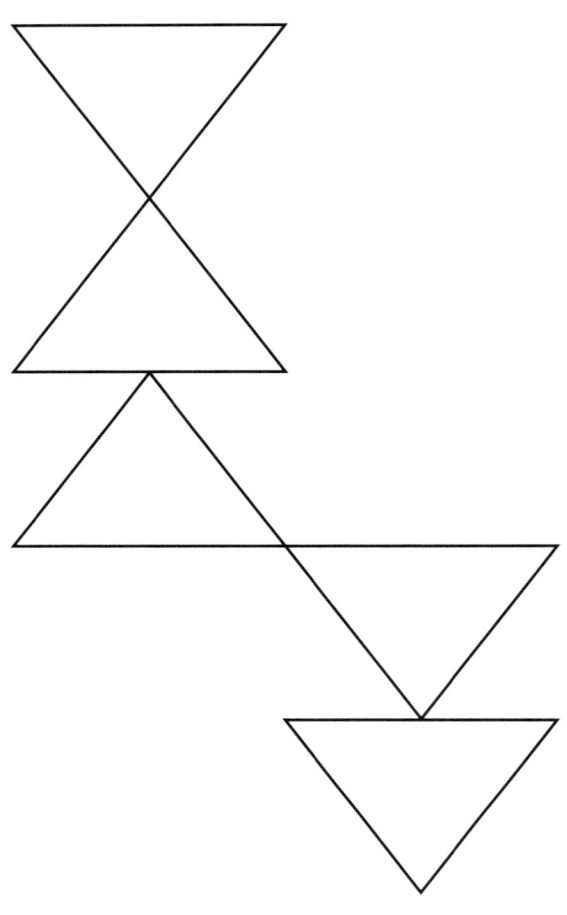

Diagram 2

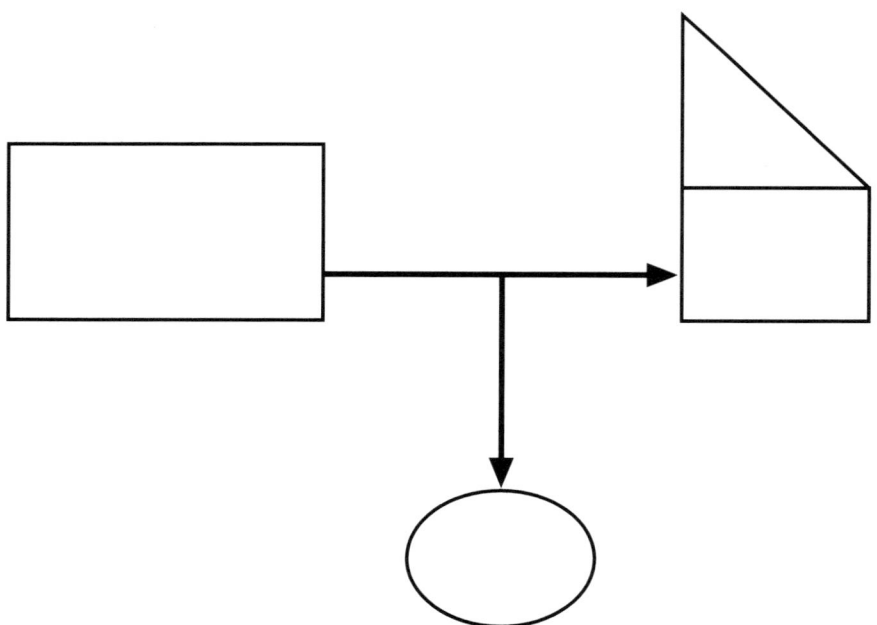

Diagram 3

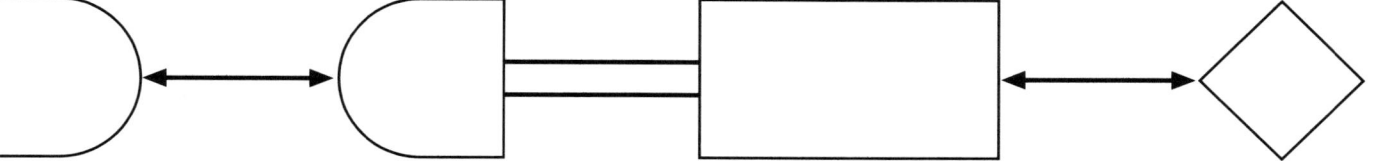

Diagram 4

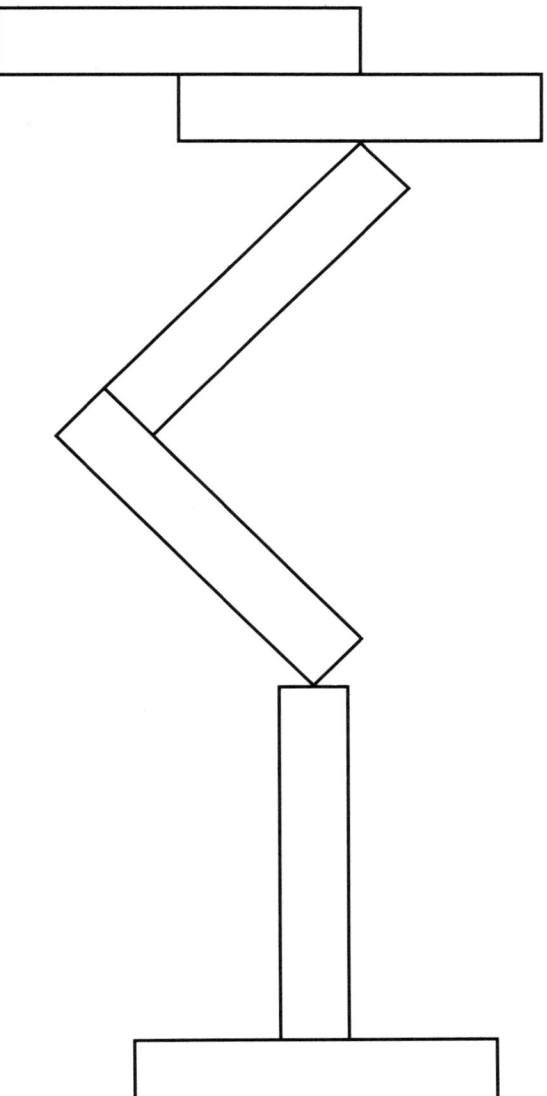

Resources for Section review, page 21, q1

Students can be given the following cards. The name and the reason for fame should be completed first. Alternatively, students can decide themselves on this aspect of the role play before they start.

Suggestions include:

Famous DJ on local or national radio.
Singer or band member – band has just had number 1 hit.

Famous model who has recently been on the cover of a national magazine.
National Lottery winner.
Business entrepreneur who has just made £1 million.
Sports personality who has just been selected for the next Olympics/famous team.
Actor/actress just landed part in TV soap or as TV newsreader.

STUDENT ROLE-PLAY PREPARATION
THE INTERVIEW
The famous ex-student

Your name is ....

You are famous because ....

You are visiting your home town and have agreed to visit your old college so that one of the students can interview you for the college magazine.

You enjoyed your time there and are happy to answer questions. However, you remember that whilst some tutors were great others were a bit boring and you also thought there were never enough computers to go round. You wonder if things have changed. You decide to think of a few awkward questions to ask your student interviewer! As you have been invited to have coffee with the Principal afterwards, you think this will give you a bit of ammunition if you want to have some fun.

STUDENT ROLE-PLAY PREPARATION
THE INTERVIEW
The student interviewee

You have been asked to interview ....

who is famous because ....

You have to ask relevant questions to write a short but interesting article for the college magazine. The editor has told you that you should ask about the celebrity's current career prospects and also find out what your interviewee remembers about the college and really liked (or disliked).

You have to make notes and then report back to the magazine editor before you write your article. This means asking questions, listening to the answers and also writing notes. You have been told that the interview shouldn't last more than about 10 minutes.

Prepare a list of about 10 questions that you think would be appropriate and also decide how you will introduce yourself at the start of the interview.

Section review, page 47, q3

Overleaf you will find a letter heading for responding to this question.

The
Malton Water Company

Beck Heights • Malton • ML5 6PD

Telephone: 01928 393839
Facsimile: 01928 489728

www.maltonwater.co.uk

4.1 – Verbal Instructions

Over to you, page 10

1 **a** Active listening = being alert when listening, concentrating so that the main points are remembered and can be repeated back accurately.

  b Job role = the type of work done by a person plus their areas of responsibility and accountability.

  c Team interdependence = the fact that members of the team are dependent upon each other for the team as a whole to be successful.

  d Implicit requirements = aspects of a task which are not spelled out because they are considered common sense or because it is assumed the person will understand they are required.

  e Line manager = the manager directly above you and to whom you are accountable for your actions.

2 No answer possible.

3 No answer possible.

4 **a** 'I don't think so' *or* 'No, sorry, I can't.'

  b 'Sorry, but I haven't had time to do it yet.'

  c 'Sorry, I haven't time to help you at the moment.'

  d 'Please can you be a bit quieter – I'm trying to concentrate on this at the moment.'

  e 'I'll tell you once more, then. Do you think you should make a note of it?'

5 Benefits (4 of): greater range of skills, people to help/support each other, social side, jobs done more quickly, can share/exchange ideas, joint problems solving. Disadvantages (4 of): have to consider/support others, team should be more important than individual glory, may have to work more slowly/differently to suit other people's way of working, may not automatically get on well with all other members, may work harder than some other members but the team as a whole will get the credit.

Section review, page 11

1 Implicit (2 of); Queries (2 of).

i Implicit: from local/usual station, presume minimum number of changes preferred, presume find out fares too. Queries: what day(s), any specific/preferred times, is fare price required.

ii Implicit: correctly addressed, appropriately wrapped, to specified addressees. Queries: have the envelopes already been prepared/is there an address list; is first or second class postage required; are any other documents to go with them (e.g. compliments slip/letter).

iii Implicit: all pages in correct order, all print readable, all print correctly aligned, no staples obscuring text. Queries: how many are required, is back-to-back preferred, have booklets to be sent out to people individually or will they be taken to the meeting by the person giving the job.

iv Implicit: from normal/agreed supplier, using official ordering system, presume white/A4. Queries: check if white/A4 required only; check quantity to be purchased, find out urgency of request (may mean order to be telephoned through or faxed).

v Implicit: from normal supplier (e.g. in-house or local shop); check the number of participants and their individual preferences, use normal payment method. Queries: check payment method if unsure, if some participants unavailable find out what they normally prefer, what drinks will be required, check meeting time if not known.

2 **a** **i** No one will be totally sure what they are doing and will probably rely on Ishmael for information.

    ii They will guess what it means. If they are lucky, they might be able to find it out from the library or online – but they may not totally cover all the aspects the tutor wants.

    iii Unless one of the others does his work for him, they will not be able to supplement their online notes with library information.

    iv This will either result in them working very quickly – may be unnecessarily – or taking their time and risking missing the deadline.

v The information sheet(s) could well be far too sketchy or too long.

vi They will either have to pay for copies or – if someone thinks quickly enough – they could print out more copies or ask their tutor for help.

b They need to liaise with the library staff for guidance, the IT staff if they need help researching online, their tutor about the number of copies and the length of the information sheet. They may also have to liaise with someone about printing/photocopying the required number of copies.

c Clarify: exact content of information sheet, whether graphics required, sources of information, number of copies required, how to produce copies, when information required by, whether tutor wants to do intermediate check before information sheet printed. Action: collect research information, agree main points to be included, draft out sheet and ask tutor to check, when master copy perfect then take copies – and make sure all of appropriate quality.

d Netiquette relates to the correct way to communicate online, particularly by email. See pages 43–4 in the CD Student Unit for information about email communication (e.g. not using all capitals or all lower case). Searching under netiquette on Google provides several useful pages with summary information. Etiquette refers to appropriate social behaviour.

4.2 – Representation in personal dealings

Over to you, page 21

1 No specific answer is possible but tutors may find the following notes helpful.

a It shouldn't matter too much whether the student mentions the Principal first or his/her parents first. The main point is that the names are stated clearly enough for the conversation to continue smoothly.

b A direct lie is not recommended, neither is putting all the blame onto the other students! The student could say there was a problem because it coincided with assessments, distract by asking how much was raised

altogether or (if sharp enough) respond with a non sequitur, e.g. 'Oh, fine. By the way my parents were very impressed with the new refectory'.

c A good strategy would be to evince interest providing it wouldn't interfere with work, e.g. 'That sounds very interesting, I'd obviously need more details of course because I've a lot of assignments to do/a part-time job this year and I wouldn't want to get behind.' If that sounds rather too much, just asking for more details at least puts off the decision!

2 Key facts are caller's name – Jackie Waring, name of daughter (Kerry), the fact that Kerry works on a Friday afternoon at Sainsbury's from 3 pm and is worried how work experience will affect this. Caller wants Julie Duerden to telephone her on 03843 592898 to clarify the situation.

3 a The main point here is that it shouldn't matter whether Alistair likes his tutor or not. He should still be professional, diplomatic and discreet. Obviously if he really likes the tutor, he could enthuse. If he does not, he could be more circumspect, e.g. 'Fine, thanks.'

b Say that Emily's parents had to leave early but would like to speak to her as soon as possible. They are worried about whether Emily is coping with the assignments. They would prefer nothing was said to Emily.

c This is more difficult – and the group will no doubt be divided in its opinions. Really, the parents shouldn't have asked Alistair to keep this confidence, especially if he is friendly with Emily. Alistair basically has three options. He can say they were just telling him they had to leave early; he can say they were sorry they had to leave early because they wanted to speak to the tutor; he can say they asked him to ask the tutor to give them a ring. The first is slightly misleading Emily (it's the truth, but not the whole truth), the second is the most pragmatic, the third is giving away the confidence he was asked to keep. The other option, of course, is to say that he can't remember and suggest Emily asks them herself when she gets home!

Section review, page 22

1 No specific answer is possible as it will depend upon the information supplied by the ex-student celebrity and the awkward questions that are asked.

2 The aim of this question is to link to the 'structured business interaction' mentioned in the assessment criteria but to make this applicable to students who are not involved in retail sales. No specific key is possible, although a range of questions should be encouraged. Some should be specific such as: what subjects do you do, do you find them interesting, how are you assessed, how long is the course, what can you do next etc. Others should be more general such as: do you enjoy it, is it easy/hard, what are the tutors like, what are the facilities like.

3 This extends the previous question by including the idea of retail sales and other 'representative' situations. These will largely depend upon the college and the part-time occupations of the students.

4.3 – Written business communication

Over to you, page 28

1 **a** He decided to **accept** the invitation. Except = not including.

b No-one could decipher his writing on the **stationery** order.

Stationary = not moving.

c He now studies art, but was **formerly** a hotel manager.

Formally = in a formal or official manner.

d I was worried he might **lose** his money. Loose = not tight.

e He wanted the **draft** document correcting immediately. Draught = current of air.

f He joined a **guerrilla** group to fight in Africa. Gorilla = large ape.

g She went to Spain to learn how to dance the **flamenco**.

Flamingo = large wading bird.

h She said his comments were **irrelevant** to the discussion.

Irreverent = without respect.

2 a, b, f, g and h are all plus points. The others are not.

a personable = friendly/pleasant

b charismatic = fascinating/appealing

c obdurate = stubborn

d neurotic = over-anxious

e impressionable = easily influenced

f presentable = well-dressed/good appearance

g urbane = sauve, elegant, debonair

h benevolent = compassionate, generous

i parsimonious = mean, tight-fisted

j diffident = shy, timid

3 **a** Jen, my best friend, is visiting us next Monday.

b In Paris last year we visited the Louvre to see the Mona Lisa, travelled on a boat on the Seine and went up the Eiffel Tower.

c Her new designs are excellent; last year's were also good.

d For her part-time course in September she has to buy three folders, a sketch pad, special artists' pencils and acrylic paints.

e The ex-MP for Stockport is dark-haired.

f I was helped by Kate Reed, our Sales Manager; Hussain Lorgat, our Production Manager; Jasper Marsh, our Distribution Manager and Sue Jackson, our Marketing Manager.

4 **a** Photos can be enlarged while you're waiting.

b You're very special to me, don't you know?

c 100s of bargains.

d It's a pity the horse can't have a rider on its back.

e The company's logo was designed by Ken's agency.

f In four weeks' time they're going to Jo's wedding.

Over to you, page 34

1

acceptable	**accommodation**	**advertisement**
allege	**awful**	benevolent
colleague	committee	**compatible**
competent	courteous	conscientious
consistent	definite	deficient
development	**environment**	**liaison**
manoeuvre	**miniature**	noticeable
occurrence	**omitted**	**permanent**
predecessor	prestigious	**questionnaire**
received	referred	**regrettable**
separate	**sincerely**	strategy
successful	unnecessary	waive

2

a In our group, Ayesha is the person **who** works the **hardest**.

b Neither of the brochures **was** any good.

c Alistair wants to know if **we** can meet him tomorrow.

d Do you know **with whom** you'll be working? (Or: **Who** will be working with you?)

e We never went **anywhere** near the palace.

f I should be grateful if you **would** call him.

g The BBC **is** going to open a studio near here.

h The train was late **because of** leaves on the line.

i He arrived for the meeting **promptly** at nine.

j I believe you saw John yesterday – how **was he**?

3 a

i Just hold on, will you? = your friend

ii Can you wait a minute? = an older relative

iii Would you mind waiting a moment? = a customer

iv I can be with you in a minute = your boss

b The following are suggested responses only.

i To your boss: 'I'm sorry I couldn't find out the information you wanted this morning because my computer was down. I am now hoping to have it by 3 pm.'

ii To a friend in another office who is the same age as you: 'Sorry I couldn't get the information to you that you wanted this morning – my computer was down. Should be able to get it by 3 pm so will get back to you.'

iii To a customer: 'I regret that I couldn't let you have the information you wanted this morning but unfortunately we had computer problems. I am now hoping to be able to obtain it for you this afternoon.'

Over to you, page 42

1 a Caller's full name (could be a problem if more than one 'Gavin'), telephone number (mobile is fine, but should be some contact number), organisation. No mention of the day he wants to start work.

b Any appropriate suggestions should be encouraged, e.g. 'Sorry, could you just give me

your full name.' 'Could I have your mobile number, please.'

c Find out who is doing Jon Scholes's work and/or pass the message on to her line manager.

d No specific answer but all key points should be included, the written message should be grammatical, all spellings should be correct and it should be written in an appropriate tone and style.

2 No specific answer possible but the message should include all the key points including the name of the caller and telephone number and the re-arranged date/time for the interview as agreed with Joel – which has been put in the diary.

3 Below are suggested alternatives.

a Not a sentence. We hope to hear from you soon.

b Not a sentence/slang. Thank you for answering our query.

c Not a sentence. Thank you for your recent letter.

d Slang. Could you come to see us next week?

e Not a sentence. We look forward to seeing you.

f Slang. We feel we have been receiving very poor service recently.

4 No specific answer but all key points should be included in a logical order. The letter should be grammatical correctly punctuated and all words should be spelled correctly. The tone and style should be suitable and appropriate paragraphs used.

Over to you, page 45

1 a A long, formal report

b An informal report

c A short, formal report

2 a ii because it is specific, rather than an opinion.

b i again it is specific and the allegation of 'late' may be hard to prove.

c i it gives the benefit of the doubt, isn't a value judgement and is legally far safer!

3 a No answer required.

b 3.2 – Paper is not stored properly. 4.3 – There are no specific policies.

c No specific answer possible but recommendations could include: better checking of documents, checking on screen, changing supplier, issuing stock strictly by rotation, improving storage, testing recycled paper, introducing 'green' policies, setting targets for saving paper, giving guidelines for saving paper, e.g. photocopying back-to-back etc. These should be written up in report style under the heading 'Recommendations'.

Over to you, page 51

1 Errors are: team, cartridges, recycled, environment, cartridges, special, boxes, donate, charities, children's foundation, sight, too, anyone, their, don't, battery, charger, grateful, appeal.

2 No specific answers possible but emails should include all relevant facts and tone/style must be appropriate.

3 No answer required – the table is given in the student notes (page 48).

Section review, page 52

1 No answer required.

2 No answer possible – it will depend upon the scenarios devised by the students.

3 No specific answer possible although each document should include all the key points mentioned, be grammatically correct, accurately spelled and punctuated and written using an appropriate tone.

4 Again no answer is possible as it will depend upon the points raised at the meeting.

4.4 – Preparation for business meetings

Over to you, page 60

1 a Postponed or deferred until a later date.

   b The person who runs the meeting/the final vote if there is a tie.

   c Everyone agreed.

   d A formal record of the discussions and decisions taken at a meeting.

   e Not held at all.

   f Put off and will be held on another date.

   g Meeting again/resuming the meeting.

2 Suggested responses are given below, but all appropriate ideas should be encouraged.

Dietary needs: vegan, vegetarian, Halal/Kosher meat, low/no salt, low fat: ensure all booking forms/notification documents include space for selecting/identifying options and inform caterers.

Hearing impairments: signer present at meeting, Typetalk service for contacts, inductive loop for hearing aid users.

Visual impairments: large print documents, dogs for the blind accepted on premises.

Wheelchair users: enough room to manoeuvre, space to turn around, special fittings in bathroom if staying overnight, choosing venue that has easy access/few or no stairs/sufficient lifts.

3 Content should be as follows:

```
Malton College
Riverside
MALTON
ML2 6KT

4 May 200-

The next meeting of the Student Council
will be held in the Percival Meeting
Room in the Technology Building at 1200
hours on Thursday, 16 May. A sandwich
lunch will be provided.

Please contact me on extension 1234 if
you cannot attend.

Agenda
1  Apologies for absence
2  Minutes of the previous meeting
3  Matters arising
4  Proposed new student diary design
5  Student car parking problems
6  Ideas for the Freshers' Fair
7  Any other business
8  Date and time of next meeting

(Student's name)
Council Secretary
```

Over to you, page 67

1 a Tilly said that the new computers were being delivered the following day.

   b Martin thought the rota would have to be changed before it could work properly.

   c Kelly said that she had spoken to Joanne Barnes. Joanne would not be able to attend the meeting the following month because she would be on holiday.

d Matt felt that the designs weren't suitable and different ones would have to be done by the following week.

e Jim said that the printers that had been delivered the previous week had to be returned because they were faulty.

2 No specific answer is possible but the summary should include all the main points, similar to the following. 'A discussion was held about a new vending machine. It was agreed that a replacement was required quickly and preferably one which provided a range of sandwiches, mainly with fish and salad options, and which gave change. The type of meat used in any meat sandwiches must be stated, i.e. whether Halal, Kosher or not. The idea of fruit was welcomed if this was an option, but several members present queried if this option was correct.'

Section review, page 68

1 The key points for the email are: Before: he needs to prepare well by clarifying the purpose of the meeting, how long it lasts and the type of discussions that are held; obtain a copy of the agenda and any preparatory papers plus the minutes of the previous meeting(s); talk to the previous chairperson, if possible, to find out if there are any main points to be aware of. At the meeting he should: start it on time, follow the agenda, introduce each topic; allow discussion, consult those present, clarify the conclusion. After the meeting he should check that the minutes are accurate and circulated to members promptly.

2 No answer possible as it depends upon the discussions held and the charities/events chosen.

In this section you will find:

Cross-referenced additional activities can be found at:

These sample assessments are designed as practice exercises to help your students understand the types of task they will be required to do for their formal assessments. For practice, tasks can be done by individuals or by groups as indicated.

There is one sample assessment for each section of the Unit:

5.1	Terms of employment contracts
5.2	Recruitment and staff development
5.3	Industrial relations
5.4	Adaptability to change

The structure and grading of the assessments reflect the grading criteria for the Unit as provided by Edexcel. Differentiation information is given where appropriate to indicate what would be required from the student to gain pass, merit or distinction grades. Tips to help the student achieve a merit or distinction grade are also given. A deadline box is provided in which you can enter a submission date to familiarise your students with the idea of working to a specified date or time.

Assessments are mainly printed one to a page so that they can be easily photocopied.

Answers to Unit 5 sample assessments

No specific answer is possible for the assessments in this unit because it will depend upon the business organisation selected by the student.

Identify a business you know well, because you work there part-time or because one of your family works there. Alternatively you could choose a business you can explore in depth on the Internet, such as Richer Sounds, or use case study materials provided by your tutor. Then undertake the following tasks.

Tasks 1 and 2 – Pass grade

1 a **Select TWO** jobs and **describe** the terms of employment.

   b Use the related job descriptions to **explain** the key features of each job.

Deadline

2 **Suggest** how the terms of employment or the features of the job may be adapted, in consultation with the job holder, to cope with:

   a temporary difficulties, such as short-staffing or emergency tasks

   b the job holder becoming more experienced and capable of carrying out additional or more responsible tasks.

Deadline

Using either the same business you chose for sample assessment 5.1, or a different business selected in agreement with your tutor, undertake the following tasks.

Tasks 1 and 2 – Pass grade

1 **a** **Describe** the recruitment procedures used by that business. **Illustrate** your findings with documentary evidence, e.g. a completed application form or job application letter on your own behalf.

   b **Explain** the appraisal or performance review system used by the business and the type of documents involved.

> **Deadline**

2 Carry out the following activities for the job you hold in the organisation *or* for a job you are interested in.

   a **Complete** a personal development plan for yourself.

   b **Identify** at least **FIVE** areas you would like to develop in that job and suggest target dates for achievement.

   c **State** how your personal development needs link with the overall business objectives.

   d **Suggest** some activities and experiences which would help you to meet your targets.

> **Deadline**

Tips to achieve a merit grade

Before you start Task 3, think about the following points:

- Recruitment procedures include writing job descriptions and person specifications, advertising, short-listing and interviewing candidates.
- There are also, usually, proper procedures at interviews to ensure all candidates are treated fairly, given equal opportunities and the best candidate is chosen. The procedures may include aptitude tests and scoring candidates.
- Monitoring procedures include appraisal interviews and the preparation of personal development plans. These enable staff to review their progress regularly and identify areas for development.
- The purpose of these procedures is to benefit both the organisation and the people who work there. The benefits become more obvious if you think about the possible consequences and problems of *not* having these procedures!

Now do Task 3.

Task 3 – Merit grade

3 For your selected business, **explain** how recruitment and monitoring procedures, like appraisals or performance reviews, help to benefit the organisation in terms of adequate and capable staff.

> **Deadline**

Tips to achieve a distinction grade

Before you start Task 4, check that you know and understand the following:

- Evaluating means assessing the strengths and weaknesses of something, based on the evidence.
- Excellent evidence of these strengths and weaknesses is whether something is effective or not. In other words, does it work? Does it achieve what it sets out to do?
- The aim of recruitment procedures is to obtain the best person for the job, to do so fairly and economically and in accordance with the law.
- Issues of discrimination and employment law also cover other aspects of the employment process, such as training and promotion.
- The aim of monitoring staff is to help staff to continually develop and improve. This benefits both them and the business. They are also less likely to become dissatisfied and leave.
- Some businesses may claim to have good procedures, but they obviously don't work if staff are unhappy and staff turnover is high.

Now do Task 4.

Task 4 – Distinction grade

4 **Evaluate** the effectiveness of the procedures for recruiting staff, monitoring staff and promoting staff in your selected business.

Do this by considering how well they achieve their aims and by identifying how well they prevent possible discrimination and ensure equality of opportunity.

Deadline

Either for one of the businesses you selected for Sample Assessments 5.1 and 5.2. or for a different business selected in agreement with your tutor, undertake the following tasks.

Tasks 1 and 2 – Pass grade

1 Assume you wish to ask for the opportunity to undergo training for a qualification. This will mean having time off work one day a week. In addition you would like your employer to pay the fees of £130 a year.

   a Decide which qualification you want to achieve and prepare a list of benefits for yourself and the organisation.

   b Practise negotiating for the outcome you wish to achieve and ask your tutor to assess your performance.

   c Assume you are now a staff representative negotiating the same issue on behalf of a colleague. Your only problem is that this colleague dropped out of a course last year so you know your manager is likely to resist your suggestion. She may also be opposed to you both doing the same qualification at the same time – although you think there are several benefits. You also have evidence that your colleague is a hard worker and keen to do well. Remember that you will need to support your arguments with facts and evidence.

Deadline

2 For the business you have selected, describe the methods you would use to negotiate a change in the conditions of employment and pay:

   a for yourself

   b as a member of a group.

In addition:

- Identify the people you would approach and the procedures you would use, particularly if you were initially unsuccessful.
- Identify any differences between the communication channels and procedures used by individual employees and those used for collective cases where most or all of the workforce is involved.

Deadline

Either for the same business you chose for the sample assessments earlier in this unit, or for a different business selected in agreement with your tutor, undertake the following tasks.

Task 1 – Pass grade

1   Describe examples of technological or structural changes that can occur in this business.

Try to identify examples of both types of changes in your answer. You may find it useful to write about some changes that have occurred in the past as well as those that could occur in the future.

Deadline

Tips for a merit grade

This question builds on the previous one.

- Think about the ways in which employees would be affected by change.
- Remember to think about both positive and negative effects.
- You may also find it useful to think about different types of employees in various jobs, e.g. junior and senior; full-time and part-time; skilled and unskilled.

Now do Task 2.

Task 2 – Merit grade

2   Explain how a particular employee may be affected by the technological or structural changes that you identified above.

Deadline

Tips for a distinction grade

For this question you have to carry out your own research and use this to make appropriate suggestions.

- There are many ways you can find out about trends. You can search on the Internet, read newspapers or journals and/or talk to people who work in an organisation.
- You may also find it useful to look back at the work you did in Unit 2, when you were learning about PESTEL analysis.
- The type of changes that occur may affect all businesses or only some of them. Remember that any changes you identify for a chosen business must be relevant to its activities.
- Then think about the way in which the business could respond. Remember that it must always operate within the law and will normally want to improve conditions for staff.

Now do Task 3.

Task 3 – Distinction grade

3   a *Either* by researching past and current trends *and/or* through reference to trade journals or news sources, **suggest** possible future technological or structural changes that could occur.

b Then **suggest** ways in which the business could prepare and adapt to these.

Deadline

5.1 – Terms of employment contracts

Over to you, page 273

1 No specific answer possible.

2 Suggestions for advantages and disadvantages include:

a Full time, permanent: advantages – security of employment often greater, career progression, get to know place/people, benefits may be better. Disadvantages: can get 'stuck in a rut', have to work many hours a week, may be little flexibility re hours/days.

b Part time, permanent: advantages – security of employment if permanent, get to know place/people, benefits should be as for full-time staff, have time for other pursuits besides work. Disadvantages: overall pay lower than full-time workers, may be less career progression, may not be as involved in social activities and may not feel as much a part of a team.

c Temporary work: advantages – useful for certain workers, e.g. specialists undertaking a specific job, those who want a stopgap, those who need extra money quickly; easier to retain independence, varied, flexible. Disadvantages: may be given all the routine jobs, no career progression, pay rates may be very variable, no security.

d Flexible hours: advantages – manage childcare and domestic commitments better, able to plan for private appointments, can work early/late depending upon temperament, may be able to set extra hours against a day off, travelling will be easier in non-peak times. Disadvantages: still have to work core time, amount of time can 'bank' for holidays will be limited, freedom to choose hours still limited, hours must be chosen in advance, no excuse for taking time off for personal appointments.

e Paid overtime: advantages – useful if need extra money, may be different rates for different times (double or treble time on occasion but less on others). Disadvantages: may not wish to work extra hours but difficult to refuse, extra pay is subject to tax, cannot be guaranteed, may be at unsocial times.

Any other appropriate suggestions should be accepted.

Over to you, page 283

1 a Flexible. No specific starting and finishing times are stated in the contract. Although the job description states normal hours it also says that some flexibility is required.

b No. The contract states that unused holiday allowance cannot be carried forward.

c It is not unfair. It is a reward for loyalty and long service and is perfectly fair if all long serving employees are treated the same.

d Inform his immediate superior by 10 am on the first day of his absence.

e Because he could work a day, then stay off sick and be paid!

f Advance warning means that either party can make alternative arrangements, i.e. the employer can replace the employee or the employee can find another job.

2 a i (3 of) Express – hours of work, holidays, notice requirement, absence procedures, disciplinary rules, health and safety policies, codes of behaviour etc.

ii (3 of) Implied – honest, reasonably competent, 'ready and willing' to do the work, reasonable care of employer's property, work towards organisation's objectives, not disclose confidential information, behave responsibly, be prepared to change when job changes.

b (3 of) Comply with contractual terms and conditions, comply with all statutory employment laws, provide a safe environment, not ask employees to take illegal actions, treat employees reasonably, consult employees about important company matters that will affect them, allow them access to their employee records (or other appropriate suggestions).

Section review, page 283

1 a Discrimination – treating someone differently and unfairly because of a reason unrelated to their job.

b Maternity leave – the statutory right to time off during pregnancy and when a baby is newborn.

c Paternity leave – the statutory right to time off for new fathers and adoptive fathers.

d Contract of employment – a legal document that defines the terms and conditions of employment for a particular job.

e Annual leave – the amount of time off allowed throughout the year for holidays, excluding bank holidays.

f Statutory employment rights – the employment rights of all British citizens through British and European laws.

g Contractual employment rights – employment rights determined by the terms and conditions stated in the contract.

h Equal opportunities policy – a commitment to treating all individuals equally and fairly at each stage of the employment process.

i Harassment – unwelcome behaviour that offends, frightens or upsets someone.

j Parental leave – the statutory right to time off for natural or adoptive parents to be with their children.

2 No specific answer required.

3 No specific answer possible as this will depend upon the information on the site at the time. It is suggested that tutors print out relevant information under each main heading which, at the time of writing, reflects the navigation of the site.

5.2 – Recruitment and staff development

Over to you, page 286

1 No specific answer possible as it will depend upon the advertisements selected.

2 a No specific answer possible, but students should be encouraged to think about 'open' questions which require a full reply, to identify questions which focus on different areas, e.g. employee's work history, reason for applying, interests and hobbies etc. and to link questions to the job requirements specified.

b No specific answer possible.

c College interview score sheets may be used as a basis for identifying areas of assessment, e.g. appearance, clarity of expression, ability to answer questions, ability to ask relevant questions etc. Suggested answers could be:

i Re-interview; assess which applicant would fit in best with the rest of the team; allow members of the panel to argue for/against each one and then take a vote.

ii Debate strengths and weaknesses in each case; compare against performance on scorecard; allow other members of panel to have 'casting votes'.

Over to you, page 292

1 Suggestions could include: (4 of) skilful, trained appraiser, easily understood/fair procedures, positive atmosphere/focus, sensible time allowed for interview (not too long/short), committed employee, business commitment to staff development.

2 No specific answer possible

Section review, page 292

1 a Job description – a document summarising the key activities and responsibilities of a job holder.

b Person specification – a summary of the essential and desirable requirements needed by a particular job applicant.

c Shortlisting – the process of reducing the number of applicants to be interviewed by assessing applications against specified criteria.

d Appraisal interview – an interview at which an employee's current performance is reviewed and future targets for achievement and training agreed.

2 a Marketing Assistant: the advertisement should be clear and identify all the essential requirements, i.e. 4 GCSEs grade C or above or equivalent qualification (BTEC First could be mentioned here!). A year's experience working in business, verbal communication skills, neat handwriting, IT skills, interest in working in Marketing, willing to undertake further study and neat and tidy appearance. Ideally some desirable aspects would also be included, e.g. GCSE English, IT qualification e-skills, previous marketing experience, use of Microsoft Office, webpage updating, friendly/outgoing personality and creative abilities. There should be clear information on how to apply, i.e. by letter/CV or completing an application form (and how to obtain one) plus a final date by which all applications must have been received.

b This should include: writing a job description and person specification, advertising the vacancy in the most suitable place, shortlisting against agreed criteria, interviewing by experienced staff so that all are asked the same questions, ensuring that no questions conflict with equal opportunities legislation, assessing and scoring applicants against agreed criteria, making an offer and notifying candidates promptly of the result.

3 No specific answer possible.

5.3 – Industrial relations

Over to you, page 296

1 No specific answer possible – it depends upon the specific college policies.

2 a Instant dismissal

b Instant dismissal (particularly if explicit term in contract, as is case for all transport workers)

c Instant dismissal

d Warning

e Warning

f Warning – although it would depend upon the seriousness of the offence and the potential consequences

g Instant dismissal

h Warning

i Warning

j Warning – although depends upon the content.

3 Any of the following: taking bribes, fraud, assault, divulging confidential information, clocking in for someone else, harassing or victimising another employee, deliberate damage to company property, serious acts of insubordination, serious negligence which causes unacceptable loss, damage or injury.

Over to you, page 300

1 a It is the employee's statutory right to have time off to deal with an emergency involving a dependant, but this does not have to be with pay. The union representative would probably see the manager to point out the situation. If the leave was still refused the employee would have a legitimate grievance.

b It is an implied right of the employer that the employee has the qualifications he claims to have and can do the job. However, the employer would be expected to assist the employee by providing appropriate training for aspects of the job which were new. If the employee refuses this training and cannot carry out the requirements of the job then he can legally be dismissed. This employee would not have a legitimate grievance.

c The sales representative is unable to carry out his job and has broken the law relating to drink driving. He can legally be dismissed and would not have a claim against his employer.

d This employee may have a genuine claim for victimisation/bullying and may also be able to bring a claim for discrimination. The union representative would ask for further details to clarify the situation but may see the supervisor (and/or the supervisor's own boss) for a discussion. The employee may be told to keep a work diary as evidence if the problem continued.

e The terms and conditions of employment should not be varied because of pregnancy to disadvantage the employee. The employee would have a legitimate grievance. If she was sacked as a result this would be classed as unfair dismissal.

2 No specific answer possible. However, students should be encouraged to follow the golden rules on page 297 of the book and prepare their case, use facts/evidence to support their view, try to negotiate a compromise and obtain a 'win/win' outcome and keep their tone and body language professional and moderate.

Section review, page 301

1 a Collective bargaining – negotiating on behalf of a large number of employees, normally by a trade union official.

b Employment tribunals – informal courts where employment disputes are heard.

c ACAS – the arbitration and conciliation service that helps two parties to find agreement over an issue.

d Gross misconduct – a serious misdemeanour that normally results in instant dismissal.

e Constructive dismissal – resigning under protest because of unfair treatment or imposed and worse terms or conditions.

f Wild-cat strike – an unofficial strike that is technically unlawful because the workers have not been balloted.

2 No specific answer possible. It may be useful for students to refer to examples (such as college policies or those of their own employers if they have a part-time job). Several of the Richer Sounds policies and rules included on the StudentZone may also be useful. As part of this exercise, where students disagree over the policy, it will be useful for them to practise their negotiation skills when devising a final answer.

3 a Unfair. The prison governor was criticised for being over-zealous.

b Fair because it would bring the name of the RSPCA and everything it stands for into disrepute.

c Unfair. This was a case of sex discrimination and the settlement was in the region of £5,000.

d Fair. It was the angry reaction rather than the singing that made the dismissal fair.

e Fair. The tribunal agreed this was misconduct.

f Unfair. The company had to reinstate the worker and compensate him for lost earnings and stress.

g Unfair. This was sex discrimination and the settlement was over £130,000 as the women was awarded £80,000 for loss of earnings and £41,000 for loss of pension rights plus extra payments for injury of feelings and aggravated damages.

5.4 – Adaptability to change

Over to you, page 306

1 a (2 of) New equipment, new software, website changes, selling goods online, taking payments online, online customer services, buying supplies online. (Or other appropriate suggestions.)

(2 of) Outsourcing of jobs, departmental reorganisation, restructure of the company, relocation.

b (3 of) Because of a merger/takeover, to remain competitive, to keep up-to-date with technology, to save money.

c (2 of) So that employees know what is happening, so that employees can contribute to the process, so that employees will be more cooperative and less anxious about the change, so that people can prepare for the change, so that people can negotiate over areas of concern.

d i (2 of) email, meetings, notices, memos, staff newsletters.

ii (2 of) local/regional/national newspaper, trade journal, letter, notice included in standard mailing, telephone call, visit by rep, information on website.

2 a Increasing the responsibilities of a job – advantages: more status/prestige, more challenging, more interesting, better promotion prospects; disadvantages: may lose previous social contacts, may need to learn new skills, may not receive commensurate pay increase, may be more stressful.

b Changing the working hours to an earlier or later start/finish – advantages: better for family commitments, better for travelling; disadvantages: worse for family commitments, worse for travelling, lose contact with previous colleagues.

c Restructuring an organisation so people work in different departments or with different teams – advantages: new challenges, may improve working relationships and extend social ties; disadvantages: lose contact with old team, insecurity and worry about relating to new team, need to adapt existing skills/learn new ones.

d Introducing new technology – advantages: new challenges, more varied/enjoyable work, up-to-date skills improve promotion prospects; disadvantages: some may be anxious about learning required skills, may be worries about job security in some areas.

e Outsourcing an operation previously done within the business – advantages: employees can concentrate on core business areas, unlikely to be missed if routine/boring tasks; disadvantages: worries about job security, staff who did this operation will be redundant or redeployed, in which case may need retraining and may have to form new working relationships.

Section review, page 306

1 **a** Structural change – a change relating to the way the business is organised or structured.

b Merger – two businesses joining together for mutual benefit.

c Take-over – one business buying another.

d E-business strategy – a plan for utilising the Internet to do business.

e Outsourcing – paying a specialist to undertake non-core business tasks or operations.

f Multiskilling – individuals having a variety of skills.

g Upskilling – improving skills level.

2 Students who have studied Unit 2.4 may recall several of these areas from their earlier work. Some suggested ideas are given below but any other appropriate suggestions and ideas should be encouraged.

a Banks: growth in automation (ATMs/automated payment machines), telephone and Internet banking. Reduced need for bank tellers. Reduced number of branches. Outsourcing of call centre operations. Jobs: changed the number/type of jobs undertaken by staff and where these are done, e.g. fewer bank tellers, more call centre staff, IT specialists for website. Future: greater emphasis on security of website transactions; greater monitoring of individual customers to enable targeted marketing approach to each person when in contact with bank.

b Schools/colleges: IT suites (and relevant hardware/software), interactive whiteboards, Internet access, laptops, data projectors for PowerPoint presentations, digital photocopiers, learning centres etc. Jobs: changed the way lessons are prepared/ delivered, the way student records are kept and administrators operate and the way students research/produce work. Future: WiFi would give Internet access throughout all educational buildings so laptops used in refectories/study areas etc.; Bluetooth = no cables required.

c Large retailers: EFTPOS/EPOS = all stock scanned in/out of system by barcodes, debit/credit card transactions processed at checkout, itemised till receipts, programmed discount offers automatically processed (e.g. 2 for price of 1 etc.), stock levels adjusted as items sold. Loyalty cards = customer data obtained for targeted marketing. Selling from website, webstore showing products, emails to inform registered customers of offers. Jobs: no need for many routine jobs e.g. pricing, stock checks etc. – although shelves still need filling. Fast processing through automated checkouts. More staff involved in website maintenance/updates, marketing and promotional activities. Future: wireless tagging/monitoring of stock to improve security; trolleys which automatically calculate contents.

d National newspapers: copy produced on laptops by journalists in situ. Copy and pictures transmitted electronically and edited on screen. Paper composed on screen and transmitted to printing section so whole process automated. Newspaper websites with updated content. Registered users enable offers to be made to customers. Jobs: fewer staff employed through more automation/ multiskilling (e.g. no typesetters, fewer machine operators, more copywriting/ inputting/editing by same staff). Greater flexibility for journalists for working off-site/submitting copy. Graphics easier/faster/ more sophisticated because of software developments. Future: option of format (tabloid/broadsheet?). More use of colour.

In this section you will find:

Cross-referenced additional activities can be found at:

These sample assessments are designed as practice exercises to help your students understand the types of task they will be required to do for their formal assessments. For practice, tasks can be done by individuals or by groups as indicated.

There is one sample assessment for each section of the Unit:

6.1	Core administrative systems
6.2	Threats to administrative effectiveness
6.3	Simple administrative systems
6.4	Health and safety at work

The structure and grading of the assessments reflect the grading criteria for the Unit as provided by Edexcel. Differentiation information is given where appropriate to indicate what would be required from the student to gain pass, merit or distinction grades. Tips to help the student achieve a merit or distinction grade are also given. A deadline box is provided in which you can enter a submission date to familiarise your students with the idea of working to a specified date or time.

Assessments are mainly printed one to a page so that they can be easily photocopied.

Answers to Unit 6 sample assessments

6.1

No specific answer possible. However, tutors should note that the administrative processes listed, and the contribution identified for each, should be specific to the business selected.

6.2

The tutor should note that neither the pass or distinction grade questions relate to a selected organisation whereas the merit grade question does. This provides more scope for students to examine a range of threats (pass grade) and then to develop these to look at precautionary measures and contingency plans (distinction grade). At merit grade the response will depend upon the organisation selected.

6.3

No specific answer possible as it will depend upon the organisation selected (pass grade) and the systems selected (merit grade).

6.4

No specific answer possible as it will depend upon the organisation selected.

For this assessment, identify an organisation you know well, such as your college, or a business where you work part-time or on work experience.

Task 1 – Pass grade

1 **a** For your selected organisation, **identify** at least **SIX** administrative processes that take place.

   b For each process you have identified, **describe** how it contributes to the smooth operation of the business.

Deadline

Task 1 – Pass grade

1 a **State** at least **FOUR** ways in which administrative effectiveness can be threatened in an organisation.

b For each threat you have identified, **describe** the possible steps that business organisations may take to protect themselves.

Deadline

Tips to achieve a merit grade

Before you start the next task, think about these points.

- You must select **five** errors, but you could suggest more.
- Bear in mind these often occur because of carelessness, poor procedures or genuine mistakes.
- There is always a direct effect (e.g. wrongly copying a number means the figure is incorrect in the document) but there may also be other implications and consequences (e.g. a customer pays the amount stated, which is actually wrong, and someone has to try to sort out the problem).
- Remember, too, that you must also consider the effect of the error on the department and the staff who work there.

Now do Task 2.

Task 2 – Merit grade

2 Select an organisation you know well, such as your college or a business where you work part-time or on a work placement.

a **Identify** at least **FIVE** errors which could occur in communication, storage or security.

b **Explain** how each of these could affect departmental effectiveness. In your answer, include the implications and possible consequences of errors, in addition to direct effects.

Deadline

Tips to achieve a distinction grade

Before you start the final task, you may find it helpful to consider the following points.

- Major threats are common to virtually all businesses. Many of them relate to IT security and ensuring that the business stays operational.
- Many measures are **precautionary** – for example, having a firewall installed.
- Other measures are taken in response to contingencies, i.e. unforeseen events. These measures are planned as part of crisis management meetings. You may find it helpful to look back at Unit 2.4 to refresh your memory about this topic.
- You can refer to your selected organisation as you write your answer but you may find it useful to include other types of businesses, too. This may give you more examples to use.

Now do Task 3.

Task 3 – Distinction grade

3 Many potential threats can affect any departmental administrative system.

    a **Identify** the main threats that an organisation may have to consider.

    b **Explain** the measures that can be taken both as a precaution and to cope with contingencies.

In your answer, include your **recommendations** for appropriate backup/retrieval procedures and other appropriate facilities.

Deadline

Select an organisation you know well. This could be your own college, an organisation where you are employed part-time or an organisation where you have undertaken work experience.

Task 1 – Pass grade

1 **Identify** a simple administrative system used within the organisation.

  a Clearly **explain** the purpose of the system.

  b Then **identify** the functions of the system.

> **Deadline**

Tips to achieve a merit grade

Before you start Task 2, you might find it useful to consider the following.

- Read the scenario carefully. Try to picture what the office must be like.
- Think about the implications of the problems. In other words, what will be their effects?
- Remember that a system takes account of each step in a process, to make sure nothing is forgotten.
- If you have thought about the problems carefully, the benefits should be fairly obvious. Especially, too, if you think about Sam's aims in running the business!

Now do Task 2.

Task 2 – Merit grade

2 Read the scenario below and then answer the questions that follow:

> You have recently agreed to help out in the office at Ritchie's Garage. The garage is owned by Sam Ritchie, a qualified mechanic, who is a friend of yours. He employs two other mechanics and runs a thriving small business, doing car repairs and MOT tests. The only problem is that the office is in chaos.
>
> Bills aren't paid on time, invoices to customers aren't issued on time (and are often incorrect!) and there are papers everywhere. There is no proper system for booking in cars which causes problems and delays for customers. There is no proper record of customers which can be used for sales or marketing purposes or for answering customer queries.
>
> You have agreed to set up some basic systems for Sam while you are there.

  a **Recommend THREE** simple administrative systems that should be set up for Sam immediately.

  b **Select ONE** of these systems and clearly explain how the system should operate. **Illustrate** how it would work either by a sequential list or by drawing a flow chart.

  c **Identify** the benefits that Sam will gain from having this system.

> **Deadline**

For a workplace you know well, such as your college, an organisation where you work part-time or where you work on work experience, undertake the following tasks.

Task 1 – Pass grade

1 a Identify and **describe** at least **FIVE** health and safety hazards which can or do exist in that workplace.

b Then **explain** the actions that have been taken to minimise the risk of anyone being harmed by each of these hazards.

Deadline

Tips to achieve a merit grade

Before you do the next task, you might find it helpful to consider the following.

- Most health and safety procedures are included in staff handbooks and explained at induction.
- You could find out more information by talking to a safety officer or safety representative.
- Notices about first aid and emergency evacuations should be easy to find.
- Remember that you have to describe the procedures – not just list them!

Now do Task 2.

Task 2 – Merit grade

2 Identify and **describe** the procedures that are used in that workplace for:

a dealing with accidents effectively

b taking action in an emergency.

Deadline

Tips to achieve a distinction grade

Before you start the final tasks, think about the following points.

- If your selected business is a very large organisation, it is impractical to think about doing a risk assessment of the whole business. Instead select a specific area and agree this with your tutor.
- You will find it easier to copy a risk assessment form from a book, rather than invent your own. This is perfectly acceptable.
- Carry out your risk assessment carefully and methodically. Remember to make careful notes on your form.
- If your form is rather scruffy afterwards, then it is better to rewrite it neatly (or type it) before you hand it in.
- Remember that your recommendations must be 'reasonably practicable'. This means that you can't expect the business to spend a lot of money when a simpler, much cheaper solution can be found.

Now do Task 3.

Tasks 3 and 4 – Distinction grade

3 Prepare a risk assessment form that you could use to assess risks in your selected business.

4 a Carry out a detailed risk assessment for your selected business.

   b Make **appropriate recommendations** for improvements.

Deadline

6.1 – Core administrative systems

Over to you, page 11

1 a Students should suggest documents such as application forms, enrolment forms and any other forms related to the registration or ID process in the college, in addition to purchase order forms, class registers, examination entry forms, course withdrawal forms etc.

b No specific answer possible as this will depend upon the structure of the college and the role/title of specific departments.

2 a 3 appropriate suggestions are needed for each business:

i A bank – customer names/addresses/account details; current interest rates on savings and loans; different types of accounts and services available; balances on customer accounts and overdrafts/loans.

ii A football club – season ticket holders names/addresses; player details and game schedules; gate receipts and other income details; invoices and expenditure details.

iii A magazine – details of regular advertisers: names/addresses of subscribers; production expenditure details, e.g. on paper, printing, distribution etc.; income details from subscription and casual sales.

iv A large bakery – purchase orders and expenditure on ingredients and consumables; sales orders and sales revenue; customer information; production plans.

v A large theme park – sales orders for consumables; maintenance plans; information on ticket sales and takings; staffing information for both permanent and seasonal staff.

b It is only expected that students will concentrate on one of the five options because many types of documents (invoices, orders, letters etc.) are common to many different types of organisation. Therefore, in the example answers below, many of the suggestions made can be used for more than one type of business.

Bank: documentary – bank account application forms, loan application forms; graphical – charts and graphs in marketing booklets, pictures of online banking screens; financial – bank statements, spreadsheets; electronic – own website, electronic payment requests; reference – banking law, currency exchange rates.

Football club: documentary – season ticket application forms, business letters; graphical – posters and adverts; financial – invoices, payroll documents; electronic – own website, database of season ticket holders; reference – newspaper reports, travel information.

Magazine: documentary – readers' letters, feature articles; graphical – drawings, photographs; financial – cash flow forecasts, expense claims; electronic – electronic orders, emails; reference – competitors' magazines, advertising regulations.

Bakery: documentary – sales orders, delivery notes; graphical – equipment use instructions, product advertisements; financial – invoices, financial forecasts; electronic – electronic orders, company Intranet; reference – health and safety manuals, equipment manuals.

Theme park: documentary – business letters, job application forms; graphical – drawings and photographs in advertisements and leaflets; financial – data related to each day's takings, spreadsheets showing projected income and expenditure; electronic – staff database, own website; reference – health and safety manuals, employment law.

3 a No specific answer possible as database systems vary, although most capture key student personal data plus enrolment/achievement information and attendance patterns. It will help students to understand the concept of reports if they can see some printed out that relate to themselves or their own group (e.g. best/worst attender in the group).

b Ideas can include: customer title, name, address, d.o.b., marital status, occupation, number of children/pets, nearest store, main interests and hobbies. Reports will be generated to target mail shots and to reflect purchasing preferences, e.g. all female customers over 35 with children, all single male customers, under 25, all customers in a given geographical area earning more than £x each year – and so on.

4   No answer possible.

Over to you, page 18

1   i   **a** No. **b** Depends on scale of error. If large tell manager, email could be sent to staff to amend data. This would be important only if marketing staff were using the data for a specific purpose.

   ii   **a** Yes. **b** Tell manager immediately and provide exact figure otherwise there is a strong likelihood the disciplinary process will be jeopardised.

   iii   **a** Yes. **b** Tell the manager, preferably before the meeting starts as important decisions could be made based on flawed data.

   iv   **a** Yes. **b** Tell the manager as it may be possible to amend the advertisement before publication or withdraw it. Too high a price will depress future sales, too low a price can create considerable consumer problems.

   v   **a** No. **b** Again it depends upon the scale. If too low a number has been calculated then no action may be taken when action is really needed – or if too high a number, unnecessary action may be taken.

   vi   **a** Yes. **b** Tell the representative and finance immediately. If the amount claimed is too low the representative will be out of pocket, if it is too high then the amount will have to be repaid. Failure to say anything in this situation is tantamount to fraud.

2   No specific answer possible as it will depend upon the individual college systems. An overview of the type of non-confidential matters that are discussed at college meetings and the type of decisions made based on these discussions and the information available at the time will illustrate the principle involved.

3   Below are suggested answers but other appropriate ideas should be accepted.

   a   (4 of) Storing and retrieving documents, photocopying, keeping customer records up-to-date, ordering office stationery and consumables, taking messages, preparing internal and external documents such as emails, reports, replies to business letters.

   b   (4 of) Information will be processed more quickly, decisions can be made based on up-to-date information, the team will have more time to concentrate on their own job roles,

Marianne will have more time to concentrate on managing the team and monitoring their performance.

4   It is recommended that tutors check each of the sites listed to check current information before this task is given to students.

   a   The Information Security Forum is an international association, funded by over 260 organisations which co-operate over practical research on information security. Samples of the projects and the names of members are found on the site.

   b   A L Digital provides a range of security solutions from firewalls to secure hosting in The Bunker (see Student Book Unit 1 page 66).

   c   The Government 'Best Practice' site provides information (mainly in pdf format) about several aspects of information security including security standards, viruses, inappropriate usage, unauthorised access, theft and systems failure. Given the amount of information on this site, you may want to sub-divide this research activity into specific areas of investigation on the site.

   d   Insight Consulting provides security solutions for businesses and several case studies are included on the site. It also advises on business continuity and risk management.

   e   This survey is carried out every two years by PriceWaterhouseCoopers and covers over 1,000 businesses. The 2004 executive summary showed that the average UK business suffers one security incident each month. Top breaches were virus infection, staff misuse, hacking, theft or fraud, systems failure and data corruption.

Section review, page 19

1   **a**   Telephone, because urgent responses are required.

   b   Email. Could include request in email that people pass the message on. A notice on the entrance to the car park would also be useful. A notice on the staff noticeboard would probably not be read by all the users.

   c   Face-to-face request is preferable, in case some negotiation is required!

   d   Leave an urgent message on his mobile phone. A safety back-up would be to ring ahead to his next appointment and leave a message there, too. The aim is to ensure contact is made as quickly as possible.

e Business letter, because this is a formal situation and the response must be in writing.

f Face-to-face because a favour is required and it may be necessary to be persuasive.

g Send a catalogue and price list by post, with a compliment slip. Speed isn't important and the customer will want printed materials to refer to over time.

h Fax them or, if they are held on computer, send them as an email attachment, because speed is important.

2 Suggested responses are given below.

Administrative process	Contribution to the business
Greeting and dealing with external visitors and callers	Good customer relations/visitors dealt with courteously and speedily
Keeping departmental planners and diaries up to date and scheduling appointments	More efficient scheduling of appointments, provides at a glance information to help planning, no important arrangements overlooked
Researching information on the Internet	Enables staff to refer to the latest information
Arranging meetings, including preparing meeting documents, booking and preparing the room and arranging for refreshments	Ensures meetings run effectively and efficiently, correct people are invited/kept informed
Organising routine travel arrangements and making hotel reservations	Enables business travel to be organised efficiently and economically
Assisting with the arrangements of special events, such as sales conferences or visits by VIPs	Enables events to run smoothly with correct documentation. Creates good impression for external visitors
Purchasing supplies of stationery and keeping stationery stock records	Ensures essential stocks are always available
Recording minor departmental expenses and arranging repayment for staff through the petty cash system	Ensures accurate accounting records are kept and staff are reimbursed promptly
Keeping staff rotas up-to-date in relation to additional working and holiday leave	Ensures adequate staff cover at all times and leave is allocated fairly amongst staff
Checking staff expense claims or invoices before they are paid	Ensures payments are correct first time
Preparing the paperwork related to departmental interviews and greeting interviewees	Ensures interview process is smooth and efficient; creates good impression with job applicants
Keeping specific departmental records and undertaking other departmental duties, such as responding to internal queries	Ensures up-to-date information available at all times and queries handled efficiently, correctly and professionally

3 No specific answer possible.

6.2 – Threats to administrative effectiveness

Over to you, page 27

1 The following are some suggestions but any other appropriate ideas should be accepted.

a **i** Contact is not made as agreed, customer has to be asked to repeat information previously given, important customer matter is not resolved as promised.

ii No one attends, some people receive forwarded notice but too late to attend, important decisions cannot be made the meeting may have to be postponed,

iii Message sent to wrong person, disclosure of confidential information to wrong person, internal information sent outside the company.

iv Customer contacts colleague at home, customer pesters colleague, colleague makes formal complaint.

v Colleague can read messages received/sent, colleague can access confidential messages, colleague can send an email in your name.

vi No one available to see the customer, important preparations before visit not carried out, customer dissatisfied with service and goes elsewhere.

vii Flight is missed because time/date is wrong, important business meeting is threatened, meeting has to be cancelled/rearranged.

viii Business is lost because quotation appears too expensive, business is gained because quotation looks cheap but then there is disagreement when invoice issued which threatens customer relations.

ix VIPs have to wait for table to become available, restaurant is fully booked and VIPs have to be taken elsewhere, VIPs not impressed with efficiency, firm's executives annoyed at looking foolish.

x Stock is pilfered, key items are taken and, because they are not noted in the system, are not replaced so are not available.

b Any appropriate ideas should be encouraged, e.g. poor quality photocopies or missing pages, faxes not sent, mail delayed, items not posted, items not franked correctly so recipient has to pay postage etc. The possibilities are virtually endless!

2 No specific answer possible as it will depend upon the exact college policies and procedures.

3 Employee records, customer records and files held by a credit reference agency. Social work records and personal databases are not covered.

4 **a**, **c** and **e**.

Over to you, page 32

1 a (4 of) Fire, vandalism, malicious damage, software virus, system failure, hacking.

b (4 of) To ensure business continuity, to prevent business information falling into the wrong hands, to prevent the destruction of important records, to prevent damage to the system, to protect the integrity of the system.

2 No specific answer possible as it will depend upon the specific college systems in place and known to students and staff.

3 No specific answers possible as it will depend upon the sites students find themselves. Tutors are, however, recommended to check the sites listed before issuing the task, to ensure they are aware of the key points which students can be expected to include in their presentations.

Section review, page 33

The aim of these tasks is to encourage students to think laterally about the major threats faced by different types of organisations and their differing needs for business continuity.

For example, the consequences of administrative errors can be appalling in a hospital – such as writing the wrong admission date on a letter or losing a patient's file. In school, there is a greater likelihood of threats to the integrity of the system from students who want to test their abilities in this area. The threat of hacking by a bank is also considerable, given the potential rewards.

With an airline, there is greater concern about system security and integrity, given that system failure can threaten passenger safety (in addition to causing major delays with knock-on effects). Whilst there is likely to be less concern about system failure in a retail store, there would obviously be considerable inconvenience for customers if payments could not be processed or if stocks could not be replenished as normal.

Measures taken by organisations differ. Hospitals need strict procedures to prevent errors and double-checking of important documents before they are issued. Security restrictions are in place in most organisations to prevent unauthorised access to confidential parts of the system by employees. All organisations invest in security measures but these are more critical in banks and airlines – though retail organisations and schools need to have protection against malicious attacks.

Any appropriate ideas should be encouraged and students encouraged to discuss and debate the issues that arise.

6.3 – Simple administrative systems
Over to you, page 35

1 a To protect the hardware, the software and the data held on the system from unauthorised access or corruption.

b Normally by the issuing of an IT policy and procedures during induction.

c (2 of) To protect the system from hackers, to prevent viruses being introduced into the system, to prevent hardware failure.

2 a To ensure that the correct items are ordered, essential items are always available, all items are stored correctly and used in sequence.

b To ensure all visitors are greeted courteously and dealt with promptly and efficiently, to ensure health and safety (e.g. by listing names of visitors, providing information on emergency evacuation procedures), to ensure security procedures are maintained, e.g. issue of visitors' passes if used.

c To ensure that all documents are stored in good condition and found quickly when required.

d To ensure that mail is sorted correctly and delivered promptly to the correct person each day.

e To ensure that outgoing mail is franked accurately and promptly despatched each day.

f To ensure that, where possible, 'found' property is reunited with its correct owner and that lost property is cleared out at regular intervals.

Over to you, page 47

1 No specific answer possible as it depends upon the college systems.

2 a Headings could be: date letter received, name of correspondent, address of correspondent, summary of topic (or heading), name of recipient, department, date of reply.

b Methods could include: receiving a copy of the reply (in some offices these are filed in a day book), receiving an email notification, record kept by person processing outgoing post, summary form to complete each day.

c Email a reminder, set up an automatic reminder system, talk to the manager, change the system (if it wasn't working or was unpopular).

3 No specific answer possible as it depends upon the departure point.

4 No specific answer possible as it depends upon countries investigated.

5

> **KATE BRETHERTON – TRAVEL SUMMARY**
>
> **Tuesday, 5 July**
> 1350   Taxi to Heathrow airport (booked)
> 1450   Check in at Terminal 3
> 1650   Depart for Copenhagen on flight SK506
> 1940   Arrive Copenhagen
> 2245   Depart Copenhagen on flight SK 273
> 2320   Arrive Aarhus
>
> **Thursday, 7 July**
> 0645   Taxi to airport
> 0745   Check in at Aarhus airport
> 0845   Depart for Copenhagen on flight SK244
> 0920   Arrive Copenhagen
>
> **Friday, 8 July**
> 1510   Taxi to airport
> 1610   Check in Copenhagen airport
> 1810   Depart for London Heathrow on flight SK1507
> 1905   Arrive London Heathrow. Taxi home (booked).

6 No specific answer possible as it depends upon student choices.

Section review, page 57

1

> **JIM KOSAK – TRAVEL ITINERARY**
>
> **Monday, 14 July**
> 1850   Check in Terminal 4, Heathrow airport
> 2150   Depart for Sydney on flight BA 0015
>
> **Wednesday, 16 July**
> 0515   Arrive Sydney
> Accommodation booked at Crowne Plaza Darling Harbour Hotel, 150 Day Street, Sydney tel: +61 2 9261 1188.
>
> **Monday, 28 July**
> 1245   Check in Terminal 4, Sydney airport
> 1545   Depart for London on flight BA0016
>
> **Tuesday, 29 July**
> 0555   Arrive London Heathrow

b The difference is due to the fact that the time in Sydney is 9 hours ahead of London. Therefore, when Jim leaves at 21.50 on Monday, it is already 6.50 am on Tuesday in Sydney.

c No specific answer possible although most tourist sites such as **www.sydney.com.au** provide information on Sydney harbour and cruises, museums and art galleries, other sights (e.g. the Opera House and Harbour Bridge, Bondi Beach and the Zoo), historic homes and day trips to areas such as the Blue Mountains.

d 9 am in London is 6 pm in Sydney. Therefore contact each morning would be best. After 2 pm or 3 pm in London it is too late to make contact. When it is 9 am in Sydney it is midnight in London.

2 a (3 of) It may be important to contact them urgently, they may be required to attend meetings in the office, an important appointment may have to be scheduled on their behalf, it may be necessary to check their schedules to answer a customer query.

b If a paper-based system is used, the system should include making contact with them regularly by phone or email to obtain an update on appointments they have scheduled. Ideally this would be daily. If a PDA or laptop is used then the information should be downloaded onto the company system each day.

3 The aim of this activity is to give students a research activity on the Internet that will help them with future Internet searches – and to illustrate the features of other search engines besides Google. The topic is too comprehensive to include specific answers and there is no requirement that all the search engines listed should be investigated. This would be inappropriate for a small group who may prefer to select just three or four alternatives.

Tutors may also wish to demonstrate how to refine searches on websites such as the BBC site.

Overture is interesting because it is a specialist company which provides paid-for content that appears on several search engines. This is why a search for, say, online gambling may bring up the same response on (currently) AOL, Freeserve, Lycos, Tiscali, MSN and Yahoo. After typing the keyword (e.g. 'credit cards' or 'online betting') into the 'Search the Web' box the Results page appears – in top right below country flag 'View Advertisers Max Bids'. When the student clicks on that and completes the security question (just copy the letters shown) the advertisers' maximum bid will then appear in the box underneath the entry. For example, at the time of writing, Capital One was paying £5.98 per click through to be at the top of the list of credit card companies. This money is shared between Overture and the search engines on which it is listed.

4 a No answer possible as it depends upon the college system.

b i To ensure the most appropriate room is reserved for the correct length of time, to prevent double-bookings.

ii To ensure refreshments are appropriate, to ensure they are served at the best time, to restore flagging spirits in a long meeting.

iii To ensure everyone who should attend is invited, to ensure people are invited in sufficient time, to ensure everyone knows the time/date/room/main business to be discussed.

iv To ensure everyone receives a copy promptly, to ensure they are accurate, to remind them of the action they have agreed to undertake.

Over to you, page 56

1 a (3 of) To coordinate appointments, to check whereabouts of staff, to prevent double-bookings, to allocate sufficient time for particular activities/arrangements.

b (2 of) Can set reminders, can search for information, can replicate 'repeat' appointments easily, different time periods can be viewed simultaneously.

2 No specific answer possible as it depends upon sites researched by students.

3 C is the correct option. The apology should be to the Chairperson for the interruption, the matter should be written down in case it is confidential, it should only be handed to the person concerned for the same reason.

4 See appropriate answers to Specialist Unit 4, page 20.

6.4 – Health and safety at work
Over to you, page 65

1 a 2d There is no longer safe access to the office.

b 2c Appropriate training has not been provided.

c **3a** and **3b** The students have not cooperated and failed to follow procedures. They are also disregarding the possible consequences.

d **3a** and **3b** As above.

e **2b** There are risks attached to the use and handling of a hazardous substance.

f **2a** This is not a safe system of work.

g **2e** There are insufficient arrangements for welfare.

h **2a** This is not safe plant (i.e. equipment).

i **2e** The working environment is no longer safe.

j **3a** and **3b**. As for **c** above.

k **3a** This disregards the consequences for the cleaner.

l **3c** This is misusing/abusing safety equipment.

2 Any appropriate ideas and suggestions should be encouraged, for example:

Shops: broken glass if item dropped, wet floor after cleaning, food hygiene issues (e.g. flies on a hot day).

Offices: licking envelopes (cutting tongue), carrying files so they obstruct vision, lifting boxes of paper (heavy), reaching files from a high shelf without appropriate safety stool.

Workshop: blocking walkways or aisles with boxes or finished goods, faulty equipment, hot/sharp objects, moving machinery.

3 No answer possible.

Over to you, page 72

1 No specific answer possible – it depends upon procedure used by the college. However, the evacuation procedures are in place to ensure the building is emptied as rapidly as possible in an orderly manner. The accident procedures are in place to ensure that the injured person receives the most appropriate attention as quickly as possible and all the key facts relating to the incident are recorded promptly.

2 No specific answer possible.

3 **i** high – it could catch fire

ii low so far as the equipment is concerned (the damage is done!), high so far as using it again is concerned!

iii medium – there is no immediate danger unless the shredder is used, so a note should be put on the shredder to prevent further use

iv high – electric/computer cables could easily be routed through the ceiling

v medium if the rip is not in a main walkway, high if it is because of the danger of tripping

vi medium to other people, high to you as it is very easy to trip over it

vii high as the glass could fall out, although if it is laminated safety glass this should mean that it wouldn't shatter

viii high, because you don't know what's wrong and shouldn't use it until you do know

ix high, because you shouldn't use it until it is repaired

x medium in winter, high in summer if computer users are affected.

4 No specific answer possible.

Section review, page 73

1 **a** The sign must be replaced as notification about first aiders is a legal requirement.

b A better mat should be fitted at the entrance. If nothing improves the flooring should be changed as the working environment isn't safe.

c Action must be taken. As a first step a warning notice should be put in the cloakroom. Again, the working environment/welfare facilities aren't safe.

d No action required. Staff are quite capable of washing their own cups.

e No action required – this would defeat the purpose of the air conditioning system!

f Action is required. Stock should be purchased and someone should be nominated to ensure there is always a supply available. PPE is an essential requirement when appropriate for handling hazardous substances.

g The only action is to purchase appropriate screen wipes, if these are not already in stock. Staff can clean their own VDUs.

h The only action required is a quiet word with the member of staff concerned.

i Action is required as the company is legally bound to provide appropriate training.

j Action is required as this equipment must, by law, be checked regularly (normally every twelve months).

2 No specific answer possible.

In this section you will find:

Cross-referenced additional activities can be found at:

These sample assessments are designed as practice exercises to help your students understand the types of task they will be required to do for their formal assessments. For practice, tasks can be done by individuals or by groups as indicated.

There is one sample assessment for each section of the Unit:

7.1	Explore sales promotion techniques
7.2	Pre-sales preparation
7.3	Sales practice
7.4	After-sales service

The structure and grading of the assessments reflect the grading criteria for the Unit as provided by Edexcel. Differentiation information is given where appropriate to indicate what would be required from the student to gain pass, merit or distinction grades. Tips to help the student achieve a merit or distinction grade are also given. A deadline box is provided in which you can enter a submission date to familiarise your students with the idea of working to a specified date or time.

Assessments are mainly printed one to a page so that they can be easily photocopied.

Answers to Unit 7 sample assessments

7.1

No specific answer possible.

7.2

Although there are obviously some common elements required in the answers for this question, it is not possible to provide a specific answer as this will depend upon the specific store chosen and the individual policies in place for each one (e.g. returns policies and/or pricing policies and discounts). In addition, the size and scale of the business will influence aspects such as security, care of the sales environment, referring customers to more experienced staff etc.

Tutors should note that despite the reference to FMCGs in the grid, students are expected to refer to a business selling consumer durables, otherwise many elements essential to the unit, such as product knowledge and negotiation skills, would not be required.

7.3

Question 3 in the relevant Over to You section should act as a useful trigger for answering this question, which satisfies the pass criteria for this part of the unit. Students will develop their answers at the end of the last section of this unit to qualify for a higher grade. Specific answers will obviously depend upon the store or business identified.

7.4

This extends the assessment activity from section 7.3. Question 2 links to the merit criteria for the assessment and question 3 to the distinction criteria. Students frequently have difficulty in recommending improvements if they select an excellent business model to investigate. In this case the question allows them to identify why this is so good – if this is the case – and to compare the business to those stores which have less exacting standards.

This links to the information provided in the delivery and assessment strategies of the Edexcel documentation, which compares the service sometimes given in some large stores (Curry's and Dixon's are mentioned) with that provided by businesses like Richer Sounds.

For this assessment you will work in a small team, as agreed by your tutor. As a first step, your team must decide a product or service to promote to a specified market.

Task 1 – Pass grade

1   **Identify** the product or service you have chosen. Then **state** your target market.

Now **decide** the main components of your sales promotion and **summarise** these in a clear promotional plan.

> **Deadline**

Tips to achieve a merit grade

Before you start Task 2, you may find it helpful to consider the following points.

* The key stages of your sales promotion are the most important points. They will include your deadline dates.
* The main features of your sales promotion are those that make it distinctive and which focus on your target market.
* Your plan needs to take account of your resources (including your team skills) and the time available.
* Bear in mind that a simple theme can often be more effective than anything that is too elaborate.
* Remember that any plan is a guide. It should be flexible enough to enable you to make changes if these are essential for success.

Now do Task 2.

Task 2 – Merit grade

2   Clearly **identify** the key stages and features of your sales promotion.

Then **carry out** your plan and **create** the materials you have identified.

> **Deadline**

Tips to achieve a distinction grade

Before you start Task 3, you are advised to read the notes below.

- Remember that an evaluation is a careful analysis of the good points and bad ones, so that you can reach a logical conclusion.
- Start by identifying all the strengths of your promotion. What worked well – and why?
- Now think about the weaknesses. Which ideas were less successful – and why?
- Now consider the team. How well did you work together? Did you meet all the deadlines? Could anything have been done better?
- Now decide what evidence you have to support your opinions. If your promotion was praised by those who saw it then this is proof of its appeal. If you had a high response rate, then this is proof of its success.

Now do Task 3.

Task 3 – Distinction grade

3 As a group, **discuss** and **evaluate** the promotion designed in Task 2 in terms of:

a its appeal and

b its success.

Then **write** your own personal account. In it you should also **identify** the improvements you think could be made next time to improve both its appeal and success.

Deadline

You have been asked to help a high street retailer which sells consumer durables, such as Richer Sounds, to prepare a booklet for new sales staff. This will be given to all new staff as part of their pre-sales preparation.

To help, you can either use the information you can access on Richer Sounds StudentZone to give you ideas or you can obtain information from another store you know well – either because you work there part-time or because a member of your family works there.

Tasks 1 and 2 – Pass grade

1   You have been asked to **identify** the key features you think should be included for *each* of the following areas:

   a Training of sales staff in customer service techniques

   b Care of the sales environment

   c Negotiating with customers and dealing with requests for discounts.

Deadline

2   Use each of the items **a** to **c** in Task 1 above as a heading. Under each heading write out the text you think should be included in the booklet. This will mean **describing** each of the key features you identified in Task 1.

Deadline

Sample assessment

For a high street store, such as Richer Sounds (or the same store you chose for your assessment for 7.2) do the following tasks.

Task 1 – Pass grade

1 a List the key features of professional practice that you would expect from their sales staff.

    b Explain why each one is important.

Keep your work safely as you will add to it when you have completed the final section of this unit.

Deadline

For the same retailer you chose for Assessment 7.3, undertake each of the following tasks to extend your answer. You should note that questions 2 and 3 refer to the information in both sections 7.3 and 7.4 of the Student Book.

Task 1 – Pass grade

1 **Describe** the key features of after-sales service you would expect to find in your chosen business.

Deadline

Tips to achieve a merit grade

Before you start Task 2, you should consider the following issues.

- This task builds on Task 1. However, you must now think about the sales staff rather than the business as a whole.
- Sales staff should obviously know all the rules, regulations and sales procedures they must follow and the guidelines laid down by the business. You can start by identifying these in relation to your own chosen organisation. This will include aspects such as time-keeping, uniform, greeting customers, handling returns and so on.
- Now identify how staff respond to everyday problems and customer queries. How do they handle these? Can they use their own initiative or do they have to ask for advice every time?
- For all the key areas you have identified, think about why these are important to the business – and to its customers.

Now do Task 2.

Task 2 – Merit grade

2 **a** **Identify** the key features of:

    i professional sales practice and

    ii after-sales service you would expect from each member of the sales staff.

  b For each feature that you identify, **explain** why you think it is important.

Deadline

Tips to achieve a distinction grade

Before you start Task 3, you may find it useful to consider the following points.

- When you evaluate, you must think about both the strengths and weaknesses to form a balanced judgement that you can support with evidence.
- Start by thinking about all the strengths – what do the sales staff do well?
- Now identify areas where you think there are weaknesses. For example, when you did Task 2, above, you may have found there are some problems staff cannot cope with on their own. Or you may have found that some staff are better than others at dealing with customers.
- Based on your findings, make appropriate recommendations.
- Remember that if you decide that no improvements can be made, you must say *why*. In this case, you are basically saying that sales practice and after-sales service are absolutely excellent in your chosen business! Identify areas where other retailers are often weak in comparison and identify at least three 'good practices' they should copy from your chosen business.

Now do Task 3.

Task 3 – Distinction grade

3 **a Evaluate** the sales service provided by your chosen retailer.

   b Suggest possible improvements that could be made to pre-sales preparation and after-sales service.

   If you feel that no improvements can be made then give a reason for your opinion. In this case either:

   - **describe** improvements that have been made in the past and explain how these now mean no further improvements can be made, *or*
   - **identify** areas where other retailers often fail to achieve best practice and recommend possible improvements that they should make to be as good as your chosen business.

Deadline

7.1 – Explore sales promotion techniques

Over to you, page 311

1 Below are suggested responses. Other appropriate answers should be accepted.

a (3 of) To build customer loyalty, to obtain/reward long-term customer loyalty, to increase sales, to stimulate interest.

b (3 of) To increase sales, to encourage impulse buying, to stimulate interest in the product, to encourage brand switching, to differentiate the product from competitors.

c (3 of) To tempt new/potential customers to visit the premises, to stimulate interest in the service, to publicise a new location and introduce staff, to make the public familiar with the business name.

d (3 of) To increase sales, to stimulate interest in the product, to link to a national promotion/well-known name, to make the public familiar with the name.

e (3 of) To increase sales, to tempt customers to try a new product, to build/reward customer loyalty, to attract new customers, to keep the public familiar with the business name.

f (3 of) To increase sales, to encourage impulse buying, to stimulate interest in the product, to encourage brand switching.

g (3 of) To increase sales, to build customer loyalty, to attract new customers, to encourage brand switching.

h (3 of) To tempt potential customers to visit the premises, to stimulate interest in the service, to keep the public familiar with the name, to introduce staff to customers, to attract new customers.

i (3 of) To increase sales (during a 'back to school' time), to encourage impulse buying, to sell/clear high levels of unsold stocks, to differentiate the products from those offered by competitors.

2 No specific answer possible as it will depend upon the details on the leaflet. However, the intended outcome will be to obtain suitable students for the course. Note: if the college does not have appropriate leaflets then the information in a course prospectus could be analysed as an alternative.

3 a Suggested USPs could be: very friendly and 'legendary' customer services by committed staff; personal and informal communications and service; excellent value for money products with guaranteed 'price beat'; technically knowledgeable staff. Other appropriate USPs should be encouraged.

b Communications, signs and promotional materials are bright, colourful and informal with catchy headings (e.g. on the website – Julian's junkyard, Richer Tips etc.). An example of an in-store catalogue is useful as evidence of the general image and style which reflects the informal culture.

Over to you, page 320

1 a Aftershave/perfume = half price luxury shower gel; organic spaghetti = free pasta sauce; packs of carrots = buy one get one free; Sunday newspaper = free CD of popular music; computer magazine = free game CD; toothpaste = free toothbrush; blank videos = multipack at discount price.

b No specific answer possible. If the group is very large tutors may prefer to split it into small groups and each group into two teams. The aim is that each team has to suggest promotional ideas for products put forward by the opposite team.

2 No specific answer possible and tutors may wish to check the websites for current information at the outset.

a ADS Visual Group undertakes all forms of corporate marketing including promotional literature, signage, DVD-video, multimedia presentations and website design.

b Ofcom is regulator for the UK communications industry. Its remit includes ensuring choice and competition in electronic communications and broadcasting, monitoring quality of provision and responding to customer complaints about offensive or harmful material. Tutors should note that this last responsibility may pass to the ASA in the future.

c ISP is the Institute of Sales Promotion which gives information on best practice and legal issues on sales promotion.

d The Office of Fair Trading provides a wide range of information on consumer rights.

e The ASA provides a wide variety of information on its role, including detailed information for school and college students.

f FootFall provides customer counting technology and statistics to retailers.

g Marley Media are sales promotion specialists who create and produce materials for a wide range of promotions.

3 No specific answer possible.

Section review, page 321

1 **a** POS displays: point of sale displays where goods or services are promoted at the checkout.

b POP displays: where products are promoted at the point of purchase to encourage people to select them.

c Promotional package: the methods and materials used for a specific promotion.

d Cross-promotional marketing: two businesses linking to promote each other's complementary goods/services.

e Above the line: advertising using all forms of media both old and new, e.g. newspapers, TV, posters, Internet etc.

f Below the line: basically all promotional methods and materials except advertising.

2 No specific answer possible. Students should be encouraged to use this task as a 'dry run' for the type of promotion they will undertake for their assessment.

7.2 – Pre-sales preparation

Over to you, page 325

1 **a** The umbrella should be returned, as under the Sale of Goods Act it could be reported to a Trading Standards Officer who technically could prosecute under the Trades Descriptions Act because it does not live up to claims made for it.

b The sofa is not satisfactory quality and can be returned under the Sale of Goods Act. It does

not matter that the delivery note was signed as customers are not expected to inspect an item in detail at the time of delivery.

c She can return one CD but will have to rely on the generosity of the shop to change it as there is no legal requirement. The shop is likely to insist the wrapping/seals are unbroken.

d The toaster is dangerous and, in addition to being returned for a refund or replacement, it can be reported to the local environmental health office under the terms of the Consumer Protection Act. The supplier is responsible, not the manufacturer, as the contract is between the buyer and the seller.

e The jeweller is liable as the loss was through negligence on the part of the sales assistant. Had the loss occurred despite all possible steps being taken to safeguard the item then the jeweller would not be liable.

f He can try to pursue his claim with the firm through the Consumer Protection (Distance Selling) Regulations but these will not be effective with a foreign site or if the firm has gone out of business. In this case he can make a claim with his credit card company who are liable under the Consumer Credit Act.

g At the time of writing this was, unfortunately, still legal but planned revisions to the Consumer Credit Act are likely to outlaw the practice.

2 **a** (3 of) Dealing with customers, product knowledge, basic consumer law, selling skills – or any other appropriate suggestions.

b (4 of) Tim will deal with specialist buyers who may be technical experts themselves; buyers will probably want to negotiate prices and extras, such as maintenance services; large orders may be placed but these can only be supplied if the goods are available; Tim will need more in-depth product knowledge, Tim will need to check customer credit ratings before agreeing sales; Tim will be expected to keep business customers informed of new developments and products that may interest them and keep customer records up-to-date.

3 **a** (3 of) Employ sales representatives to visit schools/colleges, attend educational conferences and book fairs; publish catalogues every spring and send to customers on their mailing list; send out promotional literature on new releases; offer discounts for multiple purchases; ask customers to review books on the website – and any other appropriate suggestions.

b (2 of) Corporate buyers allowed 30 days' credit, goods sent by mail order, can arrange fitting/installation, orders can be faxed through.

Over to you, page 333

1 No specific answer possible as it will depend upon the particular systems used in the college and in the stores identified. However, the point should be made that whereas a specialist service provider (e.g. college, solicitor and so on) may be able to arrange an appointment at a later date this would not be viable for most retail stores as, in most cases, the customer would probably go elsewhere if he/she could not be dealt with immediately.

2 All reasonable suggestions should be encouraged. For example, roosters need rapid attention and to be treated as 'special'; foxes are better dealt with by experienced staff; dogs should be fussed over; sheep should be recommended the most 'popular' item; jackdaws should be given lots of information/no pressure to buy; bulls should be handled with care (get help if necessary); Mr and Mrs Farmer need humouring – try to identify which one is the boss!

3 No specific answer possible.

4 Excellent booklets can be downloaded at the Home Office site in pdf format. In addition, further hints and tips can be obtained from links to specialist security companies. A key point for discussion can be what to do when a person is suspected of shoplifting in a small shop with no specialist staff.

Students should be encouraged to think about measures such as: proper opening/locking up procedures which includes setting/deactivating the alarm; grilles/shutters to protect door and windows; protecting stock from pilferage by keeping it in locked cabinets with restricted access; if possible not working alone; training staff to be alert for suspicious behaviour; mirrors to reduce blind spots in the shop; installation of CCTV/dummy cameras; use of dummy display cartons or disabling goods on display (e.g. remove working parts if possible); warning signs to deter thieves; forming a partnership with other businesses in the area; emptying tills regularly

and leaving empty/open overnight; installing a safe for valuables; checking the position of tills (so that drawer can't be reached by customers, cashier isn't in vulnerable place).

Over to you, page 339

1 No specific answer is possible as it will depend upon the local shops identified by the students. The material on the DRC site is extensive and students should enjoy the 'Little Shop of Horrors' game. There are several booklets that can be downloaded which cover case studies on a clothes shop, newsagent, hairdressing salon and café. Ideally these could be copied for students to study in groups to identify the key points relevant to different types of outlets and common aspects such as entrance width/type, lighting, layout for wheelchair access, labelling, obstructions/hazards, payment area etc.

2 No specific answer possible but students will enjoy this more if they are provided with appropriate resources to produce designs and models to illustrate their ideas.

3 No specific answer possible but hopefully students will see some common elements between local superstores, and which elements are appropriate for copying by convenience stores and which are not.

Section review, page 340

1 a Pricing policy: the policy on the prices that are charged, which may include discounts for large purchases.

b Supply constraints: the factors which could prevent goods being available for a time.

c FMCGs: fast moving consumer goods such as bread, milk, washing powder.

d Consumer durables or SMCGs: slow moving consumer goods such as televisions, washing machines, carpets.

e Buyer behaviour: the way in which customers behave when they are shopping.

f Power aisles: main through aisles in a large store on which there are major displays of merchandise.

2 As many appropriate ideas as possible should be encouraged. Many students may be able to contribute from their own experiences of retail training. Suggestions may include: (10 of) customer protection legislation, product knowledge, safety (including layout and good housekeeping), security (including vigilance), processing a sale (i.e. using the till), greeting customers, negotiating with customers, personal appearance, pricing policies, referring customers to more experienced staff, dealing with returns/exchanges.

7.3 – Sales practice

Over to you, page 346

1 a This is a legitimate opportunity to attempt upselling.

b This is unethical as it will frighten the old people. Using scare tactics to sell is never ethical.

c This is acceptable so long as the sales person is honest that the preferred brand/model is not stocked as alternative brands and models may be just as good if not better. It is up to the customer whether he/she insists on sticking to the original plan.

d This is unethical as the salesperson has deliberately misled the customer to achieve the sale. If the customer states 'time is of the essence' and nominates a specific delivery date the store will be in breach if the goods arrive late.

e This is cross-selling and is quite ethical. The customer is free to refuse.

f This is unethical and, if reported, would normally be a disciplinary offence in an ethical organisation.

g This is unethical but not illegal, unfortunately.

2 No specific answer possible.

3 No specific answer possible.

Section review, page 347

1 a NVC is body language, i.e. communicating by means of facial expressions, gestures, posture etc.

b Pace of interaction: the overall speed of communication and discussions between the customer and the salesperson.

c Customer contact details: basic contact information e.g. name, address, telephone number.

d Written quotations or estimates: itemised list which gives details of the costs of the items and the total amount.

2 No specific answer possible.

3 Suggestions may include: (10 of) appearance and manner, approaching customers in the store, how to cope on busy days, not forming judgements, how to ask question, how to cope if the customer is doubtful, how to give extra help, how to cope with technical questions, how to handle payments, how to deal with customers' rights, how to arrange demonstrations, providing written quotations.

7.4 – After-sales service

Over to you, page 353

1 a Suggestions should include items such as: name, address, telephone number, date of complaint, nature of complaint, action taken, name of staff recording complaint. It should be analysed regularly (e.g. weekly/monthly) by a manager to identify common areas of complaint which can be addressed.

b Returns are the opposite of a sale so must be recorded in the accounts (see returns day books in Unit 3, page 261). In addition, if goods are sub-standard the issue must be raised with the supplier and the goods may be returned for replacement by the supplier.

2 a Apologise and obtain the customer's telephone number so that you can contact him/her when it arrives and prevent further unnecessary journeys. Investigate why the delay has occurred and try to improve matters. If there is a genuine reason then communicate this to the customer. If possible offer the customer a voucher to compensate for the inconvenience.

b Refer the problem to your supervisor. You may be allowed to give a voucher or credit note in exchange but should not do this without permission.

c Apologise to the customer but remain loyal to Simon. Dishing the dirt about a colleague is unprofessional, no matter how tempting. If several complaints are received about Simon then have a quiet word with the supervisor.

d Apologise and check the address details in case it has been sent to the wrong address. Then put one in the post yourself.

e Apologise and try to find out when the next delivery is due. Offer to reserve one for the customer with no obligation to purchase. This means he is not under pressure to call in the moment it arrives.

Section review, page 353

1 a Dealer network: maintenance/spare parts facility operated on behalf of several manufacturers and in several locations throughout the country.

b Complaints procedures: the steps to follow to handle a complaint.

c After-sales service: the services required after a purchase has been made, e.g. maintenance, repairs or replacements.

d Extended warranty: additional policy to cover the repair of goods after the original guarantee has expired.

2 All will have policies for dealing with returns/exchanges and complaints. Specific services may include:

a Garden centre: guarantees/repairs/ installation service on durables (e.g. greenhouses), advice and information on plants sold/garden problems, repeat/follow-up purchases e.g. restocking hanging baskets on request.

b Furniture store: replacement/repairs e.g. re-covering service, advice on care and maintenance; stain/scratch removal e.g. French polishing.

c Computer supplier: dealer network for repairs, advice on software/security, emergency recovery service (in customer's own home for additional fee), advice on software/hardware updates, spare parts service, telephone faults diagnosis service.

d Designer clothes shop: alterations service, mailing list for new fashions, fashion shows and notification of special offers.

e Mail order company: postage-free returns service; advice on sizes/fittings for replacement items (if clothes), mailing latest edition of catalogue to regular customers.

These sample assessments are designed as practice exercises to help your students understand the types of task they will be required to do for their formal assessments. For practice, tasks can be done by individuals or by groups as indicated.

There is one sample assessment for each section of the Unit:

8.1	Online business activity
8.2	The benefits of an online business presence
8.3	The potential disadvantages of an online business presence
8.4	Considering the business feasibility of going online

The structure and grading of the assessments reflect the grading criteria for the Unit as provided by Edexcel. Differentiation information is given where appropriate to indicate what would be required from the student to gain pass, merit or distinction grades. Tips to help the student achieve a merit or distinction grade are also given. A deadline box is provided in which you can enter a submission date to familiarise your students with the idea of working to a specified date or time.

Assessments are mainly printed one to a page so that they can be easily photocopied.

Answers to Unit 8 sample assessments

8.1

No specific answer possible as it will depend upon the online operation selected.

8.2 – Task 1 Pass grade

This task requires a description of the various types of benefits that can be gained by an online presence. At least one appropriate example should be given to illustrate each point. A case study has not been used as this would constrain students to identifying the type of benefits which could sensibly be achieved by one operation. An open question enables students to identify and discuss a wider range of possible benefits.

8.2 – Task 2 Merit grade

This task should not present too many difficulties for students who have answered question 4 of the section review. Focusing on three different types of organisations should help students to think about a range of benefits from e-procurement (e.g. chocolates, climbing equipment) to taking bookings online.

8.2 – Tasks 3 and 4 Distinction grade

No specific answer is possible for Task 3 as this will depend upon the organisation selected. Students selecting Richer Sounds can identify their main aims and objectives from the StudentZone. It may be useful to discuss the main aims and objectives of the College with students who choose that option, although the key ones should be appreciated. The aims of the NSPCC and Amazon are relatively easy to establish from the lists provided in the Student Book and the content of their websites.

Additional features of the Richer Sounds online operation include its intranet, email, EPOS systems and the StudentZone! Tutors may be able to guide students on 'college' operations e.g. remote access to email etc.

Answers to Task 4 should include identifying the aims and objectives of the charity – linked to raising money and awareness. Students should then look at the ways a website would help, e.g. giving information, asking for volunteers, asking for donations, promoting events, asking for people to register on the site, submitting ideas for fund-raising and so on.

8.3

The answer to this question should link to the type of problems covered in this section. The section actually covers four main areas, i.e. problems relating to exposure, vulnerability to hostile attack, potential unpopularity with staff and financial uncertainties, so students could discuss each main area.

8.4 – Task 1 Pass grade

No specific answer possible as it will depend upon the additional factors researched from local competitors' sites for the case study; and upon the specific factors relating to any business chosen by the student.

8.4 – Task 2 Merit grade

a   The inclusion of pitfalls related to a larger business has been included to give the student rather more scope for answering the question – as problems relating to budget overspends, missing target deadlines, important security issues and staffing problems are more likely to apply to a larger operation. In this case the focus should be more on keeping the site simple to start with, usability, a realistic timescale, ensuring that anticipated benefits are achieved – the pitfalls relate to being over-ambitious, not focusing on the customer, not setting a realistic budget plus dealing with any 'people' problems which occur in relation to company employees.

b   In this case, the pitfalls should specifically relate to the chosen business and be linked to the SWOT analysis prepared for Task 1.

8.4 – Task 3 Distinction grade

The first part of the task is similar to the merit criteria, except that the student needs to separate those problems which are linked to implementation (e.g. budget problems, design of the site, features and usability etc.) and those concerned with having a permanent online presence, e.g. coping with customer demand, security, keeping the site up-to-date etc.

The second part should look at how a carefully structured implementation plan, which is drawn up after all the relevant factors have been considered, can help the business to prepare for/overcome problems associated with implementation. Examples include 'testing' a site; asking staff for feedback (or employing specialists to do this); consulting/training all staff involved; including web monitoring to check the success of the site; asking customers for feedback on the site itself; setting appropriate benchmarks or targets; promoting the site online and offline so that customers are aware of its presence. The plan should also include identifying/training a 'webmaster' or person responsible for the site, ensuring that security remains high, customer needs are met, the site is regularly updated and that progress towards achieving benchmarks and targets is regularly measured and action taken if these are not being achieved.

For this assessment you will need to select an online business of your choice. You may find it easier to do this assessment if you choose a simple online *retail* business rather than any other type.

Task 1 – Pass grade

1 **a** **Investigate** the website of your chosen online business.

    b **Identify** and **describe** its key features. You may find it helpful to do this by explaining how the business operates online.

Deadline

Task 1 – Pass grade

1 **Identify** and **describe FIVE** principal benefits that businesses gain by having a simple online presence. **Illustrate** your answer with appropriate examples.

Deadline

Tips to help achieve a merit grade

Before you start Task 2, you may find it helpful to consider the following.

- There are certain general benefits of operating online for all businesses. Many, for example, see this as essential to keep pace with their competitors. You should have found it quite easy to find five benefits for Task 1.
- For Task 2, you have to think about additional benefits. These may be because of the type of business, because of the type of features which could be included on the website or because of promotional opportunities.
- In many cases, an online presence can change the way the business operates – from purchasing stock or raw materials to selling.
- You may find it useful to research online sites the businesses similar to those of the business you have chosen. This will help to give you examples to use in your answer.

Now do Task 2.

Task 2 – Merit grade

2 Each of the following businesses currently operates only offline, mainly serving a local area.

- **a** A hire car business
- **b** A recruitment agency
- **c** A producer of luxury chocolates
- **d** A retailer of specialist climbing equipment
- **e** A family hotel

Each owner is now thinking of operating online as well.

Select THREE of the above businesses. Then, for each one, **identify TWO** additional and specific benefits that the owner could expect to achieve by taking this step. Again **illustrate** your answer with appropriate examples.

Deadline

Tips to achieve a distinction grade

You may find it helpful to read the notes below, before you do Tasks 3 and 4.

- To contribute to the success of the business, an online operation must help the business to achieve its aims and objectives.
- In Task 3, you will establish how the online operation is linked to the aims and objectives in a major business. In Task 4 you can then use your experience to make recommendations.
- The first step in Task 3 is to establish the aims and objectives of the business. Remember these always link to the key activity. You may find it a helpful reminder to look back at Unit 1.
- Next examine the business's website and identify the key features. There should be an obvious link between the two. Then include any of its other online features such as email or an intranet.
- Explain how these features are helping the business.
- Include any other online operations you know about, e.g. email, a staff intranet or an EPOS system.
- For Task 4, imagine yourself the charity's organiser. Think about the key aims and objectives and then the features of an online operation that could link to these. Then make your recommendations.

Now do the tasks below.

Tasks 3 and 4 – Distinction grade

3   **Select one** of the following businesses or, *with the agreement of your tutor,* another business of your choice.

- Richer Sounds
- Your own college
- NSPCC
- Amazon.com

   a   **Identify** the main aims and objectives of the business.

   b   **Identify** the main features of its online operation.

   c   Using your information from **a** and **b suggest FOUR** ways in which the online operation is helping to achieve these aims and objectives.

4   Your college group is involved in helping to raise money for a local children's hospice. The organisers are thinking of developing a simple website if this would help to achieve the aims and objectives.

   Recommend at least **THREE** ways in which an online presence could benefit the appeal.

Deadline

Task 1 – Pass grade

1   Many businesses still hesitate about having an online presence. Describe **FOUR** key disadvantages of having an online operation that can cause this.

Deadline

Either use the case study below, or select a small business in your own area that you know well and undertake the following tasks.

Case study

Rob Castle and his wife, Soraya, are qualified vets. They have regularly produced newsletters and sent these out to customers but Rob now fancies the idea of setting up a passive website. He thinks that this will give him and Soraya the opportunity to provide lots of useful information for animal owners, a map to help people get to the practice, updates and news, links to relevant sites on the web and warnings about pet information on the Internet that isn't so good! He can also promote the fact that he specialises in dealing with exotic pets as well as domestic animals. Soraya is a specialist in animal behaviour and also runs puppy training sessions. They also employ three veterinary nurses, have excellent surgical and hospitalisation facilities plus x-ray and ultrasound scanning facilities.

Rob is aware that many of the vets in the area now have a website, although some of the practices are larger than his. He also knows his IT skills aren't very good and he would need help to create the site and keep it up-to-date. This would mean talking one of the administrators into learning how to do it.

Task 1 – Pass grade

1 a If you are using the case study, **research** the sites of at least **THREE** vets in your area and **list** the typical website features offered by Rob's competitors. You can find website addresses of local vets by looking in your local *Yellow Pages* (or listings at **www.yell.com**). You can also try a good search engine. If you are using a different business, **identify THREE** local competitors and **research** their sites to find out and **list** the type of presence they have on the Internet.

b **Prepare** a SWOT analysis of a passive online presence for the business.

Hints and tips about preparing a SWOT analysis

- A SWOT analysis is the identification of the strengths and weaknesses of businesses, plus relevant opportunities and threats.
- Remember that the strengths and weaknesses are internal. For the case study, this information is given in the scenario. If you are using a business you know well, talk to the owner to identify internal strengths and weaknesses.
- The opportunities and threats relate to external factors. You can obtain this information from your research about their competitors. Opportunities are good ideas that can be copied or new features that competitors don't have. Threats are those areas your business will struggle to compete against.

Tips to achieve a merit grade

Before you start Task 2, you might find it useful to read the following notes.

- For the Unit 8.3 assessment for you have identified some key disadvantages of an online operation. A major pitfall is forgetting to consider these and thinking that there are only advantages to operating online! You may find it useful to look back at your answer for that question when you start.
- Other pitfalls can relate to the type of website, the speed of change, the staff involved and so on.
- Some pitfalls are more likely to apply to certain types of businesses than others. For example, a passive brochureware site does not have to think about pitfalls relating to accepting payments online.
- You will find it easier to identify potential pitfalls if you take into account the results of your SWOT analysis. You should also think about the features of the online operation that you are trying to achieve.

Now do Task 2.

Task 2 – Merit grade

You know that there are several pitfalls with e-business implementation although these do not always apply to a small business.

2 **a** **Identify FOUR** common pitfalls that can relate to any businesses that decide to go online.

b **Select FOUR** additional pitfalls which could specifically apply to your chosen business. For each one, **explain** why each would apply to that business.

Deadline

Tips to achieve a distinction grade

The following notes may help you to do Task 3.

- There are always possible problems with an online presence. You have identified these in Task 2.
- These are considered when an implementation plan is drawn up.
- An implementation plan identifies the best way forward.
- All the main factors must be considered when the plan is drawn up, as well as the time-scale. The key factors are always specific to a particular business, e.g. aims and objectives and competitors.
- Many factors will have been identified in the SWOT analysis.
- It is sensible to divide the key issues into those which must be considered at the outset and those which can be left until after implementation.
- There are obvious benefits from proper planning. If you think about the possible effects of *not* planning and just going ahead anyway, then this may help you to identify the benefits more easily!

Now do Task 3.

Task 3 – Distinction grade

3 **a** For the business you selected for Tasks 1 and 2, **list** the main problems to be considered:

    i before and during implementation

    ii after implementation

b **Explain** how good planning and the creation of an implementation plan can help your business prepare for and overcome some of these problems.

Illustrate your answer with specific examples.

Deadline

8.1 – Online business activity

Over to you, page 367

1 **a** Home page: normally used to refer to the main (starting) web page of a website which gives information about the content and links to other pages on the site. Can also be used to refer to a user's own preferences for the page which appears on their browser when they first connect to the Internet.

b Hypertext: a link in web page to another site or web page. These are shown by images or by underlined text or text in a different colour.

c Portal: a website which acts as a gateway to other services and information on the Internet.

d EDI (Electronic Data Interchange): a secure method used by business buyers and sellers to buy and pay for goods electronically by the exchange of structured electronic documents.

2 No specific answer is possible, as this will depend upon the sites selected by the students. The aim of this task is to begin to stimulate discussions about the features of online businesses, knowledge of which is part of the pass criteria of this section.

3 **a** No specific answer is possible as this will depend upon the key points identified by students. However, all the main fundamental issues should be included, e.g. for the child – not disclosing personal details, never arranging to meet someone, not assuming people tell the truth, telling parents if they are worried or scared. For parents – knowing about children's online activities, siting the computer in a family area, setting computer home page to a child friendly site, showing an interest in child's online activities, monitoring software/parental controls available and so on.

b The object of this question is to stimulate discussion, which could be based on the fact that restricting or warning about activities is sometimes seen as a challenge by some young people. Any appropriate suggestions (e.g. focusing on positive ideas/trust/good communications rather than over-zealous restrictions) should be encouraged.

4 No specific answer possible.

Over to you, page 375

1 **a** Local estate agent – **i** operations unlikely to be large enough to warrant anything more sophisticated.

b Language college – **ii** so that business contacts can check availability and make an online reservation.

c Virtual holiday company – **iv** so customer can build own package.

d Central London hotel – **ii** so spare capacity can be advertised online and reservations can be made by people searching online.

e National toy retailer – **iii** so visitors can shop and buy online.

f Specialist food company – **iii** so can sell goods over wider area.

2 Waste of time because (2 of): people don't buy designer labels because of their website; some designer products rarely bought online (e.g. Rolex watches); money spent on website could be spent better in other areas. Good business sense because (2 of): another (cost-effective) form of promotion; jazzy website adds to/complements image; important to try to keep the competitive edge especially if major competitors are also operating online.

3 **a** The features will vary but will generally include an online reservation facility; separate business/leisure facilities; links to other offices/global sites.

b This will concentrate on advertising the products and prices online (i.e. a brochureware site) with contact numbers.

c The key point is that the local car hire facility only has a local market, so is using the site merely as a method of promotion/additional advertising. For large national/international car hire companies, their target market is far wider and comprises different types of customers with different needs.

4 **a** They have several options. They could have a simple brochureware site and customers contact them to buy items. Alternatively they could set up a site where customers can buy online, sell records they want to exchange and/or bid to buy collectors' items. They will need to develop distribution facilities for items they sell online. They will also need to arrange to take payments online (covered later in the unit). They will also need to keep their product list up-to-date and have terms and conditions of business that ensure they are complying with their legal responsibilities. The greater the number of features, the more complex the operation and the greater the number of areas that need to be considered. Any other appropriate suggestions should be encouraged.

b Hopefully, the number of considerations discussed in **a** will help students to understand the problems that can be inherent with starting an online presence without thinking through the implications (which are the focus of later sections of the unit).

Section review, page 376

1 Some features are given below but other appropriate alternatives may be suggested.

Site 1   NHS Direct: public sector; online health information, enquiry service, further information about NHS Direct, contact information (but no facility to contact a health specialist immediately via the website).

Site 2   Richer Sounds: private sector; information on products/prices, special offers, store map, ability to order and pay online.

Site 3   college website: public sector; probably information on courses, student facilities, ability to obtain prospectus/application form online, job vacancies. Will obviously depend upon specific college site.

Site 4   Guide Dogs for the Blind: voluntary sector; information about the organisation, appeal information, becoming a helper, educational information for children.

Site 5   Thorntons: private sector; chocolate (and flower) promotions, online ordering and payment, sending a present to another address (including a multiple address upload feature), gift search feature.

Site 6   Samaritans: voluntary sector; information about the Samaritans, nearest local branch information, email contact facility, appeal for supporters

2 This activity has been designed to enable students to think about the way in which an online presence must complement and be supported by the offline activities. In addition, the online presence must link to the business's main purpose and aims/objectives. This aspect is developed in the next section of this unit.

Tutors may like to develop the activity by asking students to look back at the six organisation studied in **1** above, and ask for suggestions as to the ways in which the online presence helps these businesses to achieve their aims and objectives. This will start to prepare students for the type of thinking required for the distinction assessment criteria of the final section of this unit.

No specific answer is possible for the smaller businesses as it will depend which ones are investigated.

3 No specific answer possible as it will depend upon the business selected. Note that the requirement for a 'simple' business relates to the type of online operation and not the size of the business. For example, a large operation like Amazon is actually very simple and straightforward. However, students should be steered away from trying to investigate the potentially complex online activities of larger corporations like banks.

This question is a rehearsal for Sample Assessment 8.1.

8.2 – The benefits of an online business presence

Over to you, page 382

1 Aims may include (2 of): attracting more customers, increasing sales/profits, increasing brand recognition. Benefits of an online presence would include (6 of): global 'round the clock' visibility to customers despite rural location, expansion of business/customer base, equality of presence with larger suppliers (e.g. can put graphics of designs on website), ability to keep up with competitors, rapid response to customer interest, may be able to source some supplies more cheaply online.

2 a The sequence of organisations/individuals involved in the supply of the product to the consumer from start to finish.

b Instead of each step taking place consecutively, suppliers are linked to each other and the buying organisation to speed up the process. For example, suppliers know current sales levels and new order requirements as they occur.

c (2 of) Can assess competition, can keep up with competitors, can promote business to customers 24/7 and expand market. (1 of) Can link to suppliers electronically to buy goods, representatives can access stock levels online, can reduce storage costs by JIT purchasing.

3 a PC World sells books, paper and other accessories – Dell does not. PC World site includes a store locator which isn't relevant to Dell's site. Dell divides up its site more obviously into computers for private individuals and small/medium/large businesses. It is also obviously an international operation. Both sites include information on terms/conditions/repair policies and so on.

b (3 of) Dell will not have to pay rent or business rates for shop premises, it deals direct with the customer so there are no middlemen, it will need fewer staff (and may outsource operations to cheaper locations, such as India), it needs less warehouse space as customised orders can't be assembled/despatched immediately.

c No specific answer is possible but the question is included to generate debate about competitive operations on the Internet. Dabs is a dot.com company which has grown to become the UK's number one online IT retailer. Originally (1990) it was a mail order company. It differentiates itself by offering a far wider range of products (over 34,000 lines), including technical items such as motherboards for those who wish to customise their own products. The dabs@work section of the site explains its b2b operations. The site has been extremely successful and consistently receives good reviews/awards.

4 The student should be expected to give reasons for choosing a PDA that links to its benefits/features, for example portable computing facilities, a touch screen, handwriting recognition, electronic diary, 'to do' list, address book, calculator, memo pad, compatibility with PCs for easy downloading, 'bluetooth compatibility' (so no wires or cables required to connect to PC). On the more expensive versions

games, photographs and video files can be stored and Word documents accessed/edited. Using a PDA or laptop means anyone working away from the business can have instant access to the online facilities.

Over to you, page 389

1 No specific answer possible but students should find this activity very interesting and informative!

2 Suggested answers are given below but other appropriate ideas should be encouraged:

a NUS – aims and objectives include: being an up-to-date information source for students, campaigning on student issues and gaining increased 'brand' awareness. Website enables it to have a higher profile, to promote its activities, to provide information to students, to provide rapid updates/responses to specific situations.

b KC Mobility – aims and objectives include: attracting new customers, increasing sales/profits, higher profile to disabled drivers, and providing a service to disabled drivers. Website enables it to link to sites which provide information/grants etc. for disabled drivers, can ensure their website address is included on information given to disabled drivers, can provide information online to disabled customers, can provide details of services and options (and keep these updated) more easily and comprehensively than in standard advertisements.

c Boots – aims and objectives include: attracting new customers, beating the competition, increasing sales/profits, reducing costs. Online presence means customers can buy 24/7, special offers can be advertised and promoted cheaply, registered customers can be targeted with marketing initiatives by email particularly linked to special occasions, e.g. Valentine's Day or Mother's Day, can supply housebound/ remote users who do not live near a store, can use e-procurement to purchase supplies more economically/quickly and reduce warehouse space required.

3 a To attract new customers, to increase sales/profits.

b (3 of) 24/7 visibility, access to customers over a wider area including those who are housebound/disabled/live in remote areas, can assess and keep up with competitors, can rapidly respond to customer enquiries.

c Brochureware showing a selection of types of displays possible with prices and contact details/email facility would be most appropriate. This is because the actual display required would need to be personally discussed with the customer so an online shopping site would not be appropriate.

d No specific answer possible but affiliations should be to linked products, e.g. national florists, wedding services/venues, wine/champagne suppliers etc.

4 No specific answer possible as it will depend upon the sites being selected. The aim of this exercise is to increase the student's appreciation of the type and design of sites, their good/bad points and how these link to online operations in general.

5 Again the point of this exercise is to involve students in exploring some of the more exciting aspects of online operations and to appreciate when these are useful and have clear benefits and when they are not. The relevant factors would include: the image of the business, the type of online/offline operations being carried out (e.g. films/digital effects versus hotel), the aims and objectives of the business, the type/style of competitors' sites, the target customer and his/her expectations.

Section review, page 390

1 Any appropriate suggestions should be encouraged for this question, the aim being to remind students of likely/appropriate aims and objectives and to link these to the benefits of an online presence. Answers may include:

To make a profit – by selling online, attracting more customers.

To increase or maximise profits – by selling online/targeting customers with email promotions.

To provide goods or services to the local community – by providing up-to-date information on council services and facilities, especially in remote areas.

To expand operations – by selling over a wider area.

To increase or maximise sales – by selling online, selling over a wider area, advertising online.

To improve quality – by updating information to customers, by online feedback from customers, by obtaining supplies from a wider range of sources.

To be more competitive – reducing price (if costs lower), checking competitors' sites, matching competitors' offers, quality of presence with larger businesses.

To attract new customers – special promotions, advertising online, wider presence.

To reduce costs – online payments can improve cash flow so less borrowing required, fewer stores required to cover remote areas, some operations could be outsourced to save money, less stock held if goods sourced using integrated e-procurement system.

To enhance the brand image and increase brand awareness – email promotions, online advertising, including web address on stationery and in adverts.

To find out more about customers – online surveys and questionnaires, asking customers to register online.

To provide charitable or voluntary service – promote range of services offered online, particularly to housebound/disabled/remote areas; enable online contact, e.g. by email (as Samaritans do).

To raise funds for a charitable or voluntary service – promote the cause online, ask for volunteers/donations, sell goods online.

To increase customer awareness of activities – special promotions, online advertising, scope of information provided on website, updated information provided on website, (paid for) high listing with search engines (see page 396).

To complement the offline business – wider choice of goods available online than in all stores, coverage of a wider area, ability to buy online through e-procurement and reduce stock held.

2 The following are suggested aims/benefits but other relevant ideas should be encouraged.

a CenterParcs. Aims will include improving profit, maximising bookings, attracting new customers, reducing costs. Online operations will offer the following benefits (3 of): 24/7 visibility, can attract customers from wide area, as site can be accessed from cybercafes and public web access points, can supply brochures online, can accept bookings/payments online, quick and easy to update publicity information, can promote website for those wanting more information, can advertise on other related sites, can promote the site to registered website visitors by email, especially special offers.

b Trutex. Aims will include improving profit, maximising sales, providing a competitive service, reducing costs. Online operations will give following benefits: 24/7 visibility to retailers, schools and private customers; ability to include special services to registered retailers online, can sell online to schools operating in direct supply programme with fewer potential bad debts, can build up online mailing list, can deal with suppliers online, can help to obtain competitive edge.

c Carphone Warehouse. Aims will include improving profits, maximising sales, meeting/beating the competition, improving market share, reducing costs. Benefits include: global 24/7 visibility, ability to monitor/keep up with the competition, access to customers over wider/remote areas without increasing retail outlets, can build up affiliations and promote site through advertising, can sell online and improve cash flow/sales, can source supplies online through e-procurement.

d Whitton Cars. Aims likely to be to make a profit, possibly to expand operations, to increase bookings, to equal or beat the competition. Benefits: 24/7 visibility to wider area, can challenge larger enterprises and have equality of presence, can rapidly respond to customer interest, can analyse online competition, can advertise/promote site through affiliations and advertisements, access to remote location users and to people accessing web over public access points, can create basic site fairly easily/cheaply.

e Help the Aged. Aims include: providing a charitable service to the elderly, providing up-to-date information to the elderly and their families, to raise money for their cause. Benefits include: 24/7 presence, accessible to disabled/housebound, can rapidly update site to take account of developments/news of interest to target group, can appeal for support (keeping up with competitors), can sell products online to increase income, can promote charity through links on relevant, related sites.

3 The main reasons included: the actions of competitors, the increased use of the Internet for finding out about suppliers and prices, 24/7

visibility, ability to promote special offers and supplement product information contained in advertisements, access to potential customers who do not live near a store, who live in a remote area or who cannot easily travel to a store.

4 This question is preparation for the merit criteria which applies to the assessment for this section.

a Benefits could include the following. Local council: updated information on services to local community, accessibility to disabled/housebound, e-procurement to reduce costs/overheads. College: advertising courses online, promoting facilities online, allowing online applications/enrolments for part-time courses, allowing students access to email/learning resources online. Dabs: 24/7 visibility, nationwide reach for local company operating in one location, keep up/beat competition, reduce costs, improve cash flow, remain in relatively low cost location (Bolton) whilst expanding operations, e-procurement of supplies as and when needed. Football club: 24/7 visibility to fans, keep up with other clubs, provide information to fans and supporters, allow supporters to buy season tickets online, to sell kit and memorabilia online to increase income, expanding market presence to customers who don't live near stores/are housebound etc., can keep up with competitors, can offer online selling/delivery to increase sales and improve cash flow.

b This question can be used to provoke a debate as to why many organisations today may feel they need a website even if it only marginally relates to their main aims and objectives. Manchester United obviously wants a global presence and has a very sophisticated website with a variety of features for fans and visitors. However, fans will still want information and news on their 'home team' and the ability to sell goods (or season tickets) online can help to increase the income of even the smallest clubs.

c No specific answer possible. However, tutors may wish to provoke discussions by suggesting a variety of different types of online operations now commonly found – from football clubs and airlines to charities, newspapers and banks. It may also be useful to refer back to the range of activities covered in the first section if students are stuck for ideas.

8.3 – The potential disadvantages of an online business presence

Over to you, page 397

1   **a** and **b** No specific answer possible. However, if a member of the college web team or IT staff can be persuaded to talk to the group about security measures, then students should be encouraged to think of appropriate questions to ask beforehand and possibly submit these in advance of the discussion. A further option would be to ask any 'techies' in the group to explain the security measures they have taken at home, particularly if they have broadband access.

2   The point of this question is to focus students on one of the main reasons why an online presence may be unsuccessful. This is because of the failure of the businesses to cope with the increased market interest and demand – often through lack of planning and poor organisation. The butcher would need to have an appropriately designed site, good supplies, good distribution network (including appropriate packaging), to keep the site up-to-date, to ensure it was secure, to make sure that the costs of sending the goods further afield were covered in the overall price, to ensure that the goods arrived in good condition, bearing in mind they are perishable. All appropriate suggestions should be encouraged.

3   No specific possible. The aim of the question is to focus the students on good practice where businesses have fully assessed the benefits and disadvantages of an online operation and then planned the best way to progress.

Section review, page 397

1   (6 of) Helps them to assess if they will benefit from an online business, helps to prevent over-ambitious goals at the start, emphasises the importance of devoting appropriate resources to supporting the operation, helps them to assess the likely costs against the proposed benefits, provides information on how to progress further, gives technical information on aspects such as designing a website, security and legal issues. Any other appropriate suggestions should be encouraged.

2   Advantages (3 of): expert skills, professional look, more effects/better graphics possible, will include aspects such as search engine optimisation/user tracking, can be created so that can be updated in-house. This wouldn't be necessary or needed

(3 of): in a large organisation with its own in-house experts, if the owner has the skills to create the site him/herself, if the owner can obtain free assistance to create the simple type of site required for that type of business operation.

3   This question is to help to prepare students for the questions in the sample assessment.

   a   Additional challenges could include (5 of): exposure to negative publicity, problems of defamation, problem of coping with increased interest/demand, security issues, unpopularity with existing staff, cost versus uncertain benefits.

   b   Other reasons could link to the attitude of the owner, fear of new technology, lack of ambition, genuine belief that an online operation would not be beneficial because of type of operation/type of customers.

   c   All appropriate suggestions should be encouraged including thorough research into possibilities; realistic planning at the outset, including analysis of benefits and potential problems; specific problems identified; technical expertise obtained in relation to aspects such as online security and payment systems; appropriate provision of resources to support the operation; ensuring good communications with staff and appropriate staff training; not being too ambitious at the outset; having a budget and monitoring ongoing expenditure.

8.4 – Considering the business feasibility of going online

Over to you, page 403

1   **a**   No specific answer possible as it depends upon the sites chosen.

   b   Problems could include: security issues (e.g. denial of service); increased demand at certain times of the year; changing user specifications to allow users to mix and match holidays themselves (see dynamic packaging page 372); payment security; redundancies/industrial relations problems if outsourcing undertaken/fewer staff needed/branches closed. Preventative action will include: security measures (firewall/sophisticated 24/7 virus monitoring etc.); ensuring capacity of browsers can cope plus siting in secure location (see page 66); obtaining feedback from customers to match site to their requirements; introducing dynamic elements; ensuring payments are secured using latest technology; consultation with unions/redeployment/retraining of staff.

2 No specific answer possible as it depends upon the case study chosen.

3 Benefits include (3 of): obtaining expert advice, sharing experiences with others, free up-to-date IT information, examples of best practice, help to avoid common problems and pitfalls.

Section review, page 404

1 a SWOT analysis for Mark and Matthew.

INTERNAL FACTORS	
Strengths	**Weaknesses**
Renowned for high quality work	No IT skills – will have to pay for website to be created
Specialist supplies + can be bought cheaper online	
EXTERNAL FACTORS	
Opportunities	**Threats**
Improve customer contact opportunities	Sophisticated competitor sites
Can display examples of 'before' and 'after' work on the site	

b No specific answer possible. Students may find the entries in the SWOT analysis on page 401 of the Student Book useful to trigger ideas.

c (3 of) They can attract customers over a wider area, it is cheaper to promote their work on the website than keep printing/distributing leaflets or paying for advertisements, they can check competitor sites for prices to ensure they are competitive – or any other appropriate suggestions.

d (2 of) Not being able to cope with the increased number of enquiries as there are only two of them, problems keeping the site up-to-date unless one of them gains more IT knowledge, security problems if neither of them understands security issues/implications, cost of the website may be more than expected/budgeted.

2 a No specific answer possible as it depends upon competition and potential business in the local area. Tutors may wish to suggest additional factors which could be incorporated into the SWOT analysis to make the task more realistic.

b The first pitfall is that there isn't an implementation plan – just a lot of enthusiasm! It is unlikely that Kerry could cope with the demand. In addition, the website needs to be kept up-to-date, she would have to have all her supplies organised before she launched the site, it would be difficult to estimate demand, she would have to have a distribution network in place to deliver the food quickly, there is no budget allocated for setting up the operation.

3 No specific answer possible as it depends upon the business ideas put forward by the students. Ideas can be gleaned from some of the case studies on other sites or by looking through *Yellow Pages* and identifying types of local businesses which may benefit from an online presence, e.g. garden centres, photographers, car hire firms and so on. The requirement that the business employs 10 staff has been included as students should consider the effect on staff of their proposals and the consultation/training that would be required. The aim is to help prepare students for the merit and distinction criteria of this section of the unit.

Tutors should note that using the DTI e-planner is suggested in the Edexcel teaching notes for this unit (See **www.dti.gov.uk/bestpractice**).

Unit 9 Starting up a new business

Cross-referenced additional activities can be found at:

These sample assessments are designed as practice exercises to help your students understand the types of task they will be required to do for their formal assessments. For practice, tasks can be done by individuals or by groups as indicated.

There is one sample assessment for each section of the Unit:

9.1	Market opportunities
9.2	Legal and financial requirements
9.3	Draft business plan
9.4	Personal qualities

The structure and grading of the assessments reflect the grading criteria for the Unit as provided by Edexcel. Differentiation information is given where appropriate to indicate what would be required from the student to gain pass, merit or distinction grades in the IVA. Tips to help the student achieve a merit or distinction grade are also given. A deadline box is provided in which you can enter a submission date to familiarise your students with the idea of working to a specified date or time.

Assessments are mainly printed one to a page so that they can be easily photocopied.

Answers to Unit 9 sample assessments

9.1

No specific answers possible for either question since the answers will depend on the type of business chosen.

9.2 – Task 1 Pass grade

No specific answers available since the answers would depend on the types of businesses chosen.

9.2 – Task 2 Pass grade

a   This answer applies to the scenario in the box. The most obvious legal structure would either be a limited liability partnership (LLP) or a private limited company. These would give them the comfort of knowing that their personal possessions are safe although there would be some extra administration. However, it would mean that they would be able to obtain a bank loan more easily, if necessary, and, if they formed a private company, they could appeal to their family for additional funds if necessary in return for shares. As a limited company they would also be able to obtain credit from their suppliers more easily.

b   A sole trader is not appropriate because they want to start a business together and an ordinary partnership is not appropriate since they would have unlimited liability.

9.3

The three exercises progressively match the pass, merit and distinction criteria for this part of the unit. The requirements are fairly demanding, particularly in relation to the amount of information which needs to be provided and it may be appropriate for the students to work in small groups. This would have to be approved if the exercise were to be used for the formal assessment.

No specific answer is possible since answers would depend on the type of business chosen and the specific circumstances it is planned to operate in.

9.4 – Task 1 Pass grade

The answers below are only suggestions – all other appropriate ideas should be accepted. If students do this task collectively then a wide range of suggestions should be encouraged.

a Uniqueness of selling point/skill base. He could have a good eye for colour and style so that he can recommend a particular carpet to a customer.

b Conscientiousness. He always arrives on the day and time agreed.

c Willingness to work long hours. He will fit a carpet in an evening because householders are out at work all day.

d Availability. He always has his mobile phone switched on so that he can answer immediately.

e Commitment to professional standards of quality. Although there does not appear to be a professional trade association, he would always complete work to the highest possible standard.

f Commitment to personal development and training. He would read literature produced by manufacturers of carpets and wooden flooring to ensure that he is up-to-date with the latest materials and technology.

g Has ability to network. Always knows whom to contact if he doesn't know the answer to a question or how to tackle a problem.

h Adequate numeracy skills. Can quickly and accurately work out his price for doing a particular job.

i Adequate interpersonal and communication skills. Gets on well with people. Few people, if anyone, dislike him.

j Decisiveness. Makes his mind up quickly, once he knows all the facts.

k Willingness to encourage/develop market demand. Is always alert for a new market opportunity and is willing to follow up every lead.

l Efficient administration. All invoices are sent as soon as the jobs are completed.

m Honesty. His prices are always fair, even when he is dealing with people who could easily be fooled.

n Business scruples. All carpet and wood scraps which are left over are used whenever possible. Those which cannot be used are re-cycled or disposed of legally.

o Ability to evaluate own achievements. Rarely makes the same mistake twice.

p Ability to identify appropriate advice. Listens very carefully to advice and can fully explain the reasons for accepting or ignoring it.

q Awareness of when to seek assistance. Would prefer to ask for assistance so that he can complete a task properly, rather than struggle on his own and make a mess of things.

9.4 – Task 2 Merit grade

No specific answer is possible since this would depend on the qualities chosen by the students.

Before you complete the following tasks, carefully read the examples of possible new business ventures below.

Then choose ONE type of business which you know something about – either from direct experience or because you know someone who runs such a business who would be prepared to give you information about it.

The type of business you choose does not have to come from the list, provided that it is one which a self-employed person could set up. For your chosen type of business carry out the following tasks.

Examples of possible new business ventures

Au pair services, building/roofing, caddying, car mechanics and valeting, caring, carpet fitting, catering, childminding, cleaning, coaching, computer troubleshooting, courier services, craftsperson, database set up/maintenance, decoration, DJ, dry-cleaning, entertainment, film/video making, function planning, gardening, graphic design, hairdressing/manicure/beautician services, kebab sales, market trading, musician services, personal sports training/educational tutoring, pet exercise/grooming, photography, plumbing, property maintenance/improvement, recording engineering, removals, retailing, street vending, tailoring, taxi service, translation, website design/maintenance, window cleaning and replacement, writing.

Task 1 – Pass grade

1 **Describe** the level of market knowledge which a new entrepreneur would need for the business to survive for at least one year.

Deadline

Tips to achieve a merit grade

You may find it useful to read the following notes before you start Task 2.

- Very few successful entrepreneurs go into business on the spur of the moment; they usually need to plan carefully.
- This involves researching the market and looking at their own resources and skills.
- The plans will vary, depending upon the market itself and the results of the research.
- In your answer, remember to concentrate on the plans that would be required for the specific market you have chosen.

Now do Task 2.

Task 2 – Merit grade

2 **Explain** how a potential new entrepreneur might plan for entry into that particular market.

Deadline

Tasks 1 and 2 – *Pass grade*

1 Choose **TWO** of the potential business start-ups from the list given in Unit 9.1. Try to choose contrasting business where one would be fairly simple to start up and one would be more complex – such as one needing special equipment or premises.

For *each* of the businesses you have chosen, **list all** the key items which would be included in the start-up costs. Put these under two headings:

- start-up capital costs
- working capital/running costs.

Deadline

2 In agreement with your tutor, *either* for one of the businesses you have chosen above, or for the scenario described below carry out the following tasks.

a **Recommend** the best legal structure for the business and **give reasons** for your choice.

b **Suggest TWO** alternative structures that would **not** be appropriate and give your reasons.

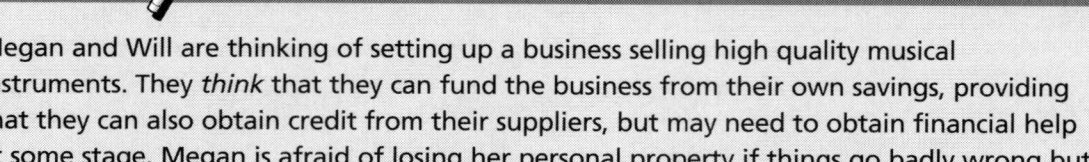

Case study

Megan and Will are thinking of setting up a business selling high quality musical instruments. They *think* that they can fund the business from their own savings, providing that they can also obtain credit from their suppliers, but may need to obtain financial help at some stage. Megan is afraid of losing her personal property if things go badly wrong but Will wants to keep administration down to a minimum.

Deadline

Your tutor may allow you to carry out these tasks as a member of a small group. All three parts are concerned with planning to start a business. You will need to choose a type of business which you know well or about which you can obtain information. It could be one that you have used for an earlier sample assessment in this unit.

Task 1 – Pass grade

1 For the business you have chosen, use the headings given below to **produce an outline business plan**.

You will probably have to invent some of the information – such as your projected cash flow. This is quite acceptable provided that the assumptions you make are reasonable.

A template for an outline business plan

1 Name and address(es) of owner(s).

2 Long term plans for the business.

3 Proposed legal status.

4 Description of nature of business/products.

5 Skill(s) of owner(s).

6 Analysis of market, i.e. size of market, competition, gap in market and customer needs/preferences.

7 Plan for marketing goods or services.

8 Financial forecasts – sales revenue, cash flow, profit and loss account.

9 List of required resources including premises, equipment and materials and estimated start-up capital and working capital required.

10 Contingency plans for coping with problems (e.g. sickness/accident/injury/market failure).

Deadline

Tips to achieve a merit grade

You may find it helpful to read the notes below, before you start Task 2.

- Your presentation should focus on the key points of your business plan.
- These should be put forward in a logical order.
- Remember to use visual aids. These will also help you to remember your key points.
- Your presentation should have a clear introduction and an appropriate conclusion.
- If you are working in a team, you will need to divide up the tasks fairly between you.
- Prepare for questions by thinking about areas which may need to be explained in more detail, particularly those related to finance and marketing.

Now do Task 2.

Task 2 – Merit grade

2 **Prepare** a presentation based on your business plan. At a time and date agreed with your tutor, **make your presentation** to the rest of your group.

Be prepared to **answer straightforward questions** from the audience.

Deadline

Tips to achieve a distinction grade

You may find it helpful to read these notes, before you start Task 3.

- Listen carefully and make notes during each presentation. This will help you to select the plan to review more easily.
- You will find the task easier to do if you choose a plan which interests you or which relates to a business area you know about or are interested in.
- Work through the plan methodically. Imagine you were investing money in the business. Which areas would concern you the most?
- Always bear in mind that the key points about a business relate to money and markets. Check the resources, the projected sales and the proposed expenses and cash flow very carefully indeed. Are they realistic or optimistic?
- Think about the worst that could occur. Has the business any plans to cope with that?
- Remember your criticism must be **constructive**. This means that you look at ways in which the plan can be improved or strengthened and make positive suggestions.

Now do Task 3.

Task 3 – Distinction grade

3 As a member of the audience, and in agreement with your tutor, **choose ONE** of the business plans presented which you think could be improved.

Ask your tutor to have a copy made for you and read it carefully. Then **note down** all of the aspects which you feel could be improved, **with reasons** for your choice.

For each point you note, **recommend** how the plan could be strengthened.

Deadline

Both of the tasks below are based on Mohammed's carpet fitting firm. This is described in the box below.

Case study

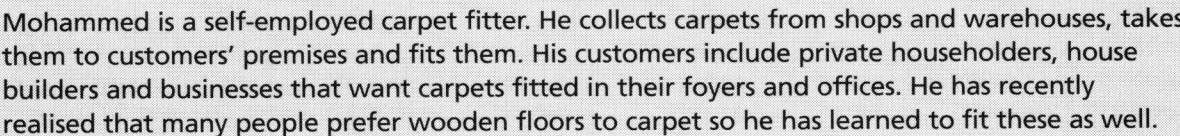

Mohammed is a self-employed carpet fitter. He collects carpets from shops and warehouses, takes them to customers' premises and fits them. His customers include private householders, house builders and businesses that want carpets fitted in their foyers and offices. He has recently realised that many people prefer wooden floors to carpet so he has learned to fit these as well.

Task 1 – Pass grade

1 Entrepreneurs need several key personal qualities to be successful. For each of the qualities listed below, **suggest ONE** type of behaviour which would show that Mohammed has that particular quality.

Use your imagination to do this. For example, the first item is 'Uniqueness of selling point/skill base'. Mohammed could demonstrate that he has this quality by being able to organise his work so that he could always fit a carpet within four days of being asked. His competitors are not so well organised and can often take up to two weeks. Now you will have to think of another example for the first item!

- **a** Uniqueness of selling point/skill base.
- **b** Conscientiousness.
- **c** Willingness to work long hours.
- **d** Availability.
- **e** Commitment to professional standards of quality.
- **f** Commitment to personal development and training.
- **g** Ability to network.
- **h** Adequate numeracy skills.
- **i** Adequate interpersonal and communication skills.
- **j** Decisiveness.
- **k** Willingness to encourage/develop market demand.
- **l** Efficient administration.
- **m** Honesty.
- **n** Business scruples.
- **o** Ability to evaluate own achievements.
- **p** Ability to identify appropriate advice.
- **q** Awareness of when to seek assistance.

Deadline

Tips to achieve a merit grade

You may find it helpful to read these notes before you start Task 2.

- Although entrepreneurs need many personal qualities, some are more crucial than others.
- The key qualities will depend upon the type of business and the work being done. For example, a graphic artist needs to be creative but an accountant needs to pay attention to details.
- A major asset for all entrepreneurs is to be able to recognise their own weaknesses. They can then take action to put them right, e.g. by obtaining training or employing someone with the skills they lack.
- Warning signs are a good way of spotting weaknesses. For example, if every document you produce is full of errors, then it is fairly certain your typing skills are poor and so are your proof-reading skills!

Now do Task 2.

Task 2 – Merit grade

2 **a** From the list given in Task 1, **select** the **FOUR** qualities that you consider to be the most important for Mohammed. **Give a reason** for choosing each one.

  b For *each* item you have chosen, **identify** *at least* one warning sign that would indicate that Mohammed lacked that particular quality to the extent that the success of the business could be threatened. In each case, **explain** why that warning sign would be significant.

Deadline

9.1 – Market opportunities

Over to you, page 9

1 **a** Jude could assess the market by personal experience (e.g. not being able to find something in shops). He might find that, the product or service does not seem to exist or that the product/service is available but it is in short supply. He might know the business and know there is scope for a new venture; know the market is growing; identify a niche market.

b He could carry out primary research by asking people or secondary research (e.g. finding out number of competitors, number of businesses who would use his services in the area etc.).

2 No specific answer possible since the answer depends on the type of business chosen.

3 **a** (6 of) How many are there? What is the market share of each? What are their USPs? What products/services do they offer? Where are they located? What is their customer profile?

b (3 of) Search on the Internet (e.g. for retail businesses use comparitive shopping sites); look in *Yellow Pages* (for local competition); research in business trade directories; contact the appropriate Trade Association; read appropriate trade/industry journals.

4

Section review, page 10

1 **a** A small specialised market within a large general market.

b A market where sales overall are increasing month by month.

c Strengths, weaknesses, opportunities, threats. A method of conducting an overall assessment of a business or potential business.

d Discovering the views of customers and potential customers on a product or service.

e General state of businesses. For example, are sales generally rising and are business people generally optimistic, or do the opposite conditions apply?

f Unique selling point. One factor which makes a product or service different from the competition.

2 Skills (2 of): knowledge of market, ability to work long hours, good at administration, ability to deal effectively with customers.

Resources (2 of): money is the ultimate resource required but it would be needed for decorating equipment, a van for transport, overalls, perhaps initial advertising.

3 This question is to help the students to think about how businesses attempt to 'profile' their customers. Their answers may vary from those below. They could be accepted if supported by sound arguments.

Type of business	Provide a personal service	Need plenty of skill and training	Every job is different	Little or no finance is needed
Recording studio	Y	Y	Y	N
Mobile hairdresser	Y	Y	N	Y
Taxi business (including base office)	N	N	N	N
Writing books	N	Y	Y	Y
Website design	N	Y	Y	N
Wedding photography	Y	Y	N	N

Type of business	Age	Income	Gender
Charity shop	Middle aged and above	Low	Probably more female than male
Keep fit centre	Mostly under 40	Probably fewer people with low income	Fairly balanced – maybe more male than female
Rugby supporters' club	Probably a wide range but fewer elderly people	Wide range	More male than females
Baby and young children's clothes shop	20s and 30s but some grandparents	Wide range	Mostly female

9.2 – Legal and financial requirements

Over to you, page 17

1 a When a business has limited liability, the owners only risk the amount of money they have invested in the firm. Their personal property is safe.

   b LLP and Ltd have limited liability.

   c Similarities (2 of): have to keep records; have to deal with the Inland Revenue; various types of legislation apply to both. Differences (2 of): limited companies have to register with Companies House and file accounts (which may have to be audited) – partnerships do not; limited companies have shares which can be sold – partnerships do not. Partnerships are formed by a Deed of Partnership – limited companies need to complete a Memorandum of Association and Articles of Association.

   d So that a self-assessment tax form, supported by evidence of earnings and expenses can be completed for the Inland Revenue. Students could also point out that records are needed of all transactions in case there is a query or customers want a refund.

2 a A franchise business is one in which a parent company allows an entrepreneur (called a franchisee) to set up business under conditions governed by a legal agreement, such as type of product/service, standards of service, advertising and training and so on in return for a fee and, normally, further payments based on the profits or sales each year.

   b Advantages (2 of): may be household name; ready-made business including brand, product/service and support/advice; easier to get loan or overdraft.

Disadvantages (2 of): franchisor takes a fee and a share of the profits; franchisee has limited scope for entrepreneurial decision making; problem with brand name will affect business.

3 (3 of) Health and safety: designed to minimise the exposure of employees and the public (and the employer themselves) to risk of injury and health problems. Fire protection: designed to minimise the risk of injury to people should there be a fire. Includes the need for alarms, fire exits, fire doors and provision of fire extinguishers. Employers' liability insurance: ensures that employees can be compensated if they are seriously injured at work or contract a chronic disease. Employee rights: ensures that employees are treated as fairly as possible. Consumer rights: to protect customers against products or services which are not up to standard. Data protection: to control the type of data which can be kept on customers and employees.

Over to you, page 26

1 a Capital (2 of): equipment, buildings, vehicles, fixtures and fittings or any other suitable answers. Working capital or running costs (2 of): stock, consumables, staff wages, deposits on utilities or any other suitable answers.

   b Owner's own money – advantages: own control over decisions, no interest charges. Disadvantages: may have to remortgage own house, may not have enough to set up the business properly.

   Partnership – advantages: access to more money, problems can be shared. Disadvantages: may not always agree, one may work harder than other(s) but only get same money. Difficult if one wants money back.

   Bank loan – advantages: can pay back over a period. Disadvantages: interest charged; may lose property if default on payments; interest rate may vary.

Bank overdraft – advantages: interest only charged daily on outstanding balance, flexible – can borrow as much or as little as needed up to an agreed limit. Disadvantages: interest rate higher than for a loan, may be told to repay it if bank suspects business may be in difficulty.

Government grants – advantages: interest free and some do not have to be repaid. Disadvantages: complex rules and paperwork, difficult to qualify for conditions required, may have to pay back if stringent conditions are not met.

Prince's Trust – advantages: low interest loans available, grants available, ongoing advice given. Disadvantages: must be young and unemployed to qualify; loan has to be paid back.

c   Employers' liability (compulsory) – to cover any staff who are employed in the case of injury; property and contents – to obtain cover in case of fire or theft (may also include consequential loss); public liability and/or product liability – in case public injured through accident on premises or using product; vehicle/goods in transit insurance – vehicle insurance is legal requirement (third party) if business has own transport; professional indemnity – to cover professionals if a claim brought against them on grounds of negligence; own life and health – mainly partners taking out life assurance to cover amount of investment in the business to cover claim on the business by their estate after death.

2   a   The closing bank balance. It is the most important because if it becomes negative, the business is paying out more than it is collecting. In addition a negative figure means that an overdraft is needed on which interest will be charged. On the other hand, a positive and increasing figure indicates that the business is making a profit.

b   It could be making a loss on trading or perhaps not collecting debts as quickly as it should. It could also be paying creditors too quickly.

3   a   A = Sales, B = Cost of sales, C = £31,000, D = Gross profit, E = Expenses, F = £3,000, G = Net profit

b   For the owner, the net profit, less tax, is his/her income. If the figure is high/increasing, this is a reflection on his/her entrepreneurial skills.

For the Inland Revenue, the figure is the one used to calculate the tax and National Insurance to be paid.

Section review, page 27

1   a   Start-up costs. The total amount of money needed to start a business. It includes capital expenditure and working capital.

b   Working capital. Also called running costs. It is the amount within the total start-up cost which pays for day-to-day expenses until the money received from customers is sufficient to cover these costs.

c   Sources of finance. The different ways in which an entrepreneur can obtain money to start a business.

d   Overdraft. A facility on a current account by agreement between the bank and a customer. It allows the customer to draw more money from the account than is actually in it. Interest is charged whenever the account is overdrawn – on a daily basis.

e   Loan. Banks will lend money to a business to help it get started or to fund development. The loan is normally for a fixed period and interest has to be paid. The bank will normally ask for an asset to be provided as surety or collateral – often the businessman's home.

f   Grant. Money provided to help a business from a government or other body. Normally does not have to be repaid. There are usually strict rules as to what situation qualifies for a grant.

g   Leasing. A capital item is 'borrowed' from the leasing company in return for monthly payments. The contract will normally include maintenance and is for a fixed period.

h   Employers' Liability Insurance. Compulsory for all businesses that employ staff. Insures employees against injury due to accidents at work or diseases caught at work.

i   Cash flow. The amount of money entering and leaving the business's bank account and particularly the effect this has on the residual balance.

j   Profit and Loss Account. A summary of all the income and expenditure for a business over a period – normally a year. The difference between the two figures is the profit – or loss.

2   *Note*: The suggestions given below are the most likely options. However, students are free to make other suggestions provided that they are prepared to support it with sound arguments.

   a   Since he is young and unemployed, he may be able to obtain a loan from the Prince's Trust. If he was made redundant he may have savings he can use.

   b   Leasing is one option since he would not have to get into debt. Alternatively he may get a loan from his bank or from a finance company linked to the garage where he buys the van.

   c   Unless she has wealthy relatives, a bank loan is the most obvious choice. The bank would normally wish to secure the loan in some way. Alternatively she could take a partner (perhaps a sleeping partner who would be prepared to invest money).

   d   Andy could set up a Deed of Partnership with his brother. This would state the share of the profit each would receive. Alternatively he could set up a private company and issue shares to his brother – and to other members of his family willing to invest in the enterprise.

3   **a**   The most common cause of cash flow problems is customers who pay their bills very late or not at all. This means that the business will eventually have no money to pay its suppliers who will then refuse to let them have goods.

   b   **i**   Sales. Total amount of money received from customers. Owners would look for a healthy sales figure – meeting forecast targets and better than the last year's figure.

   ii   Gross profit. The figure calculated by deducting the total amount paid to other businesses for raw materials etc., called cost of sales, from the sales revenue. The cost of sales amount is generally considered to be outside the control of the owners.

   iii   Total expenses. The sum of all the additional costs the business has incurred on wages, utilities etc. This amount is reckoned to be under the control of the owners. In other words, they might be able to reduce it to increase profits.

   iv   Net profit. The amount left over after all expenses have been deducted from the sales income. The money belongs to the owner(s) – *after* income tax and national insurance have been paid.

   c   Drawings – amount withdrawn from profit by sole trader or partner for personal use. Reserves – amount of profit retained in the business. The sentence means that Sam is taking out as little as possible to live on so that she can build up her reserves and use this money to finance her future expansion.

4   No specific answer possible.

9.3 – Draft business plan

Over to you, page 33

1   **a**   (3 of)Total size of market. Is market growing/saturated/declining? Customer profile. Number of potential customers. Predicted sales and income level.

   b   (3 of) How many competitors? Their location. Market share of each. USP of each. Strengths and weaknesses.

   c   (3 of) Which medium or combination of media to use? How much to spend? Local/regional or national? Timing relative to launch of business? How to measure effectiveness?

2   **a**   Sales revenue forecast. This figure is achieved by multiplying the projected number of sales with the respective price(s). It is the fundamental figure which is used to calculate cash flow and profit and loss.

   b   Cash flow. Shows how much money should be in the bank account at the end of each month. This is a measure of the success of the business. It may also highlight the need for an overdraft facility to cover any negative balance prediction. High negative cash flow can cripple a potentially healthy business.

   c   Profit and loss account. This is the test of how well a business is performing over a reasonably long period. A healthy profit means that the owner(s) can make a decent living and still have money left over for investing in the business to help it to grow. Most new businesses are not very profitable in the first few months, but after a year the figures should be looking healthy.

3   **a**   Interest rate increase. This normally only happens when the Bank of England increases the base rate. These type of changes are

normally made very cautiously and can often be anticipated. So people should not normally be taken by surprise. In this case, other businesses will also probably be affected. The owner has to decide whether he/she can afford to pay the extra interest without increasing prices. They may also try to pay off the loan quickly instead of using profits to re-invest in the business.

b Major customer goes out of business. This highlights the danger of being over reliant on one customer. It is good practice to try to have several medium sized customers so that the risk is spread. If a firm goes out of business its own customers will have to look elsewhere. The entrepreneur needs to find out who is supplying them and where they are looking to place their business. If the shortfall cannot be made up then costs may have to be cut for at least the time being.

c New competitor. If the market is growing, there may be enough room for everyone. If it is not, a lot depends on how aggressive the new business is and what its USP is. The entrepreneur needs to find out as much as possible about the new business and make sure that he/she is competitive on price, quality of service or whatever is necessary to meet the new challenge. In the short term, profits may have to fall as the action taken may cost money.

d Illness of the owner. This will depend upon the types of trade/business and whether there are any employees who can continue key operations in the owner's absence. Contact may be possible online or by mobile phone. However, sickness is a major problem for many small enterprises, especially where the owner has specialist skills (e.g. computer troubleshooter) and in that situation there would not only be no revenue during that period but business may be lost as potential customers seek out competitors who can help them during this time. It may also be possible to take out insurance.

Over to you, page 37

1 a Business Link is a government body with branches throughout England. It is a 'one stop shop' which co-ordinates various business initiatives and support mechanisms. Its main aim is to ensure that all requests for support receive the best attention.

b The prime function of Enterprise Agencies is to support business start-ups by offering advice, counselling and training. More specifically they help with the writing of a business plan and grant applications. Some offer managed workspaces and also consultancy services to established businesses.

c Each trade association exists to safeguard the interests of that particular type of trade by providing advice on insurance and legal matters, setting standards of service, offering training to update techniques and in some instances offering the services of local branch networks. All of these aspects would be useful for someone planning to set up a business.

2 a Banks offer advice and will lend money if they think that the business is viable. The loan would attract standard interest rates. Business Angels are people with business experience and money to invest. They want to take an active role in businesses which they invest in as well as taking a share of the profit. The Prince's Trust offers loans and small grants to people between 18 and 30 who are unemployed and have a good idea for starting a business.

The Prince's Trust would probably be Chloe's best starting point since the repayments on any loan or investment would be less. All three would offer advice. The other criterion that she must meet is the age band restriction.

b Both solicitors and accountants deal with businesses on a regular basis so they would each be able to offer general business advice. In addition, the solicitor should know about legal business matters (company formation etc.) and the accountant about business financial matters (cash flow, income tax etc.).

3 No specific answer possible as some of the contact information will be regional.

Section review, page 38

1 a Business plan. A document which contains information about all of the main aspects of the planned enterprise, such as the service/product, marketing and finance.

b Personal objectives. These are the personal goals to which the entrepreneur aspires. Most want to make money but probably have other equally strong aims such as self-fulfilment and to provide work for family members.

c   Legal status. Which legally defined category the business falls into – sole trader, partnership, LLP or limited company.

d   Marketing plan. How the business will be marketed, e.g. advertising in the press, direct mail shots, posters – and how much the different options will cost.

e   Mentoring. Similar to advising. It is a one-to-one relationship between an experienced business person and an entrepreneur.

f   Learning curve. The rate at which an entrepreneur learns the practicalities of running a business. The curve is normally steep in the early days and becomes less so as the individual becomes more accomplished.

2   a   (3 of) Writing things down forces the entrepreneur to consider all the aspects of the business. Something in writing to show to people such as banks and potential investors. Same argument as above to people whose advice is sought. To set performance targets against which actual results can be measured. To anticipate events/situations which could cause problems to the business.

b   To spell out what the USP is. Hence it is not sufficient to give a general description of the business. The description has to be specific enough to establish why customers should choose it before competitors.

c   Sales revenue forecast, cash flow forecast, profit and loss account.

d   Risk assessment is the identification of potential problems which a business could face. Its main purpose is to force the entrepreneur to be realistic about the prospects of the business and not to assume that all will be plain sailing. The assessment could be developed to include ideas as to what could be done if a particular problem arose.

3   a   Businesses contribute to the economic success of local areas and the country as a whole. They do this by employing and paying local people, buying goods and services and paying business rates and taxes.

b   Mentors/advisers can use their own experience of running businesses to give sound, practical advice to entrepreneurs. They will be aware of the problems and pitfalls facing a new business.

9.4 – Personal qualities

Over to you, page 47

1   There is no right answer to this exercise. It is designed to get the students to think about themselves in relation to the topic of this section – the qualities needed to be a successful entrepreneur. The temptation will be to tick everything. In any event, the exercise could be developed by asking the students to challenge each other by asking for examples of behaviour which illustrates a particular quality claimed. For example someone who is often late for lessons could hardly tick J!

2   Any one from (there are probably others):

a   Wrongly estimating the price of a job. Unable to calculate invoices to be sent, or check invoices received. Problems with sales revenue calculations, cash flow calculations, profit and loss accounts.

b   Losing stock and paperwork, getting behind with administration in general. An untidy workplace – a particular problem if working in a customer's home/premises.

c   Customers will be lost if they are annoyed or upset. There may also be problems with suppliers. There could also be problems with relationships with anyone in the network – or even no network at all.

d   Would fall behind the times from a professional point of view. Would also not learn from mistakes.

e   Dishonesty is normally discovered eventually. Someone who acquires a reputation for dishonesty will have problems dealing with customers, suppliers etc.

Section review, page 48

1   a   USP (relevant to personal attributes). Something special about the entrepreneur personally that makes their business different from other competitors.

b   Conscientiousness. Doing everything that they ought to do. In particular, honouring any promises made.

c   Working long hours. People who are employed normally work 35 to 40 hours per week. Self-employed people often work considerably more than this. They also often work unsocial hours.

d Professional standards of workmanship. These are standards of service which are accepted as the norm. They are often set by law or by trade associations.

e Personal development for professionals. Professional people keeping themselves up to date with the standards and techniques of their trade. Increasingly, professional bodies expect members formally to report actions they take to update themselves. The reports have normally to be submitted once a year.

f Networking. Entrepreneurs build up a set of contacts of people to whom they can turn to for help, advice and information. The entrepreneur would also be expected to reciprocate.

g Decisiveness. The ability to make a decision when as much information as possible is available and there is no point in procrastinating.

h Business scruples. Acting in an ethical way. This covers a wide spectrum of situations where business people can behave ethically or otherwise. In other words, it is the choice that they make.

2 a Being indecisive. The two weeks' delay cost him the opportunity to rent the premises. As far as we know, all the facts necessary to make the decision were available from the start. Nothing was to be gained by waiting. In future, once as many facts as possible are known, a decision must be made.

b As with many small businesses, the plumber has to come to terms with the fact that he will probably have to work long and unsocial hours to make his business work. In this instance, he needs to have flexible domestic arrangements so that he can, if necessary, work late to finish a job. If he does this, customers will be happy, but his family life could suffer.

c Sam and Angie are part of each other's network of contacts. Having a relationship with someone in this sort of way often means that people help each other on a reciprocal basis. In this instance, it seems that Sam has not helped Angie when she needed it. Now that he needs help she does not see why see should co-operate. In future Sam should always try to help anyone in his support network since he never knows when he might need help himself.

d Fly tipping is dumping waste materials at the roadside or similar public places. It is normally done to save time and/or the expense of taking the waste to a municipal site (which makes a charge for tipping). It is unscrupulous/unethical – and illegal! In this instance the church, which sets highs standards of ethical behaviour, does not wish to be associated with a business that breaks the law. Pete should use the accepted procedure for tipping in future. Memories of his conviction will fade and he may even get the church contract back in a couple of years.

e Caroline's administration is very poor. She should be sending out invoices as soon as she has delivered the photographs. She should also check bank statements as soon as they arrive and have a filing system to store all documents properly. A useful way of achieving all this is to set aside a few minutes each day to deal with these type of matters.

 **Richer Sounds StudentZone** *for BTEC 1st*

In 2002, Richer Sounds plc, the UK's largest specialist retailer of hi-fi equipment and related separates, liaised with Heinemann and business studies authors Carol Carysforth and Mike Neild to create a StudentZone on its website at www.richersounds.com. This has now been extended especially for Heinemann BTEC First students and designed to meet the specific criteria of the BTEC First scheme. Students simply need to enter the password contained in the student book to access information on the StudentZone.

The site covers the requirements of both the core and specialist units. Detailed information relating to the topics covered in the core units enable your students to investigate Richer Sounds to understand how business principles are applied in practice and to help them prepare for their IVA and other assessment requirements. The StudentZone is particularly valuable for students studying specialist Unit 5 and Unit 7, as comprehensive information is provided both in relation to employment at Richer Sounds as well as sales and customer service.

Special Offer!

The BTEC First Business book helps to introduce students to the business practices and principles followed by reputable companies, such as Richer Sounds. The StudentZone, which accompanies it, draws extensively from the philosophies of Julian Richer, the founder of Richer Sounds. More information is available in two books, written about Richer Sounds by Julian himself. The Richer Way, the first book, has been listed as recommended reading for Unit 7 by Edexcel. Both provide useful information on the business and its operations and will provide tutors with greater insight about the business than can be obtained from the StudentZone alone.

Heinemann are pleased to be able to offer both books at a 20% discount to all tutors. Simply complete the form below and return it to JR Books Offer, Freepost SE5508, London SE1 4BR.

Name:
....

School/College...

Address ....

....

.........................Postcode ....

Daytime contact number ....

Email ....

Please indicate which titles and the quantity you require:

(Please tick box)	QUANTITY	COVER PRICE	20% DISCOUNT
The Richer Way	☐ ____	£7.99	**£6.49**
Richer on Leadership	☐ ____	£9.99	**£7.99**
Both titles	☐ ____	£17.98	**£14.48**

Please enclose a cheque made payable to: JR Books Ltd or call 08700 1 12345 to order with a credit card.